CLASSIC TEXTS SERIES

INTEGRAL CALCULUS FOR BEGINNERS

JOSEPH EDWARDS

arihant
SUCCESS AND NOTHING LESS

ARIHANT PRAKASHAN (Series), MEERUT

Administrative & Production Offices

Regd. Office

'Ramchhaya' 4577/15, Agarwal Road, Darya Ganj, New Delhi -110002
Tele: 011- 47630600, 43518550

Head Office

Kalindi, TP Nagar, Meerut (UP) - 250002
Tel: 0121-7156203, 7156204

Sales & Support Offices

Agra, Ahmedabad, Bengaluru, Bareilly, Chennai, Delhi, Guwahati, Hyderabad, Jaipur, Jhansi, Kolkata, Lucknow, Nagpur & Pune.

PRICE ₹175.00

PO No : TXT-59-T065575-06-25

Published by Arihant Publications (India) Ltd.

For further information about the books published by Arihant, log on to www.arihantbooks.com or e-mail at info@arihantbooks.com

Follow us on

PREFACE

The present volume is intended to form a sound introduction to a study of the Integral Calculus, suitable for a student beginning the subject. Like its companion, the *Differential Calculus for Beginners*, it does not therefore aim at completeness, but rather at the omission of all portions of the subject which are usually regarded as best left for a later reading.

It will be found, however, that the ordinary processes of integration are fully treated, as also the principal methods of Rectification and Quadrature, and the calculation of the volumes and surfaces of solids of revolution. Some indication is also afforded to the student of other useful applications of the Integral Calculus, such as the general method to be employed in obtaining the position of a Centroid, or the value of a Moment of Inertia.

As it seems undesirable that the path of a student in Applied Mathematics should be blocked by a want of acquaintance with the methods of solving elementary Differential Equations, and at the same time that his course should be stopped for a systematic study of the subject in some complete and exhaustive treatise, a brief account has been added of the ordinary methods of solution of the more elementary forms occurring, leading up to and including all such kinds as the student is likely to meet with in his reading of Analytical Statics, Dynamics of a Particle, and the elementary parts of Rigid Dynamics. Up to the solution of the general Linear Differential Equation with Constant Coefficients, the subject has been treated as fully as is consistent with the scope of the present work.

The examples scattered throughout the text have been carefully made or selected to illustrate the articles which they immediately follow. A considerable number of these examples should be worked by the student so that the several methods explained in the "book-work" may be firmly fixed in the mind before attacking the somewhat harder sets at the ends of the chapters. These are generally of a more miscellaneous character, and call for greater originality and ingenuity, though few present any considerable difficulty. A large proportion of these examples have been actually set in examinations, and the sources to which I am indebted for them are usually indicated.

PREFACE

To The Third Edition...

My acknowledgments are due in some degree to the works of many of the modern writers on the subjects treated of, but more especially to the Treatises of Bertrand and Todhunter, and to Professor Greenhill's interesting *Chapter on the Integral Calculus*, which the more advanced student may consult with great advantage.

My thanks are due to several friends who have kindly sent me valuable suggestions with regard to the desirable scope and plan of the work.

JOSEPH EDWARDS.

CONTENTS

INTEGRAL CALCULUS

ABBREVIATION.

To indicate the sources from which many of the examples are derived, in cases where a group of colleges have held an examination in common, the references are abbreviated as follows :—

(α) ≡ St. Peter's, Pembroke, Corpus Christi, Queen 's, and St. Catharine's.

(β) ≡ Clare, Caius, Trinity Hall, and King's.

(γ) ≡ Jesus, Christ's, Magdalen, Emanuel, and Sidney Sussex.

(δ) ≡ Jesus, Christ's, Emanuel, and Sidney Sussex.

(ε) ≡ Clare, Caius, and King's.

INTEGRAL CALCULUS

CHAPTER I.

NOTATION, SUMMATION, APPLICATIONS.

1. Use and Aim of the Integral Calculus.

The Integral Calculus is the outcome of an endeavour to obtain some general method of finding the area of the plane space bounded by given curved lines.

In the problem of the determination of such an area it is necessary to suppose this space divided up into a very large number of very small elements. We then have to form some method of obtaining the limit of the sum of all these elements when each is ultimately infinitesimally small and their number infinitely increased.

It will be found that when once such a method of summation is discovered, it may be applied to other problems such as the finding of the length of a curved line, the areas of surfaces of given shape and the volumes bounded by them, the determination of moments of inertia, the positions of Centroids, etc.

Throughout the book all coordinates axes will be supposed rectangular, all angles will be supposed measured in circular measure, and all logarithms supposed Napierian, except when otherwise stated.

2. Determination of an Area. Form of Series to be Summed. Notation.

Suppose it is required to find the area of the portion of space bounded by a given curve AB, defined by its Cartesian equation, the ordinates AL and BM of A and B, and the x-axis.

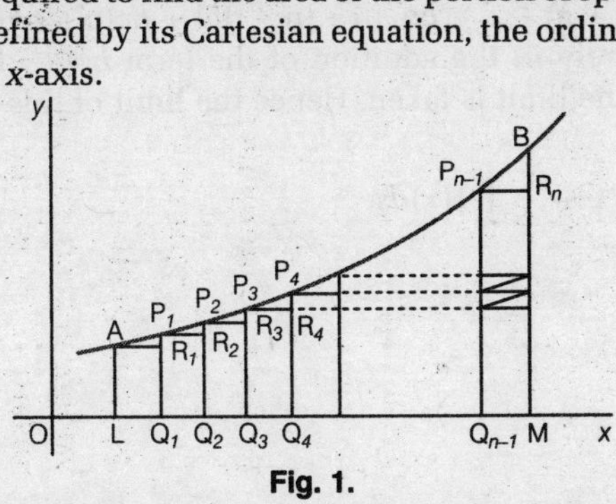

Fig. 1.

Let LM be divided into n equal small parts, LQ_1, Q_1Q_2, Q_2Q_3,..., each of length h, and let a and b be the abscissae of A and B. Then $b - a = nh$. Also if $y = \phi(x)$ be the equation of the curve, the ordinates LA, Q_1P_1, Q_2P_2, etc., through the several points L, Q_1, Q_2, etc., are of lengths $\phi(a)$, $\phi(a + h)$, $\phi(a + 2h)$, etc. Let their extremities be respectively A, P_1, P_2, etc., and complete the rectangles AQ_1, P_1Q_2, P_2Q_3, etc.

Now the sum of these n rectangles falls short of the area sought by the sum of the n small figures, AR_1P_1, $P_1R_2P_2$, etc. Let each of these be supposed to slide parallel to the x-axis into a corresponding position upon the longest strip, say $P_{n-1}Q_{n-1}MB$. Their sum is then less than the area of this strip, *i.e.* in the limit less than an infinitesimal of the first order, for the breadth $Q_{n-1}M$ is h and is ultimately an infinitesimal of the first order, and the length MB is supposed finite.

Hence, the area required is the limit when h is zero (and therefore n infinite) of the sum of the series of n terms

$h\phi(a) + h\phi(a + h) + h\phi(a + 2h) + \ldots + h\phi\{a + (n - 1)h\}$.

The sum may be denoted by

$$\underset{a+rh=a}{\overset{a+rh=b-h}{S}} \phi(a + rh)\cdot h \quad \text{or} \quad \sum_{a+rh=a}^{a+rh=b-h} \phi(a + rh)\cdot h$$

where S or Σ denotes the sum between the limits indicated.

Regarding $a + rh$ as a variable x, the infinitesimal increment h may be written as δx or dx. It is customary also upon taking the limit to replace the symbol S by the more convenient sign $\int$, and the limit of the above summation when h is diminished indefinitely is then written

$$\int_a^b \phi(x)dx,$$

and read as "the integral of $\phi(x)$ with regard to x [or of $\phi(x)dx$] between the limits $x = a$ and $x = b$," or more shortly "from a to b."

b is called the "upper" or "superior limit."

a is called the "lower" or "inferior limit."

The sum of the $n + 1$ terms,

$h\phi(a) + h\phi(a + h) + \ldots + h\phi\ \{a + (n - 1)h\} + h\phi(a + nh)$, differs from the above series merely in the addition of the term $h\phi(a + nh)$ or $h\phi(b)$ which vanishes when the limit is taken. Hence the limit of this series may also be written

$$\int_a^b \phi(x)\,dx.$$

3. Integration from the Definition.

This summation may sometimes be effected by elementary means, as we now proceed to illustrate:—

Ex. 1. Calculate $\int_a^b e^x dx$.

Here we have to evaluate

$$Lt_{h=0} h[e^a + e^{a+h} + e^{a+2h} + \dots + e^{a+\overline{n-1}h}],$$

where $\quad b = a + nh.$

This $\quad = Lt_{h=0} h \dfrac{e^{nh} - 1}{e^h - 1} e^a$

$$= Lt_{h=0} (e^b - e^a) \frac{h}{e^h - 1} = e^b - e^a.$$

[*By Diff. Calc. for Beginners*, Art. 15.]

Ex. 2. To find $\int_a^b x dx$ we have to find $Lt \sum_{r=0}^{r=n-1} (a + rh)h$, where $nh = b - a$.

Now $\quad \sum (a + rh)h = ah \cdot n + h^2 \cdot \dfrac{n(n-1)}{2}$

$$= a(b-a) + \frac{(b-a)}{2}(b - a - h),$$

and in the limit becomes

$$a(b-a) + \frac{(b-a)^2}{2} = \frac{(b-a)(b+a)}{2}$$

$$= \frac{b^2}{2} - \frac{a^2}{2}.$$

Ex. 3. To find $\int_a^b \frac{1}{x^2} dx$ we have to obtain the limit when h indefinitely diminished of

$$\left[\frac{1}{a^2} + \frac{1}{(a+h)^2} + \frac{1}{(a+2h)^2} + \dots + \frac{1}{b^2}\right]h.$$

This is $> \left[\dfrac{1}{a(a+h)} + \dfrac{1}{(a+h)(a+2h)} + \dots + \dfrac{1}{b(b+h)}\right]h,$

i.e. $\quad > \left(\dfrac{1}{a} - \dfrac{1}{a+h}\right) + \left(\dfrac{1}{a+h} - \dfrac{1}{a+2h}\right) + \dots + \left(\dfrac{1}{b} - \dfrac{1}{b+h}\right)$

$$> \frac{1}{a} - \frac{1}{b+h}$$

and $\quad < \left[\dfrac{1}{(a-h)a} + \dfrac{1}{a(a+h)} + \dots + \dfrac{1}{(b-h)b}\right]k$

$$< \left(\frac{1}{a-h} - \frac{1}{a}\right) + \left(\frac{1}{a} - \frac{1}{a+h}\right) + \ldots + \left(\frac{1}{b-h} - \frac{1}{b}\right)$$

$$< \frac{1}{a-h} - \frac{1}{b},$$

and when h diminishes without limit, each of these becomes

$$\frac{1}{a} - \frac{1}{b}.$$

Thus $$\int_a^b \frac{1}{x^2} dx = \frac{1}{a} - \frac{1}{b}$$

Ex. 4. Prove *ab initio* that

$$\int_a^b \sin x \, dx = \cos a - \cos b.$$

We now are to find the limit of

$$[\sin a + \sin(a+h) + \sin(a+2h) + \ldots \text{ to } n \text{ terms}]h,$$

i.e. of $$\frac{\sin\left(a + \overline{n-1}\frac{h}{2}\right)\sin n\frac{h}{2}}{\sin\frac{h}{2}} h \text{ where } nh = b - a.$$

This expression $$= \left[\cos\left(a - \frac{h}{2}\right) - \cos\left\{a + (2n-1)\frac{h}{2}\right\}\right] \frac{\frac{h}{2}}{\sin\frac{h}{2}}$$

$$= \left[\cos\left(a - \frac{h}{2}\right) - \cos\left(b - \frac{h}{2}\right)\right] \frac{\frac{h}{2}}{\sin\frac{h}{2}},$$

which when h is indefinitely small ultimately takes the form $\cos a - \cos b$.

EXAMPLES

Prove by summation that

1. $\int_a^b e^{-x} dx = e^{-a} - e^{-b}$.

2. $\int_a^b \sinh x dx = \cosh b - \cosh a$.

3. $\int_a^b x^2 dx = \frac{b^3 - a^3}{3}$.

4. $\int_a^b \frac{1}{\sqrt{x}} dx = 2(\sqrt{b} - \sqrt{a})$.

5. $\int_a^b \cos\theta d\theta = \sin b - \sin a$.

4. Integration of x^m.

As a further example we next propose to consider the limit of the sum of the series

$$h[a^m + (a+h)^m + (a+2h)^m + \dots + (a+\overline{n-1}h)^m],$$

where $$h = \frac{b-a}{n},$$

and n is made indefinitely large, $m+1$ not being zero.

[*Lemma* – The limit of $\dfrac{(y+h)^{m+1} - y^{m+1}}{hy^m}$ is $m+1$ when h is indefinitely diminished, whatever y may be, provided it be of finite magnitude.]

For the expression may be written

$$y\frac{\left(1+\frac{h}{y}\right)^{m+1} - 1}{h},$$

and since h is to be ultimately zero we may consider $\dfrac{h}{y}$ to be less than unity, and we may therefore apply the Binomial Theorem to expand $\left(1+\dfrac{h}{y}\right)^{m+1}$, whatever be the value of $m+1$.

(See *Diff. Calc. for Beginners*, Art. 13.) Thus the expression becomes

$$= \frac{y}{h}\left[(m+1)\frac{h}{y} + \frac{(m+1)m}{1\cdot 2}\frac{h^2}{y^2} + \dots\right]$$

$$= m + 1 + \frac{h}{y} \times \textbf{(a convergent series)}$$

$$= m + 1 \text{ when } h \text{ is indefinitely diminished.]}$$

In the result $$Lt_{h=0}\frac{(y+h)^{m+1} - y^{m+1}}{hy^m} = m+1,$$

put y successively $= a, a+h, a+2h$, etc. ... $a+(n-1)h$, and we get

$$Lt\frac{(a+h)^{m+1} - a^{m+1}}{ha^m} = Lt\frac{(a+2h)^{m+1} - (a+h)^{m+1}}{h(a+h)^m}$$

$$= Lt\frac{(a+3h)^{m+1} - (a+2h)^{m+1}}{h(a+2h)^m} = \dots$$

$$= Lt\frac{(a+nh)^{m+1} - (a+\overline{n-1}h)^{m+1}}{h(a+\overline{n-1}h)^m}$$

$$= m+1;$$

or adding numerators for a new numerator and denominators for a new denominator,

$$Lt \frac{(a+nh)^{m+1} - a^{m+1}}{h[a^m + (a+h)^m + (a+2h)^m + \ldots + (a+n-1h)^m]} = m+1,$$

or

$$Lt_{h=0} h[a^m + (a+h)^m + (a+2h)^m + \ldots + (a+\overline{n-1}h)^m]$$

$$= \frac{b^{m+1} - a^{m+1}}{m+1}.$$

In accordance with the notation of Art. 2, this may be written

$$\int_a^b x^m dx = \frac{b^{m+1} - a^{m+1}}{m+1}.$$

The letters a and b may represent any finite quantities whatever, provided x^m does not become infinite between $x = a$ and $x = b$.

When a is taken as exceedingly small and ultimately zero, it is necessary in the proof to suppose h an infinitesimal of higher order, for it has been assumed that in the limit $\frac{h}{y}$ is zero for all the values given to y.

When $b = 1$ and $a = 0$, ultimately the theorem becomes

$$\int_0^1 x^m dx = \frac{1}{m+1} \text{ if } m+1 \text{ be positive,}$$

or $= \infty$ if $m+1$ be negative.

This theorem may be written also

$$Lt_{n=\infty} \frac{1}{n}\left[\left(\frac{1}{n}\right)^m + \left(\frac{2}{n}\right)^m + \ldots + \left(\frac{n-1}{n}\right)^m\right] = \frac{1}{m+1} \text{ or } \infty$$

according as $m+1$ is positive or negative. The limit

$$Lt_{n=\infty} \frac{1}{n}\left[\left(\frac{1}{n}\right)^m + \left(\frac{2}{n}\right)^m + \ldots + \left(\frac{n}{n}\right)^m\right]$$

or, which is the same thing,

$$Lt_{n=\infty} \frac{1^m + 2^m + 3^m + \ldots + n^m}{n^{m+1}},$$

differs from the former by $\frac{1}{n}$, *i.e.* by 0 in the limit, and is therefore also $\frac{1}{m+1}$, or ∞ according as $m+1$ is positive or negative. The case when $m+1=0$ will be discussed later.

Ex. 1. Find the area of the portion of the parabola $y^2 = 4ax$ bounded by the curve, the x-axis, and the ordinate $x = c$.

Let us divide the length c into n equal portions of which NM is the $(r + 1)$v, and erect ordinates NP, MQ. Then if

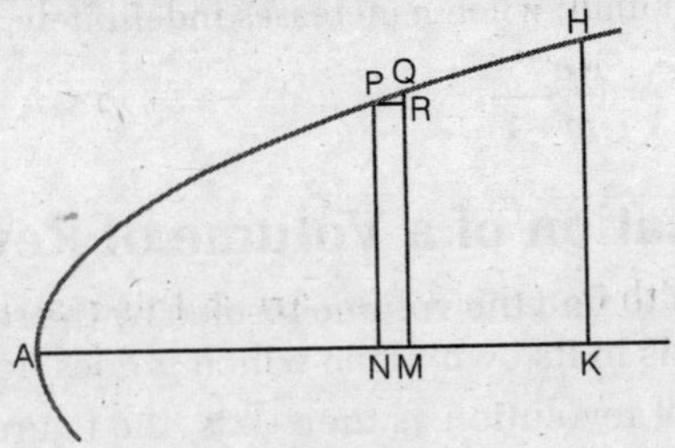

Fig. 2.

PR be drawn parallel to NM, the area required is the limit when n is infinite of the sum of such rectangles as PM (Art. 2),

$$i.e. \qquad Lt\ \Sigma PN \cdot NM \text{ or } Lt \sum_{r=0}^{r=(n-1)} \sqrt{4a \cdot rh}\ h,$$

where $nh = c$.

Now, $Lt_{h=0}[\sqrt{h} + \sqrt{2h} + \sqrt{3h} + \ldots + \sqrt{(n-1)h}]h$

$$= Lt_{n=\infty} \frac{1^{\frac{1}{2}} + 2^{\frac{1}{2}} + 3^{\frac{1}{2}} + \ldots + (n-1)^{\frac{1}{2}}}{n^{\frac{3}{2}}} \cdot c^{\frac{3}{2}} = \frac{2}{3} \cdot c^{\frac{3}{2}}. \text{ [By Art. 4.]}$$

$$\therefore \qquad \text{Area} = \frac{2}{3}\sqrt{4a}\ c^{\frac{3}{2}} = \frac{2}{3} c\sqrt{4ac}$$

$= \frac{2}{3}$ of the rectangle of which the extreme ordinate and abscissa of the area are adjacent sides.

Ex. 2. Find the mass of a rod whose density varies as the mth power of the distance from one end.

Let a be the length of the rod, ω its sectional area supposed uniform. Divide the rod into n elementary portions each of length $\frac{a}{n}$. The volume of the $(r + 1)$th element from the end of zero density is $\omega\frac{a}{n}$, and its density varies from $\left(\frac{ra}{n}\right)^m$ to $\left(\frac{\overline{r+1}\,a}{n}\right)^m$. Its mass is therefore intermediate between

$$\omega a^{m+1} \frac{r^m}{n^{m+1}} \text{ and } \omega a^{m+1} \frac{(r+1)^m}{n^{m+1}}.$$

Thus the mass of the whole rod lies between

$$\omega a^{m+1}\frac{1^m + 2^m + 3^m + \ldots + (n-1)^m}{n^{m+1}}$$

and $$\omega a^{m+1}\frac{1^m + 2^m + 3^m + \ldots + n^m}{n^{m+1}},$$

and in the limit, when n increases indefinitely, becomes

$$\frac{\omega\, a^{m+1}}{m+1}.$$

5. Determination of a Volume of Revolution.

Let it be required to find the volume formed by the revolution of a given curve AB about an axis in its own plane which it does not cut.

Taking the axis of revolution as the x-axis, the figure may be described exactly as in Art. 2.

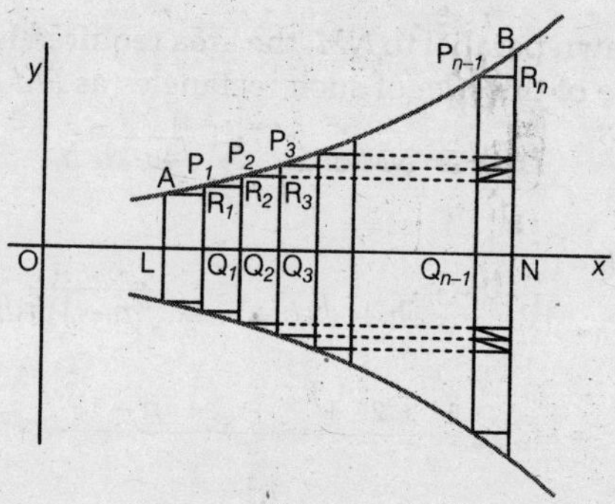

Fig. 3.

The elementary rectangles AQ_1, P_1Q_2, P_2Q_3, etc., trace in their revolution circular discs of equal thickness, and of volumes $\pi AL^2 \cdot LQ_1 \cdot \pi P_1Q_1^2 \cdot Q_1Q_2 \cdot$ etc. The several annular portions formed by the revolution of the portions AR_1P_1, $P_1R_2P_2$, $P_2R_3P_3$, etc., may be considered made to slide parallel to the x-axis into a corresponding position upon the disc of greatest radius, say that formed by the revolution of the figure $P_{n-1}Q_{n-1}NB$. Their sum is therefore less than this disc, *i.e.* in the limit less than an infinitesimal of the first order, for the breadth $Q_{n-1}N$ is h, and is ultimately an infinitesimal of the first order, and the length NB is supposed finite.

Hence the volume required is the limit, when h is zero (and therefore n infinite), of the sum of the series

$$\pi\{\phi(a)\}^2 h + \pi\{\phi(a+h)\}^2 h + \pi\{\phi(a+2h)\}^2\, h + \ldots + \pi\{\phi(a+\overline{n-1}\, h)\}^2 h.$$

or as it may be written $\pi\int_a^b [\phi(x)]^2 dx$ or $\pi\int_a^b y^2 dx$.

Ex. 1. The portion of the parabola $y^2 = 4ax$ bounded by the line $x = c$ revolves about the axis. Find the volume generated.

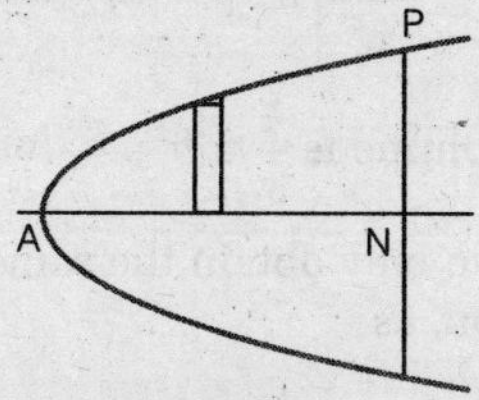

Fig. 4.

Let the portion required be that formed by the revolution of the area APN, bounded by the parabola and an ordinate PN.

Then dividing as before into elementary circular laminae, we have

$$\text{Volume } = \pi\int_0^c y^2 dx = 4a\pi\int_0^c x\,dx = 4a\pi\,\frac{c^2}{2} \qquad \text{[Art. 4.]}$$

$$= 2\pi ac^2 = \frac{1}{2}\pi PN^2 AN$$

$$= \frac{1}{2} \text{ cylinder of radius } PN \text{ and height } AN.$$

[Or if expressed as a series

$$\text{Volume} = 4a\pi\int_0^c x\,dx$$

$$= 4a\pi \; Lt\;\frac{1}{n}\left[\left(\frac{1}{n}\right)+\left(\frac{2}{n}\right)+\left(\frac{3}{n}\right)+\ldots+\left(\frac{n-1}{n}\right)\right]c^2$$

$$= 4a\pi\cdot\frac{c^2}{2} = 2a\pi c^2.] \qquad \text{[Art. 4.]}$$

Ex. 2. Find the volume of the prolate spheroid formed by the revolution of the ellipse $\frac{x^2}{a^2} + \frac{y^2}{b^2} = 1$ about the x-axis.

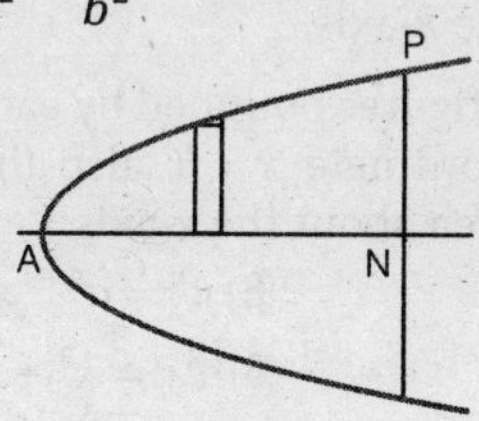

Fig. 5.

Dividing as before into elementary circular laminae whose axes coincide with x-axis, the volume is twice

$$\int_0^a \pi y^2 dx.$$

Now $\quad \int_0^a \pi y^2 dx = \int_0^a \pi\,\frac{b^2}{a^2}(a^2 - x^2)\,dx$

which, according to Article 4, is equal to

$$\frac{\pi b^2}{a^2}\left[a^2\cdot(a-0)-\frac{a^3-0^3}{3}\right] \text{ or } \frac{2}{3}\pi ab^2,$$

and the whole volume is $\frac{4}{3}\pi ab^2$;

[or if desirable we may obtain the same result without using the sign of integration, as

$$2.\ Lt_{n=\infty}\sum_{\frac{r}{n}=0}^{\frac{r}{n}=\frac{n-1}{n}}\pi\frac{b^2}{a^2}\left(a^2.\frac{a}{n}-\frac{r^2a^3}{n^3}\right)=2\frac{\pi b^2}{a^2}\left(\frac{a^3}{1}-\frac{a^3}{3}\right) \quad \text{[By Art. 4.]}$$

$$\doteq\frac{4}{3}\pi ab^2].$$

EXAMPLES

1. Find the area bounded by the curve $y=e^x$, the x-axis, and the ordinates $x=a$, $x=b$.

2. If the area in Question 1 revolve round the x-axis find the volume of the solid formed.

3. Find by the method of Art. 2, the area of the triangle formed by the line $y=x\tan\theta$, the x-axis and the line $x=a$.

Find also the volume of the cone formed when this triangle revolves about the x-axis.

4. Find the volume of the reel-shaped solid formed by the revolution about the y-axis of that part of the parabola $y^2=4ax$ cut off by the latus-rectum.

5. Find the volume of the sphere formed by the revolution of the circle $x^2+y^2=a^2$ about the x-axis.

6. Find the areas of the figures bounded by each of the following curves, the x-axis, and the ordinate $x=h$; also the volume formed by the revolution of each area about the x-axis:

(α) $y^3=a^2x$. (β) $y^n=a^{n-1}x$.

(γ) $a^{n-1}y=x^n$. (δ) $a^2y=x^3+ax^2$.

7. Find the mass of a circular disc of which the density at each point varies as the distance from the centre.

8. Find the mass of the prolate spheroid formed by the revolution of the ellipse $x^2/a^2+y^2/b^2=1$ about the x-axis, supposing the density at each point to be μx.

CHAPTER II.

GENERAL METHOD. STANDARD FORMS.

6. Before proceeding further with applications of the Integral Calculus, we shall establish a general theorem which will in many cases enable us to infer the result of the operation indicated by

$$\int_a^b \phi(x)dx$$

without having recourse to the usually tedious, and often difficult, process of Algebraic or Trigonometrical Summation.

7. PROP. Let $\phi(x)$ be any function of x which is finite and continuous between given finite values a and b of the variable x; let a be $<b$, and suppose the difference $b-a$ to be divided into n portions each equal h, so that $b-a=nh$. It is required to find *the limit of the sum* of the series

$$h[\phi(a)+\phi(a+h)+\phi(a+2h)+\ldots+\phi(b-h)+\phi(b)],$$

when h is diminished indefinitely, and therefore n increased without limit.

[It may at once be seen that this limit is finite, for if $\phi(a+rh)$ be the greatest term the sum is

$$<(n+1)h\phi(a+rh)$$

i.e. $$<(b-a)\phi(a+rh)+h\phi(a+rh),$$

which is finite, since by hypothesis $\phi(x)$ is finite for all values of x intermediate between b and a.]

Let $\psi(x)$ be another function of x such that $\phi(x)$ is its differential coefficient, *i.e.* such that

$$\phi(x)=\psi'(x).$$

We shall then prove that

$$Lt_{h=0}h[\phi(a)+\phi(a+h)+\phi(a+2h)+\ldots+\phi(b)]=\psi(b)-\psi(a).$$

By definition $\phi(a)=Lt_{h=0}\dfrac{\psi(a+h)-\psi(a)}{h}$,

and therefore $\phi(a)=\dfrac{\psi(a+h)-\psi(a)}{h}+a_1$,

where a_1 is a quantity whose limit is zero when h diminishes indefinitely; thus

$$h\phi(a)=\psi(a+h)-\psi(a)+ha_1.$$

Similarly

$$h\phi(a+h)=\psi(a+2h)-\psi(a+h)+ha_2,$$
$$h\phi(a+2h)=\psi(a+3h)-\psi(a+2h)+ha_3,$$
etc.,
$$h\phi(a+\overline{n-1}h)=\psi(a+nh)-\psi(a+\overline{n-1}h)+ha_n,$$

where the quantities $a_2, a_3, \ldots, a_n$ are all, like a_1, quantities whose limits are zero when h diminishes indefinitely.

By addition,

$$h[\phi(a)+\phi(a+h)+\phi(a+2h)+\ldots+\phi(b-h)]$$
$$=\psi(a+nh)-\psi(a)+h[a_1+a_2+\ldots+a_n],$$

Let a be the greatest of the quantities $a_1, a_2, \ldots, a_n$, then

$h[a_1+a_2+\ldots+a_n]$ is $< nha$, *i.e.* $<(b-a)a$, and therefore vanishes in the limit. Thus

$$Lt_{h=0}h[\phi(a)+\phi(a+h)+\phi(a+2h)+\ \ldots+\phi(b-h)]=\psi(b)-\psi(a).$$

The term $h\phi(b)$ is in the limit zero; hence if we desire, it may be added to the left-hand member of this result, and it may then be stated that

$$Lt_{h=0}h[\phi(a)+\phi(a+h)+\ldots+\phi(b-h)+\phi(b)]=\psi(b)-\psi(a),$$

i.e. $$\int_a^b \phi(x)\,dx=\psi(b)-\psi(a).$$

This result $\psi(b)-\psi(a)$ is frequently denoted by the notation $[\psi(x)]_a^b$.

From this result it appears that when the form of the function $\psi(x)$ (of which $\phi(x)$ is the differential coefficient) is obtained, the process of algebraic or trigonometric summation to obtain $\int_a^b \phi(x)\,dx$ may be avoided.

The letters b and a are supposed in the above work to denote *finite* quantities. We shall now *extend our notation*, so as to let $\int_a^\infty \phi(x)dx$ express the limit when b becomes infinitely large of $\psi(b)-\psi(a)$, *i.e.*

$$\int_a^\infty \phi(x)\,dx=Lt_{b=\infty}\int_a^b \phi(x)\,dx.$$

Similarly by $\int_\infty^b \phi(x)\,dx$ we shall be understood to mean

$$Lt_{a=\infty}[\psi(b)-\psi(a)]$$

or $$Lt_{a=\infty}\int_a^b \phi(x)\,dx.$$

Ex. 1. The differential coefficient of $\dfrac{x^{m+1}}{m+1}$ is plainly x^m.

Hence if $\phi(x) = x^m$ we have

$$\psi(x) = \frac{x^{m+1}}{m+1} \text{ and}$$

$$\int_a^b x^m dx = \frac{b^{m+1}}{m+1} - \frac{a^{m+1}}{m+1} = \frac{b^{m+1} - a^{m+1}}{m+1}.$$

Ex. 2. The quantity whose differential coefficient is $\cos x$ is known to be $\sin x$. Hence

$$\int_a^b \cos x \, dx = \sin b - \sin a.$$

Ex. 3. The quantity whose differential coefficient is e^x is itself e^x.

Hence $\int_a^b e^x dx = e^b - e^a$.

Ex. 4. $\int_0^\infty e^{-x} dx = Lt_{\left.\begin{subarray}{l} b=\infty \\ a=0 \end{subarray}\right\}} [-e^{-x}]_a^b = (-e^{-\infty}) - (-e^{-0}) = 1.$

EXAMPLES

Write down the values of

1. $\int_a^b x^{10} dx,$

2. $\int_0^1 x^{10} dx,$

3. $\int_1^2 x^n dx,$

4. $\int_2^3 \frac{1}{x} dx,$

5. $\int_0^2 \cos x \, dx,$

6. $\int_0^{\frac{\pi}{4}} \sec^2 x \, dx,$

7. $\int_0^{\frac{\pi}{4}} \sec x \tan x \, dx,$

8. $\int_0^1 \frac{1}{1+x^2} dx,$

9. $\int_0^1 \frac{1}{\sqrt{1-x^2}} dx,$

10. $\int_a^b (x + \cos x) dx.$

8. Geometrical Illustration of Proof.

The proof of the above theorem may be interpreted geometrically thus:—

Let *AB* be a portion of a curve of which the ordinate is finite and continuous at all points between *A* and *B*, as also the tangent of the angle which the tangent to the curve makes with the *x*-axis.

Let the abscissae of *A* and *B* be *a* and *b* respectively. Draw ordinates *AN*, *BM*.

Let the portion NM be divided into n equal portions each of length h. Erect ordinates at each of these points of division cutting the curve in P, Q, R, ..., etc. Draw the successive tangents AP_1, PQ_1, QR_1, etc., and the lines AP_2, PQ_2, QR_2, ...,

parallel to the x-axis and let the equation of the curve be $y = \psi(x)$, and let $\psi'(x) = \phi(x)$,

then $\phi(a)$, $\phi(a+h)$, $\phi(a+2h)$, etc., are respectively

$\tan P_2AP_1$, $\tan Q_2PQ_1$, etc.

and $h\phi(a)$, $h\phi(a+h)$, ..., are respectively the lengths

P_2P_1, Q_2Q_1, R_2R_1, etc.

Now it is clear that the algebraic sum of P_2P, Q_2Q, R_2R, ..., is $MB - NA$, *i.e.* $\psi(b) - \psi(a)$.

Hence $P_2P_1 + Q_2Q_1 + R_2R_1 + \ldots + [P_1P + Q_1Q + \ldots] = \psi(b) - \psi(a)$.

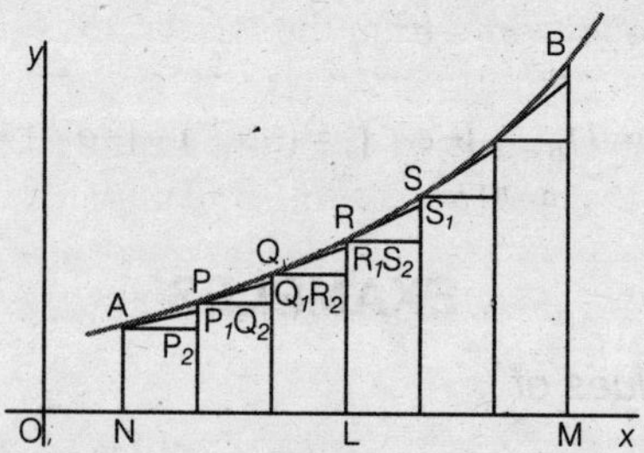

Fig. 6.

Now the portion within square brackets may be shewn to diminish indefinitely with h. For if R_1R for instance be the greatest of the several quantities P_1P, Q_1Q, etc., the sum

$$[P_1P + Q_1Q + \ldots] \text{ is } < nR_1R, \text{ i.e. } < (b-a)\frac{R_1R}{h}.$$

But if the abscissa of Q be called x, then $LR_2 = \psi(x)$, $R_2R_1 = h\psi'(x)$,

$$\text{and } LR = \psi(x+h) = \psi(x) + h\psi'(x) + \frac{h^2}{2!}\psi''(x+\theta h),$$

[*Diff. Calc. for Beginners*, Art. 185.]

$$\text{so that } R_1R = \frac{h^2}{2!}\psi''(x+\theta h) = \frac{h^2}{2!}\phi'(x+\theta h),$$

$$\text{and } (b-a)\frac{R_1R}{h} = \frac{(b-a)}{2}h\phi'(x+\theta h),$$

which is an infinitesimal in general of the first order.

Thus $\quad Lt_{h=0}[P_2P_1 + Q_2Q_1 + R_2R_1 + \ldots] = \psi(b) - \psi(a)$,

or $\quad Lt_{h=0}h[\phi(a) + \phi(a+h) + \phi(a+2h) + \ldots + \phi(b-h)] = \psi(b) - \psi(a)$.

Also since $Lt_{h=0}h\phi(b) = 0$, we have, by addition,

$$Lt_{h=0}h[\phi(a) + \phi(a+h) + \phi(a+2h) + \ldots + \phi(b)] = \psi(b) - \psi(a).$$

9. Interrogative Character of the Integral Calculus.

In the differential calculus the student has learnt how to differentiate a function of any assigned character with regard to the independent variable contained. In other words, having given $y = \psi(x)$, methods have been there explained of obtaining the form of the function $\psi'(x)$ in the equation

$$\frac{dy}{dx} = \psi'(x).$$

The proposition of Art. 7 shews that, if we can *reverse this operation* and obtain the form of $\psi(x)$ when $\psi'(x)$ is given we shall be able to perform the operation

$$\int_a^b \phi(x)\,dx,\ i.e.\ \int_a^b \psi'(x)\,dx,$$

by merely taking the function $\psi(x)$, substituting b and a alternately for x and subtracting the latter result from the former, thus obtaining

$$\psi(b) - \psi(a).$$

We shall therefore confine our attention for the next few chapters to the problem of *reversing the operations of the differential calculus.*

Further, the quantity b has been assumed to have any value whatever provided it be finite; we may therefore replace it by x and write the result of the proposition of Art. 7. as

$$\int_a^x \phi(x)dx = \psi(x) - \psi(a).$$

10. When the lower limit a is not specified and we are merely enquiring the form of the (at present) unknown function $\psi(x)$, whose differential coefficient is the known function $\phi(x)$, the notation used is

$$\int \phi(x)dx = \psi(x),$$

the limits being omitted.

11. Nomenclature.

The nomenclature of these expressions is as follows:

$$\int_a^b \phi(x)\,dx \quad \text{or} \quad \psi(b) - \psi(a)$$

is called the "**definite**" integral of $\phi(x)$ between limits a and b ;

$$\int_a^x \phi(x)\,dx \quad \text{or} \quad \psi(x) - \psi(a)$$

where the upper limit is left undetermined is called a "**corrected**" integral;

$$\int \phi(x)\,dx \quad \text{or} \quad \psi(x)$$

without any specified limits and regarded merely as the reversal of an operation of the differential calculus is called an "**indefinite**" or "**uncorrected**" integral.

12. Addition of a Constant.

It will be obvious that if $\phi(x)$ is the differential coefficient of $\psi(x)$, it is also the differential coefficient of $\psi(x) + C$ where C is any constant whatever; for the differential coefficient of any constant is zero. Accordingly we might write

$$\int \phi(x)dx = \psi(x) + C.$$

This constant is however not usually written down but will be understood to exist in all cases of indefinite integration though not expressed.

13. Different processes of indefinite integration will frequently give results of different form ; for instance $\int \frac{1}{\sqrt{1-x^2}}dx$ is $\sin^{-1} x$ or $-\cos^{-1} x$, for $\frac{1}{\sqrt{1-x^2}}$ is the differential coefficient of either of these expressions. Yet it is not to be inferred that

$$\sin^{-1} x = -\cos^{-1} x,$$

But what is really true is that $\sin^{-1} x$ and $-\cos^{-1} x$ differ by a constant, for

$$\sin^{-1} x + \cos^{-1} x = \frac{\pi}{2}$$

so that
$$\int \frac{1}{\sqrt{1-x^2}}dx = \sin^{-1} x + C$$

or
$$\int \frac{1}{\sqrt{1-x^2}}dx = -\cos^{-1} x + C',$$

the arbitrary constants being different.

14. Inverse Notation.

Agreeably with the accepted notation for the inverse Trigonometrical and inverse Hyperbolic functions, we might express the equation

$$\int \phi(x)dx = \psi(x), \quad \text{as} \quad \left(\frac{d}{dx}\right)^{-1} \phi(x) = \psi(x),$$

$$D^{-1}\phi(x) = \psi(x), \quad \text{or} \quad \frac{1}{D}\phi(x) = \psi(x);$$

and it is occasionally useful to employ this notation.

which very well expresses the interrogative character of the operation we are conducting.

15. General Laws satisfied by the Integrating Symbol $\int dx$.

(1) It will be plain from the meaning of the symbols that $\dfrac{d}{dx}\int \phi(x)dx$ is $\phi(x)$, but that $\int \dfrac{d}{dx}\phi(x)dx$ is $\phi(x) +$ any arbitrary constant.

(2) The operation of integration is **distributive**; for if u, v, w be any functions of x,

$$\frac{d}{dx}\left\{\int u\,dx + \int v\,dx + \int w\,dx\right\} = u + v + w; \text{ and therefore}$$

(omitting constants) $\int u\,dx + \int v\,dx + \int w\,dx = \int (u + v + w)dx.$

(3) The operation of integration is **commutative** with regard to constants. For if $\dfrac{du}{dx} = v$, and a be any constant, we have $\dfrac{d}{dx}(au) = a\dfrac{du}{dx} = av;$

so that (omitting any constant of integration)

$$au = \int av\,dx, \text{ or } a\int v dx = \int av\,dx,$$ which establishes the theorem.

16. We now proceed to a detailed consideration of several elementary special forms of functions.

17. Integration of x^n.

By differentiation of $\dfrac{x^{n+1}}{n+1}$ we obtain $\dfrac{d}{dx}\dfrac{x^{n+1}}{n+1} = x^n.$

Hence (as has been already seen in Art. 4 and in Art. 7, Ex. 1)

$$\int x^n dx = \frac{x^{n+1}}{n+1}.$$

Thus the rule for the integration of any constant power of x is, *Increase the index by unity and divide by the index so increased.*

For example,

$$\int x^3 dx = \frac{x^4}{4}; \qquad \int x^{\frac{5}{6}} dx = \frac{6}{11}x^{\frac{11}{6}}; \qquad \int x^{-5} dx = \frac{x^{-4}}{-4} = -\frac{1}{4x^4}.$$

EXAMPLES

Write down the integrals of

1. $x, 1, 0, x^{99}, x^{999}, x^{1000}$.
2. $x^{-11}, x^{-101}, x^{-99}$.
3. $x^{\frac{1}{2}}, x^{\frac{3}{5}}, x^{\frac{5}{8}}$.
4. $x^{-\frac{1}{2}}, x^{-\frac{5}{6}}, x^{-\frac{2}{3}}$.
5. $ax + \dfrac{b}{x^2}, a + bx + \dfrac{c}{x^{10}}$.
6. $\dfrac{ax^2 + bx + c}{x^3}, \dfrac{ax^{-2} + bx^{-1} + c}{x^{-3}}$.

18. The Case of x^{-1}.

It will be remembered that x^{-1} or $\frac{1}{x}$ is the differential coefficient of $\log x$.

Thus $$\int \frac{1}{x}dx = \log x.$$

This therefore forms an *apparent* exception to the general rule

$$\int x^n dx = \frac{x^{n+1}}{n+1}.$$

19.

The result, however, may be deduced as a limiting case. Supplying the arbitrary constant, we have

$$\int x^n dx = \frac{x^{n+1}}{n+1} + C = \frac{x^{n+1}-1}{n+1} + A, \text{ where } A = C + \frac{1}{n+1},$$

and is still an *arbitrary* constant.

Taking the limit when $n+1=0$,

$\frac{x^{n+1}-1}{n+1}$ takes the form $\log x$, [*Diff. Calc. for Beginners,* Art. 15.]

and as *C is arbitrary*, we may suppose that it contains a negatively infinite portion $-\frac{1}{n+1}$ together with another *arbitrary* portion *A*.

Thus $Lt_{n=-1}\int x^n dx = \log x + A.$

20.

In the same way as in the integration of x^n we have

$$\frac{d}{dx}(ax+b)^{n+1} = (n+1)a(ax+b)^n \text{ and } \frac{d}{dx}\log(ax+b) = \frac{a}{ax+b},$$

and therefore $\int (ax+b)^n dx = \frac{(ax+b)^{n+1}}{(n+1)a}$ and $\int \frac{dx}{ax+b} = \frac{1}{a}\log(ax+b)$.

[For convenience we shall often find

$\int \frac{1}{ax+b}dx$ printed as $\int \frac{dx}{ax+b}$, $\int \frac{1}{\sqrt{a^2+x^2}}dx$ as $\int \frac{dx}{\sqrt{a^2+x^2}}$, etc.]

EXAMPLES

Write down the integrals of

1. $ax, x^a, a+x, a-x, a-x^a.$

2. $\frac{a}{x}, \frac{x}{a}, \frac{a+x}{x}, \frac{1}{a+x}.$

3. $\frac{x}{a+x}, \frac{1}{a-bx}, \frac{1}{(a-x)^2}, \frac{1}{(a-x)^n}.$

4. $\frac{1}{a+x}+\frac{1}{a-x}, \frac{1}{x+a}+\frac{1}{x-a}, \frac{1}{(a+x)^2}+\frac{1}{(a-x)^2}.$

21. We may next remark that since the differential coefficients of $[\phi(x)]^{n+1}$ and of $\log \phi(x)$ are respectively

$$(n+1)[\phi(x)]^n \phi(x) \text{ and } \frac{\phi'(x)}{\phi(x)},$$

we have, $\int [\phi(x)]^n \phi'(x) dx = \dfrac{[\phi(x)]^{n+1}}{n+1}$ and $\int \dfrac{\phi'(x)}{\phi(x)} dx = \log \phi(x)$.

The second of these results especially is of great use. It may be put into words thus :— *the integral of any fraction of which the numerator is the differential coefficient of the denominator is*

log (*denominator*).

For example, $\displaystyle\int \frac{2ax+b}{ax^2+bx+c} dx = \log(ax^2+bx+c)$,

$$\int \cot x \, dx = \int \frac{\cos x}{\sin x} dx = \log \sin x,$$

$$\int \tan x \, dx = -\int \frac{-\sin x}{\cos x} dx = -\log \cos x = \log \sec x,$$

$$\int \frac{e^x - e^{-x}}{e^x + e^{-x}} dx = \log(e^x + e^{-x}).$$

EXAMPLES

Write down the integrals of

1. $(e^x + a)^n e^x, \dfrac{e^x}{e^x + a}, (ax^2+bx+c)^n(2ax+b)$.

2. $\dfrac{e^x + e^{-x}}{e^x - e^{-x}}, \dfrac{\sec^2 x}{\tan x}, \dfrac{2ax+b}{(ax^2+bx+c)^2}$.

3. $\dfrac{\frac{1}{1+x^2}}{\tan^{-1} x}, \dfrac{1}{\sqrt{1-x^2}\sin^{-1} x}, \dfrac{1}{x \log x}$.

22. It will now be perceived that the operations of the Integral Calculus are of a tentative, nature, and that success in integration depends upon a knowledge of the results of differentiating the simple functions. It is therefore necessary to learn the table of standard forms which is now appended. It is practically the same list as that already learnt for differentiation, and the proofs of these results lie in differentiating the right hand members of the several results. The list will be gradually extended and a supplementary list given later.

PRELIMINARY TABLE OF RESULTS TO BE COMMITTED TO MEMORY.

23.

$$\int x^n dx = \frac{x^{n+1}}{n+1}.$$

$$\int \frac{1}{x} dx = \log_e x.$$

$$\int a^x dx = \frac{a^x}{\log_e a}.$$

$$\int e^x dx = e^x.$$

$$\left.\begin{aligned}
&\int \cos x\, dx = \sin x. \\
&\int \sin x\, dx = -\cos x. \\
&\int \sec^2 x\, dx = \tan x. \\
&\int \operatorname{cosec}^2 x\, dx = -\cot x. \\
&\int \frac{\sin x}{\cos^2 x} dx = \sec x. \\
&\int \frac{\cos x}{\sin^2 x} dx = -\operatorname{cosec} x. \\
&\left.\begin{aligned}&\int \tan x\, dx = \log \sec x. \\ &\int \cot x\, dx = \log \sin x.\end{aligned}\right\} \text{Art. 21.}
\end{aligned}\right]$$

$$\left.\begin{aligned}
&\int \frac{dx}{\sqrt{a^2 - x^2}} = \sin^{-1}\frac{x}{a} \text{ or } -\cos^{-1}\frac{x}{a}. \\
&\int \frac{dx}{a^2 + x^2} = \frac{1}{a}\tan^{-1}\frac{x}{a} \text{ or } -\frac{1}{a}\cot^{-1}\frac{x}{a}. \\
&\int \frac{dx}{x\sqrt{x^2 - a^2}} = \frac{1}{a}\sec^{-1}\frac{x}{a} \text{ or } -\frac{1}{a}\operatorname{cosec}^{-1}\frac{x}{a}. \\
&\int \frac{dx}{\sqrt{2ax - x^2}} = \operatorname{vers}^{-1}\frac{x}{a} \text{ or } -\operatorname{covers}^{-1}\frac{x}{a}.
\end{aligned}\right\}$$

24. It is a help to the memory to observe that all those integrals of the above list which begin with the letters "co", as $\cos x$, $\cos^{-1}\frac{x}{a}$, $\operatorname{covers}^{-1}\frac{x}{a}$, etc., have a negative sign prefixed to them. The reason is obvious. Each of these functions decreases as x increases through the first quadrant; their differential coefficients are therefore negative.

Also it is a further help to observe the dimensions of each side.

For instance, x and a being supposed linear, $\int \frac{dx}{\sqrt{a^2 - x^2}}$ is of zero dimensions. There could therefore be no $\frac{1}{a}$ prefixed to the integral. Again $\int \frac{dx}{a^2 + x^2}$ is of dimensions -1. Hence the result of integration must be of dimensions -1. Thus the integral could not be $\tan^{-1} \frac{x}{a}$ (which is of zero dimensions). The student should therefore have no difficulty in remembering in which cases the factor $\frac{1}{a}$ is to be prefixed.

EXAMPLES

Write down the indefinite integrals of the following functions :—

1. $\frac{1}{x+1}, \frac{x}{x+1}, \frac{x}{x^2+1}, \frac{x^2}{x^3+1}, \frac{x^{n-1}}{x^n+a^n}$.

2. $2^x, x^3 + 3^x, a + b^x + c^{2x}$.

3. $\cos^2 \frac{x}{2}, \cos^3 x . \sin x, \tan^n x \sec^2 x$.

4. $\cot x + \tan x, \cos x\left(\frac{1}{\sin x} + \frac{1}{\sin^2 x}\right)$.

5. $\frac{1}{\sqrt{1-x^2}}, \frac{1}{9+x^2}, \frac{1}{x\sqrt{x^2-4}}$.

6. $\frac{1}{\sqrt{x-x^2}}, \frac{1}{x\sqrt{2x^2-8}}, \frac{1}{\sqrt{8-2x^2}}, \frac{x^2}{4+x^2}$.

7. $\frac{\tan^{-1} x}{1+x^2}, \frac{\sin^{-1} x}{\sqrt{1-x^2}}, \frac{\sec^{-1} x}{x\sqrt{x^2-1}}$.

8. $\frac{x^{e-1} + e^{x-1}}{x^e + e^x}, \frac{\cot x}{\log \sin x}, \frac{1}{x \sec^{-1} x . \sqrt{x^2-1}}$.

CHAPTER III.

METHOD OF SUBSTITUTION.

25. Change of the Independent Variable.

The independent variable may be changed from x to z by the change $x = F(z)$, by the formula

$$\int V\,dx = \int V\frac{dx}{dz}dz,$$

V being any function of x.

Or if we write $V = f(x)$,

the formula will be

$$\int f(x)dx = \int f\{F(z)\}\,F'(z)dz.$$

To prove this, it is only necessary to write

$$u = \int V dx;$$

then $$\frac{du}{dx} = V.$$

But $$\frac{du}{dz} = \frac{du}{dx}\frac{dx}{dz} = V\frac{dx}{dz},$$

whence $$u = \int V\frac{dx}{dz}dz.$$

Thus to integrate $\int \frac{e^{\tan^{-1}x}}{1+x^2}dx$, let $\tan^{-1} x = z$. Then

$$\frac{1}{1+x^2}\frac{dx}{dz} = 1,$$

and the integral becomes

$$\int \frac{e^{\tan^{-1}x}}{1+x^2}\frac{dx}{dz}dz = \int e^z dz = e^z = e^{\tan^{-1}x}.$$

26.

In using the formula

$$\int f(x)dx = \int f\{F(z)\}F'(z)dz,$$

after choosing the form of the transformation $x = F(z)$, it is usual to make use of differentials, writing the equation

$$\frac{dx}{dz} = F'(z) \text{ as } dx = F'(z)dz;$$

the formula will then be reproduced by replacing dx of the left hand side by $F'(z)\,dz$, and x by $F(z)$.

Thus in the preceding example, after putting $\tan^{-1} x = z$, we may write

$$\frac{dx}{1+x^2} = dz$$

and $$\int \frac{e^{\tan^{-1}x}}{1+x^2} dx = \int e^z dz = \text{etc.}$$

27. We next consider the case when the integration is a definite one between specified limits.

The result obtained above, when $x = F(z)$ is

$$\int f(x)dx = \int f\{F(z)\} F'(z)dz.$$

Let $$f(x) = \psi'(x),$$

then $$\int f(x)dx = \psi(x) + C;$$

and if the limits for x be a and b, we have

$$\int_a^b f(x)dx = \psi(b) - \psi(a).$$

Now when $$x = a, z = F^{-1}(a);$$

and when $$x = b, z = F^{-1}(b).$$

Also $$f\{F(z)\} = \frac{d}{dx}\psi\{F(z)\},$$

and $$f\{F(z)\} F'(z) = \frac{d}{dx}\psi\{F(z)\}\frac{dx}{dz} = \frac{d}{dz}\psi\{F(z)\},$$

whence $$\int_{F^{-1}(a)}^{F^{-1}(b)} f\{F(z)\} F'(z)dz = \int_{F^{-1}(a)}^{F^{-1}(b)} \frac{d}{dz}\psi\{F(z)\}dz$$

$$= \psi[F\{F^{-1}(b)\}] - \psi[F\{F^{-1}(a)\}]$$

$$= \psi(b) - \psi(a);$$

so that the result of integrating $f\{F(z)\} F'(z)$ with regard to z between limits $F^{-1}(a)$ and $F^{-1}(b)$ is identical with that of integrating $f(x)$ with regard to x between the limits a and b.

Ex. 1. Evaluate $\int \frac{1}{\sqrt{x}} \cos\sqrt{x}\, dx$.

Let $x = z^2$, and therefore $dx = 2z\, dz$;

$$\therefore \int \frac{1}{\sqrt{x}}\cos\sqrt{x}\, dx = \int \frac{1}{z}\cos z \,.\, 2z\, dz = 2\int \cos z\, dz = 2\sin z = 2\sin\sqrt{x}.$$

Ex. 2. Evaluate $\int x^2 \cos x^3 dx$.

Let $x^3 = z$, and therefore $3x^2 dx = dz$;

$$\therefore \int x^2 \cos x^3 dx = \frac{1}{3}\int \cos z\, dz = \frac{1}{3}\sin z = \frac{1}{3}\sin x^3.$$

Ex. 3. Evaluate $\int_0^1 \frac{x}{\sqrt{1+x^2}}\,dx$.

Put $x = \tan\theta$, then $dx = \sec^2\theta\, d\theta$;

when $x = 0$, we have $\theta = 0$,

when $x = 1$, we have $\theta = \frac{\pi}{4}$;

$$\therefore \quad \int_0^1 \frac{x}{\sqrt{1+x^2}}\,dx = \int_0^{\frac{\pi}{4}} \frac{\tan\theta}{\sec\theta}\sec^2\theta\, d\theta = \int_0^{\frac{\pi}{4}} \sec\theta\tan\theta\, d\theta$$

$$= [\sec\theta]_0^{\frac{\pi}{4}} = \sec\frac{\pi}{4} - \sec 0 = \sqrt{2} - 1.$$

Ex. 4. Evaluate $\int_0^1 \frac{dx}{e^x + e^{-x}}$ [i. e. $\frac{1}{2}\int_0^1 \operatorname{sech} x\, dx$].

Let $e^x = z$, then $e^x\, dx = dz$. When $x = 0$, $z = 1$, and when $x = 1$, $z = e$. Hence

$$\int_0^1 \frac{dx}{e^x + e^{-x}} = \int_1^e \frac{dz}{1+z^2} = [\tan^{-1} z]_1^e = \tan^{-1} e - \tan^{-1} 1 = \tan^{-1}\frac{e-1}{e+1}.$$

The indefinite integral is $\tan^{-1} e^x$.

EXAMPLES

1. Integrate $e^x \cos e^x$ (Put $e^x = z$),

   $nx^{n-1}\cos x^n$ (Put $x^n = z$),

   $\frac{1}{x}\cos(\log x)$ (Put $\log x = z$).

2. Evaluate $\int \frac{2x}{1+x^4}\,dx$ (Put $x^2 = z$), $\int \frac{3x^2 dx}{1+x^6}$ (Put $x^3 = z$).

3. Integrate $a\cos x + \frac{bx^3}{1+x^8}$, $ae^x \sin e^x + b\tanh x$.

4. Evaluate $\int_0^1 \frac{dx}{3+2x+x^2}$. (Put $x + 1 = z$).

5. Evaluate $\int_0^1 \frac{dx}{\sqrt{5-2x-x^2}}$ (Put $x + 1 = z$).

6. Evaluate $\int_2^3 \frac{dx}{(x-1)\sqrt{x^2-2x}}$ (Put $x - 1 = z$).

7. Evaluate $\int \frac{1}{2\sqrt{x}\,(1+x)}\,dx$ (Put $x = z^2$).

8. Evaluate $\int \frac{1}{2\sqrt{x}\,\sqrt{1-x}}\,dx$.

9. Evaluate $\int \frac{1}{2x\sqrt{x-1}}\,dx$.

NOTE ON THE HYPERBOLIC FUNCTIONS.

28. Definitions.

For purposes of integration it is desirable that the student shall be familiar with the definitions and fundamental properties of the direct and inverse hyperbolic functions.

By analogy with the exponential values of the sine, cosine, tangent, etc., the exponential functions

$$\frac{e^x - e^{-x}}{2}, \frac{e^x + e^{-x}}{2}, \frac{e^x - e^{-x}}{e^x + e^{-x}}, \text{etc.}$$

are respectively written $\sinh x$, $\cosh x$, $\tanh x$, etc.

29. Elementary Properties.

We clearly have

$$\cosh^2 x - \sinh^2 x = \left(\frac{e^x + e^{-x}}{2}\right)^2 - \left(\frac{e^x - e^{-x}}{2}\right)^2 = 1$$

$$\operatorname{sech}^2 x + \tanh^2 x = \left(\frac{2}{e^x + e^{-x}}\right)^2 + \left(\frac{e^x - e^{-x}}{e^x + e^{-x}}\right)^2 = 1$$

$$\tanh x = \frac{e^x - e^{-x}}{e^x + e^{-x}} = \frac{\sinh x}{\cosh x}$$

$$\coth x = \frac{e^x + e^{-x}}{e^x - e^{-x}} = \frac{\cosh x}{\sinh x} = \frac{1}{\tanh x}$$

$$\cosh^2 x + \sinh^2 x = \left(\frac{e^x + e^{-x}}{2}\right)^2 + \left(\frac{e^x - e^{-x}}{2}\right)^2 = \frac{e^{2x} + e^{-2x}}{2} = \cosh 2x,$$

$$2\sinh x \cosh x = 2\frac{e^x - e^{-x}}{2} \cdot \frac{e^x + e^{-x}}{2} = \frac{e^{2x} - e^{-2x}}{2} = \sinh 2x,$$

with many other results analogous to the common formulae of Trigonometry.

30. Inverse Forms.

Let us search for the meaning of the inverse function $\sinh^{-1} x$.

Put $$\sinh^{-1} x = y,$$

then $$x = \sinh y = \frac{e^y - e^{-y}}{2};$$

$\therefore$ $$e^{2y} - 2xe^y - 1 = 0, \quad \text{and} \quad e^y = x \pm \sqrt{1 + x^2}.$$

Thus $$y = \log(x \pm \sqrt{1 + x^2}),$$

and we shall take this expression with a positive sign, viz., $\log(x + \sqrt{1 + x^2})$ as $\sinh^{-1} x$.

31. Similarly, putting $\cosh^{-1} x = y$, we have

$$x = \cosh y = \frac{e^y + e^{-y}}{2}$$

and $e^{2y} - 2xe^y + 1 = 0$

and $e^y = x \pm \sqrt{x^2 - 1}$,

whence $y = \log(x \pm \sqrt{x^2 - 1})$,

and we shall take this expression with a positive sign, viz.,

$$\log(x + \sqrt{x^2 - 1}) \text{ as } \cosh^{-1} x.$$

32. Again, putting $\tanh^{-1} x = y$, we have

$$x = \tanh y = \frac{e^y - e^{-y}}{e^y + e^{-y}},$$

and therefore $e^{2y} = \dfrac{1+x}{1-x}$

whence $\tanh^{-1} x = \dfrac{1}{2} \log \dfrac{1+x}{1-x}$.

Similarly $\coth^{-1} x = \dfrac{1}{2} \log \dfrac{x+1}{x-1}$.

33. We shall thus consider

$\sinh^{-1} \dfrac{x}{a}$ synonymous with $\log \dfrac{x + \sqrt{x^2 + a^2}}{a}$,

$\cosh^{-1} \dfrac{x}{a}$ synonymous with $\log \dfrac{x + \sqrt{x^2 - a^2}}{a}$,

$\tanh^{-1} \dfrac{x}{a}$ synonymous with $\dfrac{1}{2} \log \dfrac{a+x}{a-x}$, and

$\coth^{-1} \dfrac{x}{a}$ synonymous with $\dfrac{1}{2} \log \dfrac{x+a}{x-a}$.

34. The Gudermannian.

Again, the function $\cos^{-1} \operatorname{sech} u$ is called the Gudermannian of u and written $\operatorname{gd} u$.

If $x = \cos^{-1} \operatorname{sech} u$,

$$\cos x = \operatorname{sech} u,$$

$$\sin x = \sqrt{1 - \operatorname{sech}^2 u} = \tanh u,$$

and $\tan x = \dfrac{\tanh x}{\operatorname{sech} u} = \sinh u$.

Hence $\operatorname{gd} u = \cos^{-1} \operatorname{sech} u = \sin^{-1} \tanh u = \tan^{-1} \sinh u$.

35. Further, if $u = \log \tan\left(\frac{\pi}{4} \pm \frac{x}{2}\right)$,

we have $$e^u = \frac{1 \pm \tan\frac{x}{2}}{1 \mp \tan\frac{x}{2}};$$

whence $$\tan\frac{x}{2} = \frac{e^u - 1}{e^u + 1},$$

and $$\tan x = \frac{2\tan\frac{x}{2}}{1 - \tan^2\frac{x}{2}} = 2\frac{\frac{e^u - 1}{e^u + 1}}{1 - \left(\frac{e^u - 1}{e^u + 1}\right)^2}$$

$$= 2\frac{e^{2u} - 1}{4e^u} = \frac{e^u - e^{-u}}{2} = \sinh u.$$

Hence $x = \tan^{-1}\sinh u = \text{gd}\, u$.

Thus $\log \tan\left(\frac{\pi}{4} + \frac{x}{2}\right) = \text{gd}^{-1} x$,

the inverse Gudermannian of x.

EXAMPLES

Establish the following results :—

1. $\int \cos\text{h}\ x\, dx = \sin\text{h}\ x.$
2. $\int \sinh x\, dx = \cosh x.$
3. $\int \text{sech}^2 x\, dx = \tanh x.$
4. $\int \text{cosech}^2 x\, dx = -\coth x.$
5. $\int \frac{\sinh x}{\cos\text{h}^2 x} dx = -\text{sech}\ x.$
6. $\int \frac{\cos\text{h}\ x}{\sin\text{h}^2 x} dx = -\text{cosech}\ x.$
7. Writing sg x for sin gd x, etc., establish the following results :—

   (α) $\int \text{cg}\ x\, dx = \text{gd}\ x.$

   (β) $\int \text{cg}^2 x\, dx = \text{sg}\ x.$

   (γ) $\int \frac{dx}{\text{cgx}} = \text{tg}\ x.$

36. Integrals of $\dfrac{1}{\sqrt{x^2+a^2}}$ and $\dfrac{1}{\sqrt{x^2-a^2}}$.

The differential coefficient of $\log_e \dfrac{x+\sqrt{x^2+a^2}}{a}$ is plainly $\dfrac{1}{\sqrt{x^2+a^2}}$.

Thus $\displaystyle\int \frac{dx}{\sqrt{x^2+a^2}} = \log\frac{x+\sqrt{x^2+a^2}}{a} = \sin h^{-1}\frac{x}{a}.$

Similarly $\displaystyle\int \frac{dx}{\sqrt{x^2-a^2}} = \log\frac{x+\sqrt{x^2-a^2}}{a} = \cos h^{-1}\frac{x}{a}.$

37. In the inverse hyperbolic forms these results resemble that for the integral $\displaystyle\int\frac{dx}{\sqrt{a^2-x^2}}$, viz., $\sin^{-1}\dfrac{x}{a}$, and the analogy is an aid to the memory.

38. We might have established the results thus:—

To find $\displaystyle\int\frac{dx}{\sqrt{x^2+a^2}}$ put $x = a\sinh u$, then

$dx = a\cos hu\, du$ and $\sqrt{x^2+a^2} = a\cosh u$.

Hence $\displaystyle\int\frac{dx}{\sqrt{x^2+a^2}} = \int du = u = \sinh^{-1}\frac{x}{a}.$

Similarly putting $x = a\cosh u$, we have

$$\int\frac{dx}{\sqrt{x^2-a^2}} = \int\frac{a\sinh u\, du}{a\sinh u} = \int du = u = \cosh^{-1}\frac{x}{a}.$$

Integrals of $\sqrt{a^2-x^2}$, $\sqrt{a^2+x^2}$, $\sqrt{x^2-a^2}$

39. To integrate $\sqrt{a^2-x^2}$.

Let $x = a\sin\theta;$

then $dx = a\cos\theta\, d\theta,$

and $\displaystyle\int\sqrt{a^2-x^2}\,dx = a^2\int\cos^2\theta\, d\theta = a^2\int\frac{1+\cos 2\theta}{2}d\theta = \frac{a^2}{4}\sin 2\theta + \frac{a^2}{2}\theta$

$$= \frac{1}{2}a\sin\theta\cdot a\cos\theta + \frac{a^2}{2}\theta$$

or $\displaystyle\int\sqrt{a^2-x^2}\,dx = \frac{x\sqrt{a^2-x^2}}{2} + \frac{a^2}{2}\sin^{-1}\frac{x}{a}.$

40. To integrate $\sqrt{a^2 + x^2}$.

Let $x = a \sinh z$,

then $dx = a \cosh z \, dz$;

then since $1 + \sinh^2 z = \cosh^2 z$,

we have
$$\int \sqrt{a^2 + x^2}\,dx = a^2 \int \cosh^2 z \, dz = \frac{a^2}{2} \int (\cosh 2z + 1)\, dz$$
$$= \frac{a^2}{4} \sinh 2z + \frac{a^2 z}{2}$$
$$= \frac{1}{2} a \sinh z \,.\, a \cosh z + \frac{a^2}{2} z,$$

i.e.
$$\int \sqrt{a^2 + x^2}\, dx = \frac{x\sqrt{a^2 + x^2}}{2} + \frac{a^2}{2} \sinh^{-1} \frac{x}{a}$$

or
$$\frac{x\sqrt{a^2 + x^2}}{2} + \frac{a^2}{2} \log \frac{x + \sqrt{x^2 + a^2}}{a}.$$

41. To integrate $\sqrt{x^2 - a^2}$.

Let $x = a \cosh z$,

then $dx = a \sinh z \, dz$;

then since $\cosh^2 z - 1 = \sinh^2 z$,

$$\int \sqrt{x^2 - a^2}\,dx = a^2 \int \sinh^2 z \, dz = \frac{a^2}{2} \int (\cosh 2z - 1)\, dz$$
$$= \frac{a^2}{4} \sinh 2z - \frac{a^2 z}{2} = \frac{1}{2} a \sinh z \cdot a \cosh z - \frac{a^2 z}{2},$$

i.e.
$$\int \sqrt{x^2 - a^2}\, dx = \frac{x\sqrt{x^2 - a^2}}{2} - \frac{a^2}{2} \cosh^{-1} \frac{x}{a}$$

or
$$\frac{x\sqrt{x^2 - a^2}}{2} - \frac{a^2}{2} \log \frac{x + \sqrt{x^2 - a^2}}{2}.$$

42. If we put $\tan x = t$, and therefore $\sec^2 x \, dx = dt$.

we have

$$\int \sec^3 x \, dx = \int \sqrt{1 + t^2}\, dt = t\frac{\sqrt{1 + t^2}}{2} + \frac{1}{2} \log(t + \sqrt{1 + t^2}), \quad \text{[by Art. 40.]}$$
$$= \frac{\tan x \sec x}{2} + \frac{1}{2} \log(\tan x + \sec x),$$

or
$$\frac{\sin x}{2\cos^2 x} + \frac{1}{4} \log \frac{1 + \sin x}{1 - \sin x}.$$

43. Integrals of cosec x and sec x.

Let $\tan\frac{x}{2} = z$; taking the logarithmic differential

$$\frac{1}{2\tan\frac{x}{2}}\sec^2\frac{x}{2}dx = \frac{dz}{z}$$

or
$$\frac{dx}{\sin x} = \frac{dz}{z}.$$

Thus $\int \operatorname{cosec} x\,dx = \int\frac{dz}{z} = \log z = \log\tan\frac{x}{2}$.

In this example let $x = \frac{\pi}{2} + y$.

Then
$$dx = dy,$$

and
$$\int \sec y\,dy = \log\tan\left(\frac{\pi}{4} + \frac{y}{2}\right).$$

Hence
$$\int \sec x\,dx = \log\tan\left(\frac{\pi}{4} + \frac{x}{2}\right)$$

or
$$\text{gd}^{-1}x.$$

44. We have now the

ADDITIONAL STANDARD FORMS,

$$\int\frac{dx}{\sqrt{x^2 + a^2}} = \log\frac{x + \sqrt{x^2 + a^2}}{a} = \sinh^{-1}\frac{x}{a}.$$

$$\int\frac{dx}{\sqrt{x^2 - a^2}} = \log\frac{x + \sqrt{x^2 - a^2}}{a} = \cosh^{-1}\frac{x}{a}.$$

$$\int\sqrt{a^2 - x^2}\,dx = \frac{x\sqrt{a^2 - x^2}}{2} + \frac{a^2}{2}\sin^{-1}\frac{x}{a}.$$

$$\int\sqrt{x^2 + a^2}\,dx = \frac{x\sqrt{a^2 + x^2}}{2} + \frac{a^2}{2}\sinh^{-1}\frac{x}{a}.$$

$$\int\sqrt{x^2 - a^2}\,dx = \frac{x\sqrt{x^2 - a^2}}{2} - \frac{a^2}{2}\cosh^{-1}\frac{x}{a}.$$

$$\int \operatorname{cosec} x\,dx = \log\tan\frac{x}{2}.$$

$$\int \sec x\,dx = \log\tan\left(\frac{\pi}{4} + \frac{x}{2}\right) = \text{gd}^{-1}x.$$

EXAMPLES

Write down the integrals of

1. $\dfrac{1}{\sqrt{1-x^2}}, \dfrac{1}{\sqrt{x^2-1}}, \dfrac{1}{\sqrt{1+x^2}}, \sqrt{1-x^2}, \sqrt{x^2-1}, \sqrt{1+x^2}$.

2. $\dfrac{1}{\sqrt{x^2+2x}}, \dfrac{1}{\sqrt{2+2x-x^2}}, \dfrac{1}{\sqrt{x^2-2x+2}}, \sqrt{x^2+2x}, \dfrac{1}{\sqrt{1-4x-x^2}}$.

3. $\dfrac{x}{\sqrt{1-x^2}}, \dfrac{x}{\sqrt{x^2-1}}, \dfrac{x^2}{\sqrt{1-x^2}}, \dfrac{x^2}{\sqrt{x^2+1}}$.

4. $x\sqrt{x^2+1}, (x+1)\sqrt{x^2+1}, \dfrac{x+1}{\sqrt{x^2+1}}$.

5. $x(x^2+a^2)^{\frac{n}{2}}, (x+1)(x^2+2x+3)^{\frac{n}{2}}$.

6. $\dfrac{x^2+2x+3}{\sqrt{1-x^2}}, \dfrac{x^2+2x+3}{\sqrt{x^2+1}}, \dfrac{x^2+2x+3}{\sqrt{x^2+x+1}}$.

7. $\sqrt{\dfrac{x+1}{x-1}}, \sqrt{\dfrac{1+x}{1-x}}, x\sqrt{\dfrac{1+x}{1-x}}, \dfrac{(x+1)\sqrt{x+2}}{\sqrt{x-2}}$.

8. $\text{cosec}\, 2x, \text{cosec}\,(ax+b), \dfrac{1}{\cos^2 x - \sin^2 x}, \dfrac{1+\tan^2 x}{1-\tan^2 x}, \dfrac{1}{3\sin x - 4\sin^3 x}$.

9. $\dfrac{1}{\sin x + \cos x}, \dfrac{1}{a\sin x + b\cos x}$.

10. Deduce $\int \text{cosec}\, x\, dx = \log \tan \dfrac{x}{2}$ by expressing cosec x as $\dfrac{1}{2}\left(\cot \dfrac{x}{2} + \tan \dfrac{x}{2}\right)$.

11. Find $\int \sec x\, dx$ by putting $\sin x = z$.

12. Show that $\int \sec x\, dx = \cosh^{-1}(\sec x)$.

13. Integrate

$$\frac{1}{x\log x}, \frac{1}{x\log x \log(\log x)}, \frac{1}{x\log x \log(\log x)\log[\log(\log x)]},$$

$$\frac{1}{xl(x)\, l^2(x)\, l^3(x) \ldots l^r(x)},$$

when $l^r x$ represents log log log ... x, the log being repeated r times.

15. Prove $\int_a^b \dfrac{\log x}{x} dx = \dfrac{1}{2}\log\left(\dfrac{b}{a}\right)\log(ab)$.

[ST. PETER'S COLL. etc., 1882.]

CHAPTER IV.

INTEGRATION BY PARTS.

45. Integration "by Parts" of a Product.

Since $$\frac{d}{dx}(uv) = u\frac{dv}{dx} + v\frac{du}{dx},$$

it follows that $uv = \int u\frac{dv}{dx}dx + \int v\frac{du}{dx}dx$

or $$\int u\frac{dv}{dx}dx = uv - \int v\frac{du}{dx}dx.$$

If $u = \phi(x)$ and $\frac{dv}{dx} = \psi(x)$, so that $v = \int \psi(x)dx$, the above rule may be written

$$\int \phi(x)\psi(x)dx = \phi(x)\left[\int \psi(x)dx\right] - \int \phi'(x)\left[\int \psi(x)dx\right]dx,$$

or interchanging $\phi(x)$ and $\psi(x)$,

$$\int \phi(x)\psi(x)dx = \psi(x)\left[\int \phi(x)dx\right] - \int \psi'(x)\left[\int \phi(x)dx\right]dx$$

Thus in integrating the product of two functions, if the integral be not at once obtainable, it is possible when the integral of either one is known, say $\psi(x)$, to connect the integral

$$\int \phi(x)\psi(x)dx$$

with a new integral $\int \phi'(x)\left[\int \psi(x)\,dx\right]dx$

which *may be more easily integrable* than the original product.

46. The rule may be put into words thus :—

Integral of the product $\phi(x)\psi(x)$

= 1st function × Integral of 2nd –

the Integral of [Diff. Co. of 1st × Int. of 2nd].

Ex. 1. Integrate $x\cos nx$.

Here it is important to connect if possible $\int x\cos nx\,dx$ with another integral in which the factor x has been removed. This may be done if x be chosen as the function $\phi(x)$, since in the second integral $\phi'(x)$, *i.e.* unity, occurs in place of x. Then

$$\phi(x) = x, \psi(x) = \cos nx,$$

$$\int \psi(x)dx = \frac{\sin nx}{n}.$$

Thus by the rule $\int x \cos nx\, dx = x\frac{\sin nx}{n} - \int 1 \cdot \frac{\sin nx}{n} dx$

$$= x\frac{\sin nx}{n} - \frac{1}{n}\left(-\frac{\cos nx}{n}\right) = x\frac{\sin nx}{n} + \frac{\cos nx}{n^2}.$$

47. Unity may be taken as one of the factors to aid an integration.

Thus
$$\int \log x\, dx = \int 1 \cdot \log x\, dx$$

$$= x \log x - \int x \frac{d}{dx}(\log x)dx$$

$$= x \log x - \int 1\, dx = x(\log x - 1) = x \log_e\left(\frac{x}{e}\right).$$

48. The operation of integrating by parts may be repeated several times.

Thus $\int x^2 \cos nx\, dx = \frac{x^2 \sin nx}{n} - \int 2x \frac{\sin nx}{n} dx$, and

$\int x \sin nx\, dx = x\left(-\frac{\cos nx}{n}\right) - \int 1.\left(-\frac{\cos nx}{n}\right) dx$; finally, $\int \cos nx\, dx = \frac{\sin nx}{n}$.

Hence $\int x^2 \cos nx\, dx = \frac{x^2 \sin nx}{n} - \frac{2}{n}\left[-\frac{x \cos nx}{n} + \frac{\sin nx}{n^2}\right]$

$$= \frac{x^2 \sin nx}{n} + \frac{2x \cos nx}{n^2} - \frac{2 \sin nx}{n^3}.$$

49. If one of the subsidiary integrals returns into the original form this fact may be utilized to infer the result of the integration.

Ex. 1. $\int e^{ax} \sin bx\, dx = \frac{e^{ax}}{a} \sin bx - \frac{b}{a}\int e^{ax} \cos bx\, dx,$

and $\int e^{ax} \cos bx\, dx = \frac{e^{ax}}{a} \cos bx + \frac{b}{a}\int e^{ax} \sin bx\, dx$;

therefore, if P and Q stand respectively for

$$\int e^{ax} \sin bx\, dx \text{ and } \int e^{ax} \cos bx\, dx,$$

we have $aP + bQ = e^{ax} \sin bx,$

and $-bP + aQ = e^{ax} \cos bx,$

whence
$$P = e^{ax} \frac{a \sin bx - b \cos bx}{a^2 + b^2}$$

$$= (a^2 + b^2)^{-\frac{1}{2}} e^{ax} \sin\left(bx - \tan^{-1}\frac{b}{a}\right)$$

and $Q = e^{ax}\dfrac{b\sin bx + a\cos bx}{a^2+b^2} = (a^2+b^2)^{-\frac{1}{2}} e^{ax}\cos\left(bx - \tan^{-1}\dfrac{b}{a}\right).$

The student will observe that these results are the same that we should obtain by putting $n = -1$ in the formulae

$$\left(\frac{d}{dx}\right)^n e^{ax} \begin{matrix}\sin\\ \cos\end{matrix}\, bx = (a^2+b^2)^{\frac{n}{2}} e^{ax} \begin{matrix}\sin\\ \cos\end{matrix}\left(bx + n\tan^{-1}\frac{b}{a}\right).$$

[*Diff. Calc. for Beginners*, Art. 61, Ex. 4.]

And this is otherwise obvious. For if to differentiate $e^{ax} \begin{matrix}\sin\\ \cos\end{matrix}(bx)$ is the same as to multiply by a factor $\sqrt{a^2+b^2}$ and to increase the angle by $\tan^{-1}\dfrac{b}{a}$, the integration, which is the inverse operation, must divide out again the factor $\sqrt{a^2+b^2}$ and diminish the angle by $\tan^{-1}\dfrac{b}{a}$.

Ex. 2. Integrate $\sqrt{a^2-x^2}$ by the rule of integration by parts.

$$\int\sqrt{a^2-x^2}\,dx = x\sqrt{a^2-x^2} - \int x\frac{d}{dx}(\sqrt{a^2-x^2})\,dx$$

$$= x\sqrt{a^2-x^2} + \int\frac{x^2}{\sqrt{a^2-x^2}}dx$$

$$= x\sqrt{a^2-x^2} + \int\frac{a^2-(a^2-x^2)}{\sqrt{a^2-x^2}}dx \qquad \text{[Note this step.]}$$

$$= x\sqrt{a^2-x^2} + a^2\sin^{-1}\frac{x}{a} - \int\sqrt{a^2-x^2}\,dx;$$

whence, transposing and dividing by 2,

$$\int\sqrt{a^2-x^2}\,dx = \frac{x\sqrt{a^2-x^2}}{2} + \frac{a^2}{2}\sin^{-1}\frac{x}{a},$$

which agrees with the result of Art. 39.

Ex. 3. Integrate $e^{3x}\sin^2 x\cos^3 x$.

Here $e^{3x}\sin^2 x\cos^3 x = \dfrac{e^{3x}}{4}\sin^2 2x\cos x$

$$= \frac{e^{3x}}{8}(1-\cos 4x)\cos x = \frac{1}{16}(2e^{3x}\cos x - e^{3x}\cos 3x - e^{3x}\cos 5x).$$

Hence, by Ex. 1, $\int e^{3x}\sin^2 x\cos^3 x\,dx = \dfrac{e^{3x}}{16}$

$$\left[\frac{2}{\sqrt{10}}\cos\left(x - \tan^{-1}\frac{1}{3}\right) - \frac{1}{3\sqrt{2}}\cos\left(3x - \frac{\pi}{4}\right) - \frac{1}{\sqrt{34}}\cos\left(5x - \tan^{-1}\frac{5}{3}\right)\right].$$

[Compare Ex. 16, p. 43, *Diff. Calc. for Beginners*, putting $n = -1$ in the result.]

EXAMPLES

Integrate by parts.

1. $xe^x, x^2e^x, x^3e^x, x\cosh x, x^2\cosh x$.
2. $x\cos x, x^2\cos x, x\cos 2x, x\cos^2 x, x\cos^3 x$.
3. $x\sin x\cos x, x\sin x\sin 2x\sin 3x$.
4. $x^2\log x, x^n\log x, x^n(\log x)^2$.
5. $e^x\sin x\cos x, e^x\sin x\cos x\cos 2x$.
6. $e^{ax}\sin px\sin qx\sin rx$.
7. Calculate $\int_0^\pi x\sin x\,dx, \int_0^\pi x\sin^2 x\,dx, \int_0^\pi x^2\sin x\,dx$.
8. Show that $\int_0^a \sqrt{a^2-x^2}\,dx = \dfrac{\pi a^2}{4}$.
9. Integrate $\int \sin^{-1} x\,dx, \int x\sin^{-1} x\,dx, \int x^2\sin^{-1} x\,dx$.

50. Geometrical Illustration.

Let PQ be any arc of a curve referred to rectangular axes Ox, Oy, and let the coordinates of P be (x_0, y_0), and of $Q\,(x_1, y_1)$.

Let PN, QM be the ordinates and PN_1, QM_1 the abscissae of the points P, Q. Then plainly

area $PNMQ$ = rect. OQ – rect. OP – area PN_1M_1Q.

But area $PNMQ = \int_{x_0}^{x_1} y\,dx$

and area $PN_1\,M_1Q = \int_{y_0}^{y_1} x\,dy$.

Thus $\int_{x_0}^{x_1} y\,dx = (x_1y_1 - x_0y_0) - \int_{y_0}^{y_1} x\,dy$.

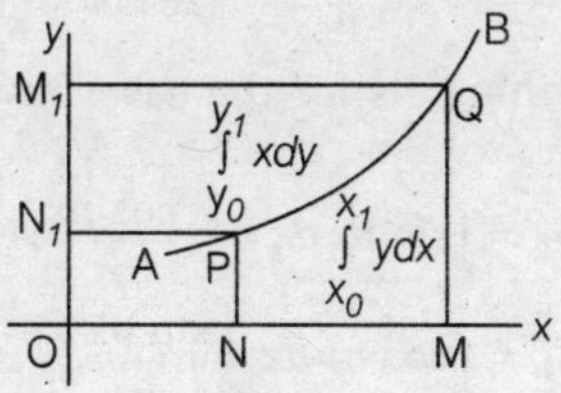

Fig. 7.

Let us now consider the curve to be defined by the equations

$$x = \phi(t) \equiv u, \text{ say},$$

and $$y = \psi(t) \equiv v, \text{ say},$$

and let t_0 and t_1 be the values of t corresponding to the values x_0, y_0, and x_1, y_1 of x and y respectively.

We then have $\int_{x_0}^{x_1} y\,dx = \int_{x_0}^{x_1} v du = \int_{t_0}^{t_1} v\frac{du}{dt}dt,$

and $\int_{y_0}^{y_1} x\,dy = \int_{x_0}^{x_1} u dv = \int_{t_0}^{t_1} u\frac{dv}{dt}dt,$

and $x_1 y_1 - x_0 y_0 = [uv]_{t_0}^{t_1}$

so that the equation above may be written

$$\int_{t_0}^{t_1} v\frac{du}{dt}dt = [uv]_{t_0}^{t_1} - \int_{t_0}^{t_1} u\frac{dv}{dt}dt;$$

and thus the rule of integration by parts is established geometrically.

51. Integrals of the Form $\int x^m \sin nx\,dx, \int x^m \cos nx\,dx.$

Reduction formulae for such integrals as the above may readily be found. Denote them respectively by S_m and C_m. Then, integrating by parts, we have at once

$$S_m = -x^m\frac{\cos nx}{n} + \frac{m}{n}C_{m-1},$$

and
$$C_m = x^m\frac{\sin nx}{n} - \frac{m}{n}S_{m-1}$$

Thus
$$S_m = -x^m\frac{\cos nx}{n} + \frac{m}{n}\left[x^{m-1}\frac{\sin nx}{n} - \frac{m-1}{n}S_{m-2}\right],$$

and
$$C_m = x^m\frac{\sin nx}{n} - \frac{m}{n}\left[-x^{m-1}\frac{\cos nx}{n} + \frac{m-1}{n}C_{m-2}\right],$$

i.e.
$$S_m = -x^m\frac{\cos nx}{n} + mx^{m-1}\frac{\sin nx}{n^2} - \frac{m(m-1)}{n^2}S_{m-2},$$

and
$$C_m = x^m\frac{\sin nx}{n} + mx^{m-1}\frac{\cos nx}{n^2} - \frac{m(m-1)}{n^2}C_{m-2}.$$

Thus when the four integrals for the cases $m = 0$ and $m = 1$ are found, viz.,

$$S_0 = \int \sin nx\,dx = -\frac{\cos nx}{n},$$

$$C_0 = \int \cos nx\,dx = \frac{\sin nx}{n},$$

$$S_1 = \int x \sin nx\,dx = -x\frac{\cos nx}{n} + \frac{\sin nx}{n^2},$$

$$C_1 = \int x \cos nx\,dx = x\frac{\sin nx}{n} + \frac{\cos nx}{n^2},$$

all others can be deduced by successive applications of the above formulae.

52. Extension of the Rule for Integration by Parts.

If u and v be functions of x and dashes denote differentiations and suffixes integrations with respect to x we may prove the following extension of the rule for integration by parts,

$$\int uv\,dx = uv_1 - u'v_2 + u''v_3 - u'''v_4 + \ldots$$
$$+ (-1)^{n-1}u^{(n-1)}v_n + (-1)^n \int u^{(n)}v_n\,dx,$$

where $u^{(n-1)}$ is written for u with $n-1$ dashes; for

$$\int uv\,dx = uv_1 - \int u'v_1dx,$$
$$\int u'v_1dx = u'v_2 - \int u''v_2dx,$$
$$\int u''v_2dx = u''v_3 - \int u'''v_3dx,$$
$$\int u'''v_3dx = u'''v_4 - \int u''''v_4dx,$$

etc. = etc.

$$\int u^{(n-2)}\,v_{n-2}\,dx = u^{(n-2)}v_{n-1} - \int u^{(n-1)}\,v_{n-1}\,dx,$$
$$\int u^{(n-1)}\,v_{n-1}\,dx = u^{(n-1)}\,v_n - \int u^{(n)}\,v_n\,dx.$$

Hence adding and subtracting alternately

$$\int uv\,dx = uv_1 - u'v_2 + u''v_3 - u'''v_4 + \ldots + (-1)^{n-1}u^{(n-1)}v_n + (-1)^n \int u^{(n)}v_n\,dx.$$

Ex. 1. If we apply this rule to $\int x^m e^{ax} dx$, we immediately obtain

$$\int x^m e^{ax}\,dx = x^m \frac{e^{ax}}{a} - mx^{m-1}\frac{e^{ax}}{a^2} + m(m-1)x^{m-2}\frac{e^{ax}}{a^3}$$
$$- m(m-1)(m-2)\,x^{m-3}\frac{e^{ax}}{a^4} + \ldots + (-1)^m m!\frac{e^{ax}}{a^{m+1}}.$$

Ex. 2. It will be at once seen that the integrals

$$\int x^m \sin nx\,dx \text{ and } \int x^m \cos nx\,dx$$

of the last article may be treated in this way.

EXAMPLES

Write down the integrals of

1. x^4e^x, $x^3 \cos h\ x$, $x^5 \sin h\ x$.
2. $x^2 \sin x$, $x^3 \sin x$, $x^3 \sin^2 x$, $x^4 \sin x \cos x$.
3. Evaluate $\int_0^\pi x^5 \sin x\,dx$, $\int_0^\pi x^5 \cos x\,dx$, $\int_0^1 x^6 e^x\,dx$.

53. The determination of the integrals

$$\int x^n e^{ax} \sin bx\,dx, \int x^n e^{ax} \cos bx\,dx,$$

may be at once effected.

For remembering $\int e^{ax} {}^{\sin}_{\cos}\, bx\,dx = \frac{e^{ax}}{r} {}^{\sin}_{\cos} (bx - \phi)$

where $r = \sqrt{a^2 + b^2}$ and $\tan\phi = \frac{b}{a}$,

we have

$$\int x^n e^{ax} \sin bx\,dx = \frac{x^n}{r} e^{ax} \sin(bx - \phi) - \frac{nx^{n-1}}{r^2} e^{ax} \sin(bx - 2\phi)$$

$$+ \frac{n(n-1)}{r^3} x^{n-2} e^{ax} \sin(bx - 3\phi) - \ldots + (-1)^n \frac{n!}{r^{n+1}} e^{ax} \sin(bx - \overline{n+1}\phi),$$

or $e^{ax} \{P \sin bx - Q \cos bx\}$

where $P = \frac{x^n}{r} \cos\phi - n\frac{x^{n-1}}{r^2} \cos 2\phi + n(n-1)\frac{x^{n-2}}{r^3} \cos 3\phi - \ldots$

$$Q = \frac{x^n}{r} \sin\phi - n\frac{x^{n-1}}{r^2} \sin 2\phi + n(n-1)\frac{x^{n-2}}{r^3} \sin 3\phi - \ldots$$

Similarly $\int x^n e^{ax} \cos bx\,dx = e^{ax} \{P \cos bx + Q \sin bx\}$.

Ex. 1. Integrate $\int x^3 e^x \sin x\,dx$.

Since $\int e^x \sin x\,dx = 2^{-\frac{1}{2}} e^x \sin\left(x - \frac{\pi}{4}\right)$,

we have

$$\int x^3 e^x \sin x\,dx = x^3\, 2^{-\frac{1}{2}} e^x \sin\left(x - \frac{\pi}{4}\right) - 3x^2\, 2^{-\frac{2}{2}} e^x \sin\left(x - \frac{\pi}{2}\right)$$

$$+ 6x.\, 2^{-\frac{3}{2}} e^x \sin\left(x - \frac{3\pi}{4}\right) - 6.\, 2^{-\frac{4}{2}} e^x \sin(x - \pi) = \text{etc}.$$

Ex. 2. Prove

$$\int x^n e^x \sin x\,dx = e^x \sum_{r=0}^{r=n} (-1)^r \frac{n!}{(n-r)!} x^{n-r} 2^{-\frac{r+1}{2}} \sin\left\{x - \frac{(r+1)\pi}{4}\right\}.$$

EXAMPLES

1. Integrate (a) $\int e^{m\sin^{-1} x}\,dx$. (b) $\int x^2 \sin^{-1} x\,dx$.

(c) $\int x \sec^2 x\,dx$. (d) $\int \tan^{-1} x\,dx$.

(e) $\int x^3 \tan^{-1} x\,dx$. (f) $\int \cos^{-1} \frac{1}{x}\,dx$.

2. Integrate (a) $\int \frac{x \sin^{-1} x}{(1-x^2)^{\frac{1}{2}}} dx$. (b) $\int \frac{x^3 \sin^{-1} x}{(1-x^2)^{\frac{3}{2}}} dx$.

(c) $\int \sin^{-1} \sqrt{\frac{x}{a+x}} dx$. (d) $\int x \sin^{-1} \frac{1}{2} \sqrt{\frac{2a-x}{a}} dx$.

3. Integrate (a) $\int \frac{e^{m \tan^{-1} x}}{1+x^2} dx$. (b) $\int \frac{e^{m \tan^{-1} x}}{(1+x^2)^2} dx$.

(c) $\int \frac{e^{m \tan^{-1} x}}{(1+x^2)^{\frac{5}{2}}} dx$. (d) $\int \frac{e^{m \tan^{-1} x}}{(1+x^2)^{\frac{3}{2}}} dx$.

4. Integrate (a) $\int e^x (\sin x + \cos x)\, dx$. (b) $\int x e^x \sin^2 x\, dx$.

(c) $\int \cosh ax \sin bx\, dx$. (d) $\int x \cosh ax \sin bx\, dx$.

(e) $\int x^2 2^x \sin 2x\, dx$. (f) $\int \cos \left\{ b \log \frac{x}{a} \right\} dx$.

5. Integrate $\int \log \frac{a}{x} \sin^{-1} x\, dx$.

6. Integrate $\int \frac{x e^x}{(x+1)^2} dx$.

7. Integrate $\int \frac{\log (\cos \theta + \sqrt{\cos 2\theta})}{1 - \cos^2 \theta} d\theta$. [α, 1891.]

8. Integrate $\int \cos 2\theta \log (1 + \tan \theta)\, d\theta$. [γ, 1882.]

9. Integrate (a) $\int e^x \frac{1 + \sin x}{1 + \cos x} dx$. [MATH. TRIPOS, 1892.]

(b) $\int e^x \frac{1 - \sin x}{1 - \cos x} dx$. [α, 1892.]

10. Prove that $\int u \frac{d^2 v}{dx^2} dx = u \frac{dv}{dx} - v \frac{du}{dx} + \int v \frac{d^2 u}{dx^2} dx$.

11. Integrate $\int (a \sin^2 x + 2b \sin x \cos x + c \cos^2 x)\, e^x dx$. [α, 1883.]

12. Show that if u be a rational integral function of x,

$\int e^{x/a} u\, dx = a e^{x/a} \left\{ u - a \frac{du}{dx} + a^2 \frac{d^2 u}{dx^2} - a^3 \frac{d^3 u}{dx^3} + \dots \right\}$, where the series within the brackets is necessarily finite. [TRIN. COLL, 1881.]

13. If $u = \int e^{ax} \cos bx\, dx$, $v = \int e^{ax} \sin bx\, dx$, prove that

$\tan^{-1} \frac{v}{u} + \tan^{-1} \frac{b}{a} = bx$, and that $(a^2 + b^2)(u^2 + v^2) = e^{2ax}$.

14. Prove that $\int x^m (\log x)^n\, dx = \dfrac{x^{m+1}}{m+1} (\log x)^n - \dfrac{n}{m+1} \int x^m (\log x)^{n-1} dx.$

Also that

$$\int x^m (\log x)^n dx = \frac{x^{m+1}}{m+1} \left[l^n - \frac{n}{m+1} l^{n-1} + \frac{n(n-1)}{(m+1)^2} l^{n-2} - \frac{n(n-1)(n-2)}{(m+1)^3} l^{n-3} + \ldots + \frac{(-1)^{n-1} n!}{(m+1)^{n-1}} l + \frac{(-1)^n n!}{(m+1)^n} \right],$$

where l stands for $\log x$.

15. Prove that

(i.) $$\int e^{ax} \cos^n bx\, dx = \frac{a \cos bx + nb \sin bx}{a^2 + n^2 b^2} e^{ax} \cos^{n-1} bx + \frac{n(n-1)}{a^2 + n^2 b^2} b^2 \int e^{ax} \cos^{n-2} bx\, dx.$$

(ii.) $$\int e^{ax} \sin^n bx\, dx = \frac{a \sin bx - nb \cos bx}{a^2 + n^2 b^2} e^{ax} \sin^{n-1} bx + \frac{n(n-1)}{a^2 + n^2 b^2} b^2 \int e^{ax} \sin^{n-2} bx\, dx.$$

[BERTRAND.]

16. Evaluate $\int x^2 \log(1 - x^2) dx$, and deduce that

$$\frac{1}{1.5} + \frac{1}{2.7} + \frac{1}{3.9} + \ldots = \frac{8}{9} - \frac{2}{3} \log_e 2.$$

[α, 1889.]

CHAPTER V.

RATIONAL ALGEBRAIC FRACTIONAL FORMS. PARTIAL FRACTIONS.

ALGEBRAIC FRACTIONAL FORMS.

54. Integration of $\dfrac{1}{x^2 - a^2}\,(x > a)$, and $\dfrac{1}{a^2 - x^2}\,(x < a)$.

Either of these forms should be thrown into Partial Fractions. Thus

$$\int \frac{dx}{x^2 - a^2} = \frac{1}{2a}\int\left(\frac{1}{x-a} - \frac{1}{x+a}\right)dx$$

$$= \frac{1}{2a}[\log(x-a) - \log(x+a)]$$

$$= \frac{1}{2a}\log\frac{x-a}{x+a}\left[= -\frac{1}{a}\coth^{-1}\frac{x}{a}\right]$$

$$\int \frac{dx}{a^2 - x^2} = \frac{1}{2a}\int\left(\frac{1}{a+x} + \frac{1}{a-x}\right)dx$$

$$= \frac{1}{2a}[\log(a+x) - \log(a-x)]$$

$$= \frac{1}{2a}\log\frac{a+x}{a-x}\left[= \frac{1}{a}\tanh^{-1}\frac{x}{a}\right].$$

(Compare the forms of the results in square brackets with the result before tabulated for $\dfrac{1}{a^2 + x^2}$ viz; $\displaystyle\int \frac{dx}{a^2 + x^2} = \frac{1}{a}\tan^{-1}\frac{x}{a}$.)

55. Integration of $\displaystyle\int \frac{dx}{ax^2 + bx + c}$.

Let $$I = \frac{1}{a}\int \frac{dx}{x^2 + \frac{b}{a}x + \frac{c}{a}} = \frac{1}{a}\int \frac{dx}{\left(x + \frac{b}{2a}\right)^2 - \frac{b^2 - 4ac}{4a^2}}$$

or $$\frac{1}{a}\int \frac{dx}{\left(x + \frac{b}{2a}\right)^2 + \frac{4ac - b^2}{4a^2}};$$

we take the former or the latter arrangement according as b^2 is > or < $4ac$. Thus if $b^2 > 4ac$,

$$I = \frac{1}{\sqrt{b^2 - 4ac}} \log \frac{2ax + b - \sqrt{b^2 - 4ac}}{2ax + b + \sqrt{b^2 - 4ac}}$$

or

$$\frac{-2}{\sqrt{b^2 - 4ac}} \coth^{-1} \frac{2ax + b}{\sqrt{b^2 - 4ac}}.$$

If $b^2 < 4ac$,

$$I = \frac{2}{\sqrt{4ac - b^2}} \tan^{-1} \frac{2ax + b}{\sqrt{4ac - b^2}}$$

or

$$-\frac{2}{\sqrt{4ac - b^2}} \cot^{-1} \frac{2ax + b}{\sqrt{4ac - b^2}}.$$

These expressions differ at most by constants, but in any given case a real form should be chosen.

56. Integrals or Expressions of The form $\dfrac{px + q}{ax^2 + bx + c}$

can be obtained at once by the following transformation

$$\frac{px + q}{ax^2 + bx + c} = \frac{p}{2a} \frac{(2ax + b)}{ax^2 + bx + c} + \frac{q - \frac{pb}{2a}}{ax^2 + bx + c},$$

the integral of the first part being

$$\frac{p}{2a} \log (ax^2 + bx + c),$$

and that of the second part being obtained by the last article.

[The beginner should notice how the above form is obtained. *It is essential that the numerator of the first fraction shall be the differential coefficient of the denominator,* and that all the x's of the numerator are thereby *exhausted.*]

Ex. $$\int \frac{x}{x^2 + 4x + 5} dx = \int \left[\frac{1}{2} \frac{2x + 4}{x^2 + 4x + 5} - \frac{2}{(x + 2)^2 + 1} \right] dx$$

$$= \frac{1}{2} \log(x^2 + 4x + 5) - 2 \tan^{-1}(x + 2).$$

57. Although the expression $px + q$ may be thrown into the form

$$\frac{p}{2a}(2ax + b) + q - \frac{pb}{2a}$$

by inspection, we might proceed thus:—

Let $px + q \equiv \lambda(2ax + b) + \mu$,

where λ and μ are constants to be determined. Then by comparing coefficients,

$$2a\lambda = p, \ \mu + \lambda b = q,$$

giving $$\lambda = \frac{p}{2a} \text{ and } \mu = q - \frac{pb}{2a}.$$

EXAMPLES

Integrate

1. $\int \frac{x\,dx}{x^2 + 2x + 3}$.

2. $\int \frac{x\,dx}{x^2 + 2x + 1}$.

3. $\int \frac{x + 1}{x^2 + 4x + 5}dx$.

4. $\int \frac{(x + 1)\,dx}{3 + 2x - x^2}$.

5. $\int \frac{(x - 1)^2}{x^2 + 2x + 2}dx$

6. $\int \frac{2x^2 + 3x + 4}{x^2 + 6x + 10}dx$.

58. General Fraction with Rational Numerator and Denominator.

Expressions of the form $\frac{f(x)}{\phi(x)}$, where $f(x)$ and $\phi(x)$ are rational integral algebraic functions of x, can be integrated by resolution into Partial Fractions.

The method of putting such an expression into Partial Fractions has been discussed in the *Differential Calculus for Beginners*, Art. 66. When the *numerator is of lower degree* than the denominator the result consists of the sum of several such terms as

$$\frac{A}{x-a}, \frac{A}{(x-a)^r}, \frac{Ax+B}{ax^2+bx+c}, \text{ and } \frac{Ax+B}{[(x+a)^2+b^2]^r}.$$

And when the numerator is of as high or higher degree than the denominator we may *divide out* until the numerator of the remaining fraction is of lower degree. The terms of the quotient can in that case be integrated at once and the remaining fraction may be put into Partial Fractions as indicated above.

Now any partical fraction of the form $\frac{A}{x - a}$ integrates at once into $A \log(x - a)$

Any fraction of the form $\dfrac{A}{(x-a)^r}$ integrates into $-\dfrac{1}{r-1}\dfrac{A}{(x-a)^{r-1}}$.

Any fraction of the form $\dfrac{Ax+B}{ax^2+bx+c}$ has been discussed in Art. 56.

And when any repeated quadratic factor such as $[(x+a)^2+b^2]^r$ occurs in $\phi(x)$ giving rise to partial fractions such as $\dfrac{Ax+B}{[(x+a)^2+b^2]^r}$ we may integrate such a fraction by the substitution $x+a=b\tan\theta$, by aid of Art. 67 or Art. 83.

But it is frequently better to factorize $(x+a)^2+b^2$ into its imaginary conjugate factors $x+a+ib$ and $x+a-ib$, and obtain conjugate pairs of partial fractions of the form $\dfrac{P+iQ}{(x+a+ib)^r}+\dfrac{P-iQ}{(x+a-ib)^r}$ which may then be integrated and the result reduced to real form by aid of De Moivre's Theorem, as in Art. 63, *Diff. Calc. for Beginners.*

59. Ex. 1. Integrate $\displaystyle\int\frac{x^2+px+q}{(x-a)(x-b)(x-c)}dx$.

We have $\dfrac{x^2+px+q}{(x-a)(x-b)(x-c)}$

$$=\frac{a^2+pa+q}{(a-b)(a-c)}\frac{1}{x-a}+\frac{b^2+pb+q}{(b-c)(b-a)}\frac{1}{x-b}$$

$$+\frac{c^2+pc+q}{(c-a)(c-b)}\frac{1}{x-c}\equiv\Sigma\frac{a^2+pa+q}{(a-b)(a-c)}\frac{1}{x-a}, \text{ say;}$$

and the integral is.

$$\Sigma\frac{a^2+pa+q}{(a-b)(a-c)}\log(x-a).$$

Ex. 2. Integrate $\displaystyle\int\frac{x}{(x-1)(x^2+4)}dx$.

Let $\dfrac{x}{(x-1)(x^2+4)}\equiv\dfrac{A}{x-1}+\dfrac{Bx+C}{x^2+4}$.

Then $A(x^2+4)+(Bx+C)(x-1)\equiv x$.

Thus $\left.\begin{aligned}A+B&=0,\\ C-B&=1,\\ 4A-C&=0;\end{aligned}\right\}$

whence $A=\frac{1}{5}, B=-\frac{1}{5}, C=\frac{4}{5}$,

and $$\frac{x}{(x-1)(x^2+4)} \equiv \frac{1}{5}\frac{1}{x-1} - \frac{1}{5}\frac{x-4}{x^2+4}$$

$$\equiv \frac{1}{5}\frac{1}{x-1} - \frac{1}{10}\frac{2x}{x^2+4} + \frac{4}{5}\frac{1}{x^2+4};$$

and the integral is $\frac{1}{5}\log(x-1) - \frac{1}{10}\log(x^2+4) + \frac{2}{5}\tan^{-1}\frac{x}{2}$.

Ex. 3. Integrate $\int \frac{x^2}{(x-1)^3(x+1)}dx.$

Put $$x - 1 = y.$$

Hence the fraction becomes $= \frac{(1+y)^2}{y^3(2+y)}$

Dividing out until y^3 is a factor of the remainder,

$$2+y)\,1+2y+y^2\left(\frac{1}{2}+\frac{3}{4}y+\frac{1}{8}y^2-\frac{1}{8}\frac{y^3}{2+y}.\right.$$

$$1+\frac{1}{2}y$$

$$\frac{3}{2}y+y^2$$

$$\frac{3}{2}y+\frac{3}{4}y^2$$

$$\frac{1}{4}y^2$$

$$\frac{1}{4}y^2+\frac{1}{8}y^3$$

$$-\frac{1}{8}y^3$$

Hence the fraction $\frac{(1+y)^2}{y^3(2+y)} = \frac{1}{2y^3} + \frac{3}{4}\frac{1}{y^2} + \frac{1}{8}\frac{1}{y} - \frac{1}{8}\frac{1}{2+y}$,

and therefore $\frac{x^2}{(x-1)^3(x+1)}$

$$= \frac{1}{2}\frac{1}{(x-1)^3} + \frac{3}{4(x-1)^2} + \frac{1}{8(x-1)} - \frac{1}{8(x+1)};$$

an the integral is $-\frac{1}{4}\frac{1}{(x-1)^2} - \frac{3}{4(x-1)} + \frac{1}{8}\log(x-1) - \frac{1}{8}\log(x+1)$.

Ex. 4. Integrate $\int \frac{x^2dx}{(x-1)^4(x^3+1)}$.

Let $x = 1 + y$; then $\frac{x^2}{(x-1)^4(x^3+1)} = \frac{1+2y+y^2}{y^4(2+3y+3y^2+y^3)}$.

We now divide out $1 + 2y + y^2$ by $2 + 3y + 3y^2 + y^3$

until y^4 is a factor of the remainder. To shorten the work we use detached coefficients:

$$\begin{array}{l}
2+3+3+1)\ 1+2+1 \qquad \left(\frac{1}{2}+\frac{1}{4}y-\frac{5}{8}y^2+\frac{5}{16}y^3.\right.\\
\quad 1+\frac{3}{2}+\frac{3}{2}+\frac{1}{2}\\
\hline
\quad \frac{1}{2}-\frac{1}{2}-\frac{1}{2}\\
\quad \frac{1}{2}+\frac{3}{4}+\frac{3}{4}+\frac{1}{4}\\
\hline
\quad -\frac{5}{4}-\frac{5}{4}-\frac{1}{4}\\
\quad -\frac{5}{4}-\frac{15}{8}-\frac{15}{8}-\frac{5}{8}\\
\hline
\quad \frac{5}{8}+\frac{13}{8}+\frac{5}{8}\\
\quad \frac{5}{8}+\frac{15}{16}+\frac{15}{16}+\frac{5}{16}\\
\hline
\quad \frac{11}{16}-\frac{5}{16}-\frac{5}{16}
\end{array}$$

Hence $$\frac{x^2}{(x-1)^4(x^3+1)}=\frac{1}{2y^4}+\frac{1}{4y^3}-\frac{5}{8y^2}+\frac{5}{16y}+\frac{1}{16}\frac{11-5y-5y^2}{x^3+1}.$$

Now $$11-5y-5y^2=11-5(x-1)-5(x-1)^2$$
$$=11+5x-5x^2,$$

and by Rule 2, p. 49, of the *Diff. Calc. for Beginners,*

$$\frac{11+5x-5x^2}{(x+1)(x^2-x+1)}=\frac{1}{3(x+1)}+\frac{X(x)}{x^2-x+1}.$$

and $$X(x)=\frac{11+5x-5x^2}{x+1}-\frac{1}{3}\frac{x^2-x+1}{x+1}=\frac{32+16x-16x^2}{3(x+1)}$$
$$=\frac{16}{3}\frac{2+x-x^2}{1+x}=\frac{16}{3}(2-x).$$

Thus $$\frac{x^2}{(x-1)^4(x^3+1)}=\frac{1}{2(x-1)^4}+\frac{1}{4(x-1)^3}-\frac{5}{8(x-1)^2}$$
$$+\frac{5}{16(x-1)}+\frac{1}{48}\frac{1}{x+1}-\frac{1}{6}\frac{(2x-1)-3}{x^2-x+1}$$

and the integral is plainly

$$=-\frac{1}{6(x-1)^3}-\frac{1}{8(x-1)^2}+\frac{5}{8(x-1)}+\frac{5}{16}\log(x-1)$$
$$+\frac{1}{48}\log(x+1)-\frac{1}{6}\log(x^2-x+1)+\frac{1}{\sqrt{3}}\tan^{-1}\frac{2x-1}{\sqrt{3}}.$$

EXAMPLES

1. Integrate with regard to x the following expressions:—

(i.) $\dfrac{x}{(x-a)(x-b)}$. (ii.) $\dfrac{1}{x(x^2-1)}$.

(iii.) $x^2(x+a)^{-1}(x+b)^{-1}$. (iv.) $\dfrac{x^2+1}{x(x^2-1)}$.

(v.) $\dfrac{x^2+1}{(2x+1)(x-1)(x+1)}$. (vi.) $\dfrac{1-3x^2}{3x-x^3}$.

(vii.) $\dfrac{x^2}{(x-a)(x-b)(x-c)}$. (viii.) $\dfrac{(x-a)(x-b)}{(x-c)(x-d)}$.

(ix.) $\dfrac{(x-a)(x-b)(x-c)}{(x-a_1)(x-b_1)(x-c_1)}$. (x.) $\dfrac{x^2}{(x+1)(x-2)(x+3)}$.

2. Evaluate

(i.) $\int \dfrac{dx}{(x-1)^2(x+1)}$. (ii.) $\int \dfrac{dx}{(x-1)^4(x+1)}$.

(iii.) $\int \dfrac{(x+1)dx}{(x-1)^2(x+2)^2}$. (iv.) $\int (ax^2+bx^3)^{-1}dx$.

(v.) $\int (x^2-1)^{-2}dx$. (vi.) $\int \dfrac{dx}{(x-a)^2(x-b)(x-c)}$.

3. Integrate

(i.) $\int \dfrac{dx}{(x^2+a^2)(x^2+b^2)}$. (ii.) $\int \dfrac{(x^2+a^2)(x^2+b^2)}{(x^2+c^2)(x^2+d^2)}dx$.

(iii.) $\int \dfrac{x^2dx}{(x^2+1)(2x^2+1)}$. (iv.) $\int \dfrac{(x^2+1)dx}{(x^2+2)(2x^2+1)}$.

4. Integrate

(i.) $\int \dfrac{x\,dx}{x^4+x^2+1}$. (ii.) $\int \dfrac{(x+1)^2}{x^4+x^2+1}dx$.

(iii.) $\int \dfrac{x^2+1}{x^4+1}dx$. (iv.) $\int \dfrac{x^2+1}{x^4-x^2+1}dx$.

(v.) $\int (x^2+a^2)(x^4+a^2x^2+a^4)^{-1}dx$.

(vi.) $\int (x^2-a^2)(x^4+a^2x^2+a^4)^{-1}dx$.

(vii.) $\int \dfrac{x^2+3x+1}{x^4+x^2+1}dx$. (viii.) $\int \dfrac{dx}{x^4+1}$.

5. Integrate

(i.) $\dfrac{x\,dx}{x^3-1}$. (ii.) $\dfrac{(3x^2+1)dx}{x(x^4-1)}$.

(iii.) $\dfrac{dx}{(x-2)(x^2+4)}$. (iv.) $\dfrac{x^5+2}{x^5-x}dx$.

(v.) $\dfrac{(x-1)dx}{(x+1)(x^2+1)}$. (vi.) $\dfrac{dx}{x^4+8x^2-9}$.

(vii.) $\dfrac{dx}{(x+1)(x^3-1)}$. (viii.) $\dfrac{dx}{(x^2+1)(x^2-x+1)}$.

(ix.) $\dfrac{dx}{1+x+x^2+x^3}$. (x.) $\dfrac{x^5dx}{(x^2+1)(x-4)}$.

6. Integrate

(i.) $\dfrac{x^2dx}{(x-2)^2(x^2-2x+4)}$. (ii.) $\dfrac{dx}{(1+x)^2(1+2x+4x^2)}$.

(iii.) $\dfrac{x^4dx}{(x-1)^2(x^2+4)}$. (iv.) $\dfrac{dx}{(x+1)^2(x^2+1)}$.

(v.) $\dfrac{dx}{(x-1)^2(x^2+1)}$. (vi.) $\dfrac{dx}{x(x-1)^2(x^2+1)}$.

(vii.) $\dfrac{dx}{x(1+3x^3+2x^6)}$. (viii.) $\dfrac{(x+a)dx}{x^2(x-a)(x^2+a^2)}$.

(ix.) $\dfrac{2x\,dx}{(1+x)(1+x^2)^2}$. (x.) $\dfrac{1}{x(x^2+1)^3}dx$.

7. Evaluate $\int_0^{\frac{\pi}{4}}\sqrt{\tan\theta}\,d\theta$ and $\int_0^{\frac{\pi}{4}}\sqrt{\cot\theta}\,d\theta$.

8. Obtain the value of $\int_0^{\frac{\pi}{4}}\dfrac{dx}{\cos^4 x-\cos^2 x\sin^2 x+\sin^4 x}$.

9. Investigate $\int_0^{\frac{\pi}{2}}\dfrac{\cos x\,dx}{(1+\sin x)(2+\sin x)}$.

10. Show that $\int_0^{\infty}\dfrac{x^2dx}{(x^2+a^2)(x^2+b^2)(x^2+c^2)}=\dfrac{\pi}{2(a+b)(b+c)(c+a)}$.

11. Prove that $\int_{-\infty}^{+\infty}\dfrac{dx}{(x^2\pm ax+a^2)(x^2\pm bx+b^2)}=\dfrac{2\pi}{\sqrt{3}}\dfrac{a+b}{ab(a^2+ab+b^2)}$.

[COLLEGES γ, 1891.]

12. Show that the sum of the infinite series

$$\frac{1}{a}-\frac{1}{a+b}+\frac{1}{a+2b}-\frac{1}{a+3b}+\ldots\ (a>0, b>0)$$

can be expressed in the form $\int_0^1\dfrac{t^{n-1}}{1+t^b}dt$;

and hence prove that $\dfrac{1}{1}-\dfrac{1}{4}+\dfrac{1}{7}-\dfrac{1}{10}+\dfrac{1}{13}-\dfrac{1}{16}+\ldots=\dfrac{1}{3}(\pi 3^{-\frac{1}{2}}+\log_e 2)$.

[OXFORD, 1887.]

CHAPTER VI.

SUNDRY STANDARD METHODS.

60. Integration of $\int \frac{dx}{\sqrt{R}}$ where $R = ax^2 + 2bx + c$.

Case I. *a* Positive.

When a is positive we may write this integral as

$$\frac{1}{\sqrt{a}}\int \frac{dx}{\sqrt{x^2 + 2\frac{b}{a}x + \frac{c}{a}}},$$

which we may arrange as

$$\frac{1}{\sqrt{a}}\int \frac{dx}{\sqrt{\left(x + \frac{b}{a}\right)^2 - \frac{b^2 - ac}{a^2}}}$$

or

$$\frac{1}{\sqrt{a}}\int \frac{dx}{\sqrt{\left(x + \frac{b}{a}\right)^2 + \frac{ac - b^2}{a^2}}}$$

according as b^2 is greater or less than ac, and the real form of the integral is therefore (Art. 36)

$$\frac{1}{\sqrt{a}}\cosh^{-1}\frac{ax + b}{\sqrt{b^2 - ac}}$$

or

$$\frac{1}{\sqrt{a}}\sinh^{-1}\frac{ax + b}{\sqrt{ac - b^2}},$$

according as b^2 is $>$ or $<$ ac.

In either case the integral may be written in the logarithmic form

$$\frac{1}{\sqrt{a}}\log(ax + b + \sqrt{a}\sqrt{ax^2 + 2bx + c}),$$

the constant $\frac{1}{\sqrt{a}}\log\sqrt{b^2 \sim ac}$ being omitted.

Also since $\cosh^{-1}z = \sinh^{-1}\sqrt{z^2 - 1}$,

and $\quad \sinh^{-1}z = \cosh^{-1}\sqrt{z^2 + 1}$,

$$\frac{1}{\sqrt{a}}\cosh^{-1}\frac{ax+b}{\sqrt{b^2-ac}}=\frac{1}{\sqrt{a}}\sinh^{-1}\frac{\sqrt{aR}}{\sqrt{b^2-ac}},$$

and $$\frac{1}{\sqrt{a}}\sinh^{-1}\frac{ax+b}{\sqrt{ac-b^2}}=\frac{1}{\sqrt{a}}\cosh^{-1}\frac{\sqrt{aR}}{\sqrt{ac-b^2}},$$

which forms therefore may be taken when a is positive and b^2 is greater or less than ac respectively.

61. Case II. *a* Negative.

If in the integral $\int\frac{dx}{\sqrt{ax^2+2bx+c}}$, a be negative, write $a=-A$. Then our integral may be written

$$\frac{1}{\sqrt{A}}\int\frac{dx}{\sqrt{-x^2+\frac{2b}{A}x+\frac{c}{A}}};$$

or $$\frac{1}{\sqrt{A}}\int\frac{dx}{\sqrt{\frac{Ac+b^2}{A^2}-\left(x-\frac{b}{A}\right)^2}},$$

or $$\frac{1}{\sqrt{A}}\sin^{-1}\frac{Ax-b}{\sqrt{Ac+b^2}}$$

i.e. $$\frac{1}{\sqrt{-a}}\sin^{-1}\frac{-ax-b}{\sqrt{b^2-ac}},$$

or omitting a constant

$$\frac{1}{\sqrt{-a}}\cos^{-1}\frac{ax+b}{\sqrt{b^2-ac}}\qquad\left[\text{for } -\sin^{-1}z=\cos^{-1}z-\frac{\pi}{2}\right].$$

Also since $$\cos^{-1}z=\sin^{-1}\sqrt{1-z^2},$$

we have $$\cos^{-1}\frac{ax+b}{\sqrt{b^2-ac}}=\sin^{-1}\frac{\sqrt{-aR}}{\sqrt{b^2-ac}}.$$

It thus appears that when $R=ax^2+2bx+c$

$$\int\frac{dx}{\sqrt{R}}=\begin{cases}\dfrac{1}{\sqrt{-a}}\sin^{-1}\dfrac{\sqrt{-aR}}{\sqrt{b^2-ac}}, & a \text{ negative},\\[2ex] \dfrac{1}{\sqrt{a}}\sinh^{-1}\dfrac{\sqrt{aR}}{\sqrt{b^2-ac}}, & a \text{ positive}, \quad b^2>ac.\\[2ex] \text{or } \dfrac{1}{\sqrt{a}}\cosh^{-1}\dfrac{\sqrt{aR}}{\sqrt{ac-b^2}}, & a \text{ positive}, \quad b^2<ac.\end{cases}$$

and the real form is to be chosen in each case.

Ex. 1. Integrate $\int \dfrac{dx}{\sqrt{2x^2 + 3x + 4}}$.

We may write this

$$= \frac{1}{\sqrt{2}} \int \frac{dx}{\sqrt{\left(x + \frac{3}{4}\right)^2 + \frac{23}{16}}}$$

$$= \frac{1}{\sqrt{2}} \sinh^{-1} \frac{4x + 3}{\sqrt{23}},$$

i.e.
$$= \frac{1}{\sqrt{2}} \cosh^{-1} \frac{2\sqrt{2}}{\sqrt{23}} \sqrt{2x^2 + 3x + 4},$$

or
$$= \frac{1}{\sqrt{2}} \log\left(\frac{4x + 3}{\sqrt{23}} + \sqrt{\frac{(4x + 3)^2 + 23}{23}}\right),$$

i.e. the integral $= \dfrac{1}{\sqrt{2}} \log(4x + 3 + 2\sqrt{2}\sqrt{2x^2 + 3x + 4})$

$\left(\text{rejecting the constant } \dfrac{1}{\sqrt{2}} \log \dfrac{1}{\sqrt{23}}\right)$.

Ex. 2. Integrate $\int \dfrac{dx}{\sqrt{4 + 3x - 2x^2}}$.

This integral may be written

$$= \frac{1}{\sqrt{2}} \int \frac{dx}{\sqrt{\frac{41}{16} - \left(x - \frac{3}{4}\right)^2}},$$

and therefore is $\dfrac{1}{\sqrt{2}} \sin^{-1} \dfrac{4x - 3}{\sqrt{41}}$,

which may also be expressed as

$$\frac{1}{\sqrt{2}} \cos^{-1} \frac{2\sqrt{2}}{\sqrt{41}} \sqrt{4 + 3x - 2x^2}.$$

EXAMPLES

1. Integrate $\int \dfrac{dx}{\sqrt{x^2 + 2x + 3}}, \int \dfrac{dx}{\sqrt{2x^2 + 2x + 3}}$.

2. Integrate $\int \dfrac{dx}{\sqrt{2 + 3x - 2x^2}}, \int \dfrac{dx}{\sqrt{2 - 3x - 2x^2}}$.

3. Integrate $\int \sqrt{a + 2bx + cx^2}\, dx$ (c positive).

4. Integrate $\int \sqrt{a + 2bx - cx^2}\, dx$ (c positive).

62. Functions of the Form $\dfrac{Ax+B}{\sqrt{ax^2+2bx+c}}$

may be integrated by first putting $Ax + B$ into the form $\lambda(ax + b) + \mu$, which may be done as in Art. 57, either by inspection or by equating coefficients; we obtain

$$Ax + B \equiv \frac{A}{a}(ax + b) + B - \frac{Ab}{a}.$$

Thus $$\frac{Ax + B}{\sqrt{ax^2 + 2bx + c}} = \frac{A}{a}\frac{ax + b}{\sqrt{ax^2 + 2bx + c}} + \frac{B - \dfrac{Ab}{a}}{\sqrt{ax^2 + 2bx + c}}.$$

The integral of the first fraction is $\frac{A}{a}.\sqrt{ax^2 + 2bx + c}$;

and that of the second has been discussed in Articles 60, 61.

EXAMPLES

Integrate

1. $\dfrac{x+1}{\sqrt{x^2+2x+3}}$.
2. $\dfrac{x}{\sqrt{x^2+a^2}}$.
3. $\dfrac{x+b}{\sqrt{x^2+a^2}}$.
4. $\dfrac{2x+3}{\sqrt{x^2-1}}$.
5. $\dfrac{2x+3}{\sqrt{x^2+x+1}}$.
6. $\dfrac{x^2+1}{\sqrt{x^2+4}}$.
7. $\dfrac{x^2+x+1}{\sqrt{x^2+2x+3}}$.
8. $\dfrac{x^3+x^2+x+1}{\sqrt{x^2+2x+3}}$.

POWERS AND PRODUCTS OF SINES AND COSINES.

63. Sine or Cosine with Positive Odd Integral Index.

Any *odd positive power of a* sine or cosine can be integrated immediately thus :—

To integrate $\int \sin^{2n+1} x\,dx$, let $\cos x = c$,

$\therefore \qquad \sin x\,dx = -dc,$

Hence $\int \sin^{2n+1} x\,dx = -\int (1-c^2)^n\,dc$

$$= -\int \left[1 - nc^2 + \frac{n(n-1)}{1\cdot 2}c^4 - ...+(-1)^n \cdot c^{2n}\right]dc$$

$$= -\cos x + n\frac{\cos^3 x}{3} - \frac{n(n-1)}{1\cdot 2}\frac{\cos^5 x}{5} + \ldots -(-1)^n \frac{\cos^{(2n+1)} x}{2n+1}.$$

Similarly, putting $\sin x = s$, and therefore $\cos x\,dx = ds$,

we have $\int \cos^{2n+1} x\,dx = \int (1-s^2)^n ds$

$$= \sin x - n\frac{\sin^3 x}{3} + \frac{n(n-1)}{1\cdot 2}\frac{\sin^5 x}{5} - \ldots + (-1)^n \frac{\sin^{2n+1} x}{2n+1}.$$

64. Product of form $\sin^p x \cos^q x$, p or q odd.

Similarly, any product of the form $\sin^p x \cos^q x$ admits of immediate integration by the same method *whenever either p or q is a positive odd integer*, whatever the other be.

For example, to integrate $\int \sin^5 x \cos^4 x\,dx$, put $\cos x = c$, and therefore $-\sin x\,dx = dc$.

Hence $\int \cos^4 x \sin^5 x\,dx = -\int c^4(1-c^2)^2 dc$

$$= -\frac{\cos^5 x}{5} + 2\frac{\cos^7 x}{7} - \frac{\cos^9 x}{9}.$$

Again to integrate $\int \sin^{\frac{3}{5}} x \cos^3 x\,dx$ we proceed thus:—

$$= \int \sin^{\frac{3}{5}} x(1-\sin^2 x)d(\sin x) = \frac{5}{8}\sin^{\frac{8}{5}} x - \frac{5}{18}\sin^{\frac{18}{5}} x.$$

65. When $p + q$ is a negative even integer,

the expression $\sin^p x \cos^q x$ admits of immediate integration in terms of $\tan x$ or $\cot x$.

For put $\tan x = t$, and therefore $\sec^2 x\,dx = dt$, and let

$p + q = -2n$, n being integral. Thus

$$\int \sin^p x \cos^q x\,dx = \int \tan^p x \cos^{p+q+2} x\,dt = \int t^p(1+t^2)^{n-1}dt$$

$$= \int (t^p + {}^{n-1}C_1 t^{p+2} + {}^{n-1}C_2 t^{p+4} + \ldots + t^{p+2n-2})\,dt$$

$$= \frac{\tan^{p+1} x}{p+1} + {}^{n-1}C_1 \frac{\tan^{p+3} x}{p+3} + {}^{n-1}C_2 \frac{\tan^{p+5} x}{p+5} + \ldots + \frac{\tan^{p+2n-1} x}{p+2n-1}.$$

Similarly, if we put $\cot x = c$, then $-\operatorname{cosec}^2 x\,dx = dc$,

and

$$\int \sin^p x \cos^q x\,dx = -\int \cot^q x \sin^{p+q+2} x\,dc = -\int c^q(1+c^2)^{n-1}dc$$

$$= -\frac{\cot^{q+1} x}{q+1} - {}^{n-1}C_1 \frac{\cot^{q+3} x}{q+3} - {}^{n-1}C_2 \frac{\cot^{q+5} x}{q+5} - \ldots - \frac{\cot^{q+2n-1} x}{q+2n-1},$$

a result the same as the former arranged in the opposite order.

Ex. 1. Integrate $\int \frac{\cos^2 x}{\sin^6 x} dx$.

This may be written $-\int \cot^2 x\,(1 + \cot^2 x)\,d\cot x$,

and the result is therefore $= -\frac{\cot^3 x}{3} - \frac{\cot^5 x}{5}$.

It may also be integrated in terms of $\tan x$ thus:—

$$\int \frac{\cos^2 x}{\sin^6 x} dx = \int \frac{1}{\tan^6 x}(1 + \tan^2 x)\,d\tan x$$

$$= -\frac{\tan^{-5} x}{5} - \frac{\tan^{-3} x}{3},$$

the result being the same as before.

Ex. 2. $\int \sec^{\frac{3}{5}}\theta \operatorname{cosec}^{\frac{7}{5}}\theta\,d\theta = \int \tan^{-\frac{7}{5}}\theta\,d\tan\theta = -\frac{5}{2}\tan^{-\frac{2}{5}}\theta = -\frac{5}{2}\cot^{\frac{2}{5}}\theta$.

66. Use of Multiple Angles.

Any positive integral power of a sine or cosine, or any product of positive integral powers of sines and cosines, can be expressed by trigonometrical means in a series of sines or cosines of multiples of the angle, and then each term may be integrated at once; for

$$\int \cos nx\,dx = \frac{\sin nx}{n} \quad \text{and} \quad \int \sin nx\,dx = -\frac{\cos nx}{n}.$$

Ex. 1. $\int \cos^2 x\,dx = \int \frac{1 + \cos 2x}{2} dx = \frac{x}{2} + \frac{\sin 2x}{4}$.

Ex. 2. $\int \cos^3 x\,dx = \int \frac{3\cos x + \cos 3x}{4} dx = \frac{3}{4}\sin x + \frac{1}{12}\sin 3x$.

Ex. 3. $\int \cos^4 x\,dx = \int \left(\frac{1 + \cos 2x}{2}\right)^2 dx$

$$= \int \frac{1 + 2\cos 2x + \frac{1 + \cos 4x}{2}}{4} dx$$

$$= \int \left(\frac{3}{8} + \frac{1}{2}\cos 2x + \frac{1}{8}\cos 4x\right) dx$$

$$= \frac{3}{8}x + \frac{1}{4}\sin 2x + \frac{1}{32}\sin 4x.$$

67. It has already been shown that when the index is odd no such transformation is necessary, thus in the second example

$$\int \cos^3 x\,dx = \int (1-\sin^2 x)d\sin x = \sin x - \frac{\sin^3 x}{3},$$

which presents the result in different form. The method we are now discussing will therefore be of more especial value for the case of $\sin^p x\cos^q x$, *where neither p nor q are odd.*

Ex. 4. Integrate $\int \sin^8 x\,dx$.

Let $\cos x + i\sin x = y$; then

$$2\cos x = y + \frac{1}{y},\ 2\cos nx = y^n + \frac{1}{y^n},$$

$$2i\sin x = y - \frac{1}{y},\ 2i\sin nx = y^n - \frac{1}{y^n}.$$

Thus $2^8 i^8 \sin^8 x = \left(y - \frac{1}{y}\right)^8$

$$= \left(y^8 + \frac{1}{y^8}\right) - 8\left(y^6 + \frac{1}{y^6}\right) + 28\left(y^4 + \frac{1}{y^4}\right) - 56\left(y^2 + \frac{1}{y^2}\right) + 70$$

$$= 2\cos 8x - 16\cos 6x + 56\cos 4x - 112\cos 2x + 70.$$

Thus $\sin^8 x = \frac{1}{2^7}(\cos 8x - 8\cos 6x + 28\cos 4x - 56\cos 2x + 35)$,

and $\int \sin^8 x\,dx = \frac{1}{2^7}\left[\frac{\sin 8x}{8} - 8\frac{\sin 6x}{6} + 28\frac{\sin 4x}{4} - 56\frac{\sin 2x}{2} + 35x\right]$.

Ex. 5. Integrate $\int \sin^6 x\cos^2 x\,dx$.

Put $\cos x + i\sin x = y$; then

$2^6 i^6 \sin^6 x \cdot 2^2\cos^2 x$

$$= \left(y - \frac{1}{y}\right)^6\left(y + \frac{1}{y}\right)^2 \qquad \text{[See Art. 68.]}$$

$$= y^8 + \frac{1}{y^8} - 4\left(y^6 + \frac{1}{y^6}\right) + 4\left(y^4 + \frac{1}{y^4}\right) + 4\left(y^2 + \frac{1}{y^2}\right) - 10$$

$$= 2\cos 8x - 8\cos 6x + 8\cos 4x + 8\cos 2x - 10,$$

and $\sin^6 x\cos^2 x = \frac{1}{2^7}\{-\cos 8x + 4\cos 6x - 4\cos 4x - 4\cos 2x + 5\}$,

whence

$$\int \sin^6 x\cos^2 x\,dx = \frac{1}{2^7}\left\{-\frac{\sin 8x}{8} + 4\frac{\sin 6x}{6} - 4\frac{\sin 4x}{4} - 4\frac{\sin 2x}{2} + 5x\right\}.$$

68. Note. It is convenient for such examples to remember that the several sets of Binomial Coefficients may be quickly reproduced in the following scheme:—

1								
1	1							
1	2	1						
1	3	3	1					
1	4	6	4	1				
1	5	10	10	5	1			
1	6	15	20	15	6	1		
1	7	21	35	35	21	7	1	
1	8	28	56	70	56	28	8	1

etc.,

each number being formed at once as the sum of the one immediately above it and the preceding one. Thus in forming the 7th row we have

$0 + 1 = 1, 1 + 5 = 6, 5 + 10 = 15, 10 + 10 = 20$, etc;

and in multiplying out such a product as $\left(y - \frac{1}{y}\right)^6 \left(y + \frac{1}{y}\right)^2$ occurring above we only need the coefficients of $(1 - t)^6(1 + t)^2$ and all the work appearing will be

coefficients of $(1 - t)^6$ are $1 - 6 + 15 - 20 + 15 - 6 + 1$,

coefficients of $(1 - t)^6(1 + t)$ are $1 - 5 + 9 - 5 - 5 + 9 - 5 + 1$,

coefficients of $(1 - t)^6(1 + t)^2$ are $1 - 4 + 4 + 4 - 10 + 4 + 4 - 4 + 1$,

each row of figures being formed according to the same law as before. The student will discover the reason of this by performing the actual multiplication of $a + bt + ct^2 + dt^3 + \ldots$ by $1 + t$, in which the several coefficients are $a, a + b, b + c, c + d$, etc.

Similarly if the coefficients in $(1 + t)^4(1 - t)^2$ were required, the work appearing would be

$$1 + 4 + 6 + 4 + 1,$$
$$1 + 3 + 2 - 2 - 3 - 1,$$
$$1 + 2 - 1 - 4 - 1 + 2 + 1,$$

and the last row are the coefficients required.

The coefficients here are formed thus:—

$$1 - 0 = 1,\ 4 - 1 = 3,$$
$$6 - 4 = 2,\ 4 - 6 = -2, \text{ etc.}$$

EXAMPLES

1. Integrate
$\sin^2 x, \sin^3 x, \sin^4 x, \sin^5 x, \sin^6 x, \sin^7 x, \sin^{2n} x, \sin^{2n+1} x$, doing those with odd indices in two ways.

2. Integrate
$\sin^2 x\cos^3 x, \sin^3 x\cos^3 x, \sin^3 x\cos^2 x, \sin^4 x\cos^4 x, \sin^4 x\cos^6 x.$

3. Integrate $\dfrac{\sin^2 x}{\cos^4 x}, \dfrac{\cos^2 x}{\sin^4 x}, \dfrac{1}{\sin^2 x\cos^2 x}, \dfrac{1}{\sin^4 x\cos^4 x}.$

4. Evaluate $\int_0^{\frac{\pi}{4}} \sin^2 x\,dx, \int_0^{\frac{\pi}{4}} \cos^5 x\,dx, \int_0^{\frac{\pi}{4}} \cos^6 x\,dx.$

5. Integrate $\sin 2x\cos^2 x, \sin 3x\cos^3 x, \sin nx\cos^2 x.$

6. Show that $\int \sin x\sin 2x\sin 3x\,dx = -\frac{1}{8}\cos 2x - \frac{1}{16}\cos 4x + \frac{1}{24}\cos 6x.$

7. Show that

(i.) $\int \sin mx\cos nx\,dx = -\dfrac{\cos(m+n)x}{2(m+n)} - \dfrac{\cos(m-n)x}{2(m-n)}.$

(ii.) $\int \sin mx\sin nx\,dx = \dfrac{\sin(m-n)x}{2(m-n)} - \dfrac{\sin(m+n)x}{2(m+n)}.$

(iii.) $\int \cos mx\cos nx\,dx = \dfrac{\sin(m-n)x}{2(m-n)} + \dfrac{\sin(m+n)x}{2(m+n)}.$

Deduce from (ii.) and (iii.) $\int \sin^2 mx\,dx$ and $\int \cos^2 mx\,dx$, and verify the results by independent integration.

INTEGRAL POWERS OF A SECANT OR COSECANT.

69. Even Positive Integral Powers of a secant or cosecant come under the head discussed in Art. 65.

Thus $\int \sec^2 x\,dx = \tan x, \int \sec^4 x\,dx = \int (1+\tan^2 x)d\tan x = \tan x + \dfrac{\tan^3 x}{3},$

$\int \sec^6 x\,dx = \int (1 + 2\tan^2 x + \tan^4 x)d\tan x = \tan x + 2\dfrac{\tan^3 x}{3} + \dfrac{\tan^5 x}{5}$, etc.,

and generally $\int \sec^{2n+2} x\,dx = \int (1+t^2)^n dt$ where $t = \tan x$

$$= t + {}^nC_1\frac{t^3}{3} + {}^nC_2\frac{t^5}{5} + \dots + \frac{t^{2n+1}}{2n+1},$$

Similarly $\int \operatorname{cosec}^2 x\,dx = -\cot x,$

$$\int \operatorname{cosec}^4 x\,dx = -\int (1+\cot^2 x)d\cot x = -\cot x - \frac{\cot^3 x}{3}, \text{ etc.}$$

and generally $\int \operatorname{cosec}^{2n+2} x\,dx = -c - {}^nC_1\dfrac{c^3}{3} - {}^nC_2\dfrac{c^5}{5} - \dots - \dfrac{c^{2n+1}}{2n+1}$

where $c = \cot x$.

70. Odd positive integral powers of a secant or cosecant can be integrated thus :—

By differentiation we have at once

$$(n+1)\sec^{n+2}x - n\sec^n x = \frac{d}{dx}(\tan x \sec^n x)$$

and $(n+1)\operatorname{cosec}^{n+2}x - n\operatorname{cosec}^n x = -\frac{d}{dx}(\cot x \operatorname{cosec}^n x)$

Whence

$$\left.\begin{aligned}(n+1)\int \sec^{n+2}x\,dx &= \tan x \sec^n x + n\int \sec^n x\,dx \\ \text{and}\quad (n+1)\int \operatorname{cosec}^{n+2}x\,dx &= -\cot x \operatorname{cosec}^n x + n\int \operatorname{cosec}^n x\,dx\end{aligned}\right\}\text{A.}$$

Thus as $\int \sec x\,dx = \log\tan\left(\frac{\pi}{4}+\frac{x}{2}\right)$,

and $\int \operatorname{cosec} x\,dx = \log\tan\frac{x}{2}$,

we may infer at once the integrals of

$$\sec^3 x, \sec^5 x, \sec^7 x, \ldots; \operatorname{cosec}^3 x, \operatorname{cosec}^5 x, \text{etc.},$$

by successively putting $n = 1, 3, 5$, etc., in the above formulae.

Thus $\int \sec^3 x dx = \frac{1}{2}\tan x \sec x + \frac{1}{2}\log\tan\left(\frac{x}{2}+\frac{\pi}{4}\right)$,

$$\int \sec^5 x dx = \frac{1}{4}\tan x \sec^3 x + \frac{3}{4}\int \sec^3 x$$

$$= \frac{1}{4}\tan x \sec^3 x + \frac{3}{8}\tan x \sec x + \frac{3}{8}\log\tan\left(\frac{x}{2}+\frac{\pi}{4}\right), \text{ etc.}$$

71. Such formulae as A are called "REDUCTION" formulae, and the student will meet with many others in Chapter 7. We postpone till that chapter the consideration of the integration of such an expression as $\sin^p x \cos^q x$ except for such cases as have been already considered.

72. Since a positive power of a secant or cosecant is a negative power of a cosine or sine, and a positive power of a cosine or sine is a negative power of a secant or cosecant it will appear that we are now able to integrate *any integral positive or negative power of a sine, cosine, secant, or cosecant.*

INTEGRAL POWER OF TANGENT OR COTANGENT.

73. Any integral power of a tangent or cotangent may be readily integrated.

For $\int \tan^n x\,dx = \int \tan^{n-2} x(\sec^2 x - 1)dx$

$$= \int \tan^{n-2} x\, d\tan x - \int \tan^{n-2} x\,dx$$

$$= \frac{\tan^{n-1} x}{n-1} - \int \tan^{n-2} x\,dx.$$

And since $\int \tan x\,dx = \log\sec x$,

and $\int \tan^2 x dx = \int (\sec^2 x - 1)dx = \tan x - x$

we may integrate $\tan^3 x$, $\tan^4 x$, $\tan^5 x$, etc.

Thus we have $\int \tan^3 x\,dx = \int \tan x\,(\sec^2 x - 1)\,dx$

$$= \frac{\tan^2 x}{2} - \log\sec x,$$

$$\int \tan^4 x\,dx = \int \tan^2 x\,(\sec^2 x - 1)\,dx$$

$$= \frac{\tan^3 x}{3} - \tan x + x, \text{ etc.}$$

By continuing this process we shall evidently obtain

$$\int \tan^{2n} x\,dx = \frac{\tan^{2n-1} x}{2n-1} - \frac{\tan^{2n-3} x}{2n-3} + \frac{\tan^{2n-5} x}{2n-5} - \ldots + (-1)^{n-1}\tan x + (-1)^n x,$$

and $$\int \tan^{2n+1} x\,dx = \frac{\tan^{2n} x}{2n} - \frac{\tan^{2n-2} x}{2n-2} + \frac{\tan^{2n-4} x}{2n-4} - \ldots + (-1)^{n-1}\frac{\tan^2 x}{2} + (-1)^n \log\sec x.$$

Similarly

$$\int \cot^n x\,dx = \int \cot^{n-2} x\,(\operatorname{cosec}^2 x - 1)\,dx = -\frac{\cot^{n-1} x}{n-1} - \int \cot^{n-2} x\,dx,$$

whilst $\int \cot x\,dx = \log\sin x$,

and $\int \cot^2 x\,dx = \int (\operatorname{cosec}^2 x - 1)\,dx = -\cot x - x$;

and therefore we may thus integrate

$\cot^3 x$, $\cot^4 x$, $\cot^5 x$, etc.

Hence *any integral power of a tangent or cotangent admits of immediate integration.*

74. Integration of $\int \frac{dx}{a+b\cos x}$, etc.

We may write $a+b\cos x$ as

$$a\left(\cos^2\frac{x}{2}+\sin^2\frac{x}{2}\right)+b\left(\cos^2\frac{x}{2}-\sin^2\frac{x}{2}\right),$$

i.e.

$$(a+b)\cos^2\frac{x}{2}+(a-b)\sin^2\frac{x}{2},$$

or

$$(a-b)\cos^2\frac{x}{2}\left[\frac{a+b}{a-b}+\tan^2\frac{x}{2}\right].$$

Thus

$$\int\frac{dx}{a+b\cos x}=\frac{2}{a-b}\int\frac{\frac{1}{2}\sec^2\frac{x}{2}\,dx}{\frac{a+b}{a-b}+\tan^2\frac{x}{2}},$$

or

$$\frac{2}{a-b}\int\frac{d\left(\tan\frac{x}{2}\right)}{\frac{a+b}{a-b}+\tan^2\frac{x}{2}} \qquad \text{...(1)}$$

Case I. If $a>b$ this becomes $\frac{2}{a-b}\frac{1}{\sqrt{\frac{a+b}{a-b}}}\tan^{-1}\frac{\tan\frac{x}{2}}{\sqrt{\frac{a+b}{a-b}}}$,

or

$$\frac{2}{\sqrt{a^2-b^2}}\tan^{-1}\left\{\sqrt{\frac{a-b}{a+b}}\tan\frac{x}{2}\right\}.$$

Since

$$2\tan^{-1}z=\cos^{-1}\frac{1-z^2}{1+z^2},$$

we may write this as $\frac{1}{\sqrt{a^2-b^2}}\cos^{-1}\frac{1-\frac{a-b}{a+b}\tan^2\frac{x}{2}}{1+\frac{a-b}{a+b}\tan^2\frac{x}{2}}$,

or

$$\frac{1}{\sqrt{a^2-b^2}}\cos^{-1}\frac{b+a\cos x}{a+b\cos x}.$$

Case II. If $a<b$, writing the integral in the form

$$\frac{2}{b-a}\int\frac{d\tan\frac{x}{2}}{\frac{b+a}{b-a}-\tan^2\frac{x}{2}}, \qquad \text{...(2)}$$

in place of the form (1), we have in this case by Art. 54,

$$\int \frac{dx}{a+b\cos x} = \frac{2}{b-a}\frac{1}{2\sqrt{\dfrac{b+a}{b-a}}}\log\frac{\sqrt{\dfrac{b+a}{b-a}}+\tan\dfrac{x}{2}}{\sqrt{\dfrac{b+a}{b-a}}-\tan\dfrac{x}{2}}$$

$$= \frac{1}{\sqrt{b^2-a^2}}\log\frac{\sqrt{b+a}+\sqrt{b-a}\tan\dfrac{x}{2}}{\sqrt{b+a}-\sqrt{b-a}\tan\dfrac{x}{2}}.$$

By Art. 33 this may be written $\dfrac{2}{\sqrt{b^2-a^2}}\tanh^{-1}\sqrt{\dfrac{b-a}{b+a}}\tan\dfrac{x}{2}$,

or, since $2\tanh^{-1} z = \cosh^{-1}\dfrac{1+z^2}{1-z^2}$,

we may still further exhibit the result as

$$\frac{1}{\sqrt{b^2-a^2}}\cosh^{-1}\frac{1+\dfrac{b-a}{b+a}\tan^2\dfrac{x}{2}}{1-\dfrac{b-a}{b+a}\tan^2\dfrac{x}{2}},$$

or
$$\frac{1}{\sqrt{b^2-a^2}}\cosh^{-1}\frac{b+a\cos x}{a+b\cos x}.$$

We therefore have

$$\int\frac{dx}{a+b\cos x} = \begin{cases} \left.\begin{array}{l} \dfrac{2}{\sqrt{a^2-b^2}}\tan^{-1}\sqrt{\dfrac{a-b}{a+b}}\tan\dfrac{x}{2}, \\ \text{i. e. } \dfrac{1}{\sqrt{a^2-b^2}}\cos^{-1}\dfrac{b+a\cos x}{a+b\cos x}; \end{array}\right\} a>b. \\ \left.\begin{array}{l} \dfrac{2}{\sqrt{b^2-a^2}}\tanh^{-1}\sqrt{\dfrac{b-a}{b+a}}\tan\dfrac{x}{2}, \\ \text{i. e. } \dfrac{1}{\sqrt{b^2-a^2}}\log\dfrac{\sqrt{b+a}+\sqrt{b-a}\tan\dfrac{x}{2}}{\sqrt{b+a}-\sqrt{b-a}\tan\dfrac{x}{2}}, \\ \text{or } \dfrac{1}{\sqrt{b^2-a^2}}\cosh^{-1}\dfrac{b+a\cos x}{a+b\cos x}. \end{array}\right\} a<b. \end{cases}$$

These forms are all equivalent, but one of the real forms is to be chosen when the formula is used.

75. The integral of $\dfrac{1}{a+b\cos x+c\sin x}$ may be immediately deduced, for

$$b\cos x+c\sin x=\sqrt{b^2+c^2}\cos\left(x-\tan^{-1}\frac{c}{b}\right),$$

and therefore the proper form of the integral can at once be written down in each of the cases a greater or less than $\sqrt{b^2+c^2}$.

Ex. $$\int\frac{dx}{13+3\cos x+4\sin x}=\int\frac{dx}{13+5\cos(x-\alpha)}\qquad\left(\text{where }\tan\alpha=\frac{4}{3}\right)$$

$$=\frac{1}{\sqrt{13^2-5^2}}\cos^{-1}\frac{5+13\cos(x-\alpha)}{13+5\cos(x-\alpha)}$$

$$=\frac{1}{12}\cos^{-1}\frac{5+13\cos(x-\alpha)}{13+5\cos(x-\alpha)},$$

$$\frac{1}{6}\tan^{-1}\left(\frac{2}{3}\tan\frac{x-\alpha}{2}\right).$$

76. The integral $\int\dfrac{dx}{a+b\sin x}$ may be easily deduced by putting

$$x=\frac{\pi}{2}+y,$$

then $$\int\frac{dx}{a+b\sin x}=\int\frac{dy}{a+b\cos y},$$

and therefore its value may be written down in both the cases $a \gtrless b$.

Of course it may be investigated also independently by first writing $a+b\sin x$ as

$$a\left(\cos^2\frac{x}{2}+\sin^2\frac{x}{2}\right)+2\,b\sin\frac{x}{2}\cos\frac{x}{2},$$

or $$\cos^2\frac{x}{2}\left(a+2b\tan\frac{x}{2}+a\tan^2\frac{x}{2}\right).$$

The integral then becomes

$$\frac{2}{a}\int\frac{d\tan\frac{x}{2}}{\left(\tan\frac{x}{2}+\frac{b}{a}\right)^2+\frac{a^2-b^2}{a^2}},$$

and two cases arise as before.

77. The integral $\int \frac{dx}{a+b\cosh x}$ may be similarly treated.

$$\int \frac{dx}{a+b\cosh x} = \int \frac{dx}{a\left(\cosh^2\frac{x}{2} - \sinh^2\frac{x}{2}\right) + b\left(\cosh^2\frac{x}{2} + \sinh^2\frac{x}{2}\right)}$$

$$= \frac{2}{b-a}\int \frac{d\left(\tanh\frac{x}{2}\right)}{\frac{b+a}{b-a} + \tanh^2\frac{x}{2}},$$

if $b > a$, this $= \frac{2}{\sqrt{b^2-a^2}}\tan^{-1}\sqrt{\frac{b-a}{b+a}}\tanh\frac{x}{2},$

which further reduces to $\frac{1}{\sqrt{b^2-a^2}}\cos^{-1}\frac{b+a\cosh x}{a+b\cosh x};$

and if $b < a$ the integral is $\frac{2}{\sqrt{a^2-b^2}}\tanh^{-1}\sqrt{\frac{a-b}{a+b}}\tanh\frac{x}{2},$

which further reduces to $\frac{1}{\sqrt{a^2-b^2}}\cosh^{-1}\frac{b+a\cosh x}{a+b\cosh x}.$

78. Similarly the integrals of $\frac{1}{a+b\sinh x}$ and of $\frac{1}{a+b\cosh x+c\sinh x}$ may be easily obtained.

EXAMPLES

1. Integrate $\int \frac{\sqrt{\tan x}}{\sin x\cos x}dx$.

2. Integrate (i.) $\int \frac{\sec x\,dx}{a+b\tan x}$. (ii.) $\int \frac{dx}{(a\sin x+b\cos x)^2}$.

3. Integrate (i.) $\int \frac{d\theta}{a+b\tan\theta}$. (ii.) $\int \frac{a\sin\theta+b\cos\theta}{c\sin\theta+e\cos\theta}d\theta$.

4. Prove that, with certain limitations on the values of the constants involved $\int_\beta^x \frac{dx}{\sqrt{(a-x)(x-\beta)}} = 2\,\text{arc}\cos\sqrt{\frac{a-x}{a-\beta}}$, and integrate $\int_a^\beta \sqrt{(x-a)(\beta-x)}\,dx$.

5. Integrate

(i.) $\int \frac{dx}{a^2 - b^2 \cos^2 x}\ a > b,$ (ii.) $\int \frac{dx}{5 + 4\cos x},$

(iii.) $\int \frac{dx}{\cos a + \cos x},$ (iv.) $\int \frac{dx}{3(1 - \sin x) - \cos x},$

(v.) $\int \frac{\sqrt{2}\, dx}{2\sqrt{2} + \cos x + \sin x},$ (vi.) $\int \frac{d\theta}{a^2 \sin^2 \theta + b^2 \cos^2 \theta},$

(vii.) $\int \frac{\cos a \cos x + 1}{\cos a + \cos x} dx,$ and

(viii.) Prove $\int_0^{\theta} \frac{dx}{1 - \cos\theta \cos x} = \frac{\pi}{2} \operatorname{cosec} \theta.$

6. Integrate (i.) $\int \frac{dx}{\sqrt{x-a} + \sqrt{x-b}}.$ (ii.) $\int \frac{dx}{\sqrt{a(x-b)} + \sqrt{b(x-a)}}.$

(iii.) $\int \frac{dx}{\sqrt{ax+b} + \sqrt{a' x + b'}}.$

7. Integrate $\int \frac{d\theta}{15\sin^2\theta - 16\cos\theta}.$

8. Integrate $\int \frac{dx}{\sin x + \sin 2x}.$

9. Integrate $\int \cos 2\theta \log \frac{\cos\theta + \sin\theta}{\cos\theta - \sin\theta} d\theta.$

10. Integrate $\int \frac{\cosh x + \sinh x \sin x}{1 + \cos x} dx.$

11. Integrate $\int \sqrt{1 + \sin x}\, dx.$

12. Integrate $\int \frac{\sin x}{\sqrt{1 + \sin x}} dx.$

13. Integrate $\int \frac{\sec x}{1 + \operatorname{cosec} x} dx.$

14. Integrate $\int \frac{\tan x\, dx}{\sqrt{a + b\tan^2 x}}.$

15. Evaluate $\int_0^{\pi} \frac{x}{1 + \sin x} dx.$

16. Integrate $\int \frac{\sec x \operatorname{cosec} x}{\log \tan x} dx.$

17. Integrate $\int \frac{\sin\theta - \cos\theta}{\sqrt{\sin 2\theta}} d\theta.$

18. Integrate $\int \frac{\cot\theta - 3\cot 3\theta}{3\tan 3\theta - \tan\theta}\,d\theta$.

19. Integrate $\int \frac{dx}{x\sqrt{a^n + x^n}}$.

20. Integrate $\int \frac{x^2 dx}{(x\sin x + \cos x)^2}$.

21. Integrate $\int \frac{\sin 2x\,dx}{(a + b\cos x)^2}$.

22. Integrate $\int \sqrt{\frac{1-\cos\theta}{\cos\theta(1+\cos\theta)(2+\cos\theta)}}\,d\theta$.

23. Integrate $\int \sqrt{\frac{1+\sin x}{1-\sin x}\cdot\frac{2+\sin x}{2-\sin x}}\,dx$.

24. Integrate $\int \frac{\sin\theta - \cos\theta}{(\sin\theta + \cos\theta)\sqrt{\sin\theta\cos\theta + \sin^2\theta\cos^2\theta}}\,d\theta$.

25. Integrate $\int \frac{\sin^3\theta\,d\theta}{(1+\cos^2\theta)\sqrt{1+\cos^2\theta+\cos^4\theta}}$.

26. Integrate $\int \sin^{-1}\frac{2x}{1+x^2}\,dx$.

27. Integrate $\int \frac{\sqrt{1+x^2}}{1-x^2}\,dx$.

28. Integrate $\int \frac{\sin x}{\sin 2x}\,dx, \int \frac{\sin x}{\sin 3x}\,dx, \int \frac{\sin x}{\sin 4x}\,dx$, and prove that

$$5\int \frac{\sin x}{\sin 5x}\,dx = \sin\frac{2\pi}{5}\log\left\{\frac{\sin\left(x-\frac{2\pi}{5}\right)}{\sin\left(x+\frac{2\pi}{5}\right)}\right\} - \sin\frac{\pi}{5}\log\left\{\frac{\sin\left(x-\frac{\pi}{5}\right)}{\sin\left(x+\frac{\pi}{5}\right)}\right\}.$$

[TBIN. COLL., 1892.]

CHAPTER VII.

REDUCTION FORMULAE.

REDUCTION FORMULAE.

79. Many functions occur whose integrals are not immediately reducible to one or other of the standard forms, and whose integrals are not directly obtainable. In some cases, however, such integrals may be linearly connected by some algebraic formula with the integral of another expression, which itself may be either immediately integrable or at any rate easier to integrate than the original function.

For instance it will be shown that $\int (a^2 + x^2)^{\frac{5}{2}} dx$ can be expressed in terms of $\int (a^2 + x^2)^{\frac{3}{2}} dx$, and this latter itself in terms of $\int (a^2 + x^2)^{\frac{1}{2}} dx$, which being a standard form the integral of $\int (a^2 + x^2)^{\frac{5}{2}} dx$ may be inferred.

Such connecting algebraical relations are called Reduction Formulae.

80. The student will realise that several reduction methods have already been used. For instance the method of Integration by parts of Chapter IV, and the formulae A of Art.70. It is proposed to consider such formulae more fully in the present chapter, and to give a ready method for the reproduction of some of the more important.

81. On the integration of $x^{m-1}X^p$, where X stands for anything of the form $a + bx^n$.

In several cases the integration can be performed directly.

I. If *p be a positive integer*, the binomial in

$$x^{m-1}(a+bx^n)^p$$

expands into a finite series, and each term is integrable.

Next suppose p fractional $= \frac{r}{s}$, r and s being integers and s positive.

II. Consider the case when $\frac{m}{n}$ is a positive integer.

Let $\qquad X = a + bx^n = z^s$

$\therefore \qquad bn\, x^{n-1} dx = s z^{s-1} dz$

and $$\int x^{m-1}X^{\frac{r}{s}}dx=\frac{s}{bn}\int x^{m-1}z^{r}\cdot\frac{z^{s-1}}{x^{n-1}}dz$$

$$=\frac{s}{bn}\int z^{r+s-1}\left(\frac{z^{s}-a}{b}\right)^{\frac{m-n}{n}}dz,$$

and when $\frac{m}{n}$ is a positive integer, this expression is directly integrable by expanding the binomial and integrating each term.

III. When $\frac{m}{n}$ is a negative integer, the expression

$$\frac{z^{r+s-1}}{(z^{s}-a)^{-\frac{m}{n}+1}}$$

may be put into partial fractions, and the integration may then be proceeded with (Art.58).

IV. If $\frac{m}{n}+\frac{r}{s}$ is an integer positive or negative, we may proceed thus:—

$$\int x^{m-1}(a+bx^{n})^{\frac{r}{s}}dx=\int x^{m+\frac{rn}{s}-1}(b+ax^{-n})^{\frac{r}{s}}dx,$$

and by cases II. and III. this is integrable when $\dfrac{m+\frac{rn}{s}}{-n}$ is either a positive or a negative integer by the substitution $b+ax^{-n}=z^{s}$. That is, the expression is integrable when $\frac{m}{n}+\frac{r}{s}$ is integral, positive, or negative.

Three cases therefore admit of integration immediately or by simple substitution.

(1) *p a positive integer.* (2) $\frac{m}{n}$ *an integer.* (3) $\frac{m}{n}+p$ *an integer.*

Ex.1. Integrate $\int x^{5}(a^{3}+x^{3})^{\frac{1}{2}}dx$.

Here $m=6$, $n=3$, and $\frac{m}{n}=$ an integer.

Let $a^{3}+x^{3}=z^{2}$,

so that $3x^{2}dx=2z\,dz$.

Then the integral becomes

$$=\int(z^{2}-a^{3})\,z\cdot\frac{2}{3}z\,dz=\frac{2}{3}\left(\frac{z^{5}}{5}-a^{3}\frac{z^{3}}{3}\right)=\text{etc.}$$

Ex. 2. Integrate $\int x^{\frac{1}{2}}(a^3+x^3)^{\frac{1}{2}}dx$.

Here $m=\frac{3}{2}$, $n=3$, $p=\frac{1}{2}$, and $\frac{m}{n}+p$ is an integer.

The integral is $\int x^2(1+a^3x^{-3})^{\frac{1}{2}}dx$.

Let $1+a^3x^{-3}=z^2$,

then $-3\frac{a^3}{x^4}dx=2z\ dz$,

and the integral becomes $-\frac{2}{3a^3}\int x^6z^2\ dz=-\frac{2}{3}a^3\int\frac{z^2}{(z^2-1)^2}dz$,

which might be put into partial fractions. If, however, z be put $=\sec\theta$, the process of putting the expression into partial fractions will be avoided and the final integration may be quickly effected (Art.70).

82. Reduction Formulae for $\int x^{m-1}(a+bx^n)^p dx$.

Let $a+bx^n=X$; then $\int x^{m-1}X^pdx$ can be connected with any of the following six integrals :—

$$\int x^{m-1}X^{p-1}dx,\ \int x^{m-1}X^{p+1}dx,\ \int x^{m-n-1}X^pdx,\ \int x^{m+n-1}X^pdx,$$

$$\int x^{m-n-1}X^{p+1}dx,\int x^{m+n-1}X^{p-1}dx,$$

according to the following rule :—

Let $P=x^{\lambda+1}X^{\mu+1}$ where λ and μ are the *smaller indices of x and X respectively* in the two expressions whose integrals are to be connected. Find $\frac{dP}{dx}$. Rearrange this as a *linear function of the expressions* whose integrals are to be connected. Integrate, and the connection is complete.

Ex. 1. Connect $\int x^{m-1}X^pdx$ with $\int x^{m-1}X^{p-1}dx$.

Let $P=x^mX^p$.

Then
$$\frac{dP}{dx}=mx^{m-1}X^p+x^mpX^{p-1}\frac{dX}{dx}$$
$$=mx^{m-1}X^p+pbnx^{m+n-1}X^{p-1}$$
$$=mx^{m-1}X^p+pnx^{m-1}(X-a)X^{p-1}$$

[Note the rearrangement "*as a linear function*, etc., etc."]

$$=(m+pn)x^{m-1}X^p-apnx^{m-1}X^{p-1}.$$

Hence $P=(m+pn)\int x^{m-1}X^pdx-apn\int x^{m-1}X^{p-1}dx$,

or
$$\int x^{m-1}X^pdx=\frac{x^mX^p}{m+pn}+\frac{apn}{m+pn}\int x^{m-1}X^{p-1}dx.$$

The advantage of this reduction is that the index of the usually troublesome factor X^p is lowered; and by successive applications of the same formula we may ultimately reduce the integral to one which has been previously worked, or which can be easily obtained.

Ex. 2. Thus, for instance, to find $\int (x^2+a^2)^{\frac{5}{2}}\,dx$ we may connect this integral with $\int (x^2+a^2)^{\frac{3}{2}}\,dx$, and this again with $\int (x^2+a^2)^{\frac{1}{2}}\,dx$, and this last is a standard form.

As the reduction is used twice, we will connect

$$\int (x^2+a^2)^{\frac{n}{2}}\,dx \text{ with } \int (x^2+a^2)^{\frac{n}{2}-1}\,dx.$$

Let $$P = x(x^2+a^2)^{\frac{n}{2}},$$

$$\frac{dP}{dx} = (x^2+a^2)^{\frac{n}{2}} + nx^2(x^2+a^2)^{\frac{n}{2}-1}$$

$$= (x^2+a^2)^{\frac{n}{2}} + n(x^2+a^2-a^2)(x^2+a^2)^{\frac{n}{2}-1}$$

[Note the preparatory step *which might be performed mentally*]

$$= (n+1)(x^2+a^2)^{\frac{n}{2}} - na^2(x^2+a^2)^{\frac{n}{2}-1}$$

[which is now "*rearranged as a linear function, etc., etc.*"].

Integrating, $P = (n+1)\int (x^2+a^2)^{\frac{n}{2}}\,dx - na^2\int (x^2+a^2)^{\frac{n}{2}-1}\,dx$

and $$\int (x^2+a^2)^{\frac{n}{2}}\,dx = \frac{x(x^2+a^2)^{\frac{n}{2}}}{n+1} + \frac{na^2}{n+1}\int (x^2+a^2)^{\frac{n}{2}-1}\,dx.$$

Putting $n=5$ and $n=3$,

$$\int (x^2+a^2)^{\frac{5}{2}}\,dx = \frac{x(x^2+a^2)^{\frac{5}{2}}}{6} + \frac{5}{6}a^2\int (x^2+a^2)^{\frac{3}{2}}\,dx,$$

$$\int (x^2+a^2)^{\frac{3}{2}}\,dx = \frac{x(x^2+a^2)^{\frac{3}{2}}}{4} + \frac{3}{4}a^2\int (x^2+a^2)^{\frac{1}{2}}\,dx$$

and $$\int (x^2+a^2)^{\frac{1}{2}}\,dx = \frac{x(x^2+a^2)^{\frac{1}{2}}}{2} + \frac{a^2}{2}\sinh^{-1}\frac{x}{a}$$

Then $$\int (x^2+a^2)^{\frac{5}{2}}\,dx = \frac{x(x^2+a^2)^{\frac{5}{2}}}{6} + \frac{5}{6.4}a^2x(x^2+a^2)^{\frac{3}{2}}$$

$$+\frac{5\cdot 3}{6\cdot 4\cdot 2}\cdot a^4x(x^2+a^2)^{\frac{1}{2}} + \frac{5\cdot 3}{6\cdot 4\cdot 2}a^6\sinh^{-1}\frac{x}{a}.$$

Ex. 3. Calculate the value of $\int_0^{2a} x^m\sqrt{2ax-x^2}dx$, m being a positive integer. We shall endeavour to connect

$$\int x^m\sqrt{2ax-x^2}dx \text{ with } \int x^{m-1}\sqrt{2ax-x^2}dx,$$

i.e.
$$\int x^{m+\frac{1}{2}}(2a-x)^{\frac{1}{2}}dx \text{ with } \int x^{m-\frac{1}{2}}(2a-x)^{\frac{1}{2}}dx.$$

Let
$$P=x^{m+\frac{1}{2}}(2a-x)^{\frac{3}{2}} \text{ according to the rule, then}$$

$$\frac{dP}{dx}=\left(m+\frac{1}{2}\right)x^{m-\frac{1}{2}}(2a-x)^{\frac{3}{2}}-\frac{3}{2}x^{m+\frac{1}{2}}(2a-x)^{\frac{1}{2}}$$

$$=(2m+1)ax^{m-\frac{1}{2}}(2a-x)^{\frac{1}{2}}-(m+2)x^{m+\frac{1}{2}}(2a-x)^{\frac{1}{2}}.$$

Hence $(m+2)\int x^{m+\frac{1}{2}}(2a-x)^{\frac{1}{2}}dx$

$$=-x^{m+\frac{1}{2}}(2a-x)^{\frac{3}{2}}+(2m+1)a\int x^{m-\frac{1}{2}}(2a-x)^{\frac{1}{2}}dx$$

or $\int_0^{2a} x^m\sqrt{2ax-x^2}dx$

$$=-\left[\frac{x^{m-1}(2ax-x^2)^{\frac{3}{2}}}{m+2}\right]_0^{2a}+\frac{2m+1}{m+2}a\int_0^{2a} x^{m-1}\sqrt{2ax-x^2}dx,$$

i.e. if $I_m=\int_0^{2a} x^m\sqrt{2ax-x^2}dx$, and m be a positive integer,

$$I_m=\frac{2m+1}{m+2}aI_{m-1}=\frac{2m+1}{m+2}\cdot\frac{2m-1}{m+1}a^2I_{m-2}$$

$$=\frac{2m+1}{m+2}\cdot\frac{2m-1}{m+1}\cdot\frac{2m-3}{m}a^3I_{m-3}=\text{etc.}$$

$$=\frac{2m+1}{m+2}\cdot\frac{2m-1}{m+1}\cdot\frac{2m-3}{m}\cdots\frac{5}{4}\cdot\frac{3}{3}\cdot a^mI_0.$$

Now to find I_0 or $\int_0^{2a}\sqrt{2ax-x^2}dx$, put $x=a(1-\cos\theta)$.

Then $dx=a\sin\theta\, d\theta$

and $\sqrt{2ax-x^2}=a\sin\theta$.

Also when $x=0$, we have $\theta=0$,

when $x=2a$, we have $\theta=\pi$.

Hence $I_0=\int_0^{\pi} a^2\sin^2\theta d\theta=\frac{a^2}{2}\int_0^{\pi}(1-\cos 2\theta)d\theta=\frac{a^2}{2}\left[\theta-\frac{1}{2}\sin 2\theta\right]_0^{\pi}=\frac{\pi a^2}{2}.$

Hence $I_m=\frac{(2m+1)(2m-1)\ldots 3}{(m+2)(m+1)\ldots 3}a^{m+2}\frac{\pi}{2}=\frac{(2m+1)!}{m!(m+2)!}\cdot\frac{\pi a^{m+2}}{2^m}.$

EXAMPLES

Apply the rule stated in Art. 82 to obtain the following reduction formulae (when $X = a + bx^n$) :—

1. $\int x^{m-1} X^p dx = -\dfrac{x^m X^{p+1}}{an(p+1)} + \dfrac{m+pn+n}{an(p+1)} \int x^{m-1} X^{p+1} dx.$

2. $\int x^{m-1} X^p dx = \dfrac{x^{m-n} X^{p+1}}{b(m+np)} - \dfrac{(m-n)a}{b(m+np)} \int x^{m-n-1} X^p dx.$

3. $\int x^{m-1} X^p dx = \dfrac{x^m X^{p+1}}{am} - \dfrac{b(m+np+n)}{am} \int x^{m+n-1} X^p dx.$

4. $\int x^{m-1} X^p dx = \dfrac{x^{m-n} X^{p+1}}{bn(p+1)} - \dfrac{m-n}{bn(p+1)} \int x^{m-n-1} X^{p+1} dx.$

5. $\int x^{m-1} X^p dx = \dfrac{x^m X^p}{m} - \dfrac{bnp}{m} \int x^{m+n-1} X^{p-1} dx.$

6. $\int x^m (\log x)^p dx = \dfrac{x^{m+1} (\log x)^p}{m+1} - \dfrac{p}{m+1} \int x^m (\log x)^{p-1} dx.$

Integrate out $x^m \log x$, $x^m (\log x)^2$, $x^m (\log x)^3$.

7. Obtain the integrals of $\int x^m \sqrt{(2ax - x^2)}\, dx$ for the cases

$m=1$, $m=2$, $m=3$ and their numerical values when the limits of integrating are 0 and $2a$.

83. Reduction formulae for $\int \sin^p x \cos^q x\, dx$.

A similar rule may be given for a reduction formula for $\int \sin^p x \cos^q x\, dx$.

This expression may be connected with any of the following six integrals:—

$$\int \sin^{p-2} x \cos^q x\, dx, \int \sin^{p+2} x \cos^q x\, dx,$$
$$\int \sin^p x \cos^{q-2} x\, dx, \int \sin^p x \cos^{q+2} x\, dx,$$
$$\int \sin^{p-2} x \cos^{q+2} x\, dx, \int \sin^{p+2} x \cos^{q-2} x\, dx,$$

by the following rule.

Put $P = \sin^{\lambda+1} x \cos^{\mu+1} x$ where λ and μ are the smaller indices of $\sin x$ and $\cos x$, respectively in the two expressions whose integrals are to be connected.

Find $\dfrac{dP}{dx}$, and *rearrange as a linear function of the expressions* whose integrals are to be connected.

Integrate and the connection is effected.

Ex. Connect the integrals

$$\int \sin^p x \cos^q x\, dx,$$
$$\int \sin^{p-2} x \cos^q x\, dx.$$

Let $\quad P = \sin^{p-1} x \cos^{q+1} x,$

$$\frac{dP}{dx} = (p-1)\sin^{p-2} x \cos^{q+2} x - (q+1)\sin^p x \cos^q x$$
$$= (p-1)\sin^{p-2} x \cos^q x(1-\sin^2 x) - (q+1)\sin^p x \cos^q x$$
$$= (p-1)\sin^{p-2} x \cos^q x - (p+q)\sin^p x \cos^q x$$

[Note the last two lines of *rearrangement as a linear function* of $\sin^p x \cos^q x$ and $\sin^{p-2} x \cos^q x$],

$$\therefore\ P = (p-1)\int \sin^{p-2} x \cos^q x\, dx - (p+q)\int \sin^p x \cos^q x\, dx.$$

Hence

$$\int \sin^p x \cos^q x\, dx = -\frac{\sin^{p-1} x \cos^{q+1} x}{p+q} + \frac{p-1}{p+q}\int \sin^{p-2} x \cos^q x\, dx.$$

It will be remembered, however, that in the case where either p or q is an odd integer the complete integration can be effected immediately [Arts. 64, 67].

The present method is useful in the case where p and q are *both even integers*.

EXAMPLES

Connect the integral $\int \sin^p x \cos^q x\, dx$ with

1. $\int \sin^{p+2} x \cos^q x\, dx.$
2. $\int \sin^p x \cos^{q-2} x\, dx.$
3. $\int \sin^p x \cos^{q+2} x\, dx.$
4. $\int \sin^{p-2} x \cos^{q+2} x\, dx.$
5. $\int \sin^{p+2} x \cos^{q-2} x\, dx.$
6. Prove that $\int \sin^n x\, dx = -\frac{\cos x \sin^{n-1} x}{n} + \frac{n-1}{n}\int \sin^{n-2} x\, dx.$

   Employ this formula to integrate $\sin^4 x$, $\sin^6 x$, $\sin^8 x$.
7. Establish a formula of reduction for $\int \cos^n x\, dx$.
8. Integrate $\sin^4 x \cos^2 x$, $\frac{\sin^4 x}{\cos^2 x}$, $\frac{1}{\sin^4 x \cos^2 x}$.

84. To calculate the integrals $S_n = \int_0^{\frac{\pi}{2}} \sin^n x\,dx$ and $C_n = \int_0^{\frac{\pi}{2}} \cos^n x\,dx$.

Connect $\int \sin^n x\,dx$ with $\int \sin^{n-2} x\,dx$.

Let $P = \sin^{n-1} x \cos x$ according to the rule; then

$$\frac{dP}{dx} = (n-1)\sin^{n-2} x \cos^2 x - \sin^n x$$

$$= (n-1)\sin^{n-2} x - n\sin^n x,$$

$$\therefore \qquad \int \sin^n x\,dx = -\frac{\sin^{n-1} x \cos x}{n} + \frac{n-1}{n}\int \sin^{n-2} x\,dx.$$

Hence since $\sin^{n-1} x \cos x$ vanishes when n is an integer not less than 2, when $x = 0$, and also when $x = \frac{\pi}{2}$, we have

$$S_n = \frac{n-1}{n} \cdot S_{n-2} = \frac{n-1}{n} \cdot \frac{n-3}{n-2} S_{n-4},$$

$$= \frac{n-1}{n} \cdot \frac{n-3}{n-2} \cdot \frac{n-5}{n-4} \cdot S_{n-6} = \text{etc,}$$

if n be even this ultimately comes to

$$S_n = \frac{n-1}{n} \cdot \frac{n-3}{n-2} \cdots \frac{5}{6} \cdot \frac{3}{4} \cdot \frac{1}{2} \int_0^{\frac{\pi}{2}} 1\,dx,$$

that is $\qquad S_n = \frac{n-1}{n} \cdot \frac{n-3}{n-2} \cdots \frac{3}{4} \cdot \frac{1}{2} \cdot \frac{\pi}{2},$

If n be odd we similarly get, $S_n = \frac{n-1}{n} \cdot \frac{n-3}{n-2} \cdots \frac{4}{5} \cdot \frac{2}{3} \int_0^{\frac{\pi}{2}} \sin x\,dx,$

and since $\qquad \int_0^{\frac{\pi}{2}} \sin x\,dx = [-\cos x]_0^{\frac{\pi}{2}} = 1$

we have $\qquad S_n = \frac{n-1}{n} \cdot \frac{n-3}{n-2} \cdots \frac{4}{5} \cdot \frac{2}{3}.$

In a similar way it may be seen that $\int_0^{\frac{\pi}{2}} \cos^n x\,dx$ has precisely the same value as the above integral in each case, n odd, n even. This may be shown too from other considerations.

These formulae are useful to write down quickly any integral of the above form.

Thus $\int_0^{\frac{\pi}{2}} \sin^{10} \theta\,d\theta = \frac{9}{10} \frac{7}{8} \frac{5}{6} \frac{3}{4} \frac{1}{2} \cdot \frac{\pi}{2}, \qquad \int_0^{\frac{\pi}{2}} \sin^9 \theta\,d\theta = \frac{8}{9} \frac{6}{7} \frac{4}{5} \frac{2}{3}.$

[The student should notice that these are written down most easily by beginning *with the denominator*. We then have the ordinary sequence of natural numbers written backwards. Thus the first of these examples is

(10 under 9) × (8 under 7) × (6 under 5), etc.,

stopping at (2 under 1), and writing a factor $\frac{\pi}{2}$. But when the first denominator is odd, in forming such a sequence it terminates with (3 under 2) and no factor $\frac{\pi}{2}$ is written.]

85. To investigate a formula for $\int_0^{\frac{p}{2}} \sin^p q \cos^q q \, dq$.

Let this integral be denoted by $f(p,q)$; then since

$$\int \sin^p\theta \cos^q\theta d\theta = -\frac{\sin^{p-1}\theta \cos^{q+1}\theta}{p+q} + \frac{p-1}{p+q}\int \sin^{p-2}\theta \cos^q\theta d\theta,$$

we have, if p and q be positive integers, and p be not less than 2

$$f(p,q) = \frac{p-1}{p+q} f(p-2,q).$$

Case I. If *p be even* $=2m$, and *q also even* $=2n$,

$$f(2m,2n) = \frac{2m-1}{2m+2n} f(2m-2,2n)$$

$$= \frac{(2m-1)(2m-3)}{(2m+2n)(2m+2n-2)} f(2m-4,2n) = \text{etc}$$

$$= \frac{(2m-1)(2m-3)\ldots 1}{(2m+2n)(2m+2n-2)\ldots(2n+2)} f(0,2n),$$

and $$f(0,2n) = \int_0^{\frac{\pi}{2}} \cos^{2n}\theta \, d\theta = \frac{2n-1}{2n}\frac{2n-3}{2n-2}\ldots\frac{1}{2}\frac{\pi}{2}$$

Thus $$f(2m,2n) = \frac{[1\cdot3\cdot5\ldots(2m-1)][1\cdot3\cdot5\ldots(2n-1)]}{2\cdot4\cdot6\ldots(2m+2n)}\frac{\pi}{2}.$$

Case II. If *p be even* $=2m$, and *q odd* $=2n-1$,

$$f(2m,2n-1) = \frac{2m-1}{2m+2n-1} f(2m-2,2n-1) = \text{etc.}$$

$$= \frac{(2m-1)(2m-3)\ldots 1}{(2m+2n-1)(2m+2n-3)\ldots(2n+1)} f(0,2n-1),$$

and $$f(0,2n-1) = \int_0^{\frac{\pi}{2}} \cos^{2n-1}\theta \, d\theta = \frac{2n-2}{2n-1}\frac{2n-4}{2n-3}\ldots\frac{2}{3},$$

i.e. $$f(2m,2n-1) = \frac{[1\cdot3\cdot5\ldots(2m-1)][2\cdot4\cdot6\ldots(2n-2)]}{1\cdot3\cdot5\ldots(2m+2n-1)}.$$

Case III. If p be *odd* $=2m-1$ and q *even* $=2n$, we obtain similarly

$$f(2m-1,2n)=\frac{[2\cdot 4\cdot 6\ldots(2m-2)][1\cdot 3\cdot 5\ldots(2n-1)]}{1\cdot 3\cdot 5\ldots(2m+2n-1)}.$$

This may also be deduced at once from Case II. by putting

$$\theta=\frac{\pi}{2}-\phi,$$

or $\int_0^{\frac{\pi}{2}}\sin^p\theta\cos^q\theta\,d\theta=\int_{\frac{\pi}{2}}^{0}\cos^p\phi\sin^q\phi(-1)\,d\phi=\int_0^{\frac{\pi}{2}}\sin^q\phi\cos^p\phi\,d\phi,$

so that $\qquad f(p,q)=f(q,p).$

Case IV. If p be *odd* $=2m-1$, and q *odd* $=2n-1$,

$$f(2m-1,2n-1)=\frac{2m-2}{2m+2n-2}f(2m-3,2n-1)$$

$$=\frac{(2m-2)(2m-4)}{(2m+2n-2)(2m+2n-4)}f(2m-5,2n-1)=\text{etc}.$$

$$=\frac{(2m-2)(2m-4)\ldots 2}{(2m+2n-2)(2m+2n-4)\ldots(2n+2)}f(1,2n-1),$$

and $\qquad f(1,2n-1)=\int_0^{\frac{\pi}{2}}\sin\theta\cos^{2n-1}\theta\,d\theta=\left[-\frac{\cos^{2n}\theta}{2n}\right]_0^{\frac{\pi}{2}}=\frac{1}{2n},$

$$\therefore\ f(2m-1,2n-1)=\frac{[2\cdot 4\cdot 6\ldots(2m-2)][2\cdot 4\cdot 6\ldots(2n-2)]}{2\cdot 4\cdot 6\ldots(2m+2n-2)}.$$

86. Expression in a single rule.

These four formulae may be expressed under one rule as follows:—

Let $\Gamma(n+1)$ be a function defined by the relations

$$\Gamma(n+1)=n\Gamma(n),\ \Gamma(1)=1,\ \Gamma\left(\frac{1}{2}\right)=\sqrt{\pi}.$$

These relations will be found to sufficiently define $\Gamma(n+1)$ where $n+1$ is either an integer or of the form $\frac{2k+1}{2}$.

k being a positive integer

For instance, $\Gamma(6)=5\Gamma(5)=5\cdot 4\Gamma(4)=5\cdot 4\cdot 3\ \Gamma(3)=5\cdot 4\cdot 3\cdot 2\,\Gamma(2)$

$$=5\cdot 4\cdot 3\cdot 2\cdot 1\,\Gamma(1)=5!$$

$$\Gamma\left(\frac{11}{2}\right)=\frac{9}{2}\Gamma\left(\frac{9}{2}\right)=\frac{9}{2}\cdot\frac{7}{2}\Gamma\left(\frac{7}{2}\right)=\frac{9}{2}\cdot\frac{7}{2}\cdot\frac{5}{2}\Gamma\left(\frac{5}{2}\right)=\frac{9}{2}\cdot\frac{7}{2}\cdot\frac{5}{2}\cdot\frac{3}{2}\Gamma\left(\frac{3}{2}\right)$$

$$=\frac{9}{2}\cdot\frac{7}{2}\cdot\frac{5}{2}\cdot\frac{3}{2}\cdot\frac{1}{2}\Gamma\left(\frac{1}{2}\right)=\frac{9}{2}\cdot\frac{7}{2}\cdot\frac{5}{2}\cdot\frac{3}{2}\cdot\frac{1}{2}\sqrt{\pi}.$$

This function is called a Gamma function, but we do not propose to enter into its properties further here.

The products $1\cdot3\cdot5\ldots2n-1, 2\cdot4\cdot6\ldots2n$

which occur in the foregoing cases of $\int_0^{\frac{\pi}{2}}\sin^p\theta\cos^q\theta\,d\theta$

may be expressed at once in terms of this function.

For $$\Gamma\left(\frac{2n+1}{2}\right)=\frac{2n-1}{2}\cdot\frac{2n-3}{2}\cdot\frac{2n-5}{2}\cdots\frac{1}{2}\Gamma\left(\frac{1}{2}\right),$$

so that $$1\cdot3\cdot5\ldots(2n-1)=\frac{2^n}{\sqrt{\pi}}\Gamma\left(\frac{2n+1}{2}\right);$$

and $$\Gamma\left(\frac{2n+2}{2}\right)=\frac{2n}{2}\cdot\frac{2n-2}{2}\cdot\frac{2n-4}{2}\cdots\frac{2}{2},$$

so that $$2\cdot4\cdot6\ldots2n=2^n\Gamma\left(\frac{2n+2}{2}\right).$$

Hence, in Case I.

$$\left.\begin{matrix}p=2m,\\ q=2n.\end{matrix}\right\}\int_0^{\frac{\pi}{2}}\sin^p\theta\cos^q\theta\,d\theta=\frac{\frac{2^m}{\sqrt{\pi}}\Gamma\left(\frac{p+1}{2}\right)\frac{2^n}{\sqrt{\pi}}\Gamma\left(\frac{q+1}{2}\right)}{2^{m+n}\Gamma\left(\frac{p+q+2}{2}\right)}\frac{\pi}{2}$$

$$=\frac{\Gamma\left(\frac{p+1}{2}\right)\Gamma\left(\frac{q+1}{2}\right)}{2\Gamma\left(\frac{p+q+2}{2}\right)}.$$

In Case II. $$\left.\begin{matrix}p=2m,\\ q=2n-1.\end{matrix}\right\}\int_0^{\frac{\pi}{2}}\sin^p\theta\cos^q\theta\,d\theta=\frac{\frac{2^m}{\sqrt{\pi}}\Gamma\left(\frac{p+1}{2}\right)\cdot2^{n-1}\Gamma\left(\frac{q+1}{2}\right)}{\frac{2^{m+n}}{\sqrt{\pi}}\Gamma\left(\frac{p+q+2}{2}\right)}$$

$$=\frac{\Gamma\left(\frac{p+1}{2}\right)\Gamma\left(\frac{q+1}{2}\right)}{2\Gamma\left(\frac{p+q+2}{2}\right)}.$$

In Case III. we evidently have the same result.

In Case IV. $$\left.\begin{matrix}p=2m-1,\\ q=2n-1.\end{matrix}\right\}\int_0^{\frac{\pi}{2}}\sin^p\theta\cos^q\theta\,d\theta=\frac{2^{m-1}\Gamma\left(\frac{p+1}{2}\right)2^{n-1}\Gamma\left(\frac{q+1}{2}\right)}{2^{m+n-1}\Gamma\left(\frac{p+q+2}{2}\right)}$$

$$=\frac{\Gamma\left(\frac{p+1}{2}\right)\Gamma\left(\frac{q+1}{2}\right)}{2\Gamma\left(\frac{p+q+2}{2}\right)}.$$

It will be noticed therefore that in every case we have the same result, viz,

$$\int_0^{\frac{\pi}{2}} \sin^p \theta \cos^q \theta \, d\theta = \frac{\Gamma\left(\frac{p+1}{2}\right)\Gamma\left(\frac{q+1}{2}\right)}{2\Gamma\left(\frac{p+q}{2}+1\right)},$$

and that the $\frac{p+q}{2}+1$ occurring in the denominator is the sum of the $\frac{p+1}{2}$ and the $\frac{q+1}{2}$ in the numerator.

This is a very convenient formula for evaluating quickly integrals of the above form.

Thus $$\int_0^{\frac{\pi}{2}} \sin^6 \theta \cos^8 \theta \, d\theta = \frac{\Gamma\left(\frac{7}{2}\right)\Gamma\left(\frac{9}{2}\right)}{2\Gamma(8)}$$

$$= \frac{\frac{5}{2}\cdot\frac{3}{2}\cdot\frac{1}{2}\sqrt{\pi}\cdot\frac{7}{2}\cdot\frac{5}{2}\cdot\frac{3}{2}\cdot\frac{1}{2}\sqrt{\pi}}{2\cdot 7\cdot 6\cdot 5\cdot 4\cdot 3\cdot 2\cdot 1} = \frac{5\pi}{2^{12}}.$$

87. The student should, however, observe (as it has been pointed out previously), that *when either p or q or both of them are odd integers,* the expression $\sin^p \theta \cos^q \theta$ is directly integrable without a reduction formula at all.

For instance, $\int \sin^6 \theta \cos^3 \theta \, d\theta = \int \sin^6 \theta (1-\sin^2 \theta) \, d \sin \theta = \frac{\sin^7 \theta}{7} - \frac{\sin^9 \theta}{9}$,

and $$\int_0^{\frac{\pi}{2}} \sin^6 \theta \cos^3 \theta \, d\theta = \frac{1}{7} - \frac{1}{9} = \frac{2}{63}.$$

Similarly, $$\int_0^{\frac{\pi}{2}} \sin^6 \theta \cos^2 \theta \, d\theta = -\int_1^0 \cos^2 \theta (1 - 2\cos^2 \theta + \cos^4 \theta) \, d \cos \theta$$

$$= \left[-\frac{\cos^3 \theta}{3} + \frac{2\cos^5 \theta}{5} - \frac{\cos^7 \theta}{7}\right]_1^0 = +\frac{1}{3} - \frac{2}{5} + \frac{1}{7} = \frac{8}{105}.$$

But when p and q are both even and the indefinite integral required, or of the limits of integration be other than 0 and $\frac{\pi}{2}$, we must either use the reduction formula of Art.83 or proceed as in Art.67.

EXAMPLES

Write down the values of

1. $\int_0^{\frac{\pi}{2}} \sin^2 x \, dx$, $\int_0^{\frac{\pi}{2}} \sin^4 x \, dx$, $\int_0^{\frac{\pi}{2}} \sin^8 x \, dx$, $\int_0^{\frac{\pi}{2}} \cos^9 x \, dx$.

2. $\int_0^{\frac{\pi}{2}} \sin^6 x \cos^4 x \, dx$, $\int_0^{\frac{\pi}{2}} \sin^6 x \cos^5 x \, dx$, $\int_0^{\frac{\pi}{2}} \sin^5 x \cos^6 x \, dx$,

$\int_0^{\frac{\pi}{2}} \sin^5 x \cos^5 x \, dx$.

3. If O_r represent the product $1\cdot3\cdot5\ldots$ to r factors, and E_r represent the product $2\cdot4\cdot6\ldots$ to r factors, prove the formulae

(1) $\int_0^{\frac{\pi}{2}} \sin^{2m}\theta\cos^{2n}\theta\,d\theta = \frac{O_m O_n}{E_{m+n}}\cdot\frac{\pi}{2}.$

(2) $\int_0^{\frac{\pi}{2}} \sin^{2m}\theta\cos^{2n-1}\theta\,d\theta = \frac{O_m E_{n-1}}{O_{m+n}} = \int_0^{\frac{\pi}{2}} \sin^{2n-1}\theta\cos^{2m}\theta\,d\theta.$

(3) $\int_0^{\frac{\pi}{2}} \sin^{2m-1}\theta\cos^{2n-1}\theta\,d\theta = \frac{E_{m-1}E_{n-1}}{E_{m+n-1}}.$

4. Write down the indefinite integrals of $\int\sin^7\theta\cos\theta\,d\theta$, $\int\sin^7\theta\cos^3\theta\,d\theta$, $\int\sin^7\theta\ \cos^5\theta\,d\theta$, $\int\sin^7\theta\cos^2\theta\,d\theta$, $\int\sin^6\theta\cos^4\theta\,d\theta$.

Evaluate

5. $\int_0^{\frac{\pi}{4}}\sin^5\theta\cos^2\theta\,d\theta$, $\int_0^{\frac{\pi}{4}}\sin^4\theta\,d\theta$, $\int_0^{\frac{\pi}{4}}\sin^2\theta\cos^4\theta\,d\theta$, $\int_0^{\frac{\pi}{3}}\sin^7\theta\,d\theta$.

6. $\int_0^{\frac{\pi}{4}}\cos^2 2\theta\,d\theta$, $\int_0^{\frac{\pi}{6}}\cos^3 3\phi\,d\phi$, $\int_0^{\frac{\pi}{6}}\cos^4 3\phi\sin^2 6\phi\,d\phi$.

7. Deduce the formulae of Art. 84 for $\int_0^{\frac{\pi}{2}}\left(\frac{\sin}{\cos}\right)^n x\,dx$ from the result

$$\frac{\Gamma\left(\frac{p+1}{2}\right)\Gamma\left(\frac{q+1}{2}\right)}{2\Gamma\left(\frac{p+q}{2}+1\right)} \text{ of Art.86.}$$

EXAMPLES

1. Prove that

(a) $\int\cos^{2n}\phi\,d\phi = \frac{1}{2n}\tan\phi\cos^{2n}\phi + \left(1-\frac{1}{2n}\right)\int\cos^{2n-2}\phi\,d\phi.$

(b) $\int\sec^{2n+1}\phi\,d\phi = \frac{1}{2n}\tan\phi\sec^{2n-1}\phi + \left(1-\frac{1}{2n}\right)\int\sec^{2n-1}\phi\,d\phi.$

2. Investigate a formula of reduction applicable to $\int x^m(1+x^2)^{\frac{n}{2}}dx$ when m and n are positive integers, and complete the integration, if $m=5$, $n=7$. [ST. JOHN'S COLL. CAMB, 1881.]

3. Investigate a formula of reduction for $\int\frac{x^{2n+1}dx}{(1-x^2)^{\frac{1}{2}}}$,

and by means of this integral show that

$$\frac{1}{2n+2}+\frac{1}{2}\cdot\frac{1}{2n+4}+\frac{1\cdot 3}{2\cdot 4}\cdot\frac{1}{2n+6}+\frac{1\cdot 3\cdot 5}{2\cdot 4\cdot 6}\cdot\frac{1}{2n+8}+\dots \text{ ad inf.}$$
$$=\frac{2\cdot 4\cdot 6\dots 2n}{3\cdot 5\cdot 7\dots 2n+1}.$$

Sum also the series $\frac{1}{2n+1}+\frac{1}{2}\cdot\frac{1}{2n+3}+\frac{1\cdot 3}{2\cdot 4}\cdot\frac{1}{2n+5}+\frac{1}{2}\cdot\frac{3}{4}\cdot\frac{5}{6}\frac{1}{2n+7}+\dots \textit{ad inf.}$

[MATH. TRIPOS. 1879.]

4. Prove that

$$\int (a^2+x^2)^{\frac{2n+1}{2}}\,dx=\frac{x}{2n+2}(a^2+x^2)^{\frac{2n+1}{2}}+\frac{2n+1}{2n+2}\,a^2\int (a^2+x^2)^{\frac{2n-1}{2}}\,dx.$$

5. If $\phi(n)=a^{2n-1}\int_0^\infty \frac{dx}{(a^2+x^2)^n}$, prove $\phi(n)=\frac{2n-3}{2n-2}\,\phi\,(n-1)$.

6. Find reduction formulae for

(α) $\int x^n(a+bx)^{p+\frac{1}{2}}\,dx$, (γ) $\int \frac{x^m dx}{(a^3+x^3)^{\frac{n}{3}}}$,

(β) $\int x^{2n}(x^2+a^2)^{\frac{2p+1}{2}}\,dx$, (δ) $\int \frac{x^m dx}{(x^3-1)^{\frac{1}{3}}}$;

and obtain the value of $\int x^8(x^3-1)^{-\frac{1}{3}}dx$. [COLLEGES, CAMB.]

7. Find a reduction formula for $\int e^{ax}\cos^n x\,dx$, where n is a positive integer, and evaluate $\int e^{ax}\cos^4 x\,dx$. [OXFORD, 1889.]

8. Find formulae of reduction for $\int x^n \sin x\,dx$ and $\int e^{ax}\sin^n x\,dx$. Deduce from the latter a formula of reduction for

$$\int \cos ax \sin^n x\,dx.$$ [COLLEGES γ, 1890.]

9. If $u_n=\int_0^{\frac{\pi}{4}}\sin^{2n} x\,dx$, prove that $u_n=\left(1-\frac{1}{2n}\right)u_{n-1}-\frac{1}{n2^{n+1}}$ and deduce

$$u_n=-\frac{1}{2^{n+1}}\left\{\frac{1}{n}+\frac{(2n-1)}{n(n-1)}+\frac{(2n-1)}{n(n-1)}\frac{(2n-3)}{(n-2)}+\dots\right\}+\frac{(2n-1)(2n-3)\dots 3}{2n(2n-2)\dots 4}\cdot\frac{\pi}{8}.$$

[MATH. TRIPOS, 1878.]

10. Show that $(m+n)(m+n-2)\int \sin^m\theta\cos^n\theta\,d\theta=(m-1)\sin^{m+1}\theta\cos^{n-1}\theta$

$$-(n-1)\sin^{m-1}\theta\cos^{n+1}\theta+(m-1)(n-1)\int \sin^{m-2}\theta\cos^{n-2}\theta\,d\theta.$$

[TRIN. COLL, CAMB., 1889.]

11. Prove that

$$\int_0^1 x^{4m+1}\sqrt{\frac{1-x^2}{1+x^2}}\,dx=\frac{1\cdot3\cdot5\ldots(2m-1)}{2\cdot4\cdot6\ldots2m}\frac{\pi}{4}-\frac{2\cdot4\cdot6\ldots2m}{3\cdot5\cdot7\ldots(2m+1)}\cdot\frac{1}{2}.$$

12. Find *a* formula of reduction for $\int_1^x \frac{x^n dx}{\sqrt{x-1}}$. Show that

$$\frac{2\cdot4\cdot6\ldots2n}{3\cdot5\cdot7\ldots(2n+1)}\left[1+\frac{1}{2}x+\frac{1\cdot3}{2\cdot4}x^2+\ldots\frac{1\cdot3\ldots(2n-1)}{2\cdot4\ldots2n}x^n\right]$$

$$\equiv 1+\frac{a_1}{3}(x-1)+\frac{a_2}{5}(x-1)^2+\ldots+\frac{1}{2n+1}(x-1)^n,$$

where $a_1, a_2, \ldots$ are the binomial coefficients. [ST. JOHN'S, 1886.]

13. Show that

$$2^m\int \cos mx\cos^m x\,dx$$

$$=C+x+m\cdot\frac{\sin 2x}{2}+\frac{m(m-1)}{1\cdot2}\cdot\frac{\sin 4x}{4}+\ldots+\frac{\sin 2mx}{2m},$$

where m is an integer. [COLLEGES α, 1885.]

14. Show that $\int_0^{\frac{\pi}{2}}\sin^{2m}\theta\cos^{2m-1}\theta\,d\theta=\frac{(2m-2)(2m-4)\ldots4\cdot2}{(4m-1)(4m-3)\ldots(2m+1)}$, m being a positive integer. [OXFORD, 1889.]

15. Prove that if $I_{m,n}=\int\cos^m x\sin nx\,dx$,

$$(m+n)I_{m,n}=-\cos^m x\cos nx+mI_{m-1,n-1},$$

and $\left[I_{m,n}\right]_0^{\frac{\pi}{2}}=\frac{1}{2^{m+1}}\left(2+\frac{2^2}{2}+\frac{2^3}{3}+\ldots+\frac{2^m}{m}\right)$. [BERTRAND.]

16. If $I_{m,n}=\int\cos^m x\cos nx\,dx$,

prove that $I_{m,n}=-\frac{\cos^2 nx}{m^2-n^2}\frac{d}{dx}\left(\frac{\cos^m x}{\cos nx}\right)+\frac{m(m-1)}{m^2-n^2}I_{m-2,n}$,

and show that $[I_{m,n}]_0^{\frac{\pi}{2}}=\frac{m(m-1)}{m^2-n^2}[I_{m-2,n}]_0^{\frac{\pi}{2}}$.

17. If $u_{m,n}=\int_0^{\frac{\pi}{2}}\cos^m x\sin nx\,dx$,

prove that $u_{m,n}=\frac{1}{m+n}+\frac{m}{m+n}u_{m-1,n-1}$.

Hence find the value (when m is a positive integer) of

$$\int_0^{\frac{\pi}{2}}\cos^m x\sin 2mx\,dx.$$ [γ, 1887.]

18. Prove that $\int_0^{\frac{\pi}{2}} \cos^n x \cos nx\, dx = \frac{\pi}{2^{n+1}}$. [BERTRAND.]

19. If $m+n$ be even, prove that $\int_0^{\frac{\pi}{2}} \cos^m \theta \cos n\theta\, d\theta = \frac{\pi}{2^{m+1}} \frac{m!}{\frac{m+n}{2}!\,\frac{m-n}{2}!}$.

[COLLEGES, 1882.]

20. Evaluate the integral $\int_{-\frac{\pi}{2}}^{\frac{\pi}{2}} e^{-nx} \cos^m x\, dx$. [COLLEGES, 1886.]

21. If $\int_0^{\frac{\pi}{2}} \cos^m x \cos nx\, dx$ be denoted by $f(m, n)$, show that

$$f(m, n) = \frac{m}{m-n} f(m-1, n+1) = \frac{m}{m+n} f(m-1, n-1).$$

[OXFORD, 1890.]

22. Prove that if n be a positive integer greater than unity.
$\int_0^{\frac{\pi}{2}} \cos^{n-2} x \sin nx\, dx = \frac{1}{n-1}$. [OXFORD, 1889.]

23. Find a reduction formula for the integral $\int \frac{\sin nx}{\sin x} dx$.

24. If $u_{m,n} = \int_0^{\infty} \frac{\sin^m x}{x^n} dx$, where m is not less than n, and m, n are either both odd or both even integers, show that
$(n-1)(n-2)u_{m,n} + m^2 u_{m,n-2} - m(m-1)u_{m-2,n-2} = 0$.

25. If $u_n = \int \frac{dx}{(a + b\cos x)^n}$,

show that $u_n = \frac{A \sin x}{(a + b\cos x)^{n-1}} + Bu_{n-1} + Cu_{n-2}$,

where $A = -\frac{1}{n-1} \frac{b}{a^2 - b^2}$, $B = \frac{(2n-3)a}{(n-1)(a^2 - b^2)}$, $C = -\frac{n-2}{n-1} \frac{1}{a^2 - b^2}$

Show that $\int_0^{\frac{\pi}{2}} \frac{d\phi}{(1 - e^2 \sin^2 \phi)^3} = \frac{8 - 8e^2 + 3e^4}{(1-e^2)^{\frac{5}{2}}} \frac{\pi}{16}$,

e being less than unity. [ST. JOHN'S COLL., 1885.]

26. Prove that $\int \frac{\sin^m x}{a + b\cos x} dx$, can be integrated in finite terms when m is an integer.

27. If $U_n = \int \frac{\sin^m x}{(a + b \cos x)^n} dx$, prove that U_n can be calculated from a formula of reduction of the form
$AU_n + BU_{n-1} + CU_{n-2} = \sin^{m+1} x(a + b \cos x)^{-n+1}$, and determine the constants A, B, C.

[β, 1891.]

28. Find a reduction formula for the integral $\int \frac{x^m dx}{(\log x)^n}$. [OXFORD, 1889.]

29. Find a reduction formula for

$$\int \frac{x^m dx}{(ax^2 + 2bx + c)^{\frac{1}{2}}}.$$

[β, 1891.]

30. Prove that, if $X = x^2 + ax + a^2$

$$\int X^{\frac{n}{2}} dx = \frac{2x + a}{2(n+1)} X^{\frac{n}{2}} + \frac{3na^2}{4(n+1)} \int X^{\frac{n}{2}-1} dx.$$

[ST. JOHN'S 1889.]

31. Find reduction formulae for

(α) $\int \tanh^n x \, dx$.

(β) $\int \frac{dx}{(a + b \cos x + c \sin x)^n}$.

(γ) $\int \frac{x}{\sin^n x} dx$.

32. Establish the following formula for double integration by parts, u and v being functions of x, and dashes denoting differentiation and suffixes integrations with respect to x :—

$$\iint uv\,(dx)^2 = uv_2 - 2u'v_3 + 3u''v_4 - 4u'''v_5 + \ldots$$

$$+ (-1)^{n-1} nu^{(n-1)} v_{n+1} + (-1)^n n \int u^{(n)} v_{n+1} dx + (-1)^n \int dx \int u^{(n)} v_n dx.$$

[α, 1888.]

CHAPTER VIII.

MISCELLANEOUS METHODS AND EXAMPLES.

INTEGRALS OF FORM $\int \frac{dx}{X\sqrt{Y}}$.

88. The integration of expressions of the form $\int \frac{dx}{X\sqrt{Y}}$ can be *readily* effected in all cases for which

I. X and Y are *both linear* functions of x.

II. *X linear, Y quadratic.*

III. *X quadratic, Y linear.*

If X and Y be *both quadratic* the integration can be performed, but the process is more troublesome.

89. Case I. *X* and *Y* both linear.

The best substitution is :—

Put $\sqrt{Y} = y.$

Let $$I = \int \frac{dx}{(ax+b)\sqrt{cx+e}}.$$

Putting $\sqrt{cx+e} = y,$

we have $$\frac{cdx}{2\sqrt{cx+e}} = dy,$$

and $$ax + b = \frac{a}{c}(y^2 - e) + b,$$

and I becomes $2\int \frac{dy}{ay^2 - ae + bc}$, which, being one of the standard forms $\int \frac{dy}{y^2 \pm \lambda^2}$, is immediately integrable.

Ex. Integrate $I = \int \frac{dx}{(x+1)\sqrt{x+2}}.$

Let $\sqrt{x+2} = y$, then $\frac{dx}{\sqrt{x+2}} = 2\,dy.$

Thus $\quad I=\int\frac{2\,dy}{y^2-1}=\int\left(\frac{1}{y-1}-\frac{1}{y+1}\right)dy$

$$=\log\frac{y-1}{y+1}=\log\frac{\sqrt{x+2}-1}{\sqrt{x+2}+1}.$$

90. The same substitution, viz, $\sqrt{Y}=y$ will suffice for the integration of $\int\frac{\phi(x)\,dx}{X\sqrt{Y}}$ when $\phi(x)$ is *any rational integral algebraic function of x, and X and Y are each linear.*

Ex. Integrate $\quad I=\int\frac{x^4}{(x-1)\sqrt{x+2}}\,dx.$

Writing $\sqrt{x+2}=y$, we have

$$\frac{dx}{\sqrt{x+2}}=2dy \text{ and } x=y^2-2,$$

so that $\quad \frac{x^4}{x-1}=\frac{y^8-8y^6+24y^4-32y^2+16}{y^2-3}$

$$=y^6-5y^4+9y^2-5+\frac{1}{y^2-3}$$

(by common division).

Thus $\quad \frac{1}{2}I=\int\left[y^6-5y^4+9y^2-5+\frac{1}{2\sqrt{3}}\left(\frac{1}{y-\sqrt{3}}-\frac{1}{y+\sqrt{3}}\right)\right]dy$

$$=\frac{y^7}{7}-y^5+3y^3-5y+\frac{1}{2\sqrt{3}}\log\frac{y-\sqrt{3}}{y+\sqrt{3}}$$

$$=\frac{1}{7}(x+2)^{\frac{7}{2}}-(x+2)^{\frac{5}{2}}+3(x+2)^{\frac{3}{2}}-5(x+2)^{\frac{1}{2}}+\frac{1}{2\sqrt{3}}\log\frac{\sqrt{x+2}-\sqrt{3}}{\sqrt{x+2}+\sqrt{3}}.$$

91. Case II. *X* linear, *Y* quadratic.

The proper substitution is:—

Put $\quad X=\frac{1}{y}.$

Let $\quad I=\int\frac{dx}{(ax+b)\sqrt{cx^2+ex+f}}.$

Putting $\quad ax+b=\frac{1}{y},$

we have, by logarithmic differentiation,

$$\frac{adx}{ax+b}=-\frac{dy}{y}$$

and $$cx^2 + ex + f = \frac{c}{a^2}\left(\frac{1}{y} - b\right)^2 + \frac{e}{a}\left(\frac{1}{y} - b\right) + f$$

$$\equiv \frac{Ay^2 + 2By + C}{y^2}, \text{ say.}$$

Hence the integral has been reduced to the known form

$$I = -\frac{1}{a}\int \frac{dy}{\sqrt{Ay^2 + 2By + C}},$$

which has been already discussed.

Ex. Integrate $I = \int \frac{dx}{(x+1)\sqrt{x^2 + 4x + 2}}$.

Let $x + 1 = y^{-1}$, then $\frac{dx}{x+1} = -\frac{dy}{y}$, and

$$I = -\int \frac{dy}{y\sqrt{\left(\frac{1}{y} + 1\right)^2 - 2}} = -\int \frac{dy}{\sqrt{1 + 2y - y^2}}$$

$$= -\int \frac{dy}{\sqrt{2 - (y-1)^2}} = \cos^{-1}\frac{y-1}{\sqrt{2}} = \cos^{-1}\left\{\frac{-x}{(x+1)\sqrt{2}}\right\}.$$

92. It will now appear that any expression of the form $\int \frac{\phi(x)}{(ax+b)\sqrt{cx^2 + ex + f}}\,dx$ can be integrated, $\phi(x)$ being any rational integral algebraic function of x. For by common division we can express $\frac{\phi(x)}{ax+b}$ in the form

$$Ax^n + Bx^{n-1} + \dots + Kx + L + \frac{M}{ax+b},$$

$Ax^n + Bx^{n-1} + \dots + L$ being the quotient and M the remainder. We thus have reduced the process to the integration of a number of terms of the class

$$\int \frac{Ex^r}{\sqrt{cx^2 + ex + f}}\,dx,$$

and one of the class

$$\int \frac{M}{(ax+b)\sqrt{cx^2 + ex + f}}\,dx.$$

The latter has been discussed in the last article, and integrals of the former class may be obtained by the reduction formula

$$F(r) = \frac{x^{r-1}(cx^2 + ex + f)^{\frac{1}{2}}}{rc} - \frac{2r-1}{2r}\frac{e}{c}F(r-1) - \frac{r-1}{r}\frac{f}{c}F(r-2),$$

where $F(r)$ stands for $\int \frac{x^r}{\sqrt{cx^2+ex+f}}\,dx.$

The proof of this is left as an exercise.

Ex. Integrate $I = \int \frac{x^2+3x+5}{(x+1)\sqrt{x^2+1}}\,dx.$

By division $\qquad \frac{x^2+3x+5}{x+1} = x+2+\frac{3}{x+1}.$

Now $\qquad \int \frac{x}{\sqrt{x^2+1}}\,dx = \sqrt{x^2+1},$

$$\int \frac{2}{\sqrt{x^2+1}}\,dx = 2\sinh^{-1}x,$$

and to integrate $\int \frac{dx}{(x+1)\sqrt{x^2+1}}$ we put $x+1=\frac{1}{y}$ and get

$$-\int \frac{dy}{y\sqrt{\frac{1}{y^2}-\frac{2}{y}+2}} \quad \text{or} \quad -\frac{1}{\sqrt{2}}\int \frac{dy}{\sqrt{y^2-y+\frac{1}{2}}},$$

i.e. $\qquad -\frac{1}{\sqrt{2}}\int \frac{dy}{\sqrt{\left(y-\frac{1}{2}\right)^2+\frac{1}{4}}}$ *i.e.* $-\frac{1}{\sqrt{2}}\sinh^{-1}(2y-1)$

Thus $\qquad I = \sqrt{x^2+1}+2\sinh^{-1}x-\frac{3}{\sqrt{2}}\sinh^{-1}\frac{1-x}{1+x}.$

93. Case III. *X* quadratic, *Y* linear.

The proper substitution is :—

Put $\qquad \sqrt{Y}=y.$

Let $\qquad I = \int \frac{dx}{(ax^2+bx+c)\sqrt{ex+f}}.$

Putting $\qquad \sqrt{ex+f}=y,\ \frac{e\,dx}{2\sqrt{ex+f}}=dy,$

and ax^2+bx+c reduces to the form

$$Ay^4+By^2+C, \text{ and } I \text{ becomes } \frac{2}{e}\int \frac{dy}{Ay^4+By^2+C}.$$

Now $\frac{1}{Ay^4+By^2+C}$ can be thrown into partial fractions as

$$\frac{\lambda y+\mu}{\alpha y^2+\beta y+\gamma}+\frac{\lambda' y+\mu'}{\alpha' y^2+\beta' y+\gamma'},$$

and each fraction is integrable by foregoing rules.

94. It is also evident that the same substitution may be made for the integration of expressions of the form

$$\int \frac{\phi(x)}{(ax^2+bx+c)\sqrt{ex+f}}\,dx,$$

where $\phi(x)$ is rational, integral and algebraic; for when $\sqrt{ex+f}$ is put equal to y, $\frac{\phi(x)}{ax^2+bx+c}$ reduces to the form $\frac{\lambda_0 y^{2n}+\lambda_1 y^{2n-2}+\ldots+\lambda_n}{Ay^4+By^2+C}$, which by division, and the rules for partial fractions, may be expressed as

$$P_0 y^{2n-4}+P_2 y^{2n-6}+\ldots+P_{2n-4}+\frac{\lambda y+\mu}{\alpha y^2+\beta y+\gamma}+\frac{\lambda' y+\mu'}{\alpha' y^2+\beta' y+\gamma'}.$$

and each term is at once integrable.

Ex. Integrate $I=\int \frac{x+2}{(x^2+3x+3)\sqrt{x+1}}\,dx.$

Putting $\sqrt{x+1}=y$, we have $\frac{dx}{\sqrt{x+1}}=2dy$, and

$$I=2\int\frac{(y^2+1)\,dy}{y^4+y^2+1}=\int\left(\frac{1}{y^2+y+1}+\frac{1}{y^2-y+1}\right)dy$$

$$=\frac{2}{\sqrt{3}}\tan^{-1}\frac{2y+1}{\sqrt{3}}+\frac{2}{\sqrt{3}}\tan^{-1}\frac{2y-1}{\sqrt{3}}=-\frac{2}{\sqrt{3}}\tan^{-1}\sqrt{3}\,\frac{\sqrt{x+1}}{x}.$$

EXAMPLES

Integrate the following expressions:–

1. $\frac{1}{x\sqrt{x+1}},\ \frac{1}{(x-1)\sqrt{x+2}},\ \frac{x+1}{(x-1)\sqrt{x+2}},\ \frac{x^2+x+1}{(x+2)\sqrt{x-1}}.$

2. $\frac{1}{x\sqrt{x^2+1}},\ \frac{1}{(x+1)\sqrt{x^2+1}},\ \frac{x}{(x+1)\sqrt{x^2+1}},\ \frac{x^2+x+1}{(x+1)\sqrt{x^2+2x+3}}.$

3. $\frac{1}{(x^2+1)\sqrt{x}},\ \frac{1}{(x^2+2x+2)\sqrt{x+1}},$

$$\frac{x}{(x^2+2x+2)\sqrt{x+1}},\ \frac{x^2+1}{(x^2+2x+2)\sqrt{x+1}}.$$

95. Case IV. *X* and *Y* both quadratic.

We do not propose to discuss in general terms the method of integration of expressions of the form

$$\int\frac{\phi(x)}{X\sqrt{Y}}dx$$

where X and Y are both quadratic and (ϕx) rational, integral and algebraic, as it is beyond the scope of the present volume. We may say, however, that the proper substitution for such cases is $\sqrt{\frac{Y}{X}} = y$, and the student will glean the method to be adopted from the following examples. *

Ex. 1. Integrate $I = \int \frac{dx}{(x^2+a^2)\sqrt{x^2+b^2}}$.

Putting $\sqrt{\frac{x^2+b^2}{x^2+a^2}} = y,$

$$\frac{1}{y}\frac{dy}{dx} = \frac{x}{x^2+b^2} - \frac{x}{x^2+a^2} = \frac{(a^2-b^2)x}{(x^2+a^2)(x^2+b^2)},$$

$$\frac{dy}{dx} = \frac{(a^2-b^2)x}{(x^2+a^2)^{\frac{3}{2}}(x^2+b^2)^{\frac{1}{2}}}.$$

The student may refer to Greenhill's "Chapter on the Integral Calculus" for a general discussion of the method.

Thus I becomes $\int \frac{(x^2+a^2)^{\frac{1}{2}}dy}{(a^2-b^2)x}$

Also $(x^2+a^2)y^2 = x^2+b^2,$

so that $x^2 = \frac{b^2-a^2y^2}{y^2-1},$

and $x^2+a^2 = \frac{b^2-a^2}{y^2-1}$

Thus I reduces further to $\frac{1}{a^2-b^2}\int \frac{\sqrt{b^2-a^2}}{\sqrt{b^2-a^2y^2}}dy,$

i.e.

$$I = \frac{1}{a\sqrt{b^2-a^2}}\cos^{-1}\frac{ay}{b}$$

$$= \frac{1}{a\sqrt{b^2-a^2}}\cos^{-1}\frac{a}{b}\sqrt{\frac{x^2+b^2}{x^2+a^2}} \quad (a<b).$$

If $a>b$, we may arrange I as

$$\frac{1}{a^2-b^2}\int \frac{\sqrt{a^2-b^2}}{\sqrt{a^2y^2-b^2}}dy,$$

i.e. $I = \frac{1}{a\sqrt{a^2-b^2}}\cosh^{-1}\frac{ay}{b} = \frac{1}{a\sqrt{a^2-b^2}}\cosh^{-1}\frac{a}{b}\sqrt{\frac{x^2+b^2}{x^2+a^2}} \quad (a>b).$

Ex. 2. Integrate $I = \int \frac{(x+1)\,dx}{(2x^2-2x+1)\sqrt{3x^2-2x+1}}$.

Putting $\sqrt{\frac{3x^2-2x+1}{2x^2-2x+1}} = y,$

we obtain
$$\frac{1}{y}\frac{dy}{dx} = \frac{3x-1}{3x^2-2x+1} - \frac{2x-1}{2x^2-2x+1}$$
$$= -\frac{x(x-1)}{(3x^2-2x+1)(2x^2-2x+1)}.$$

The maximum and minimum values y_1^2 and y_2^2 of y^2 are given by $x = 1$ and $x = 0$, and are respectively 2 and 1, so that for real values of x, y^2 must be not greater than 2 and not less than 1.

$$\left.\begin{aligned} \text{Now} \quad y_1^2 - y^2 &\equiv 2 - y^2 = \frac{(x-1)^2}{2x^2-2x+1}, \\ \text{and} \quad y^2 - y_2^2 &\equiv y^2 - 1 = \frac{x^2}{2x^2-2x+1}. \end{aligned}\right\}$$

Thus I becomes

$$-\int \frac{(3x^2-2x+1)(2x^2-2x+1)}{x(x-1)} \sqrt{\frac{2x^2-2x+1}{3x^2-2x+1}} \frac{x+1}{(2x^2-2x+1)\sqrt{3x^2-2x+1}}\,dy,$$

or
$$-\int \frac{x+1}{x(x-1)}\sqrt{2x^2-2x+1}\,dy.$$

Now $\frac{x+1}{x(x-1)}\sqrt{2x^2-2x+1}$
$$= \left(\frac{2}{x-1} - \frac{1}{x}\right)\sqrt{2x^2-2x+1} = \frac{2}{\sqrt{2-y^2}} - \frac{1}{\sqrt{y^2-1}}.$$

Thus
$$I = \int\left(\frac{1}{\sqrt{y^2-1}} - \frac{2}{\sqrt{2-y^2}}\right)dy$$
$$= \cosh^{-1} y + 2\cos^{-1}\frac{y}{\sqrt{2}}$$
$$= \cosh^{-1}\sqrt{\frac{3x^2-2x+1}{2x^2-2x+1}} + 2\cos^{-1}\frac{1}{\sqrt{2}}\sqrt{\frac{3x^2-2x+1}{2x^2-2x+1}}.$$

EXAMPLES

Integrate

1. $\dfrac{x}{(x^2+a^2)\sqrt{x^2+b^2}}$.

2. $\dfrac{1}{(x^2-1)\sqrt{x^2+1}}$.

3. $\dfrac{1}{(x^2+1)\sqrt{(x+1)(x-1)}}$.

4. $\dfrac{1}{x^2\sqrt{x^2-1}}$.

5. $\dfrac{1}{(x^2+2ax+b^2)\sqrt{x^2+2ax+c^2}}$.

6. $\dfrac{1}{(x-1)^{3/2}(x+1)^{3/2}}$.

7. $\dfrac{3x+4}{(5x^2+8x)\sqrt{4x^2-2x+1}}$.

96. Fractions of form $\dfrac{a+b\sin x+c\cos x}{a_1+b_1\sin x+c_1\cos x}$.

This fraction can be thrown into the form

$$\frac{A}{(a_1+b_1\sin x+c_1\cos x)}+\frac{B(b_1\cos x-c_1\sin x)}{(a_1+b_1\sin x+c_1\cos x)}+C,$$

where A, B, C are constants so chosen that

$A+Ca_1=a, -Bc_1+Cb_1=b, Bb_1+Cc_1=c,$

and each term is then integrable.

97. Similarly the expression

$$\frac{a+b\sin x+c\cos x}{(a_1+b_1\sin x+c_1\cos x)^n} \text{ may be arranged as } \frac{A}{(a_1+b_1\sin x+c_1\cos x)^n}$$

$$+\frac{B(b_1\cos x-c_1\sin x)}{(a_1+b_1\sin x+c_1\cos x)^n}+\frac{C}{(a_1+b_1\sin x+c_1\cos x)^{n-1}},$$

and the first and third fractions may be reduced by a reduction formula [Ex. 25, Ch. VII.], while the second is immediately integrable.

98. Similar remarks apply to fractions of the form

$$\frac{a+b\sinh x+c\cosh x}{a_1+b_1\sinh x+c_1\cosh x}, \frac{a+b\sinh x+c\cosh x}{(a_1+b_1\sinh x+c_1\cosh x)^n}.$$

99. Some Special Forms.

It is easy to show that

$$\frac{\sin x}{\sin(x-a)\sin(x-b)\sin(x-c)}=\sum\frac{\sin a}{\sin(a-b)\sin(a-c)}\cot(x-a),$$

and $\dfrac{\sin^2 x}{\sin(x-a)\sin(x-b)\sin(x-c)}$

$$=\sum\frac{\sin^2 a}{\sin(a-b)\sin(a-c)}\frac{1}{\sin(x-a)},$$

whence $\displaystyle\int\frac{\sin x\,dx}{\sin(x-a)\sin(x-b)\sin(x-c)}$

$$=\sum\frac{\sin a}{\sin(a-b)\sin(a-c)}\log\sin(x-a),$$

and $\displaystyle\int\frac{\sin^2 x\,dx}{\sin(x-a)\sin(x-b)\sin(x-c)}$

$$=\sum\frac{\sin^2 a}{\sin(a-b)\sin(a-c)}\log\tan\frac{x-a}{2}.$$

100. More generally Hermite has shown * how to integrate any expression of the form

$$\frac{f(\sin\theta,\cos\theta)}{\sin(\theta-a_1)\sin(\theta-a_2)\ldots\sin(\theta-a_n)},$$

where $f(x, y)$ is any homogeneous function of x, y of $n-1$ dimensions. For by the ordinary rules of partial fractions

$$\frac{f(t,1)}{(t-a_1)(t-a_2)\ldots(t-a_n)}=\frac{f(a_1,1)}{(a_1-a_2)(a_1-a_3)\ldots(a_1-a_n)}$$

$$\times\frac{1}{t-a_1}+\frac{f(a_2,1)}{(a_2-a_1)(a_2-a_3)\ldots(a_2-a_n)}\frac{1}{t-a_2}+\ldots,$$

which may be written $\displaystyle\sum_{r=1}^{r=n}\frac{f(a_r,1)}{(a_r-a_1)(a_r-a_2)\ldots(a_r-a_n)}\frac{1}{t-a_r}$

(the factor a_r-a_r being omitted in the denominator of the above coefficient).

Putting $t=\tan\theta$, $a_1=\tan\alpha_1$, $a_2=\tan\alpha_2$, etc., this theorem becomes

$$\frac{f(\sin\theta,\cos\theta)}{\sin(\theta-\alpha_1)\sin(\theta-\alpha_2)\ldots\sin(\theta-\alpha_n)}$$

$$=\sum_{r=1}^{r=n}\frac{f(\sin\alpha_r,\cos\alpha_r)}{\sin(\alpha_r-\alpha_1)\ldots\sin(\alpha_r-\alpha_n)}\frac{1}{\sin(\theta-\alpha_r)}.\ *$$

Thus $\displaystyle\int\frac{f(\sin\theta,\cos\theta)}{\sin(\theta-\alpha_1)\ \ldots\sin(\theta-\alpha_n)}d\theta$

$$=\sum_{r=1}^{r=n}\frac{f(\sin\alpha_r,\cos\alpha_r)}{\sin(\alpha_r-\alpha_1)\ldots\sin(\alpha_r-\alpha_n)}\log\tan\frac{\theta-\alpha_r}{2}.$$

Proc. Lond. Math. Soc., 1872.

*See Hobson's *Trigonometry*, page 111.

EXAMPLES

Integrate

1. $\dfrac{\sin x}{\sin\left(x-\dfrac{\pi}{6}\right)\sin\left(x+\dfrac{\pi}{6}\right)}$.

2. $\dfrac{\cos 2x - \cos 2a}{\cos x - \cos a}$.

3. $\dfrac{\cos 3x - \cos 3a}{\cos x - \cos a}$.

4. $\dfrac{\cos nx - \cos na}{\cos x - \cos a}$.

5. $\dfrac{\sin 2x - \sin 2a}{\sin x - \sin a}$.

6. $\dfrac{\cos^2 x}{\sin x\,(\sin^2 x - \sin^2 a)}$.

GENERAL PROPOSITIONS.

101. There are certain general propositions or integration which are almost self evident from the definition of integration or from the geometrical meaning. Thus

102. I. $\int_a^b \phi(x)\,dx = \int_a^b \phi(z)\,dz,$

for each is equal to $\psi(b) - \psi(a)$ if $\phi(x)$ be the differential coefficient of $\psi(x)$. The result being ultimately independent of x it is plainly immaterial whether x or z is used in the process of obtaining the indefinite integral.

103. II. $\int_a^b \phi(x)\,dx = \int_a^c \phi(x)\,dx + \int_c^b \phi(x)\,dx.$

For, if $\psi(x)$ be the indefinite integral of $\phi(x)$
the left side is $\psi(b) - \psi(a)$,
and the right side is $\psi(c) - \psi(a) + \psi(b) - \psi(c)$,
which is the same thing.

Let us illustrate this fact geometrically.

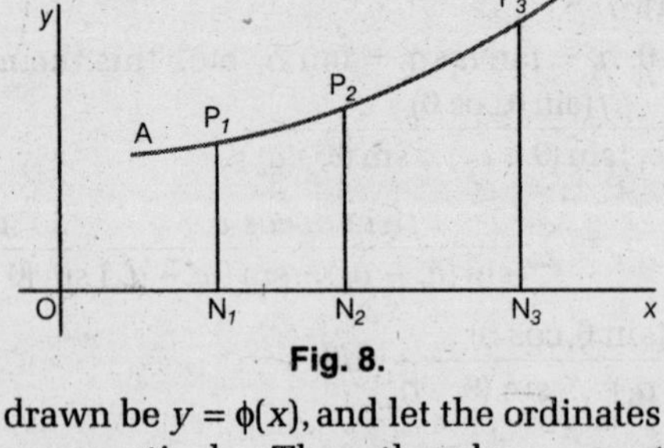

Fig. 8.

Let the curve drawn be $y = \phi(x)$, and let the ordinates N_1P_1, N_2P_2, N_3P_3 be $x = a$, $x = c$, $x = b$, respectively. Then the above equation expresses the obvious fact that

Area $N_1N_3P_3P_1$ = area $N_1N_2P_2P_1$ + area $N_2N_3P_3P_2$.

104. III. $\int_a^b \phi(x)\,dx = -\int_b^a \phi(x)\,dx.$

For with the same notation as before
the left hand side is $\psi(b)-\psi(a)$,
and the right hand side is $-[\psi(a)-\psi(b)]$.

105. IV. $\int_0^a \phi(x)\,dx = \int_0^a \phi(a-x)\,dx$

For if we put $x = a - y$,
we have $dx = -dy$; and if $x = a, y = 0$,
if $x = 0, y = a$.

Hence $\int_0^a \phi(x)\,dx = -\int_a^0 \phi(a-y)\,dy$

$$= \int_0^a \phi(a-y)\,dy \text{ (by III.)} = \int_0^a \phi(a-x)\,dx \qquad \text{(by I.)}$$

Geometrically this expresses the obvious fact that, in estimating the area $OO'QP$ between the y and x axes,

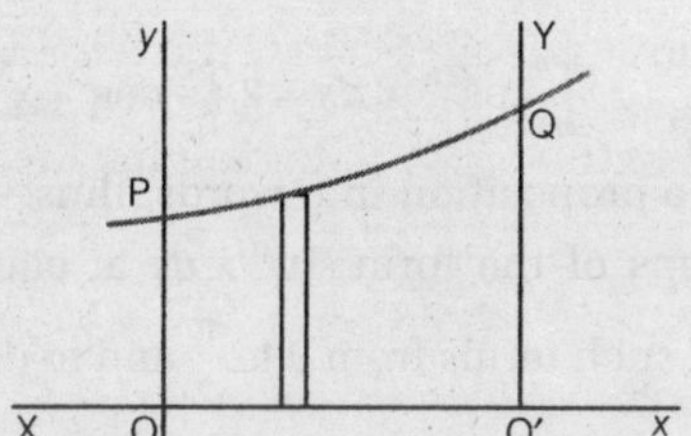

Fig. 9.

an ordinate $O'Q$, and a curve PQ, we may if we like take our origin at O', $O'Q$ as our Y-axis, and $O'X$ as our positive direction of the X-axis.

106. V. $\int_0^{2a} \phi(x)\,dx = \int_0^a \phi(x)\,dx + \int_0^a \phi(2a-x)\,dx.$

For by II.

$$\int_0^{2a} \phi(x)\,dx = \int_0^a \phi(x)\,dx + \int_a^{2a} \phi(x)\,dx,$$

and if we put $2a - x = y$,
we have $dx = -dy$,
and when $x = a, y = a$,
when $x = 2a, y = 0$.

Thus $\int_a^{2a} \phi(x)\,dx = -\int_a^0 \phi(2a-y)\,dy$

$$= \int_0^a \phi(2a-y)\,dy = \int_0^a \phi(2a-x)\,dx$$

Hence $$\int_0^{2a}\phi(x)\,dx = \int_0^{a}\phi(x)\,dx + \int_0^{a}\phi(2a-x)\,dx.$$

We leave the obvious geometrical interpretation to the student.

107. VI. Plainly if $\phi(x)$ be such that $\phi(2a-x) = \phi(x)$

this proposition becomes $\int_0^{2a}\phi(x)\,dx = 2\int_0^{a}\phi(x)\,dx,$

and if $\phi(x)$ be such that $\phi(2a-x) = -\phi(x)$,

$$\int_0^{2a}\phi(x)\,dx = 0.$$

Thus since $$\sin^n x = \sin^n(\pi - x),$$

$$\int_0^{\pi}\sin^n x\,dx = 2\int_0^{\frac{\pi}{2}}\sin^n x\,dx;$$

and since $$\cos^{2n+1} x = -\cos^{2n+1}(\pi - x),$$

and $$\cos^{2n} x = \cos^{2n}(\pi - x),$$

$$\int_0^{\pi}\cos^{2n+1} x\,dx = 0,$$

and $$\int_0^{\pi}\cos^{2n} x\,dx = 2\int_0^{\frac{\pi}{2}}\cos^{2n} x\,dx.$$

We may put such a proposition into words, thus:—

To add up all terms of the form $\sin^n x\,dx$ at equal intervals between 0 and π is to add up all such terms from 0 to $\frac{\pi}{2}$ and to double. For the second quadrant sines are merely repetitions of the first quadrant sines in the reverse order. Or geometrically, the curve $y = \sin^n x$ being symmetrical about the ordinate $x = \frac{\pi}{2}$, the whole area between 0 and π is double that between 0 and $\frac{\pi}{2}$.

Similar geometrical illustrations will apply to other cases.

108. VII. If $\phi(x) = \phi(a+x)$

$$\int_0^{na}\phi(x)dx = n\int_0^{a}\phi(x)dx.$$

For, drawing the curve $y = \phi(x)$, it is clear that it consists of an infinite series of repetitions of the part lying between the ordinates OP_0 $(x = 0)$ and N_1P_1 $(x = a)$ and the areas bounded by the successive portions of the curve, the corresponding ordinates and the x-axis are all equal.

Thus $$\int_0^{a}\phi(x)dx = \int_a^{2a}\phi(x)dx = \int_{2a}^{3a}\phi(x)dx = \text{etc.}$$

and $$\int_0^{na} \phi(x)\,dx = n\int_0^a \phi(x)\,dx.$$

Thus, for instance,

$$\int_0^{2\pi} \sin^{2n} x\,dx = 2\int_0^{\pi} \sin^{2n} x\,dx = 4\int_0^{\frac{\pi}{2}} \sin^{2n} x\,dx = 4\,\frac{2n-1}{2n}\cdot\frac{2n-3}{2n-2}\cdots\frac{1}{2}\cdot\frac{\pi}{2}.$$

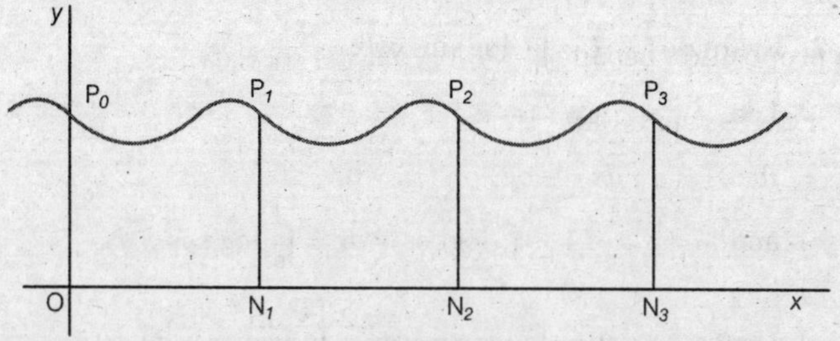

Fig. 10.

SOME ELEMENTARY DEFINITE INTEGRALS.

109. We have seen that whenever the indefinite integration $\int \phi(x)\,dx$ can be performed, the value of the definite integral $\int_a^b \phi(x)\,dx$ can at once be inferred.

In many cases, however, the value of the definite integral can be inferred without performing the indefinite integration, and even when it cannot be performed.

We propose to give a few elementary illustrations.

Ex. 1. Evaluate $I = \int_0^{2a} (2ax - x^2)^{\frac{n}{2}} \text{vers}^{-1} \frac{x}{a}\,dx$.

Writing $x = 2a - y$,

we have $dx = -\,dy$,

$$2ax - x^2 = 2ay - y^2, \text{ and } \quad \text{vers}^{-1}\frac{x}{a} = \pi - \text{vers}^{-1}\frac{y}{a}.$$

Hence $$I = -\int_{2a}^{0} (2ay - y^2)^{\frac{n}{2}}\left(\pi - \text{vers}^{-1}\frac{y}{a}\right)dy$$

$$= \pi\int_0^{2a} (2ay - y^2)^{\frac{n}{2}}\,dy - I.$$

Hence $$I = \frac{\pi}{2}\int_0^{2a} (2ay - y^2)^{\frac{n}{2}}\,dy.$$

Putting $y = a(1 - \cos\theta),\ dy = a\sin\theta\,d\theta,$

and we obtain $I = \frac{\pi}{2} a^{n+1} \int_0^{\pi} \sin^{n+1}\theta\, d\theta = \pi a^{n+1} \int_0^{\frac{\pi}{2}} \sin^{n+1}\theta d\theta$

$$= \pi a^{n+1} \frac{n}{n+1} \frac{n-2}{n-1} \frac{n-4}{n-3} \ldots \text{ down to } \frac{2}{3} \text{ or } \frac{1}{2}\frac{\pi}{2},$$

according as n is even or odd.

Ex. 2. Evaluate $\quad I = \int_0^{\frac{\pi}{2}} \log \sin x\, dx.$

Let $\quad x = \frac{\pi}{2} - y,$

then $\quad dx = -dy;$

and $\quad I = -\int_{\frac{\pi}{2}}^{0} \log \cos y\, dy = \int_0^{\frac{\pi}{2}} \log \cos x\, dx.$

Hence $\quad 2I = \int_0^{\frac{\pi}{2}} \log \sin x\, dx + \int_0^{\frac{\pi}{2}} \log \cos x\, dx$

$$= \int_0^{\frac{\pi}{2}} \log \sin x \cos x\, dx = \int_0^{\frac{\pi}{2}} (\log \sin 2x - \log 2)\, dx$$

$$= \int_0^{\frac{\pi}{2}} \log \sin 2x\, dx - \frac{\pi}{2} \log 2\,.$$

Put $\quad 2x = z,$

then $\quad dx = \frac{1}{2} dz\,;$

then $\quad \int_0^{\frac{\pi}{2}} \log \sin 2x\, dx = \frac{1}{2} \int_0^{\pi} \log \sin z\, dz = \int_0^{\frac{\pi}{2}} \log \sin x\, dx = I.$

Thus $\quad 2I = I - \frac{\pi}{2} \log 2\,, \quad$ or $\quad I = \frac{\pi}{2} \log \frac{1}{2}.$

Thus $\quad \int_0^{\frac{\pi}{2}} \log \sin x\, dx = \int_0^{\frac{\pi}{2}} \log \cos x\, dx = \frac{\pi}{2} \log \frac{1}{2}.$

Ex. 3. Evaluate $\quad I = \int_0^1 \frac{\log(1-x)}{x} dx.$

Expanding the logarithm, we have

$$I = -\int_0^1 \left(1 + \frac{x}{2} + \frac{x^2}{3} + \frac{x^3}{4} + \ldots \text{ to } \infty\right) dx$$

$$= -\left(\frac{1}{1^2} + \frac{1}{2^2} + \frac{1}{3^2} + \frac{1}{4^2} + \ldots\right) = -\frac{\pi^2}{6}.$$

If we put $\quad x = 1 - y,$

we have $\quad I = -\int_1^0 \frac{\log y}{1-y} dy = \int_0^1 \frac{\log x}{1-x} dx\,.$

Hence we also have $\int_0^1 \frac{\log x}{1-x} dx = -\frac{\pi^2}{6}.$

Ex. 4. Evaluate $I = \int_0^\infty \log\left(x + \frac{1}{x}\right)\frac{dx}{1+x^2}$.

Put $\quad x = \tan\theta,$

$\therefore \quad dx = \sec^2\theta d\theta;$

$$\therefore \quad I = \int_0^{\frac{\pi}{2}} \log(\tan\theta + \cot\theta)\,d\theta = \int_0^{\frac{\pi}{2}} \log\frac{2}{\sin 2\theta}\,d\theta$$

$$= -\int_0^{\frac{\pi}{2}} (\log\sin\theta + \log\cos\theta)\,d\theta$$

$$= -2\int_0^{\frac{\pi}{2}} \log\sin\theta\,d\theta = \pi\log 2.$$

110. Differentiation under an Integral Sign.

Suppose the function to be integrated to be $\phi(x, c)$ containing a quantity c which is independent of x.

Suppose also that the limits a and b of the integration *are finite* quantities, and independent of c.

Then will $\quad \frac{\partial}{\partial c}\int_a^b \phi(x,c)\,dx = \int_a^b \left[\frac{\partial}{\partial c}\phi(x,c)\right]dx.$

For let $$u = \int_a^b \phi(x,c)\,dx.$$

Then $$u + \delta u = \int_a^b \phi(x, c + \delta c)\,dx,$$

and $$\frac{\delta u}{\delta c} = \int_a^b \frac{\phi(x, c+\delta c) - \phi(x,c)}{\delta c}\,dx,$$

which, by Taylor's theorem, $= \int_a^b \left[\frac{\partial\phi(x,c)}{\partial c} + \frac{\delta c}{2}\frac{\partial^2\phi(x,c)}{\partial c^2} + \ldots\right]dx$

$$= \int_a^b \frac{\partial\phi(x,c)}{\partial c}\,dx + \frac{\delta c}{2}\int_a^b \left[\frac{\partial^2\phi}{\partial c^2} + \ldots\right]dx$$

And if z, say, be the greatest value of which $\frac{\partial^2\phi}{\partial c^2} + \ldots$ be capable,

$$\delta c\int_a^b \left[\frac{\partial^2\phi}{\partial c^2} + \ldots\right]dx < \delta c\,(b-a)\,z,$$

and vanishes in the limit when δc is indefinitely diminished. Thus, in the limit

$$\frac{\partial u}{\partial c} = \int_a^b \frac{\partial\phi(x,c)}{\partial c}\,dx.$$

111. The case in which the limits a and b also contain c is somewhat beyond the scope of the present volume.

112. This proposition may be used to deduce many new integrations when one has been performed.

Thus since

$$\int \frac{1}{(x+c)\sqrt{x-a}}\,dx = \frac{2}{\sqrt{c+a}}\tan^{-1}\sqrt{\frac{x-a}{c+a}}\ (c+a>0),$$

we have, by differentiating n times with regard to c,

$$\int \frac{1}{(x+c)^{n+1}\sqrt{x-a}}\,dx = \frac{2(-1)^n}{n!}\frac{\partial^n}{\partial c^n}\left\{\frac{1}{\sqrt{c+a}}\tan^{-1}\sqrt{\frac{x-a}{c+a}}\right\}.$$

Also, differentiating n times with regard to a, we obtain

$$\int \frac{1}{(x+c)(x-a)^{\frac{2n+1}{2}}}\,dx = \frac{2^{n+1}}{1.3.5\ldots(2n-1)}\frac{\partial^n}{\partial a^n}\left\{\frac{1}{\sqrt{c+a}}\tan^{-1}\sqrt{\frac{x-a}{c+a}}\right\}.$$

Similarly, differentiating this latter p times with regard to c, we obtain

$$\int \frac{dx}{(x+c)^{p+1}(x-a)^{\frac{2n+1}{2}}} = \frac{2^{n+1}(-1)^p}{(p!)\cdot 1\cdot 3\ldots(2n-1)}\frac{\partial^{n+p}}{\partial c^p\partial a^n}\left\{\frac{1}{\sqrt{c+a}}\tan^{-1}\sqrt{\frac{x-a}{c+a}}\right\}.$$

EXAMPLES

1. Obtain the following integrals:—

(i.) $\int (1+x)^{-1}x^{-\frac{1}{2}}\,dx.$ (ii.) $\int (1+x)^{-1}(1+2x)^{-\frac{1}{2}}dx.$

(iii.) $\int x^{-1}(2-3x+x^2)^{-\frac{1}{2}}\,dx.$ (iv.) $\int \frac{dx}{(1+x)\sqrt{1+x+x^2}}.$

(v.) $\int \frac{\sqrt{1+x+x^2}}{1+x}\,dx.$ (vi.) $\int \frac{x^2+x-1}{(x+1)\sqrt{x^2-1}}\,dx.$

(vii.) $\int \frac{dx}{x\sqrt{a^n+x^n}}.$ (viii.) $\int \frac{1-x}{1+x}\cdot\frac{1}{\sqrt{x+x^2+x^3}}\,dx.$

2. Integrate

(i.) $\dfrac{x}{(a^2+b^2-x^2)\sqrt{(a^2-x^2)(x^2-b^2)}}.$ [ST. JOHN'S, 1888.]

(ii.) $\dfrac{x+b}{(x^2+a^2)\sqrt{x^2+c^2}}.$ [ST. JOHN'S, 1889.]

(iii.) $\dfrac{1}{\sin\theta\sqrt{a\cos^2\theta+b\sin^2\theta+c}}.$ [TRINITY, 1888.]

3. Find the values of

(i.) $\int \dfrac{\sin x \, dx}{(\cos x + \cos \alpha)\sqrt{(\cos x + \cos \beta)(\cos x + \cos \gamma)}}$.

(ii.) $\int \dfrac{dx}{\cos (x + \alpha) \sqrt{\cos (x + \beta) \cos (x + \gamma)}}$. [γ, 1890.]

4. Prove that, with certain limitations on the values of the constants involved,

$$\int \frac{dx}{(x - p)(ax^2 + 2bx + c)^{\frac{1}{2}}} = \frac{1}{(-ap^2 - 2bp - c)^{\frac{1}{2}}} \text{ arc sin } \frac{(ap + b)x + bp + c}{(x - p)(b^2 - ac)^{\frac{1}{2}}}$$ [TRINITY, 1886.]

5. Prove that $\int (\cos x)^n \, dx$ may be expressed by the series

$$\sin x - N_1 \frac{\sin^3 x}{3} + N_2 \frac{\sin^5 x}{5} - N_3 \frac{\sin^7 x}{7} + \ldots \text{etc.},$$

$N_1, N_2, N_3, \ldots$ being the coefficients of the expansion $(1 + a)^{\frac{n-1}{2}}$, and n having any real value positive or negative. [SMITH'S PRIZE, 1876.]

6. Evaluate the following definite integrals:—

(i.) $\int_0^1 \dfrac{dx}{1 + 2x + 2x^2 + 2x^3 + x^4}$. [ST. JOHN'S 1888.]

(ii.) $\int_0^a \dfrac{a^2 - x^2}{(a^2 + x^2)^2} dx$.

(iii.) $\int_0^\infty \dfrac{\sqrt{x} \, dx}{(1 + x)(2 + x)(3 + x)}$. [OXFORD, 1888.]

7. Prove that $\int_0^1 \dfrac{dx}{(1 + x^2)(1 - x^2)^{\frac{1}{2}}} = \dfrac{\pi}{2\sqrt{2}}$.

8. Show that $\int_{\sqrt{3}}^{2\sqrt{3}} z^3 (z^2 - 3)^{\frac{3}{2}} \, dz = \dfrac{16038}{35}$. [OXFORD, 1888.]

9. Evaluate (i.) $\int_0^{\frac{\pi}{2}} \dfrac{dx}{2 + \cos x}$. [I.C.S., 1889.]

(ii.) $\int_0^{\frac{\pi}{2}} \dfrac{dx}{4 + 5 \sin x}$. (iii.) $\int_0^\pi \dfrac{dx}{1 - 2a \cos x + a^2}$. [I.C.S., 1888.]

10. Prove that $\int_0^{\pi} \cos^n x\,dx$ is equal to zero or $\pi(n!)/2^n\left(\frac{1}{2}n!\right)^2$ according as n is odd or even.

If S denote the sum of the infinite series

$\sin^2 x + \frac{\sin^4 x}{3^2} + \frac{\sin^6 x}{5^2} + \ldots$, prove that $\int_0^{\frac{\pi}{2}} S\,dx = \frac{\pi^2}{4} - \frac{\pi}{2}$.

[OXFORD, 1890.]

11. Prove that if c be < 1,

(i.) $\int_0^{\frac{\pi}{2}} \sin^{-1}(c\cos x)\,dx = \frac{c}{1^2} + \frac{c^3}{3^2} + \frac{c^5}{5^2} + \frac{c^7}{7^2} + \ldots$.

(ii.) $\frac{1}{\pi}\int_0^{\frac{\pi}{2}} [\sin^{-1}(c\cos x)]^2\,dx = \frac{c^2}{2^2} + \frac{c^4}{4^2} + \frac{c^6}{6^2} + \frac{c^8}{8^2} + \ldots$.

12. Prove that $\int_0^{\frac{\pi}{2}} \left(\frac{\theta}{\sin\theta}\right)^2 d\theta = \pi \log 2$.

13. Find a reduction formula for $\int_0^{\pi} e^{-x} \sin^n x\,dx$. [ST. JOHN'S, 1888.]

14. Evaluate

(i.) $\int_0^{\frac{\pi}{2}} \sin x \log \sin x\,dx$. [δ, 1883.]

(ii.) $\int_0^{\frac{\pi}{2}} \tan x \log \sin x\,dx$. [ST. JOHN'S, 1882.]

(iii.) $\int_0^{\frac{\pi}{2}} \sin 2x \log \tan x\,dx$. [ST. JOHN'S, 1886.]

15. Evaluate

(i.) $\int_0^{\frac{\pi}{2}} \frac{dx}{a^2\sin^2 x + b^2\cos^2 x}$. [I.C.S., 1887.]

(ii.) $\int_0^{\frac{\pi}{4}} \frac{\sin 2\theta}{\sin^4\theta + \cos^4\theta}\,d\theta$. [I.C.S., 1891.]

16. Prove

(i.) $\int_0^{\pi} \frac{x\tan x\,dx}{\sec x + \cos x} = \frac{\pi^2}{4}$. [POISSON.]

(ii.) $\int_0^{\pi} \frac{x\,dx}{a^2 - \cos^2 x} = \frac{\pi^2}{2a\sqrt{a^2-1}}$,

a being supposed greater than unity. [OXFORD, 1890.]

17. Prove

(i.) $\int_0^1 \frac{\log x}{1+x}\,dx = -\frac{\pi^2}{12}$.   (ii.) $\int_0^\infty \left(\frac{\log x}{1-x}\right)^2 dx = \frac{2}{3}\pi^2$.

18. Prove that

$$\int_0^1 \frac{a\,dz}{1+a^2(1-z^2)} = a - \frac{2}{3}a^3 + \frac{2\cdot 4}{3\cdot 5}a^5 - \frac{2\cdot 4\cdot 6}{3\cdot 5\cdot 7}a^7 + \ldots.$$ [OXFORD, 1889.]

19. Prove that

$$\frac{2}{\pi}\int_0^{\frac{\pi}{2}} \frac{d\theta}{(1-e^2\cos^2\theta)^{\frac{1}{2}}} = 1 + \frac{1^2}{2^2}e^2 + \frac{1^2.3^2}{2^2.4^2}e^4 + \frac{1^2\cdot 3^2\cdot 5^2}{2^2\cdot 4^2\cdot 6^2}e^6 + \ldots,$$

e being supposed < 1.

20. Prove that $\int_0^1 v^{xz}dv = 1 - \frac{x}{2^2} + \frac{x^2}{3^3} - \frac{x^3}{4^4} + \frac{x^4}{5^5}$ – etc.

[MATH. TRIPOS, 1878.]

21. Prove that

$$1 - \frac{1}{7} + \frac{1}{9} - \frac{1}{15} + \frac{1}{17} - \ldots \textit{ad inf.} = \frac{\pi}{8}(1+\sqrt{2}).$$ [β, 1888.]

22. If $\phi(x) = -\phi(2a-x)$, $\int_b^{2a}\phi(x)\,dx = -\int_0^b \phi(x)\,dx$. [TRIN. HALL, etc, 1886.]

23. Prove that $\int_b^c \frac{\phi(x-b)}{\phi(c-x)}\,dx = \int_b^c \frac{\phi(c-x)}{\phi(x-b)}\,dx$, provided $\phi(x)$ remains finite when x vanishes. [ST. JOHN'S, 1883.]

24. Prove that $\int_0^{2a}\phi(x)\,dx = \int_0^a \{\phi(x) + \phi(2a-x)\}\,dx$, and illustrate the theorem geometrically.

25. If $f(x) = f(a+x)$, show that $\int_a^{na} f(x)\,dx = (n-1)\int_0^a f(x)\,dx$,

and illustrate geometrically.

26. Show that $\int_a^b \phi(x)\,dx = \frac{b-a}{q-p}\int_p^q \phi\left(\frac{aq-bp}{q-p} + \frac{b-a}{q-p}x\right)dx$.

27. Determine by integration the limiting value of the sums of the following series when n is indefinitely great :—

(i.) $\frac{1}{n+1} + \frac{1}{n+2} + \frac{1}{n+3} + \ldots + \frac{1}{n+n}$. [α, 1884.]

(ii.) $\frac{n}{n^2+1^2} + \frac{n}{n^2+2^2} + \frac{n}{n^2+3^2} + \ldots + \frac{n}{n^2+n^2}$. [OXFORD, 1888.]

(iii.) $\frac{1}{\sqrt{2n-1^2}} + \frac{1}{\sqrt{4n-2^2}} + \frac{1}{\sqrt{6n-3^2}} + \ldots + \frac{1}{\sqrt{2n^2-n^2}}$.

[CLARE, etc., 1882.]

(iv.) $\frac{1}{n}\left\{\sin^{2k}\frac{\pi}{2n} + \sin^{2k}\frac{2\pi}{2n} + \sin^{2k}\frac{3\pi}{2n} + \ldots + \sin^{2k}\frac{\pi}{2}\right\}$,

k being an integer. [ST. JOHN'S, 1886.]

28. Show that the limit when n is increased indefinitely of

$$\frac{(n-m)^{\frac{1}{3}}}{n} + \frac{(2^n n - m)^{\frac{1}{3}}}{2n} + \frac{(3^2 n - m)^{\frac{1}{3}}}{3n} + \ldots + \frac{(n^3 - m)^{\frac{1}{3}}}{n^2} \text{ is } \frac{3}{2}.$$

[COLLEGES, 1892.]

29. Show that the limit when n is infinite of

$$\left\{\phi(a)\cdot\phi\left(a+\frac{h}{n}\right)\cdot\phi\left(a+\frac{2h}{n}\right)\ldots\phi\left(a+\frac{nh}{n}\right)\right\}^{\frac{1}{n}} \text{ is } e^{\frac{1}{h}\int_a^{a+h}\log\phi(x)dx}.$$

Apply this result to find the limit of

$$\left\{\left(1+\frac{1}{n^2}\right)\left(1+\frac{2^2}{n^2}\right)\left(1+\frac{3^2}{n^2}\right)\ldots\left(1+\frac{n^2}{n^2}\right)\right\}^{\frac{1}{n}}$$

[CLARE, etc., 1886.]

30. Find the limiting value of $(n!)^{\frac{1}{n}}/n$ when n is infinite.

31. Find the limiting value when n is infinite of the n th part of the sum of the n quantities

$$\frac{n+1}{n}, \frac{n+2}{n}, \frac{n+3}{n}, \ldots, \frac{n+n}{n};$$

and show that it is to the limiting value of the nth root of the product of the same quantities as $3e : 8$, where e is the base of the Napierian logarithms.

[OXFORD, 1886.]

32. If na is always equal to unity and n is indefinitely great, show that the limiting value of the product

$$\{1+a^4\}\{1+(2a)^4\}^{\frac{1}{2}}\{1+(3a)^4\}^{\frac{1}{3}}\{1+(4a)^4\}^{\frac{1}{4}}\ldots\{1+(na)^4\}^{\frac{1}{n}} \text{ is } e^{\frac{\pi^2}{48}}.$$

[OXFORD, 1888.]

CHAPTER IX.

RECTIFICATION, ETC.

113. In the course of the next four chapters we propose to illustrate the foregoing method of obtaining the limit of a summation by application of the process of integration to the problems of finding the lengths of curved lines, the areas bounded by such lines, finding surfaces and volumes of solids of revolution, etc.

114. Rules for the Tracing of a Curve.

As we shall in many cases have to form some rough idea of the shape of the curve under discussion, in order to properly assign the limits of integration, we may refer the student to the author's larger *Treatise on the Differential Calculus*, Chapter XII., for a full discussion of the rules of procedure.

The following rules, however, are transcribed for convenience of reference, and will in most cases suffice for present requirements:—

115. I. For Cartesian Equations.

1. A glance will suffice to detect symmetry in a curve.

(a) If no odd powers of y occur, the curve is symmetrical with respect to the axis of x. Similarly for symmetry about the y-axis.

Thus $y^2 = 4ax$ is symmetrical about the x-axis.

(b) If all the powers of both x and y which occur be even, the curve is symmetrical about both axes, *e.g.*, the ellipse

$$\frac{x^2}{a^2} + \frac{y^2}{b^2} = 1.$$

(c) Again, if on changing the signs of x and y, the equation of the curve remains unchanged, there is symmetry in opposite quadrants, *e.g.*, the hyperbola $xy = a^2$, or the cubic $x^3 + y^3 = 3ax$.

If the curve be not symmetrical with regard to either axis, consider whether any obvious transformation of coordinates could make it so.

2. Notice whether the curve passes through the origin; also the points *where it crosses the coordinate axes*, or; in fact any points whose coordinates present themselves as obviously satisfying the equation to the curve.

3. Find the asymptotes; first, those parallel to the axes, next, the oblique ones.
4. If the curve pass through the origin equate to zero the terms of lowest degree. These terms will give the tangent or tangents at the origin.
5. Find $\frac{dy}{dx}$; and where it vanishes or becomes infinite; i.e., find where the tangent is parallel or perpendicular to the x-axis.
6. If we can solve the equation for one of the variables, say y, in terms of the other, x, it will be frequently found that radicals occur in the solution, and that the range of admissible values of x which give real values for y is thereby limited. The *existence of loops* upon a curve is frequently detected thus.
7. Sometimes the equation is much simplified when *reduced to the polar form.*

116. II. For Polar Curves.

It is advisable to follow some such routine as the following:—

1. If possible, *form a table* of corresponding values of r and θ which satisfy the curve for chosen values of θ, such as $\theta = 0, \pm\frac{\pi}{6}, \pm\frac{\pi}{4}, \pm\frac{\pi}{3}$, etc. Consider both positive *and negative* values of θ.
2. Examine whether there be symmetry about the initial line. This will be so when a change of sign of θ leaves the equation unaltered, *e.g.*, in the cardioide $r = a(1 - \cos\theta)$.
3. It will frequently be obvious from the equation of the curve that the values of r or θ are confined *between certain limits.* If such exist they should be ascertained, *e.g.*, if $r = a \sin n\theta$, it is clear that r must lie in magnitude between the limits 0 and a, and the curve lie wholly within the circle $r = a$.
4. Examine whether the curve has any asymptotes, rectilinear or circular.

RECTIFICATION.

117. The process of finding the length of an arc of a curve between two specified points is called rectification.

Any formula expressing the differential coefficient of s proved in the differential calculus gives rise at once by integration to a formula in the integral calculus for finding s. We add a list of the most common. (The references are to the author's *Diff. Calc. for Beginners*.)

118. In each case the limits of integration are the values of the independent variable corresponding to the two points which terminate the arc whose length is sought:

Formula in the Diff. Calc.	Formula in the Int. Calc.	Reference.	Observations.
$\frac{ds}{dx} = \sqrt{1 + \left(\frac{dy}{dx}\right)^2}.$	$s = \int \sqrt{1 + \left(\frac{dy}{dx}\right)^2}\, dx.$	P.79.	For Cartesian Equations of form $y = f(x)$.
$\frac{ds}{dy} = \sqrt{1 + \left(\frac{dx}{dy}\right)^2}.$	$s = \int \sqrt{1 + \left(\frac{dx}{dy}\right)^2}\, dy.$	P.79.	For Cartesian Equations of form $x = f(y)$.
$\frac{ds}{d\theta} = \sqrt{r^2 + \left(\frac{dr}{d\theta}\right)^2}.$	$s = \int \sqrt{r^2 + \left(\frac{dr}{d\theta}\right)^2}\, d\theta.$	P.81.	For Polar Equations of form $r = f(\theta)$.
$\frac{ds}{dr} = \sqrt{1 + r^2\left(\frac{d\theta}{dr}\right)^2}.$	$s = \int \sqrt{1 + r^2 \left(\frac{d\theta}{dr}\right)^2}\, dr.$	P.81.	For Polar Equations of form $\theta = f(r)$.
$\frac{ds}{dt} = \sqrt{\left(\frac{dx}{dt}\right)^2 + \left(\frac{dy}{dt}\right)^2}.$	$s = \int \sqrt{\left(\frac{dx}{dt}\right)^2 + \left(\frac{dy}{dt}\right)^2}\, dt.$	P.80.	For case when curve is given as $x = f(t), y = F(t)$.
$\frac{ds}{dr} = \sec\phi = \frac{r}{\sqrt{r^2 - p^2}}.$	$s = \int \frac{r\, dr}{\sqrt{r^2 - p^2}}.$	Pp81, 82.	For use when Pedal Equation is given.
$\frac{ds}{d\psi} = p + \frac{d^2 p}{d\psi^2}.$	$s = \frac{dp}{d\psi} + \int p\, d\psi.$	P.115.	For use when Tangential Polar Equation is given.

119. We add illustrative examples :—

Ex. 1. Find the length of the arc of the parabola $x^2 = 4ay$ extending from the vertex to one extremity of the latus-rectum.

$y = \frac{x^2}{4a}$, $y_1 = \frac{x}{2a}$, and the limits are $x = 0$ and $x = 2a$. Hence

$$\text{arc} = \int_0^{2a} \sqrt{1 + \frac{x^2}{4a^2}}\, dx$$

$$= \frac{1}{2a}\left[\frac{x\sqrt{x^2 + 4a^2}}{2} + \frac{4a^2}{2}\log\left(x + \sqrt{x^2 + 4a^2}\right)\right]_0^{2a}$$

$$= \frac{1}{4a}\left[2a\sqrt{8a^2} + 4a^2 \log(1 + \sqrt{2})\right]$$

$$= a\left[\sqrt{2} + \log(1 + \sqrt{2})\right].$$

Ex. 2. Obtain the same result by taking y as the independent variable.

$x = \sqrt{4ay}, \frac{dx}{dy} = \sqrt{\frac{a}{y}}$, and the limits are $y = 0$ and $y = a$. Hence

$$\text{arc} = \int_0^a \sqrt{1 + \frac{a}{y}}\, dy$$

(Put $y = a\tan^2\theta$, and $\therefore dy = 2a\tan\theta\sec^2\theta\, d\theta$.)

$$= \int_0^{\frac{\pi}{4}} 2a\sec^3\theta d\theta = 2a\left[\frac{\tan\theta\cdot\sec\theta}{2} + \frac{1}{2}\log(\tan\theta + \sec\theta)\right]_0^{\frac{\pi}{4}}$$

$$= a[\sqrt{2} + \log(1 + \sqrt{2})].$$

Ex. 3. Find the perimeter of the cardioide $r = a(1 - \cos\theta)$.

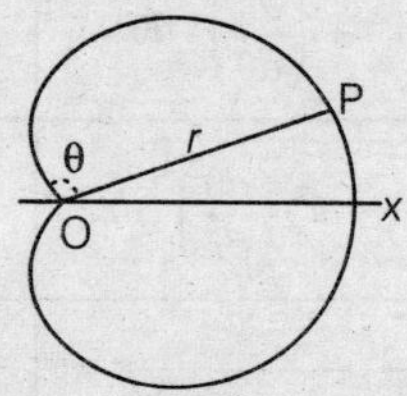

Fig. 11.

The curve is symmetrical about the initial line, and θ varies from 0 to π for the upper half.

$$\frac{dr}{d\theta} = a\sin\theta .$$

Hence $$\text{arc} = 2\int_0^{\pi} \sqrt{a^2(1 - \cos\theta)^2 + a^2\sin^2\theta\, d\theta}$$

$$= 2a\cdot\int_0^{\pi} 2\sin\frac{\theta}{2} d\theta = \left[-8a\cos\frac{\theta}{2}\right]_0^{\pi} = 8a$$

Ex. 4. Find the length of the arc of the equiangular spiral $p = r\sin a$ between the points at which the radii vectores are r_1 and r_2.

Here $$\text{arc} = \int_{r_1}^{r_2} \frac{r\, dr}{\sqrt{r^2 - r^2\sin^2 a}} = \frac{r_2 - r_1}{\cos a}.$$

Ex. 5. Find the length of any arc of the involute of a circle, whose equation is $p = A\psi + B$.

Here $$s = \left[\frac{dp}{d\psi} + \int p d\psi\right]_{\psi_1}^{\psi_2}$$

$$= \frac{A}{2}(\psi_2^2 - \psi_1^2) + B(\psi_2 - \psi_1),$$

where ψ_1 and ψ_2 are the values of ψ at the beginning and end of the arc respectively.

120. Formula for Closed Curve.

In using the formula

$$s = \frac{dp}{d\psi} + \int p\,d\psi$$

in the case of a closed oval, the origin being within the curve, it may be observed that the length of the whole contour is given by $\int_0^{2\pi} p\,d\psi$, for the portion $\left[\frac{dp}{d\psi}\right]$ disappears when the limits are taken.

Ex. Show that the perimeter of an ellipse of small eccentricity e exceeds by $\frac{3e^4}{64}$ of its length that of a circle having the same area.

[γ, 1889.]

Here $p^2 = a^2\cos^2\alpha + b^2\sin^2\alpha = a^2(1 - e^2\sin^2\alpha) = a^2(1 - e^2\cos^2\psi)$,

where α is the angle which p makes with the major axis.

Hence $$p = a\left(1 - \frac{1}{2}e^2\cos^2\psi - \frac{1}{8}e^4\cos^4\psi - \ldots\right)$$

Hence $$s = 4a\left\{\frac{\pi}{2} - \frac{1}{2}e^2\cdot\frac{1}{2}\frac{\pi}{2} - \frac{1}{8}e^4\cdot\frac{3}{4}\frac{1}{2}\frac{\pi}{2} - \ldots\right\}$$

$$= 2\pi a\left(1 - \frac{1}{4}e^2 - \frac{3}{64}e^4\ldots\right).$$

The radius (r) of a circle of the same area is given by

$$r^2 = ab = a^2(1 - e^2)^{\frac{1}{2}},$$

and its circumference $= 2\pi a\left(1 - \frac{1}{4}e^2 - \frac{3}{32}e^4\ldots\right)$

$\therefore$ Circumf. ellipse − circumf. circle $= \left(\frac{3}{16} - \frac{3}{32}\right)\pi a e^4 = \frac{3e^4}{64}\cdot 2\pi a$

$= \frac{3e^4}{64}$ [circ. of circle], as far as terms involving e^4.

EXAMPLES

1. Find by integration the length of the arc of the circle $x^2 + y^2 = a^2$, intercepted between the points where $x = a\cos\alpha$ and $x = a\cos\beta$.
2. Show that in the catenary $y = c\cosh\frac{x}{c}$ the length of arc from the vertex (where $x = 0$) to any point is given by $s = c\sinh\frac{x}{c}$.

3. In the evolute of a parabola, viz., $4(x-2a)^3 = 27ay^2$, show that the length of the curve from its cusp $(x = 2a)$ to the point where it meets the parabola is $2a(3\sqrt{3}-1)$.

4. Show that the length of the arc of the cycloid, $\left.\begin{array}{l} x = a(\theta + \sin\theta), \\ y = a(1-\cos\theta), \end{array}\right\}$ between the points for which $\theta = 0$ and $\theta = 2\psi$, is $s = 4a\sin\psi$.

5. Show that in the epicycloid for which

$$\left.\begin{array}{l} x = (a+b)\cos\theta - b\cos\dfrac{a+b}{b}\theta, \\ y = (a+b)\sin\theta - b\sin\dfrac{a+b}{b}\theta, \end{array}\right\}$$

$s = \dfrac{4b(a+b)}{a}\cos\dfrac{a}{2b}\theta$, s being measured from the point at which $\theta = \pi b/a$. When $b = -\dfrac{a}{4}$, show that $x^{\frac{2}{3}} + y^{\frac{2}{3}} = a^{\frac{2}{3}}$; and that if s be measured from a cusp which lies on the y-axis, $s^3 \propto x^2$.

6. Show that in the ellipse $x = a\cos\theta$, $y = b\sin\theta$, the perimeter may be expressed as $2a\pi\left\{1 - \dfrac{1}{2^2}e^2 - \dfrac{1^2\cdot 3}{2^2\cdot 4^2}e^4 - \dfrac{1^2\cdot 3^2\cdot 5}{2^2\cdot 4^2\cdot 6^2}e^6 - \ldots \text{ to } \infty\right\}$.

7. Find the length of any arc of the curves

(i.) $r = a\cos\theta$. (ii.) $r = ae^{m\theta}$.

(iii.) $r = a\theta$. (iv.) $r = a\sin^2\dfrac{\theta}{2}$.

8. Apply the formula $s = \dfrac{dp}{d\psi} + \int p\,d\psi$ to rectify the cardioide whose equation is $r = a(1+\cos\theta)$. [TRINITY, 1888.]

9. Two radii vectores OP, OQ of the curve $r = 2a\cos^3\left(\dfrac{\pi}{4} + \dfrac{\theta}{3}\right)$ are drawn equally inclined to the initial line; prove that the length of the intercepted arc is $a\alpha$, where α is the circular measure of the angle POQ. [ASPARAGUS, *Educ. Times.*]

10. Show that the length of an arc of the curve $y^n = x^{m+n}$ can be found in finite terms in the cases when $\dfrac{n}{2m}$ or $\dfrac{n}{2m} + \dfrac{1}{2}$ is an integer.

11. Find the length of the arc between two consecutive cusps of the curve $(c^2 - a^2)p^2 = c^2(r^2 - a^2)$. [Epicycloid.]

12. Find the whole length of the loop of the curve $3ay^2 = x(x-a)^2$. [OXFORD, 1889.]

13. Show that the length of the arc of the hyperbola $xy = a^2$ between the limits $x = b$ and $x = c$ is equal to the arc of the curve $p^2(a^4 + r^4) = a^4r^2$ between the limits $r = b, r = c$. [OXFORD, 1888.]

14. Show that in the parabola $\frac{2a}{r} = 1 + \cos\theta, \frac{ds}{d\psi} = \frac{2a}{\sin^3\psi}$, and hence show that the arc intercepted between the vertex and the extremity of the latus rectum is $a\{\sqrt{2} + \log(1 + \sqrt{2})\}$. [I.C.S, 1882.]

121. Length of the Arc of an Evolute.

It has been shown (*Diff. Calc. for Beg.*, Art. 157) that the difference between the radii of curvature at

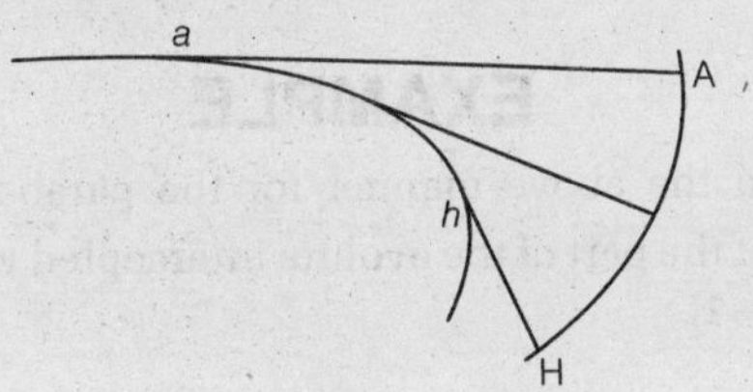

Fig. 12.

two points of a curve is equal to the length of the corresponding arc of the evolute;

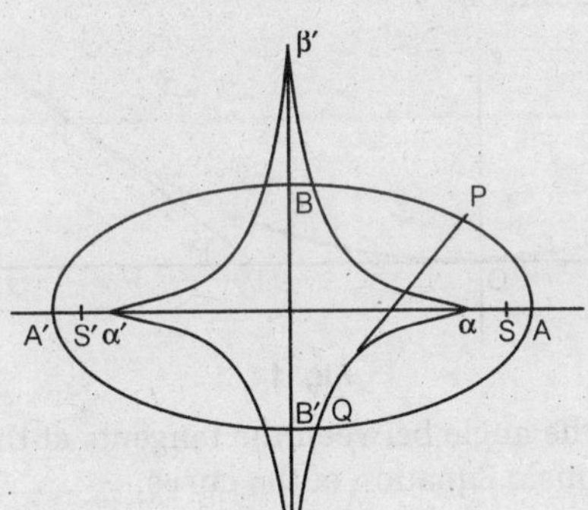

Fig. 13.

i.e., if ah be the arc of the evolute of the portion AH of the original curve, then (Fig. 12)

arc $ah = Aa - Hh$, *i.e.*, $\rho(\text{at } A) - \rho(\text{at } H)$,

and if the evolute be regarded as a rigid curve, and a string be unwound from it, being kept tight, then the points of the unwinding string describe a system of parallel curves one of which is the original curve AH.

Ex. Find the length of the evolute of the ellipse.

Let $\alpha, \alpha', \beta, \beta'$ be the centres of curvature corresponding to the extremities of the axes, viz., A, A', B, B', *respectively. The arc* $\alpha\beta$ *of the evolute corresponds to, the arc AB* of the curve, and we have (Fig. 13)

$$\text{arc} \quad \alpha\beta = \rho\,(\text{at } B) - \rho(\text{at A}) = \frac{a^2}{b} - \frac{b^2}{a}$$

[for rad. of curv. of ellipse $= \dfrac{a^2b^2}{p^3}$. Ex. 3; p.118, *Diff. Calc. for. Beg.*]

Thus the length of the entire perimeter of the evolute

$$= 4\left(\frac{a^2}{b} - \frac{b^2}{a}\right).$$

EXAMPLE

Show in the above manner for the parabola $y^2 = 4ax$ that the length of the part of the evolute intercepted within the parabola is $4a(3\sqrt{3} - 1)$.

122. Intrinsic Equation.

The relation between s, the length of the arc of a given curve, measured from a given fixed point on

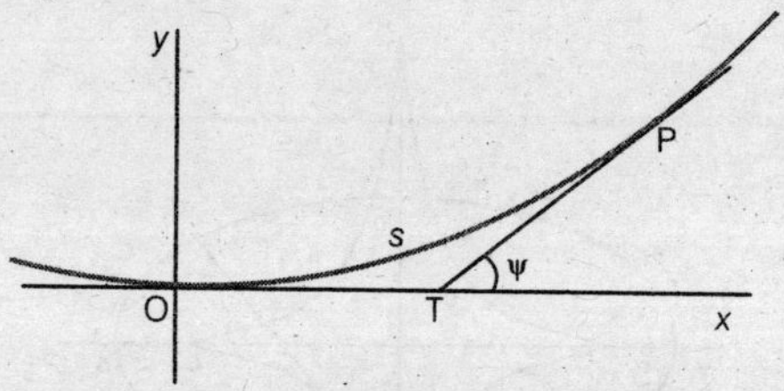

Fig. 14.

the curve, and the angle between the tangents at the extremities of the arc is called the Intrinsic Equation of the curve.

123. To obtain the Intrinsic Equation from the Cartesian.

Let the equation of the curve be given as $y = f(x)$. Suppose the x-axis to be a tangent at the origin, and the length of the arc to be measured from the origin.

Then $\qquad \tan\psi = f'(x), \qquad$ ...(1)

also $\qquad s = \int_0^x \sqrt{1 + [f'(x)]^2}\, dx \qquad$ ...(2)

If s be determined by integration from (2), and x eliminated between this result and equation (1), the required relation between s and ψ will be obtained.

Ex. 1. Intrinsic equation of a circle.

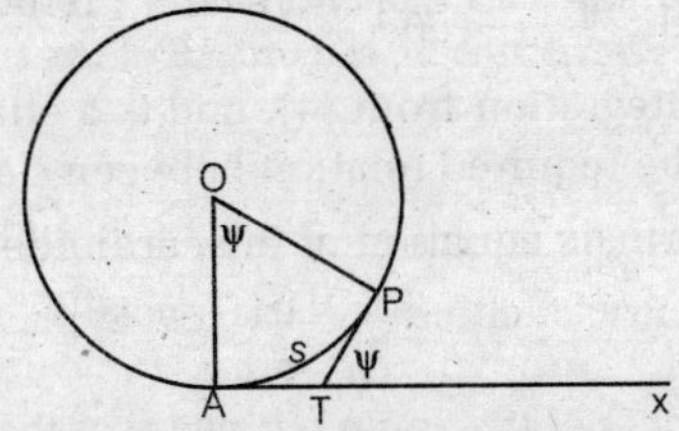

Fig. 15.

If ψ be the angle between the initial tangent at A and the tangent at the point P, and a the radius of the circle, we have

$$P\hat{O}A = P\hat{T}X = \psi,$$

and therefore $\quad s = a\psi$.

Ex. 2. In the case of the catenary $y + c = c\cosh\dfrac{x}{c}$, the intrinsic equation is $s = c\tan\psi$.

For $\quad \tan\psi = \dfrac{dy}{dx} = \sinh\dfrac{x}{c}$

and $\quad \dfrac{ds}{dx} = \sqrt{1 + \sinh^2\dfrac{x}{c}} = \cosh\dfrac{x}{c},$

and therefore $\quad s = c\sinh\dfrac{x}{c},$

the constant of integration being chosen so that x and s vanish together, whence $s = c\tan\psi$.

124. To obtain the Intrinsic Equation from the Polar.

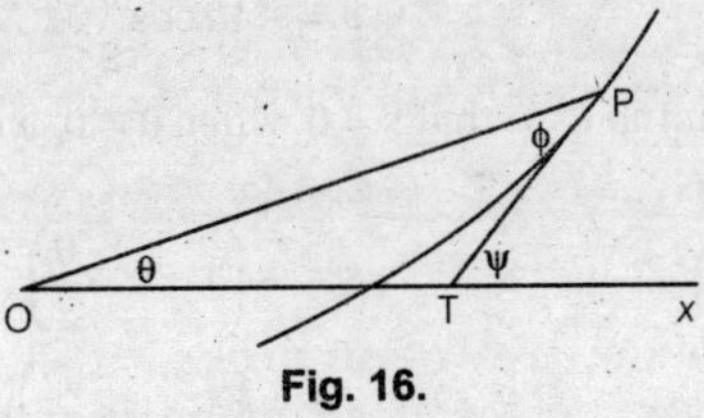

Fig. 16.

Take the initial line parallel to the tangent at the point from which the arc is measured. Then with the usual notation we have

$$r = f(\theta), \text{ the equation to the curve,} \qquad \text{... (1)}$$

$$\psi = \theta + \phi, \qquad \text{...(2)}$$

$$\tan\phi = r\frac{d\theta}{dr} = \frac{f(\theta)}{f'(\theta)}, \qquad \text{...(3)}$$

$$\frac{ds}{d\theta} = \sqrt{r^2 + \left(\frac{dr}{d\theta}\right)^2} = \sqrt{[f(\theta)]^2 + [f'(\theta)]^2}, \qquad \ldots(4)$$

If s be found by integration from (4), and θ, ϕ eliminated by means of equations (2) and (3), the required relation between s and ψ will be found.

Ex. Find the intrinsic equation of the cardioide

$$r = a(1 - \cos\theta).$$

Here $$\psi = \theta + \phi$$

and $$\tan\phi = \frac{a(1-\cos\theta)}{a\sin\theta} = \tan\frac{\theta}{2}.$$

Hence $$\phi = \frac{\theta}{2},$$

and $$\psi = \theta + \frac{\theta}{2} = \frac{3\theta}{2},$$

$\therefore$ $$\theta = \frac{2}{3}\psi.$$

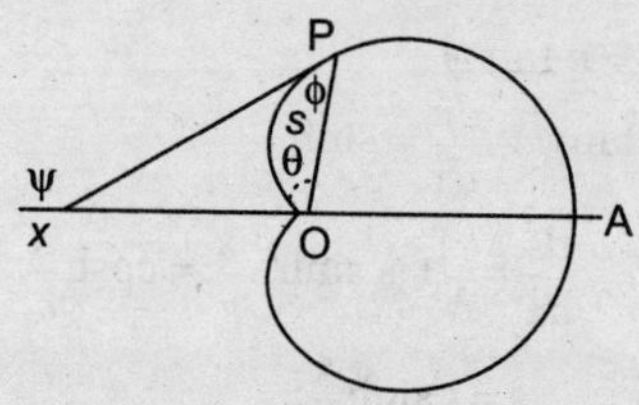

Fig. 17.

Also $$\frac{ds}{d\theta} = \sqrt{a^2(1-\cos\theta)^2 + a^2\sin^2\theta}$$

$$= 2a\sin\frac{\theta}{2},$$

and $$s = -4a\cos\frac{\theta}{2} + C.$$

If we determine C so that $s = 0$ when $\theta = 0$, we have

$$C = 4a,$$

$\therefore$ $$s = 4a\left(1 - \cos\frac{\theta}{2}\right),$$

or $$s = 4a\left(1 - \cos\frac{\psi}{3}\right).$$

the intrinsic equation sought.

We may notice that if A be the vertex, the arc AP is $4a\cos\dfrac{\psi}{3}$.

125. When the Equation of the Curve is given as

$$x = f(t),\ y = \phi(t),$$

we have $$\tan\psi = \frac{dy}{dx} = \frac{\phi'(t)}{f'(t)} \quad \ldots(1)$$

Also $$\frac{ds}{dt} = \sqrt{\left(\frac{dx}{dt}\right)^2 + \left(\frac{dy}{dt}\right)^2} = \sqrt{[f'(t)]^2 + [\phi'(t)]^2} \quad \ldots(2)$$

By means of equation (2) s may be found by integration in terms of t.

If then, between the result and equation (1) t be eliminated, we shall obtain the required relation between s and ψ.

Ex. In the cycloid

$$x = a(t + \sin t),\ y = a(1 - \cos t),$$

we have $$\tan\psi = \frac{\sin t}{1 + \cos t} = \tan\frac{t}{2},$$

$\therefore$ $$t = 2\psi.$$

Also $$\frac{ds}{dt} = a\sqrt{(1 + \cos t)^2 + \sin^2 t} = 2a\cos\frac{t}{2},$$

whence $s = 4a\sin\frac{t}{2}$ if s be measured from the origin where $t = 0$.

Hence $s = 4a\sin\psi$ is the equation required.

126. Intrinsic Equation of the Evolute.

Let $s = f(\psi)$ be the equation of the given curve. Let s' be the length of the arc of the evolute measured from some fixed point A to any other point Q. Let O and P be the points on the original curve corresponding to the points A, Q on the evolute; ρ_0, ρ the radii of curvature at O and P; ψ', the angle the tangent QP makes with OA produced, and ψ the angle the tangent PT makes with the tangent at O.

Then $$\psi' = \psi, \text{ and } s' = \rho - \rho_0 = \frac{ds}{d\psi} - \rho_0,$$

or $$s' = f'(\psi') - \rho_0.$$

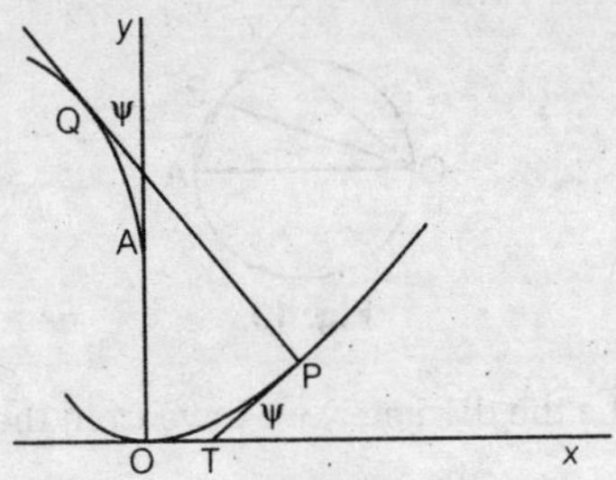

Fig. 18.

127. Intrinsic Equation of an Involute.

With the same figure, if the curve AQ be given by the equation $s' = f(\psi')$, we have

$$\rho = s' + \rho_0,\ \rho = \frac{ds}{d\psi},\ \text{and } \psi = \psi',$$

whence $$s = \int \{f(\psi) + \rho_0\} d\psi.$$

Ex. The intrinsic equation of the catenary is $s = c \tan\psi$ (Art. 123).

Hence the intrinsic equation of its evolute is

$$s = c\sec^2\psi - \rho_0,$$

and $$\rho_0 = \text{radius of curvature at the vertex}$$

$$= c\left[\rho = \frac{ds}{d\psi} = c\sec^2\psi \text{ and } \psi = 0\right],$$

$\therefore$ the evolute is $s = c(\sec^2\psi - 1)$, or $s = c\tan^2\psi$.

The intrinsic equation of an involute is

$$s = \int (c\tan\psi + A) d\psi$$

$$= c\log\sec\psi + A\psi + \text{constant};$$

and if s be so measured that $s = 0$, when $\psi = 0$, we have

$$s = c\log(\sec\psi) + A\psi.$$

128. Length of Arc of Pedal Curve.

If p be the perpendicular from the origin upon the tangent to any curve, and χ the angle it makes with the initial line, we may regard p, χ as the current polar coordinates of a point on the pedal curve.

Hence, the length of the pedal curve may be calculated by the formula

$$\int \sqrt{p^2 + \left(\frac{dp}{d\chi}\right)^2}\, d\chi.$$

Ex. Apply the above method to find the length of any arc of the pedal of a circle with regard to a point on the circumference (*i.e.* a cardioide).

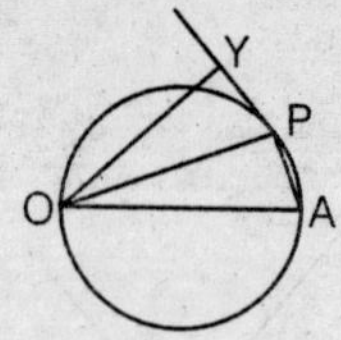

Fig. 19.

Here, if $2a$ be the diameter, we have from the figure

$$p = OP\cos\frac{\chi}{2} = 2a\cos^2\frac{\chi}{2}.$$

Hence arc of pedal

$$= \int 2\sqrt{a^2 \cos^4 \frac{\chi}{2} + a^2 \sin^2 \frac{\chi}{2} \cos^2 \frac{\chi}{2}}\, d\chi$$

$$= \int 2a \cos \frac{\chi}{2} d\chi = 4a \sin \frac{\chi}{2} + C.$$

The limits for the upper half of the curve are $\chi = 0$ and $\chi = \pi$. Hence the whole perimeter of the pedal

$$= 2\left[4a \sin \frac{\chi}{2}\right]_0^\pi = 8a.$$

EXAMPLES

1. Find the length of any arc of the curve $y^2 (a - x) = x^3$. [α, 1888.]

2. Find the length of the complete cycloid given by $\left.\begin{aligned} x &= a\theta + a \sin \theta, \\ y &= a - a \cos \theta. \end{aligned}\right\}$

3. Find the curve for which the length of the arc measured from the origin varies as the square root of the ordinate.

4. Show that the intrinsic equation of the parabola is $s = a \tan \psi \sec \psi + a \log(\tan \psi + \sec \psi)$.

5. Interpret the expressions

   (i.) $\int y \frac{dx}{ds} ds$, (ii.) $\int x \frac{dy}{ds} ds$,

   (iii.) $\int \left(\frac{x}{r^2} \frac{dy}{ds} - \frac{y}{r^2} \frac{dx}{ds} \right) ds$,

   wherein the line integrals are taken round the perimeter of a given closed curve. [ST. JOHN'S. 1890.]

6. The major axis of an ellipse is 1 foot in length, and its eccentricity is 1/10. Prove its circumference to be 3.1337 feet nearly. [TRINITY, 1883.]

7. Show that the length of the arc of that part of the cardioide $r = a(1 + \cos \theta)$, which lies of the side of the line $4r = 3a \sec \theta$ remote from the pole, is equal to $4a$. [OXFORD, 1888.]

8. Find the length of an arc of the cissoid $r = a \frac{\sin^2 \theta}{\cos \theta}$.

9. Find the length of any arc of the curve $x^{\frac{2}{3}} - y^{\frac{2}{3}} = a^{\frac{2}{3}}$.

10. Show that the intrinsic equation of the semicubical parabola $3ay^2 = 2x^3$ is $9s = 4a(\sec^3 \psi - 1)$.

11. In a certain curve $\left.\begin{aligned} x &= e^{\theta}\sin\theta, \\ y &= e^{\theta}\cos\theta, \end{aligned}\right\}$

show that $s = e^{\theta}\sqrt{2} + C.$

12. Show that the length of an arc of the curve $x\sin\theta + y\cos\theta = f'(\theta)$,

$x\cos\theta - y\sin\theta = f''(\theta)$

is given by $s = f(\theta) + f''(\theta) + C.$

13. Show that in the curve $y = a\log\sec\dfrac{x}{a}$ the intrinsic equation is $s = a\,\text{gd}^{-1}\psi.$

14. Show that the length of the arc of the curve $y = \log\cot h\dfrac{x}{2}$ between the points $(x_1, y_1), (x_2, y_2)$ is $\log\dfrac{\sin h\, x_2}{\sin h\, x_1}$.

15. Trace the curve $y^2 = \dfrac{x}{3a}(a-x)^2$, and find the length of that part of the evolute which corresponds to the loop. [ST. JOHN'S, 1881 and 1891.]

16. Find the length of an arc of an equiangular spiral $(p = r\sin\alpha)$ measured from the pole.

Show that the arcs of an equiangular spiral measured from the pole to the different points of its intersection with another equiangular spiral having the same pole but a different angle will form a series in geometrical progression. [TRINITY, 1884.]

17. Show that the curve whose pedal equation is $p^2 = r^2 - a^2$ has for its intrinsic equation $s = a\dfrac{\psi^2}{2}$.

18. Show that the whole length of the limacon $r = a\cos\theta + b$ is equal to that of an ellipse whose semi-axes are equal in length to the maximum and minimum radii vectores of the limacon.

19. Prove that the length of the nth pedal of a loop of the curve $r^{mn} = a^m \sin m\theta$ is

$$a(mn+1)\int_0^{\frac{\pi}{m}} (\sin m\theta)^{\frac{mn-m+1}{m}}\, d\theta.$$ [∈, 1883.]

20. Show that the length of a loop of the curve

$3x^2y - y^3 = (x^2+y^2)^3$ is $2\displaystyle\int_0^1 \frac{d\xi}{\sqrt{1-\xi^6}}$. [ST. JOHN'S, 1881.]

CHAPTER X.

QUADRATURE, ETC.

129. Areas. Cartesians.

The process of finding the area bounded by any portion of a curve is termed quadrature.

It has been already shown in Art. 2 that the area bounded by any curved line $[y = \phi(x)]$, any pair of ordinates $[x = a$ and $x = b]$ and the axis of x, may be considered as the limit of the sum of an infinite number of inscribed rectangles; and that the expression for the area is

$$\int_a^b y\,dx \quad \text{or} \quad \int_a^b \phi(x)\,dx.$$

In the same way the area bounded by any curve, two given abscissae $[y = c, y = d]$ and the y-axis is

$$\int_c^d x\,dy.$$

130. Again, if the area desired be bounded by two given curves $[y = \phi(x)$ and $y = \psi(x)]$ and two given ordinates $[x = a$ and $x = b]$, it will be clear by similar reasoning that this area may be also considered as the limit of the sum of a series of rectangles constructed as indicated in the figure. The expression for the area will accordingly be

$$Lt \sum_{x=a}^{x=b} PQ\,dx \qquad \text{or} \qquad \int_a^b [\phi(x) - \psi(x)]dx.$$

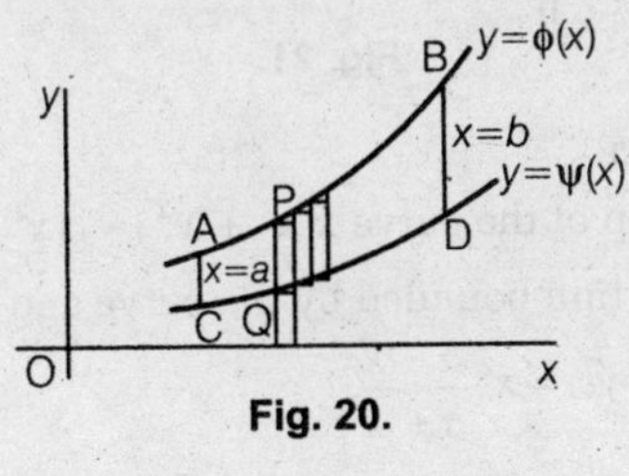

Fig. 20.

Ex. 1. Find the area bounded by the ellipse $\dfrac{x^2}{a^2} + \dfrac{y^2}{b^2} = 1$, the ordinates $x = c$, $x = d$ and the x-axis.

$$\text{Here area} = \int_c^d \frac{b}{a}\sqrt{a^2 - x^2}\,dx = \frac{b}{a}\left[\frac{x\sqrt{a^2 - x^2}}{2} + \frac{a^2}{2}\sin^{-1}\frac{x}{a}\right]_c^d$$

$$= \frac{b}{2a}\left[d\sqrt{a^2 - d^2} - c\sqrt{a^2 - c^2} + a^2\left(\sin^{-1}\frac{d}{a} - \sin^{-1}\frac{c}{a}\right)\right].$$

For a quadrant of the ellipse we must put $d = a$ and $c = 0$ and the above expression becomes

$$\frac{b}{2a}\cdot a^2\cdot\frac{\pi}{2} \quad \text{or} \quad \frac{\pi ab}{4},$$

giving πab for the area of the whole ellipse.

Ex. 2. Find the area above the x-axis included between the curves $y^2 = 2ax - x^2$ and $y^2 = ax$.

The circle and the parabola touch at the origin and cut again at (a, a). So the limits of integration are from $x = 0$ to $x = a$.

The area sought is therefore,

$$\int_0^a [\sqrt{2ax - x^2} - \sqrt{ax}]dx.$$

Now putting $x = a(1 - \cos\theta)$,

$$\int_0^a \sqrt{2ax - x^2}\,dx = \int_a^{\pi/2} a^2 \sin^2\theta\, d\theta = a^2\frac{1}{2}\frac{\pi}{2} = \frac{\pi a^2}{4},$$

and $$\int_0^a \sqrt{ax}\,dx = \sqrt{a}\left[\frac{x^{\frac{3}{2}}}{\frac{3}{2}}\right]_0^a = \frac{2}{3}a^2.$$

Thus the area required is $a^2\left(\frac{\pi}{4} - \frac{2}{3}\right)$.

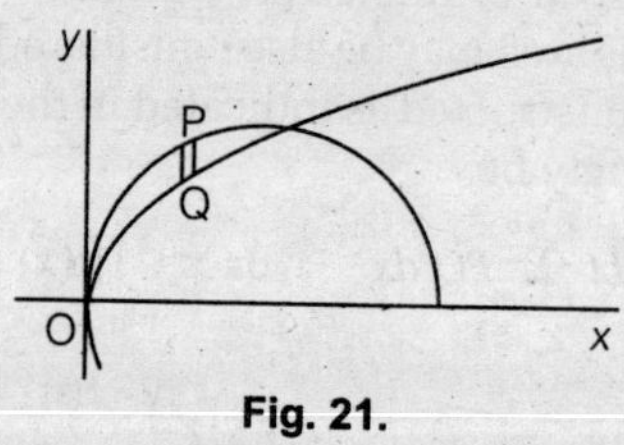

Fig. 21.

Ex. 3. Find the area

(1) of the loop of the curve $x(x^2 + y^2) = a(x^2 - y^2)$;

(2) of the portion bounded by the curve and its asymptote.

Here $$y^2 = x^2\frac{a - x}{a + x}.$$

To trace this curve we observe :—

(1) It is symmetrical about the x-axis.

(2) No real part exists for points at which x is $> a$ or $< -a$.

(3) It has an asymptote $x + a = 0$.

(4) It goes through the origin, and the tangents there are $y = \pm x$.

(5) It crosses the x-axis where $x = a$, and at this point $\frac{dy}{dx}$ is infinite.

(6) The shape of the curve is therefore that shown in the figure (Fig. 22).

Hence for the loop the limits of integration are 0 to a, and then double the result so as to include the portion below the x-axis.

For the portion between the curve and the asymptote the limits are $-a$ to 0, and double as before.

For the loop we therefore have

$$\text{area} = 2\int_0^a x\sqrt{\frac{a-x}{a+x}}\,dx;$$

for the portion between the curve and the asymptote,

$$\text{area} = -2\int_{-a}^0 x\sqrt{\frac{a-x}{a+x}}\,dx.$$

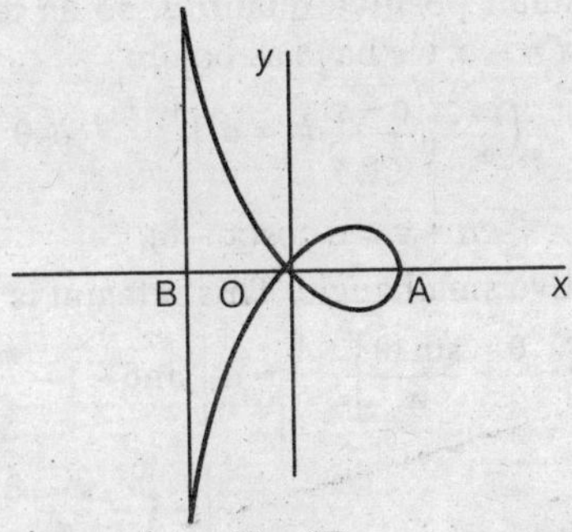

Fig. 22.

To integrate $\int x\sqrt{\frac{a-x}{a+x}}\,dx$, put $x = a\cos\theta$ and $dx = -a\sin\theta\,d\theta$.

Then $\int_0^a x\sqrt{\frac{a-x}{a+x}}\,dx = -\int_{\frac{\pi}{2}}^0 a\cos\theta\sqrt{\frac{(1-\cos\theta)^2}{1-\cos^2\theta}}\,a\sin\theta\,d\theta$

$$= a^2\int_0^{\frac{\pi}{2}}(\cos\theta-\cos^2\theta)d\theta = a^2\left(1-\frac{1}{2}\frac{\pi}{2}\right) = \left(1-\frac{\pi}{4}\right)a^2,$$

and area of loop $= 2a^2\left(1-\frac{\pi}{4}\right)$.

Again, $\int_{-a}^0 x\sqrt{\frac{a-x}{a+x}}\,dx = -\int_{\pi}^{\frac{\pi}{2}} a\cos\theta\sqrt{\frac{(1-\cos\theta)^2}{1-\cos^2\theta}}\,a\sin\theta\,d\theta$

$$= a^2\int_{\frac{\pi}{2}}^{\pi}(\cos\theta-\cos^2\theta)d\theta = -a^2\left(1+\frac{\pi}{4}\right).$$

[The meaning of the negative sign is this:— In choosing the + sign before the radical in $y = x\sqrt{\frac{a-x}{a+x}}$ we are tracing the portion of the curve below the x-axis on the left of the origin and above the axis on the right of the origin.

Hence y being negative between the limits referred to, it is to be expected that we should obtain a negative value for the expression

$$Lt \sum_{x=-a}^{x=0} y\delta x.]$$

Thus the whole area required is

$$2a^2\left(1+\frac{\pi}{4}\right).$$

[It must, also be observed in this example that the greatest ordinate is an infinite one. In Art. 2 it was assumed that every ordinate was finite. Is then the result for the area bounded by the curve and the asymptote rigorously true?

To examine this more closely let us integrate between limits $-a+\varepsilon$ and 0, where ϵ is some small positive quantity, so as to exclude the infinite ordinate at the point $x = -a$, we have as before

$$\int_{-a}^{0} x\sqrt{\frac{a-x}{a+x}}\,dx = a^2\int_{\frac{\pi}{2}}^{\pi-\delta} (\cos\theta - \cos^2\theta)d\theta$$

where $$-a+\varepsilon = a\cos(\pi-\delta),$$

so that δ is a positive small angle. This integral is

$$a^2\left[\sin\theta - \frac{\theta}{2} - \frac{\sin 2\theta}{4}\right]_{\frac{\pi}{2}}^{\pi-\delta} = a^2\left[\sin\delta - 1 - \frac{\pi-\delta}{2} + \frac{\pi}{4} + \frac{\sin 2\delta}{4}\right]$$

$$= a^2\left[-1-\frac{\pi}{4}+\frac{\delta}{2}+\sin\delta+\frac{\sin 2\delta}{4}\right],$$

which approaches indefinitely close to the former result

$$-a^2\left(1+\frac{\pi}{4}\right)$$

when δ is made to diminish without limit.]

EXAMPLES

1. Obtain the area bounded by a parabola and its latus rectum.
2. Obtain the areas bounded by the curve, the x-axis, and the specified ordinates in the following cases:—

(*a*) $y = c\cosh\dfrac{x}{c}$, $x = 0$ to $x = h$.

(*b*) $y = e^x$, $x = 0$ to $x = h$.

(*c*) $y = \dfrac{b}{a}\sqrt{a^2 - x^2}$, $x = \sqrt{a^2 - b^2}$ to $x = a$.

(*d*) $y = xe^{x^2}$, $x = 0$ to $x = h$.

(*e*) $y = \log x$, $x = a$ to $x = b$.

(*f*) $xy = k^2$, $x = a$ to $x = b$.

3. Obtain the area bounded by the curves $y^2 = 4ax$, $x^2 = 4ay$.

4. Find the areas of the portions into which the ellipse $x^2/a^2 + y^2/b^2 = 1$ is divided by the line $y = c$.

5. Find the whole area included between the curve $x^2y^2 = a^2(y^2 - x^2)$ and its asymptotes.

6. Find the area between the curve $y^2(a + x) = (a - x)^3$ and its asymptote.

7. Find the area of the loop of the curve $y^2x + (x + a)^2(x + 2a) = 0$.

131. Sectorial Areas. Polars.

When the area to be found is bounded by a curve $r = f(\theta)$ and two radii vectores drawn from the origin in given directions, we divide the area into elementary sectors with the same small angle $\delta\theta$, as shown in the figure. Let the area to be found be bounded by the arc PQ and the radii vectores OP, OQ. Draw radii vectores $OP_1, OP_2, \ldots OP_{n-1}$ at equal angular intervals.

Then by drawing with centre O the successive circular arcs PN, P_1N_1, P_2N_2, etc., it may be at once seen that the limit of the sum of the circular sectors OPN, OP_1N_1, OP_2N_2, etc., is the area required. For the remaining elements $PNP_1, P_1N_1P_2, P_2N_2P_3$, etc., may be made to rotate about O so as to occupy new positions on the greatest sector say $OP_{n-1}Q$ as indicated in the figure. Their sum is plainly less than this sector; and in the limit when the angle of the sector is indefinitely diminished its area also diminishes without limit provided the radius vector OQ remains finite.

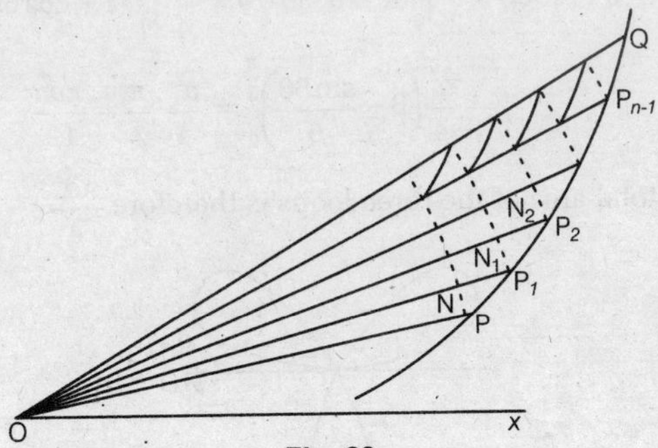

Fig. 23.

The area of a circular sector is $\frac{1}{2}$ (radius)^2 × circular meas. of angle of sector.

Thus the area required $= \frac{1}{2} Lt\Sigma r^2 \,\delta\theta$, the summation being conducted for such values of θ as lie between $\theta = xOP$ and $\theta = xOP_{n-1}$, *i.e.*, xOQ in the limit, Ox being the initial line.

In the notation of the integral calculus, if $x\hat{O}P = \alpha$, and $x\hat{O}Q = \beta$, this will be expressed as

$$\frac{1}{2}\int_{\alpha}^{\beta} r^2 d\theta \quad \text{or} \quad \frac{1}{2}\int_{\alpha}^{\beta} \{f(\theta)\}^2 d\theta.$$

Ex. 1. Obtain the area of the semicircle bounded by $r = a\cos\theta$ and the initial line.

Here the radius vector sweeps over the angular interval from $\theta = 0$ to $\theta = \frac{\pi}{2}$.

Hence the area is

$$\frac{1}{2}\int_0^{\frac{\pi}{2}} a^2\cos^2\theta \, d\theta = \frac{a^2}{2}\cdot\frac{1}{2}\cdot\frac{\pi}{2} = \frac{\pi a^2}{8}, \textit{ i.e.}, \ \frac{1}{2}\pi\,(\text{radius})^2.$$

Ex. 2. Obtain the area of a loop of the curve $r = a\sin 3\theta$.

This curve will be found to consist of three equal loops as indicated in the figure (Fig. 24).

The proper limits for making the integration extend over the first loop are $\theta = 0$ and $\theta = \frac{\pi}{3}$, for these are two successive values of θ for which r vanishes.

$$\therefore \ \text{Area of loop} = \frac{1}{2}\int_0^{\frac{\pi}{3}} a^2\sin^2 3\theta \, d\theta = \frac{a^2}{4}\int_0^{\frac{\pi}{3}} (1 - \cos 6\theta) d\theta$$

$$= \frac{a^2}{4}\left(\theta - \frac{\sin 6\theta}{6}\right)_0^{\frac{\pi}{3}} = \frac{a^2}{4}\cdot\frac{\pi}{3} = \frac{\pi a^2}{12}.$$

The total area of the three loops is therefore $\frac{\pi a^2}{4}$.

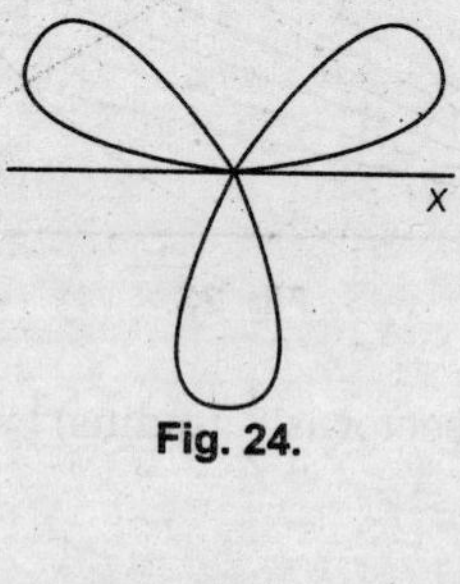

Fig. 24.

EXAMPLES

Find the areas bounded by

1. $r^2 = a^2 \cos^2\theta + b^2 \sin^2\theta$.
2. One loop of $r = a \sin 2\theta$.
3. One loop of $r = a \sin 4\theta$.
4. One loop of $r = a \sin n\theta$.
5. The portion of $r = ae^{\theta \cot \alpha}$ bounded by the radii vectores $\theta = \beta$ and $\theta = \beta + \gamma$ (γ being less than 2π).
6. Any sector of $r^{\frac{1}{2}}\theta = a^{\frac{1}{2}}$ ($\theta = \alpha$ to $\theta = \beta$).
7. Any sector of $r\theta^{\frac{1}{2}} = a$ ($\theta = \alpha$ to $\theta = \beta$).
8. Any sector of $r\theta = a$ ($\theta = \alpha$ to $\theta = \beta$).
9. The cardioide $r = a(1 - \cos\theta)$.
10. If s be the length of the curve $r = a \tanh\frac{\theta}{2}$ between the origin and $\theta = 2\pi$, and A the area between the same points, show that $A = a(s - a\pi)$. [OXFORD, 1888.]

132. Area of a Closed Curve.

Let (x, y) be the Cartesian coordinates of any point P on a closed curve; $(x + \delta x, y + \delta y)$ those of an adjacent point Q. Let (r, θ), $(r + \delta r, \theta + \delta\theta)$ be the corresponding polar coordinates. Also, we shall suppose that in travelling along the curve from P to Q along the infinitesimal are PQ the direction of rotation of the radius vector OP is counter-clockwise (*i.e.* that the

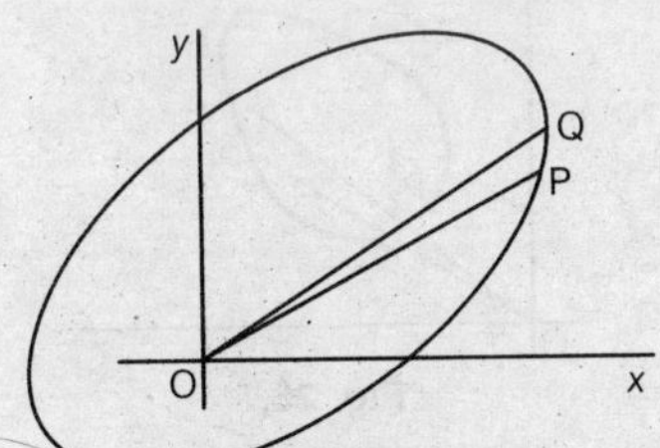

Fig. 25.

area is on the *left* hand to a person travelling in this direction). Then the element

$$\frac{1}{2}r^2\delta\theta = \Delta OPQ = \frac{1}{2}(x\,\delta y - y\,\delta x).$$

Hence another expression for the area of a closed curve is

$$\frac{1}{2}\int(xdy - ydx),$$

the limits being such that the point (x, y) travels once completely round the curve.

133. If we put $y = vx$ so that $\frac{xdy - ydx}{x^2} = dv$, we may write the above expression as $\frac{1}{2}\int x^2 dv$, where x is to be expressed in terms of v and the limits of integration so chosen that the current point (x, y) travels once completely round the curve. As v is really $\tan\theta$ and becomes infinite when θ is a right angle care must be taken not to integrate *through* the value ∞.

Ex. Find by this method the area of the ellipse

$$x^2/a^2 + y^2/b^2 = 1.$$

Putting $y = vx$, we have $x^2\left(\frac{1}{a^2} + \frac{v^2}{b^2}\right) = 1$

and area $= \frac{1}{2}\int x^2 dv = \frac{1}{2}\int \frac{b^2 dv}{\frac{b^2}{a^2} + v^2} = \left[\frac{ab}{2}\tan^{-1}\frac{av}{b}\right]$

between properly chosen limits.

Now, in the first quadrant v varies from 0 to ∞. Hence

area of quadrant $= \frac{ab}{2}\cdot\frac{\pi}{2}$,

and therefore area of ellipse $= \pi ab$.

134. If the origin lie without the curve, as the current point P travels round we obtain triangular elements such as OP_1Q_1, including portions of space such as OP_2Q_2 shown in the figure which lie outside

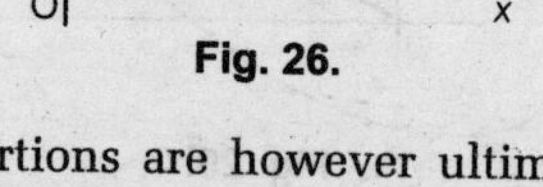

Fig. 26.

the curve. These portions are however ultimately removed from the whole integral when the point P travels over the element P_2Q_2, for the triangular element OP_2Q_2 is reckoned negatively as θ is decreasing and $\delta\theta$ is negative.

135. If however the curve cross itself, the expression

$\frac{1}{2}\int(xdy - ydx)$, taken round the whole perimeter, no longer represents the sum of the areas of the several loops. For draw two contiguous radii vectores OP_1, OQ_1 cutting the curve again at Q_2, P_3, Q_4 and P_2, Q_3, P_4 respectively. Then in travelling continuously through the complete perimeter we obtain positive elements, such as OP_1Q_1 and OP_3Q_3, and negative elements such as OP_2Q_2 and OP_4Q_4.

Now $\quad OP_1Q_1 - OP_2Q_2 + OP_3Q_3 - OP_4Q_4$ = quadl. $P_1Q_1P_4Q_4$ – quadl. $P_2Q_2P_3Q_3$, and in integrating for the whole curve we therefore obtain the difference of the two loops.

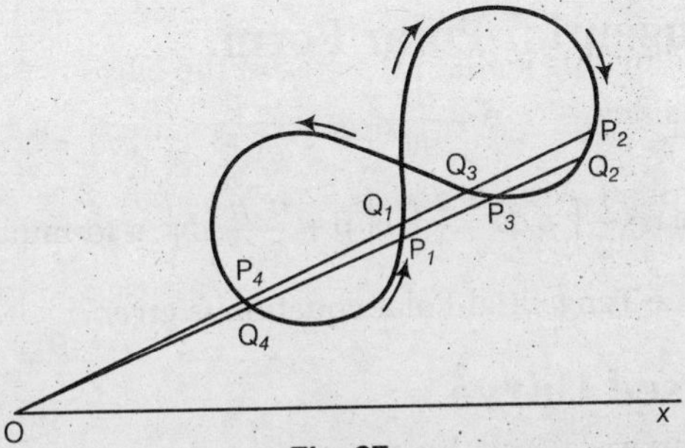

Fig. 27.

Similarly, if the curve cuts itself more than once, this integral gives the difference of the sum of the odd loops and the sum of the even loops.

To obtain the absolute area of such a curve we must therefore obtain that of each loop separately and then add the results.

Of course in curves with several *equal* loops it is sufficient to find the area of any one, and to ascertain the number of such loops.

136. Other Expressions for an Area.

Many other expressions may be deduced for the area of a plane curve, or proved independently, specially adapted to the cases when the curve is defined by other systems of coordinates.

If PQ be an element δs of a plane curve, and OY the perpendicular from the pole on the chord PQ,

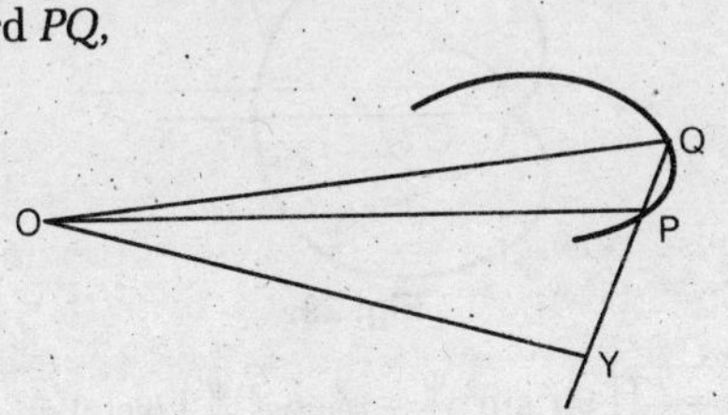

Fig. 28.

$\Delta OPQ = \frac{1}{2} OY \cdot PQ$, and any sectorial area $= \frac{1}{2} Lt \Sigma OY \cdot PQ$ the summation being conducted along the whole bounding arc. In the notation of the Integral Calculus this is $\frac{1}{2}\int p\, ds$.

[This may be at once deduced from $\frac{1}{2}\int r^2 d\theta$, thus:—

$$\int r^2 d\theta = \int r^2 \frac{d\theta}{ds} ds = \int r \sin\phi \, ds$$

(where ϕ is the angle between the tangent and the radius vector)

$$= \int p\, ds.]$$

137. Tangential-Polar Form.

Again, since $\rho = \dfrac{ds}{d\psi} = p + \dfrac{d^2 p}{d\psi^2}$,

we have area $= \frac{1}{2}\int p\, ds = \frac{1}{2}\int p\left(p + \frac{d^2p}{d\psi^2}\right) d\psi$, a formula suitable for use when the Tangential-Polar equation is given.

138. Closed Curve.

When the curve is closed this expression admits of some simplification.

For $\displaystyle\int p \frac{d^2 p}{d\psi^2} d\psi = \left[p \frac{dp}{d\psi}\right] - \int \left(\frac{dp}{d\psi}\right)^2 d\psi$,

and in integrating round the whole perimeter the first term disappears. Hence when the curve is *closed* we have

$$\text{area} = \frac{1}{2}\int \left\{p^2 - \left(\frac{dp}{d\psi}\right)^2\right\} d\psi.$$

Ex. By Ex. 23, p. 89, *Diff. Calc. for Beginners*, the equation of the one-cusped epicycloid (*i.e.*, the cardioide) may be expressed as

$$p = 3a \sin\frac{\psi}{3}.$$

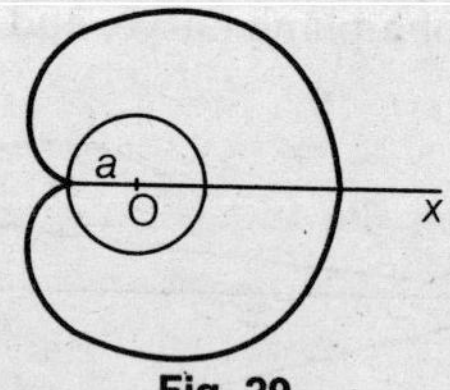

Fig. 29.

Hence its whole area $= \frac{1}{2}\int\left(9a^2 \sin^2\frac{\psi}{3} - a^2\cos^2\frac{\psi}{3}\right) d\psi$ taken between limits $\psi = 0$ and $\psi = \dfrac{3\pi}{2}$ and doubled.

Putting $\psi = 3\theta$, this becomes $= 3a^2 \int_0^{\frac{\pi}{2}} (9\sin^2\theta - \cos^2\theta)\, d\theta = 6\pi a^2$.

139. Pedal Equation.

Again, for curves given by their pedal equations, we have

$$A=\frac{1}{2}\int p\,ds=\frac{1}{2}\int p\frac{ds}{dr}dr=\frac{1}{2}\int p\sec\phi\,dr=\frac{1}{2}\int\frac{rp}{\sqrt{r^2-p^2}}dr.$$

Ex. In the equiangular spiral $p=r\sin a$.

Hence any sectorial area $=\frac{1}{2}\int_{r_1}^{r_2}\frac{r^2\sin a\,dr}{r\cos a}=\frac{1}{4}(r_2^2-r_1^2)\tan\alpha.$

140. Area included between a curve, two radii of curvature and the evolute.

In this case we take as our element of area the elementary triangle contained by two contiguous radii of curvature and the infinitesimal arc ds of the curve.

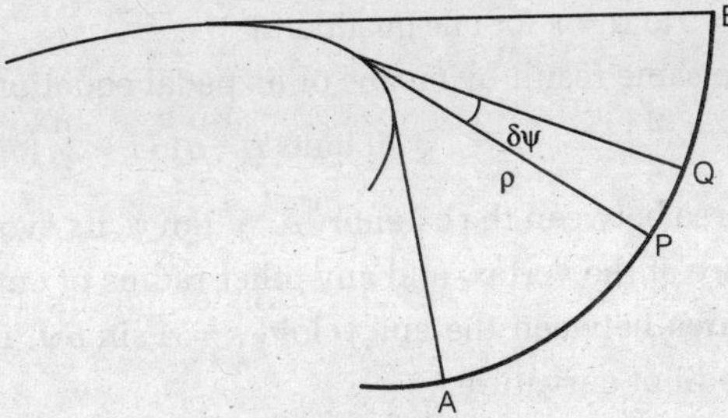

Fig. 30.

To first order infinitesimals this is $\frac{1}{2}\rho^2\delta\psi$, and the area

$$=Lt\Sigma\frac{1}{2}\rho^2\delta\psi,\text{ i.e. }\frac{1}{2}\int\rho^2d\psi\text{ or }\frac{1}{2}\int\rho\,ds.$$

Ex. 1. The area between a circle, its involute, and a tangent to the circle is (Fig. 31)

$$\frac{1}{2}\int_0^{\psi}(a\psi)^2d\psi=\frac{a^2\psi^3}{6}.$$

Ex. 2. The area between the tractrix and its asymptote is found in a similar manner.

The tractrix is a curve such that the portion of its tangent between the point of contact and the x-axis is of constant length c.

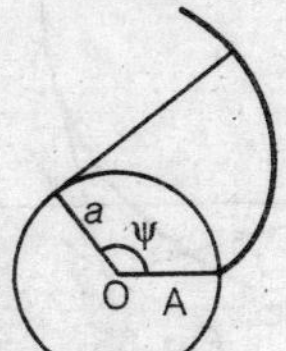

Fig. 31.

Taking two adjacent tangents and the axis of x as forming as elemental triangle (Fig. 32)

$$\text{area} = 2 \cdot \frac{1}{2}\int_{\frac{\pi}{2}}^{\pi} c^2 d\psi = \frac{\pi c^2}{2}.$$

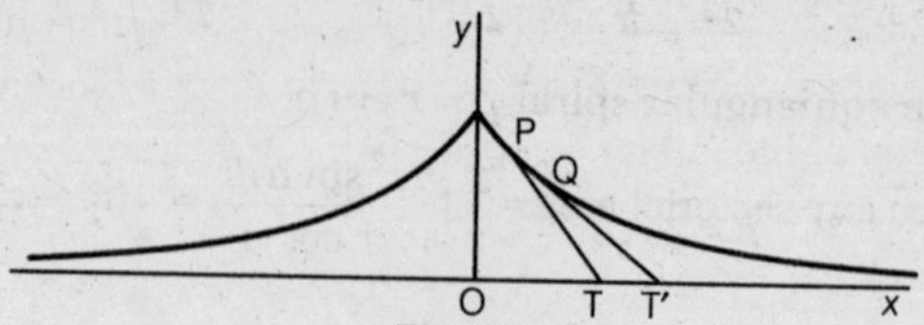

Fig. 32.

EXAMPLES

1. Find the area of the two-cusped epicycloid $p = 2a \sin \frac{\psi}{2}$.

   [Limits $\psi = 0$ to $\psi = \pi$ for one quadrant.]

2. Obtain the same result by means of its pedal equation

   $r^2 = a^2 + \frac{3}{4}p^2$. [Limits $r = a$ to $r = 2a$ for one quadrant.]

3. Find the area between the catenary $s = c \tan \psi$, its evolute, the radius of curvature at the vertex, and any other radius of curvature.

4. Find the area between the epicycloid $s = A \sin B\psi$, its evolute, and any two radii of curvature.

5. Find the area between the equiangular spiral $s = A_e B\psi$, its evolute, and any two radii of curvature.

AREAS OF PEDALS.

141. Area of Pedal Curve.

If $p = f(\psi)$ be the tangential-polar equation (*Diff. Calc. for Beginners*, Art. 130) of a given curve, $\delta\psi$ will be the angle between the perpendiculars on two contiguous tangents, and the area of the pedal may be expressed as $\frac{1}{2}\int p^2 d\psi$ (compare Art. 131).

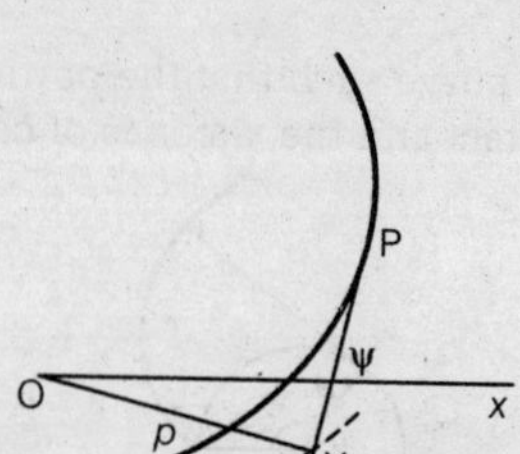

Fig. 33.

Ex. Find the area of the pedal of a circle with regard to a point on the circumference (the cardioide).

Here if OY be the perpendicular on the tangent at P, and OA the diameter (= $2a$), it is geometrically obvious that OP bisects the angle AOY. Hence, calling $Y\hat{O}A = \psi$, we have for the tangential polar equation of the circle

$$p = 2a\cos^2\frac{\psi}{2}.$$

Hence $$\text{area} = \frac{1}{2}\int 4a^2\cos^4\frac{\psi}{2}d\psi,$$

where the limits are to be taken as 0 and π, and the result to be doubled so as to include the lower portion of the pedal.

Thus $$A = 4a^2\int_0^{\pi}\cos^4\frac{\psi}{2}d\psi = 4a^2\cdot 2\int_0^{\frac{\pi}{2}}\cdot\cos^4\theta\, d\theta = 8a^2\,\frac{3}{4}\frac{1}{2}\frac{\pi}{2} = \frac{3}{2}\pi a^2.$$

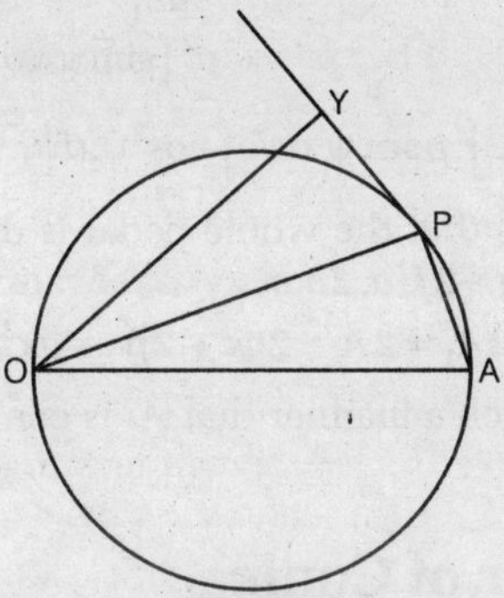

Fig. 34.

142. Locus of Origins of Pedals of given Area.

Let O be a fixed point. Let p, ψ be the polar coordinates of the foot of a perpendicular OY upon any tangent to a given curve.

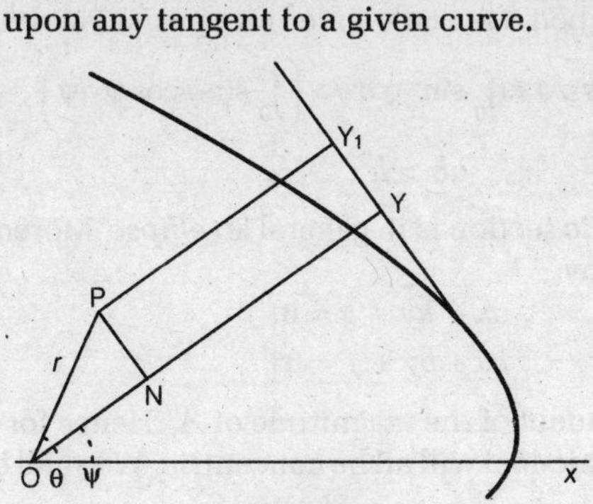

Fig. 35.

Let P be any other fixed point, $PY_1(=p_1)$ the perpendicular from P upon the tangent. Then the areas of the pedals with O and P, respectively as origins are

$$\frac{1}{2}\int p^2 d\psi \quad \text{and} \quad \frac{1}{2}\int p_1^2 d\psi$$

taken between certain definite limits. Call these areas A and A_1, respectively. Let r, θ be the polar coordinates of P with regard to O, and x, y their Cartesian equivalents. Then

$$p_1 = p - r\cos(\theta - \psi) = p - x\cos\psi - y\sin\psi,$$

and p is a known function of ψ. Hence

$$\begin{aligned} 2A_1 = \int p_1^2 d\psi &= \int (p - x\cos\psi - y\sin\psi)^2 d\psi \\ &= \int p^2 d\psi - 2x\int p\cos\psi d\psi - 2y\int p\sin\psi d\psi \\ &\quad + x^2\int\cos^2\psi d\psi + 2xy\int\cos\psi\sin\psi\, d\psi \\ &\quad + y^2\int\sin^2\psi\, d\psi. \end{aligned}$$

Now $2\int p\cos\psi\, d\psi, 2\int p\sin\psi\, d\psi, \int\cos^2\psi\, d\psi, \ldots$

between such limits that the whole pedal is described will be definite constants. Call them $-2g, -2f, a, 2h, b$,

and we thus obtain $2A_1 = 2A + 2gx + 2fy + ax^2 + 2hxy + by^2$.

If then P move in such a manner that A_1 is constant, its locus must be a conic section.

143. Character of Conic.

It is a known result in inequalities that

$$(p^2 + q^2 + r^2 + \ldots + k^2)(p_1^2 + q_1^2 + r_1^2 + \ldots + k_1^2) \nless (pp_1 + qq_1 + \ldots + kk_1)^2$$

Hence it will be obvious that if $p, q, r, \ldots,$ stand for $\cos h, \cos 2h, \cos 3h, \ldots, \cos nh$, and $p_1, q_1, r_1, \ldots$, for $\sin h, \sin 2h$, etc., we shall have in the limit when h is made indefinitely small and nh finite $= \psi$, say.

$$\int_0^\psi \cos^2\psi\, d\psi \times \int_0^\psi \sin^2\psi\, d\psi > \left(\int_0^\psi \sin\psi\cos\psi\, d\psi\right)^2,$$

i.e. $\qquad ab > h^2.$

Hence our conic section is in general an *ellipse*. Moreover the position of its centre is given by

$$\left.\begin{aligned} ax + hy + g = 0 \\ hx + by + f = 0 \end{aligned}\right\},$$

and is independent of the magnitude of A_1. Hence for different values of A_1 these several conic-loci will all be concentric. We shall call this centre Ω.

144. Closed Oval.

Next suppose that our original curve is a closed oval curve, and that the point P is within it. Then the limits of integration are 0 and 2π.

Thus $$a = \int_0^{2\pi} \cos^2\psi \, d\psi = \pi = \int_0^{2\pi} \sin^2\psi \, d\psi = b$$

and $$h = \int_0^{2\pi} \cos\psi \sin\psi \, d\psi = 0.$$

Hence the conic becomes

$$\pi(x^2 + y^2) + 2gx + 2fy + 2(A - A_1) = 0,$$

i.e. a circle whose centre is at the point

$$\frac{1}{\pi}\int_0^{2\pi} p\cos\psi \, d\psi, \frac{1}{\pi}\int_0^{2\pi} p\sin\psi \, d\psi.$$

145. Connexion of Areas.

The point Ω having been found, let us transfer our origin from O to Ω. The linear terms of the conic will thereby be removed. Thus Ω is a point such that the integrals $\int p\cos\psi \, d\psi$ and $\int p\sin\psi \, d\psi$ both vanish, and if Π be the area of the pedal whose pole is Ω we have for any other

$$2A_1 = 2\Pi + ax^2 + 2hxy + by^2$$

in the general case. The area of this conic is

$$\frac{2\pi(A_1 - \Pi)}{\sqrt{ab - h^2}}$$

(Smith's *Conic Sections*, Art. 171). Thus

$$A_1 = \Pi + \frac{\sqrt{ab - h^2}}{2\pi} \text{ (area of conic).}$$

For the particular case of any closed oval the equation of the conic becomes

$$2A_1 = 2\Pi + \pi(x^2 + y^2),$$

whence $A_1 = \Pi + \dfrac{\pi r^2}{2}$, where r is the radius of the circle on which P lies for constant values of A_1, *i.e.* the distance of P from Ω.

146. Position of the Point Ω for Centric Oval.

In any oval which has a centre the point Ω is plainly at that centre, for when the centre is taken as origin, the integrals $\int p\cos\psi \, d\psi$ and $\int p\sin\psi \, d\psi$ both vanish when the integration is performed for the complete oval (opposite elements of the integration cancelling).

147. **Ex. 1.** Find the area of the pedal of a circle with regard to any point within the circle at a distance c from the centre (a limacon).

Here $$A_1 = \Pi + \frac{\pi r^2}{2},$$

and $$\Pi = \pi a^2.$$

Hence $$A_1 = \pi a^2 + \frac{\pi c^2}{2}.$$

Ex. 2. Find the area of the pedal of an ellipse with regard to any point at distance c from the centre.

In this case Π is the area of the pedal with regard to the centre

$$= 2\int_0^{\frac{\pi}{2}} (a^2 \cos^2\theta + b^2 \sin^2\theta)\, d\theta = (a^2 + b^2)\frac{\pi}{2}.$$

Hence $$A_1 = \frac{\pi}{2}(a^2 + b^2 + c^2).$$

Ex. 3. The area of the pedal of the cardioide $r = a(1 - \cos\theta)$ taken with respect to an internal point on the axis at a distance c from the pole is

$$\frac{3\pi}{8}(5a^2 - 2ac + 2c^2).$$ [MATH. TRIPOS, 1876.]

Let O be the pole, P the given internal point; p and p_1 the two perpendiculars OY_2 and PY_1 on any tangent from O and P respectively; ϕ the angle $Y_2\hat{O}P$ and $OP = c$; then

$$p_1 = p - c\cos\phi, \text{ and } 2A_1 = 2A - 2c\int p\cos\phi\, d\phi + \int c^2\cos^2\phi\, d\phi.$$

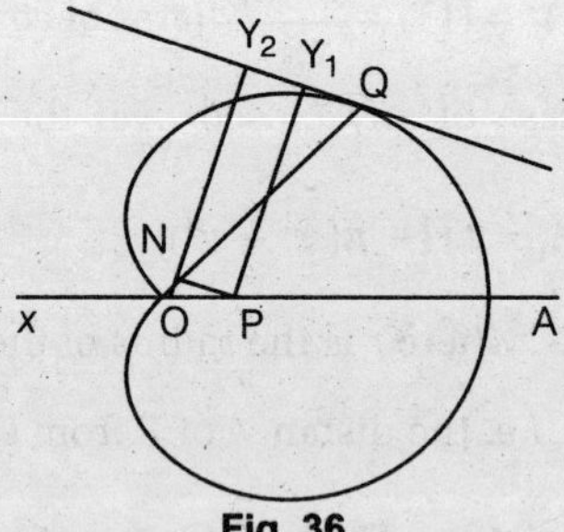

Fig. 36.

Now in order that p may sweep out the whole pedal we must integrate between limits $\phi = 0$ and $\phi = \frac{3\pi}{2}$ and double. Now in the cardioide (Fig. 36)

$$p = OQ \sin Y_2QO = OQ \sin\frac{1}{2}xOQ.$$ [*Diff. Calc.*, p. 143.]

For $\quad Y_2QO = \frac{1}{2}xOQ = \frac{\theta}{2}.$

Hence $\quad \frac{\pi}{2} - \{\phi - (\pi - \theta)\} = \frac{\theta}{2},$

or $\quad \frac{3\pi}{2} - \phi = \frac{3\theta}{2}, \quad \text{and} \quad \frac{\theta}{2} = \frac{\pi}{2} - \frac{\phi}{3},$

so $\quad p = r\sin\frac{\theta}{2} = 2a\sin^3\frac{\theta}{2} = 2a\cos^3\frac{\phi}{3}.$

Hence
$$\int p\cos\phi\, d\phi = 2\int_0^{\frac{3\pi}{2}} 2a\cos^3\frac{\phi}{3}\cos\phi\, d\phi$$
$$= 4a \times 3\int_0^{\frac{\pi}{2}} \cos^3 z\cos 3z\, dz$$
$$= 12a\int_0^{\frac{\pi}{2}} [4\cos^6 z - 3\cos^4 z]dz$$
$$= 12a\left[4\frac{5}{6}\frac{3}{4}\frac{1}{2}\frac{\pi}{2} - 3\frac{3}{4}\frac{1}{2}\frac{\pi}{2}\right] = \frac{3\pi a}{4}.$$

Also
$$\int c^2\cos^2\phi\, d\phi = 3\cdot 2c^2\frac{1}{2}\frac{\pi}{2} = \frac{3\pi c^2}{2}.$$

Finally
$$2A = 2\int_0^{\frac{3\pi}{2}} 4a^2\cos^6\frac{\phi}{3}d\phi = 24a^2\int_0^{\frac{\pi}{2}}\cos^6 z\, dz,$$
$$A = 12a^2\frac{5}{6}\frac{3}{4}\frac{1}{2}\frac{\pi}{2} = \frac{15\pi a^2}{8}.$$

Thus
$$A_1 = \frac{15\pi a^2}{8} - \frac{3\pi ac}{4} + \frac{3\pi c^2}{4}$$
$$= \frac{3}{8}\pi(5a^2 - 2ac + 2c^2).$$

148. Origin for Pedal of Minimum Area.

When Ω is taken as origin, it appears that
$$2A_1 = 2\Pi + \int (x\cos\psi + y\sin\psi)^2 d\psi.$$

Hence, as the term $\int (x\cos\psi + y\sin\psi)^2 d\psi$ is necessarily positive, it is clear that A_1 can never be less than Π. Ω is therefore the origin for which the corresponding pedal curve has a minimum area.

149. Pedal of an Evolute of a Closed Oval.

The formula for the area of any closed oval proved in Art. 138 is

$$\text{area of oval} = \frac{1}{2}\int\left\{p^2 - \left(\frac{dp}{d\psi}\right)^2\right\}d\psi.$$

Hence, $$\frac{1}{2}\int p^2 d\psi = \text{oval} + \frac{1}{2}\int\left(\frac{dp}{d\psi}\right)^2 d\psi.$$

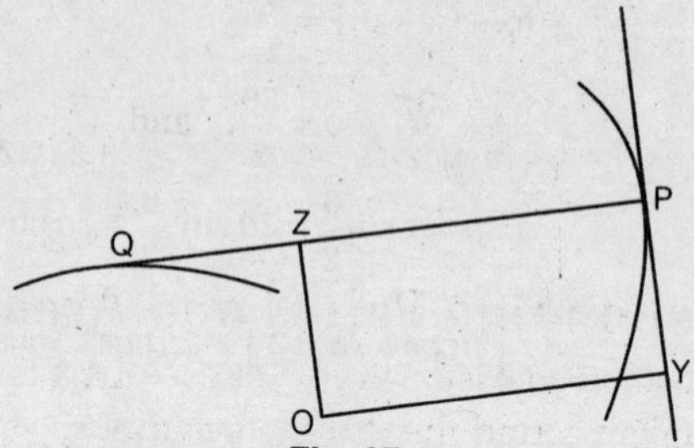

Fig. 37.

which plainly expresses that the area of any pedal of an oval curve is equal to the area of the oval itself together with the area of the pedal of the evolute (for $\frac{dp}{d\psi}$ is the radius vector of the pedal of the evolute).

This also admits of elementary geometrical proof.

Ex. Find the area of the pedal of the evolute of an ellipse with regard to the centre.

The above article shows that

area of pedal of evolute = area of pedal of ellipse – area of ellipse

$$= \frac{\pi}{2}(a^2 + b^2) - \pi ab = \frac{\pi}{2}(a - b)^2.$$

150. Area bounded by a Curve, its Pedal, and a pair of Tangents.

Let P, Q be two contiguous points on a given curve, Y, Y' the corresponding points of the pedal of any origin O. Then since (with the usual notation) $PY = \frac{dp}{d\psi}$ the elementary triangle bounded by two contiguous tangents PY, QY' and the chord YY' is to the first order of infinitesimals

$$\frac{1}{2}\left(\frac{dp}{d\psi}\right)^2 \delta\psi.$$

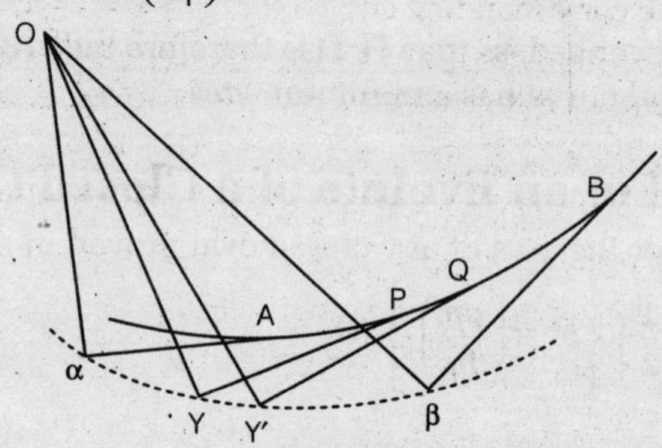

Fig. 38.

Hence the area of any portion bounded by the two curves and a pair of tangents to the original curve may be expressed as

$$\frac{1}{2}\int\left(\frac{dp}{d\psi}\right)^2 d\psi,$$

and is the *same as the corresponding portion of the area of the pedal of the evolute.*

151. Corresponding Points and Areas.

Let $f(x, y) = 0$ be any closed curve. Its area (A_1) is expressed by the line-integral $\int y\,dx$ taken round the complete contour.

If the coordinates of the current point (x, y) be connected with those of a second point (ξ, η) by the relations $x = m\xi$, $y = n\eta$, this second point will trace out the curve $f(m\xi, n\eta) = 0$ whose area (A_2) is expressed by the line-integral $\int \eta\,d\xi$ taken round its contour.

And we have $$A_1 = \int y\,dx = \int n\eta\,m\,d\xi = mn\int \eta\,d\xi = mnA_2,$$

whence it appears that the area of any closed curve $f(x, y) = 0$ is mn times that of $f(mx, ny) = 0$.

152. Ex. 1. Apply this method to find the area of the ellipse

$$\frac{x^2}{a^2} + \frac{y^2}{b^2} = 1.$$

Putting $$\frac{x}{a} = \frac{\xi}{r},\ \frac{y}{b} = \frac{\eta}{r},$$

the corresponding point ξ, η traces out the circle $\xi^2 + \eta^2 = r^2$,

and area of ellipse $= \dfrac{ab}{r^2} \times$ area of circle $= \dfrac{ab}{r^2} \times \pi r^2 = \pi ab$.

Ex. 2. Find the area of the curve $(m^2x^2 + n^2y^2)^2 = a^2x^2 + b^2y^2$.

Let $$mx = \xi,\ ny = \eta,$$

then the corresponding curve is $(\xi^2 + \eta^2)^2 = \dfrac{a^2}{m^2}\xi^2 + \dfrac{b^2}{n^2}\eta^2$,

or in polars $$r^2 = \frac{a^2}{m^2}\cos^2\theta + \frac{b^2}{n^2}\sin^2\theta,$$

the central pedal of an ellipse, symmetrical about both axes.

Hence the area of the first curve

$$= \frac{1}{mn} \times \text{area of second} = \frac{1}{mn}\cdot 2\cdot\int_0^{\frac{\pi}{2}}\left(\frac{a^2}{m^2}\cos^2\theta + \frac{b^2}{n^2}\sin^2\theta\right)d\theta$$

$$= \frac{\pi}{2mn}\left(\frac{a^2}{m^2} + \frac{b^2}{n^2}\right).$$

EXAMPLES

1. Find the area of the loop of the curve $ay^2 = x^2(a - x)$. [I.C.S., 1882.]

2. Find the whole area of the curve $a^2y^2 = a^2x^2 - x^4$. [I.C.S., 1881.]

3. Trace the curve $a^2x^2 = y^3(2a - y)$, and prove that its area is equal to that of the circle whose radius is a. [I.C.S., 1887 and 1890.]

4. Trace the curve $a^4y^2 = x^5(2a - x)$, and prove that its area is to that of the circle whose radius is a as 5 to 4.

5. Find the whole area of the curve $y^2 = x^2 \dfrac{a^2 - x^2}{a^2 + x^2}$. [CLARE, etc., 1892.]

6. By means of the integral $\int y\,dx$ taken round the contour of the triangle formed by the intersecting lines

$$y = a_1x + b_1, \quad y = a_2x + b_2, \quad y = a_3x + b_3,$$

show that they enclose the area

$$\frac{(b_1 - b_3)^2}{2(a_1 - a_3)} + \frac{(b_2 - b_1)^2}{2(a_2 - a_1)} + \frac{(b_3 - b_2)^2}{2(a_3 - a_2)}.$$ [SM. PRIZE, 1876.]

7. Find the area between $y^2 = \dfrac{x^3}{a - x}$ and its asymptote.

8. If ψ be the angle the tangent makes with the axis of x, show that the area of an oval curve is

$$\pm\int y\cos\psi\,ds \quad \text{or} \quad \mp\int x\sin\psi\,ds,$$

the integration being taken all round the perimeter.

9. Find the areas of the curves

(i) $x = a\cos^3 t, y = b\sin^3 t$; (ii) $\left(\dfrac{x}{a}\right)^{\frac{2}{5}} + \left(\dfrac{y}{b}\right)^{\frac{2}{5}} = 1$;

(iii) $\left(\dfrac{x}{a}\right)^{\frac{2}{m}} + \left(\dfrac{y}{b}\right)^{\frac{2}{m}} = 1$.

10. Find the areas bounded by

$x^2 + y^2 = 4a^2, x^2 + y^2 = 2ay, x = a$. [H.C.S., 1881.]

11. The parabola $y^2 = ax$ cuts the hyperbola $x^2 - y^2 = 2a^2$ at the points P, Q; and the tangent at P to the hyperbola cuts the parabola again in R. Find the area of the curvilineal triangle PQR. [OXFORD. 1889.]

12. Find the area common to the ellipses

$x^2 + 2y^2 = 2c^2, 2x^2 + y^2 = 2c^2$. [OXFORD, 1888.]

13. Find the two portions of area bounded by the straight line $y = c$, and the curves whose equations are

$$x^2 + y^2 = c^2, \; y^2 + 4x^2 = 4c^2.$$ [I.C.S., 1891.]

14. Find by integration the area lying on the same side of the axis of x as the positive part of the axis of y, and which is contained by the lines $y^2 = 4ax$, $x^2 + y^2 = 2ax$, $x = y + 2a$.

Express the area both when x is the independent variable and when y is the independent variable. [PETERHOUSE, etc., 1882.]

15. If A is the vertex, O the centre, and P any point on the hyperbola $x^2 / a^2 - y^2 / b^2 = 1$, prove that

$$x = a \cosh \frac{2S}{ab},\ y = b \sinh \frac{2S}{ab},$$

where S is the sectorial area AOP. [MATH. TRIPOS, 1885.]

16. An ellipse of small eccentricity has its perimeter equal to that of a circle of radius a. Show that its area is

$$\pi a^2 (1 - \frac{3}{32} e^4) \text{ nearly.}$$ [α, 1883.]

17. Find the curvilinear area enclosed between the parabola $y^2 = 4ax$ and its evolute.

18. Show that the area of the pedal of an ellipse with regard to its centre is one half of the area of the director circle.

19. Prove that the area of the locus of intersections of tangents at right angles for the curve $x^{\frac{2}{3}} + y^{\frac{2}{3}} = a^{\frac{2}{3}}$ is $\frac{1}{4} \pi a^2$. [MATH. TRIPOS, 1888.]

20. Prove that if s be the arc of the curve $\left.\begin{array}{l} r = a \sec \alpha, \\ \theta = \tan \alpha - \alpha, \end{array}\right\}$

where α is a variable parameter, measured from the initial line to a point P on the curve; and if A be the area bounded by the curve, the initial line, and the radius vector to P, then $9A^2 = 2as^3$.

21. Find the area of the closed portion of the Folium

$$r = \frac{3a \sin\theta \cos\theta}{\sin^3 \theta + \cos^3 \theta}.$$ [I.C.S., 1884.]

In what ratio does the line $x + y = 2a$ divide the area of the loop?

[OXFORD, 1889.]

22. Find the area of the curve $r = a\theta e^{b\theta}$ enclosed between two given radii vectores and two successive branches of the curve.

[TRINITY, 1881.]

23. Find the area of the loop of the curve $r = a\theta \cos \theta$ between

$$\theta = 0 \text{ and } \theta = \frac{\pi}{2}.$$ [OXFORD, 1890.]

24. Show that the area of a loop of the curve $r = a \cos n\theta$ is $\frac{\pi a^2}{4n}$, and state the total area in the cases n odd, n even.

25. Find the area of a loop of the curve $r = a\cos 3\theta + b\sin 3\theta$.

[I.C.S., 1890.]

26. Show that the area contained between the circle $r = a$ and the curve $r = a\cos 5\theta$ is equal to three-fourths of the area of the circle.

[OXFORD, 1888.]

27. Prove that the area of the curve

$$r^2(2c^2\cos^2\theta - 2ac\sin\theta\cos\theta + a^2\sin^2\theta) = a^2c^2 \text{ is equal to } \pi ac.$$

[I.C.S., 1879.]

28. Find the whole area of the curve represented by the equation $r = a\cos\theta + b$, assuming $b > a$.

29. Find the area included between the two loops of the curve $r = a(2\cos\theta + \sqrt{3})$. [OXFORD, 1889.]

30. Find the area between the curve $r = a(\sec\theta + \cos\theta)$ and its asymptote.

31. Prove that the area of one loop of the pedal of the lemniscate $r^2 = a^2\cos 2\theta$ with respect to the pole is a^2. [OXFORD, 1885.]

32. Find the area of the loop of the curve

$$(x + y)(x^2 + y^2) = 2axy.$$

[OXFORD, 1890.]

33. Prove that the area of the loop of the curve

$$x^5 + y^5 = 5ax^2y^2 \text{ is } \frac{5}{2}a^2.$$

[e, 1884.]

34. Find the whole area contained between the curve $x^2(x^2 + y^2) = a^2(y^2 - x^2)$ and its asymptotes. [OXFORD, 1888.]

35. Show that the area of the ellipse $\frac{a^2b^2}{p^2} = a^2 + b^2 - r^2$ included between the curve, the semi-major axis, and a radius vector r from the centre, is $\frac{ab}{2}\tan^{-1}\sqrt{\frac{a^2 - r^2}{r^2 - b^2}}$, a, b being the semi-axes of the ellipse.

[CLARE, etc., 1882]

36. Show that the area included between the curve $s = a\tan\psi$, its tangent at $\psi = 0$ and its tangent at $\psi = \phi$, is

$$\frac{1}{2}a^2\tan\phi + a^2\tan\frac{\phi}{2} - a^2\log(\sec\phi + \tan\phi).$$

[TRINITY, 1892]

37. Show that the area of the space between the epicycloid $p = A\sin B\psi$ and its pedal curve taken from cusp to cusp is $\frac{1}{4}\pi A^2B$.

38. Show that the curve $r = a\left(\frac{1}{2}\sqrt{3} + \cos\frac{1}{2}\theta\right)$ has three loops whose areas are $a^2\left(\frac{5}{4}\pi + 2\sqrt{3}\right)$, $a^2\left(\frac{5}{6}\pi - \frac{5}{4}\sqrt{3}\right)$, $a^2\left(\frac{5}{12}\pi - \frac{3}{4}\sqrt{3}\right)$ respectively.

[COLLEGES, 1892.]

39. Find the area of a loop of the curve $x^4 + y^4 = 2a^2xy$. [OXFORD, 1888.]

40. Find the area of the pedal of the curve [EVOl. of Ell.]

$$(ax)^{\frac{2}{3}} + (by)^{\frac{2}{3}} = (a^2 - b^2)^{\frac{2}{3}},$$ the origin being taken at $x = \sqrt{a^2 - b^2}$, $y = 0$.

[OXFORD, 1888.]

41. Find the area included between one of the branches of the curve $x^2y^2 = a^2(x^2 + y^2)$ and its asymptotes. [α, 1887.]

42. Find the whole area of the curve $x^4 + y^4 = a^2(x^2 + y^2)$. [α, 1887.]

43. Find the area of a loop of the curve

$$(m^2x^2 + n^2y^2)^2 = a^2x^2 - b^2y^2.$$ [ST. JOHN'S 1887.]

44. Trace the shape of the following curves, and find their areas:—

(i.) $(x^2 + y^2)^3 = axy^4$.

(ii.) $(x^2 + 2y^2)^3 = axy^4$. [BELL, etc., SCHOLARSHIPS, 1887.]

45. Prove that the area of $\frac{x^2}{a^4} + \frac{y^2}{b^4} = \frac{1}{c^2}\left(\frac{x^2}{a^2} + \frac{y^2}{b^2}\right)^2$ is $\frac{\pi c^2}{2ab}(a^2 + b^2)$.

46. Prove that the area in the positive quadrant of the curve

$$(a^2x^2 + b^2y^2)^{\frac{3}{2}} = mx^3 + ny^3 \text{ is } \frac{1}{3ab}\left(\frac{m}{a^3} + \frac{n}{b^3}\right).$$ [α, 1890.]

47. Prove that the area of the curve

$$(a^2x^2 + b^2y^2)^2 = c^6(x^2 - y^2) \text{ is } \frac{c^6}{a^3b^3}\left\{ab + (b^2 - a^2)\tan^{-1}\frac{b}{a}\right\}.$$

[ST. JOHN'S, 1883.]

48. Prove that the area of the curve

$$\left(c^2 + \frac{a^2y^2}{b^2} + \frac{b^2x^2}{a^2}\right)\left(\frac{x^2}{a^2} + \frac{y^2}{b^2}\right) = \left(\frac{a^2y^2}{b^2} + \frac{b^2x^2}{a^2}\right),$$

where c is less than both a and b, is $\pi(ab - c^2)$. [OXFORD, 1890.]

49. Prove that the area of the curve $x^4 - 3ax^3 + a^2(2x^2 + y^2) = 0$ is $\frac{3}{8}\pi a^2$.

[MATH. TRIPOS, 1893.]

50. Prove that the areas of the two loops of the curve

$r^2 - 2ar\cos\theta - 8ar + 9a^2 = 0$ are $(32\pi + 24\sqrt{3})a^2$,

and $(16\pi - 24\sqrt{3})a^2$. [MATH. TRIPOS, 1875.]

[Note on Ex. 45. Locus of mid-points of chords of an ellipse which touch a fixed circle.

Note on Ex. 48. Locus of mid-points of chords of length $2c$ of an ellipse. Therefore, area required $= \pi ab - \int_0^{2\pi} \frac{1}{2}c^2 d\theta$. Hence result. But the student may use Art. 151.]

CHAPTER XI.

SURFACE AND VOLUMES OF SOLIDS OF REVOLUTION.

153. Volumes of Revolution about the x-axis.

It was shown in Art. 5 that if the curve $y = f(x)$ revolve about the axis of x the portion between the ordinates $x = x_1$ and $x = x_2$ is to be obtained by the formula

$$\int_{x_1}^{x_2} \pi y^2 \cdot dx.$$

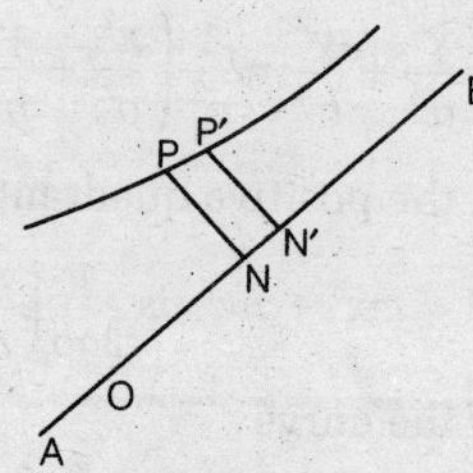

Fig. 39.

154. About any axis.

More generally, if the revolution be about any line AB, and if PN be any perpendicular drawn from a point P on the curve upon the line AB and $P'N'$ a contiguous perpendicular, the volume is expressed as

$$Lt\ \Sigma \pi PN^2 \cdot NN',$$

or if O be a given point on the line $AB = \int \pi PN^2 d(ON)$.

155. Ex. 1. Find the volume formed by the revolution of the loop of the curve $y^2 = x^2 \dfrac{a - x}{a + x}$ (Art. 130, Ex. 3) about the x-axis.

Here volume $= \int_0^a \pi y^2 dx = \pi \int_0^a x^2 \dfrac{a - x}{a + x} dx.$

Putting $a + x = z$, this becomes

$$= \pi \int_a^{2a} \frac{(z - a)^2 (2a - z)}{z} dz$$

$$= \pi\int_a^{2a}\left(\frac{2a^3}{z} - 5a^2 + 4az - z^2\right)dz$$

$$= \pi\left[2a^3 \log z - 5a^2 z + 2az^2 - \frac{z^3}{3}\right]_a^{2a}$$

$$= 2\pi\alpha^3\left[\log 2 - \frac{2}{3}\right].$$

Ex. 2. Find the volume of the spindle formed by the revolution of a parabolic arc about the line joining the vertex to one extremity of the latus rectum.

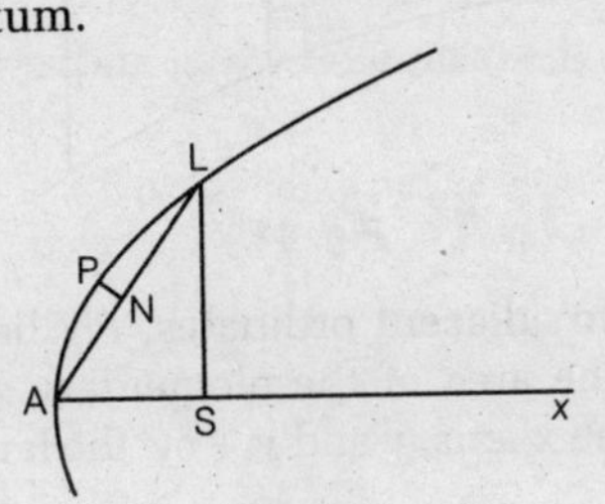

Fig. 40.

Let the parabola be $y^2 = 4ax$.

Then the axis of revolution is $y = 2x$,

and $$PN = \frac{y - 2x}{\sqrt{5}}.$$

Also $$AN = \sqrt{x^2 + y^2 - \left(\frac{y - 2x}{\sqrt{5}}\right)^2}$$

$$= \sqrt{x^2 + 4y^2 + 4xy} / \sqrt{5} = \frac{2y + x}{\sqrt{5}},$$

$\therefore$ $$d(AN) = \frac{dx + 2dy}{\sqrt{5}} = \frac{dx + 2\sqrt{\frac{a}{x}}\,dx}{\sqrt{5}},$$

$$PN = \frac{2(\sqrt{ax} - x)}{\sqrt{5}},$$

and volume $$= \int \pi PN^2 \cdot dAN$$

$$= \pi\int_0^a \frac{4}{5}x\,(\sqrt{a} - \sqrt{x})^2\left(1 + 2\frac{\sqrt{a}}{\sqrt{x}}\right)\frac{1}{\sqrt{5}}dx$$

$$= \frac{4\pi}{5\sqrt{5}} \times \frac{a^3}{6} = \frac{2\pi a^3\sqrt{5}}{75}.$$

156. Surfaces of Revolution.

Again, if S be the curved surface of the solid traced out by the revolution of any arc AB about the x-axis.

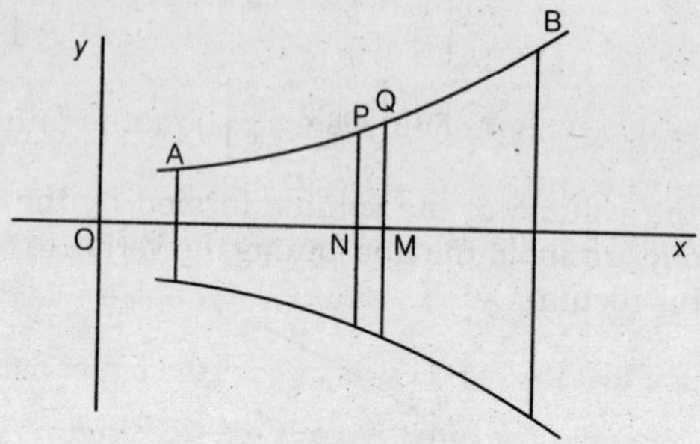

Fig. 41.

suppose PN, QM two adjacent ordinates, PN being the smaller, δs the elementary arc PQ, δS the area of the elementary zone traced out by the revolution of PQ about the x-axis, y and $y + \delta y$ the lengths of the ordinates of P and Q.

Now we may take it as axiomatic that the area traced out by PQ in its revolution is greater than it would be if each point of it were at the distance PN from the axis, and less than if each point were at a distance QM from the axis.

Then δS lies between $2\pi y\, \delta s$ and $2\pi(y + \delta y)\delta s$, and therefore in the limit we have

$$\frac{dS}{ds} = 2\pi y \quad \text{or} \quad S = \int 2\pi y\, ds.$$

This may be written as

$$\int 2\pi y \frac{ds}{dx} dx, \int 2\pi y \frac{ds}{dy} dy, \int 2\pi y \frac{ds}{d\theta} d\theta, \int 2\pi y \frac{ds}{dr} dr, \text{etc.,}$$

as may happen to be convenient in any particular example, the values of $\frac{ds}{dx}, \frac{ds}{dy}, \frac{ds}{d\theta}$, etc., being obtained from the differential calculus.

157.

Ex. 1. Find the surface of a belt of the paraboloid formed by the revolution of the curve $y^2 = 4ax$ about the x-axis.

Here $\qquad \frac{dy}{dx} = \sqrt{\frac{a}{x}} \cdot \frac{ds}{dx} = \sqrt{1 + \frac{a}{x}},$

and surface $\qquad = 2\pi \int_{x_1}^{x_2} y \frac{ds}{dx} dx$

$$= 4\pi\sqrt{a}\int_{x_1}^{x_2}\sqrt{x+a}\,dx = \frac{8\pi}{3}a^{\frac{1}{2}}\left[(x+a)^{\frac{3}{2}}\right]_{x_1}^{x_2}$$

$$= \frac{8}{3}\pi a^{\frac{1}{2}}\{(x_2+a)^{\frac{3}{2}} - (x_1+a)^{\frac{3}{2}}\}.$$

Ex. 2. The curve $r = a(1+\cos\theta)$ revolves about the initial line. Find the volume and surface of the figure formed.

Here volume $= \int \pi y^2 dx = \pi\int r^2 \sin^2\theta \, d\,(r\cos\theta)$

$$= \pi\int a^2(1+\cos\theta)^2 \sin^2\theta \, a\, d(\cos\theta + \cos^2\theta),$$

the limits being such that the radius sweeps over the upper half of the curve.

Hence volume $= \pi a^3 \int_0^{\pi} (1+\cos\theta)^2(1+2\cos\theta)\sin^3\theta\, d\theta$

$$= \pi a^3 \int_0^{\pi} (1 + 4\cos\theta + 5\cos^2\theta + 2\cos^3\theta)\sin^3\theta\, d\theta$$

$$= 2\pi a^3 \int_0^{\frac{\pi}{2}} (1 + 5\cos^2\theta)\sin^3\theta\, d\theta$$

$$= 2\pi a^3\left\{\frac{2}{3} + 5\frac{\Gamma\left(\frac{3}{2}\right)\Gamma(2)}{2\Gamma\left(\frac{7}{2}\right)}\right\} = 2\pi a^3\left(\frac{4}{3}\right) = \frac{8\pi a^3}{3}.$$

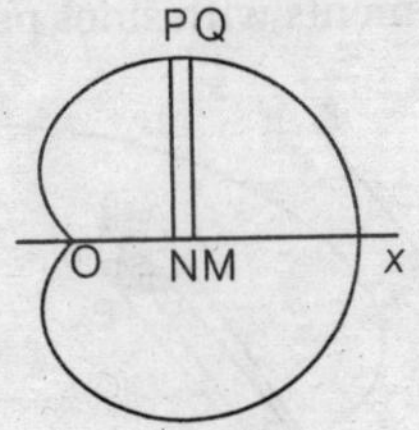

Fig. 42.

The surface $= 2\pi\int y\, ds = 2\pi\int_0^{\pi} r\sin\theta \frac{ds}{d\theta} d\theta$

$$= 2\pi\int_0^{\pi} a(1+\cos\theta)\sin\theta\sqrt{a^2(1+\cos\theta)^2 + a^2\sin^2\theta}\, d\theta$$

$$= 2\pi a^2 \int_0^{\pi} (1+\cos\theta)\sin\theta\cdot 2\cos\frac{\theta}{2} d\theta$$

$$= 16\pi a^2 \int_0^{\pi} \cos^4\frac{\theta}{2}\sin\frac{\theta}{2} d\theta$$

$$= 32\pi a^2\left[-\frac{\cos^5\frac{\theta}{2}}{5}\right]_0^{\pi} = \frac{32}{5}\pi a^2.$$

EXAMPLES

1. Obtain the surface of a sphere of radius a (i.) by Cartesians, (ii.) by polars, taking the origin on the circumference.
2. A quadrant of a circle, of radius a, revolves round its chord. Show that the surface of the spindle generated

$$= 2\pi a^2\sqrt{2}\left(1-\frac{\pi}{4}\right),$$

and that its volume $= \dfrac{\pi a^3}{6\sqrt{2}}(10-3\pi)$.

3. The part of the parabola $y^2 = 4ax$ cut off by the latus rectum revolves about the tangent at the vertex. Find the curved surface and the volume of the reel, thus generated.

THEOREMS OF PAPPUS OR GULDIN.

158. I. *When any closed curve revolves about a line in its own plane, which does not cut the curve, the* **volume** *of the ring formed is equal to that of a cylinder whose base is the curve and whose height is the length of the path of the centroid of the* **area** *of the curve.*

Let the x-axis be the axis of rotation. Divide the area (A) up into infinitesimal rectangular elements with sides parallel to the coordinate axes, such as

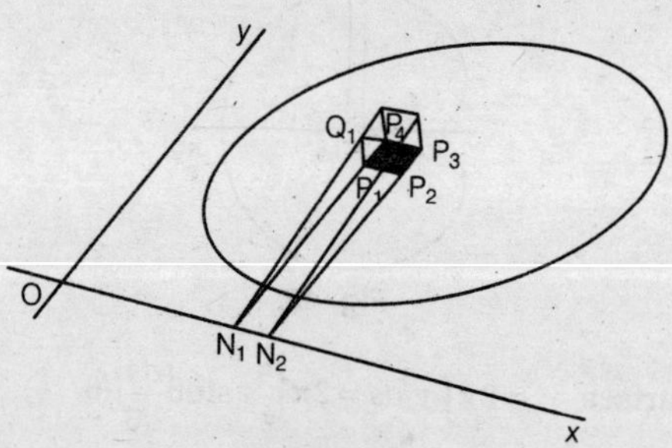

Fig. 43.

$P_1P_2P_3P_4$, each of area δA. Let the ordinate $P_1N_1 = y$. Let rotation take place through an infinitesimal angle $\delta\theta$. Then the elementary solid formed is on base δA and its height to first order infinitesimals is $y\delta\theta$, and therefore to infinitesimals of the third order its volume is $\delta A \cdot y\delta\theta$.

If the rotation be through any finite angle α we obtain by summation $\delta A \cdot y \cdot \alpha$.

If this be integrated over the whole area of the curve we have for the volume of the solid formed

$$\alpha\int y\, dA.$$

Now, the formula for the ordinate of the centroid of a number of masses $m_1, m_2, \ldots$, with ordinates $y_1, y_2, \ldots$, is $\bar{y} = \dfrac{\Sigma\, my}{\Sigma\, m}$. If then we seek the value of the ordinate of centroid of the *area* of the curve, each element δA is to be multiplied by its ordinate and the sum of all such products formed, and divided by the sum of the elements, and we have

$$\bar{y} = \frac{Lt\ \Sigma\, y\, \delta A}{Lt\ \Sigma\, \delta A},$$

or in the language of the Integral Calculus

$$\bar{y} = \frac{\int y dA}{\int dA} = \frac{\int y\, dA}{A}$$

Thus $\int y\, dA = A\bar{y}.$

Therefore volume formed $= A\ (a\bar{y})$.

But A is the area of the revolving figure and $a\bar{y}$ is the length of the path of its centroid.

This establishes the theorem.

COR. If the curve perform a complete revolution, and form a solid ring, we have $a = 2\pi$ and volume $= A(2\pi\bar{y})$.

159. II. *When any closed curve revolves about a line in its own plane which does not cut the curve, the curved* **surface** *of the ring formed in equal to that of the cylinder whose base is the curve and whose height is the length of the path of the centroid of the* **perimeter** *of the curve.*

Let the x-axis be the axis of rotation. Divide the perimeter s up into infinitesimal elements such as P_1P_2 each of length δs. Let the ordinate P_1N_1 be called y. Let rotation take place through an infinitesimal angle $\delta\theta$. Then the elementary area formed is ultimately a rectangle with sides δs and $y\,\delta\theta$, and to infinitesimals of the second order its area is $\delta s \cdot y\delta\theta$.

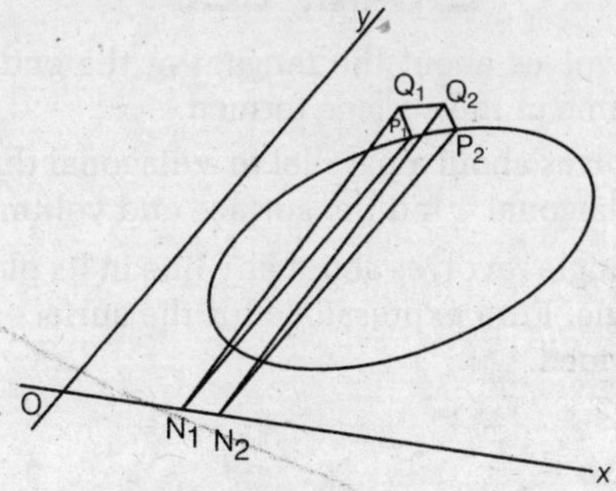

Fig. 44.

If the rotation be through any finite angle a we obtain by summation $\delta s \cdot ya$.

If this be integrated over the whole perimeter of the curve we have for the curved surface of the solid formed

$$a\int y\,ds.$$

If we seek the value of the ordinate ($\overline{\eta}$) of the centroid of the *perimeter* of the curve, each element δs is to be multiplied by its ordinate, and the sum of all such products formed, and divided by the sum of the elements, and we have

$$\overline{\eta} = \frac{Lt\,\Sigma\,y\,\delta s}{Lt\,\Sigma\,\delta s},$$

or in the language of the Integral Calculus

$$\overline{\eta} = \frac{\int y\,ds}{\int ds} = \frac{\int y\,ds}{s}.$$

Thus $$\int y\,ds = s\overline{\eta},$$

and the surface formed $= s(a\overline{\eta})$.

But s is the perimeter of the revolving figure, and $a\overline{\eta}$ is the length of the path of the centroid *of the perimeter.*

This establishes the theorem.

COR. If the curve perform a complete revolution and form a solid ring, we have $a = 2\pi$ and surface $= s(2\pi\overline{\eta})$.

Ex. The volume and surface of an anchor-ring formed by the revolution of a circle of radius a about a line in the plane of the circle at distance d from the centre are respectively

volume $= \pi a^2 \times 2\pi d = 2\pi^2 a^2 d$,

surface $= 2\pi a \times 2\pi d = 4\pi^2 ad$.

EXAMPLES

1. An ellipse revolves about the tangent at the end of the major axis. Find the volume of the surface formed.
2. A square revolves about a parallel to a diagonal through an extremity of the other diagonal. Find the surface and volume formed.
3. A scalene triangle revolves about any line in its plane which does not cut the triangle. Find expressions for the surface and volume of the solid thus formed.

160. Revolution of a Sectorial Area.

When any sectorial area OAB revolves about the initial line we may divide the revolving area up into infinitesimal sectorial elements such as OPQ, whose area may be denoted to first order infinitesimals by $\frac{1}{2}r^2\delta\theta$. Being ultimately a triangular element, its centroid is $\frac{2}{3}$ of the way from O along its median, and in a complete revolution the centroid travels a distance

$$2\pi\left(\frac{2}{3}r\sin\theta\right) \text{ or } \frac{4}{3}\pi r\sin\theta.$$

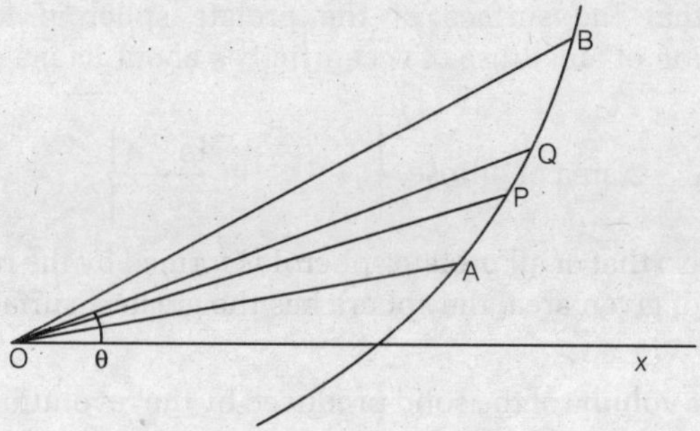

Fig. 45.

Thus by Guldin's first theorem the volume traced by the revolution of this element is

$$\frac{1}{2}r^2\delta\theta\cdot\frac{4}{3}\pi r\sin\theta$$

to first order infinitesimals, and therefore the volume traced by the revolution of the whole area OAB is

$$\frac{2}{3}\pi\int r^3\sin\theta\, d\theta.$$

161. If we put

$$x = r\cos\theta,\ y = r\sin\theta, \text{ and } t = \tan\theta,$$

we have $\quad r^3\sin\theta\,\delta\theta = r^3\sin\theta\,\delta\,(\tan^{-1}t)$

$$= r^3\sin\theta\cdot\frac{\delta t}{1+t^2} = r^3\cos^3\theta t\,\delta t = x^3 t\,\delta t,$$

and the volume may therefore be expressed as

$$\frac{2}{3}\pi\int x^3 t\, dt.$$

EXAMPLES

1. Find by integration the volume and surface of the right circular cone formed by the revolution of a right-angled triangle about a side which contains the right angle.

2. Determine the entire volume of the ellipsoid which is generated by the revolution of an ellipse around its axis major. [I.C.S., 1887.]

3. Prove that the volume of the solid generated by the revolution of an ellipse round its minor axis, is a mean proportional between those generated by the revolution of the ellipse and of the auxiliary circle round the major axis. [I.C.S., 1881.]

4. Prove that the surface of the prolate spheroid formed by the revolution of an ellipse of eccentricity e about its major axis is equal to

$$2.\text{area of ellipse.}\left\{\sqrt{1-e^2}+\frac{\sin^{-1}e}{e}\right\}.$$

Prove also that of all prolate spheroids formed by the revolution of an ellipse of given area, the sphere has the greatest surface.

[I.C.S., 1891.]

5. Find the volume of the solid produced by the revolution of the loop of the curve $y^2 = x^2\dfrac{a+x}{a-x}$ about the axis of x. [I.C.S., 1892.]

6. Find the surface and volume of the reel formed by the revolution of the cycloid round a tangent at the vertex

$$\begin{Bmatrix} x = a\theta + a\sin\theta, \\ y = a(1-\cos\theta). \end{Bmatrix}.$$

7. Show that the volume of the solid formed by the revolution of the cissoid $y^2(2a-x) = x^3$ about its asymptote is equal to $2\pi^2a^3$.

[TRINITY, 1886.]

8. Find the volume of the solid formed by the revolution of the curve $(a-x)y^2 = a^2x$ about its asymptote. [I.C.S., 1883.]

9. If the curve $r = a + b\cos\theta$ revolve about the initial line, show that the volume generated is $\dfrac{4}{3}\pi a(a^2+b^2)$ provided a be greater than b.

[α, 1884.]

10. Find the volume of the solid formed by the revolution about the prime radius of the loop of the curve $r^3 = a^3\theta\cos\theta$ between $\theta = 0$ and $\theta = \dfrac{\pi}{2}$. [OXFORD, 1890.]

11. Show that if the area lying within the cardioide $r = 2a(1 + \cos\theta)$, and without the parabola $r(1 + \cos\theta) = 2a$, revolves about the initial line, the volume generated is $18\pi a^3$.

[TRINITY, 1892.]

12. The loop of the curve $2ay^2 = x(x - a)^2$ revolves about the straight line $y = a$. Find the volume of the solid generated. [OXFORD, 1890.]

13. Show that the coordinates of the centroid of the sectorial area of $r = f(\theta)$ bounded by the vectors $\theta = \alpha, \theta = \beta$, has for its coordinates

$$\bar{x} = \frac{\frac{2}{3}\int_\alpha^\beta r^3 \cos\theta \, d\theta}{\int_\alpha^\beta r^2 d\theta}, \bar{y} \frac{\frac{2}{3}\int_\alpha^\beta r^3 \sin\theta \, d\theta}{\int_\alpha^\beta r^2 d\theta},$$

14. Show that the centroid of the cardioide $r = a(1 - \cos\theta)$ is on the initial line at a distance $\frac{5a}{6}$ from the origin.

15. If the cardioide $r = a(1 - \cos\theta)$ revolve round the line $p = r\cos(\theta - \gamma)$, prove that the volume generated is $3p\pi^2a^2 + \frac{5}{2}\pi^2a^3\cos\gamma$.

[ST.JOHN'S, 1882.]

16. The curve $r = a(1 - e\cos\theta)$, where e is very small, revolves about a tangent parallel to the initial line. Prove that the volume of the solid thus generated is approximately $2\pi^2a^3(1 + e^2)$. [I.C.S., 1892.]

17. The lemniscate $r^2 = a^2\cos 2\theta$ revolves about a tangent at the pole. Show that the volume generated is $\frac{\pi^2a^3}{4}$.

CHAPTER XII.

SURFACE INTEGRALS. SECOND-ORDER ELEMENTS OF AREA. MISCELLANEOUS APPLICATIONS.

162. Use of Second Order Infinitesimals as Elements of Area.

For many purposes it is found necessary to use for our elements of area second order infinitesimals.

163. Suppose, for instance, we desire to find the mass of the area bounded by a given curve, the x-axis, and a pair of ordinates, when there is a distribution of surface-density over the area not uniform, but represented at any point by $\sigma = \phi\,(x, y)$, say, where (x, y) are the coordinates of the point in question.

Let Ox, Oy be the coordinate axes, AB any arc of the curve whose equation is $y = f(x)$; $\{a, f(a)\}$ and $\{b, f(b)\}$ the coordinates of the points A, B upon it; AJ and BK the ordinates of A and B. Let PN, QM be any contiguous ordinates of the curve, and $x, x + \delta x$ the abscissae of the points P and Q. Let R, U be contiguous points on the ordinate of P whose ordinates are $y, y + \delta y$. And we shall suppose $\delta x, \delta y$ small quantities of the first order of smallness.

Draw RS, UT, PV parallel to the x-axis. Then the area of the rectangle $RSTU$ is $\delta x \cdot \delta y$, and its mass may be regarded (to the second order of smallness) as $\phi(x, y)\,\delta x \delta y$.

Then the mass of the strip $PNMV$ may be written

$$Lt_{\delta y = 0}[\Sigma\,\phi\,(x, y)\,\delta y]\,\delta x,$$

or in conformity with the notation of the Integral Calculus

$$\left[\int \phi(x, y)\,dy\right]\delta x.$$

between the limits $y = 0$ and $y = f(x)$. In performing this integration (with regard to y) x is to be regarded as constant, for we are finding the limit of the sum of the masses of all elements in *the elementary strip PM*, *i.e.* the mass of the strip PM.

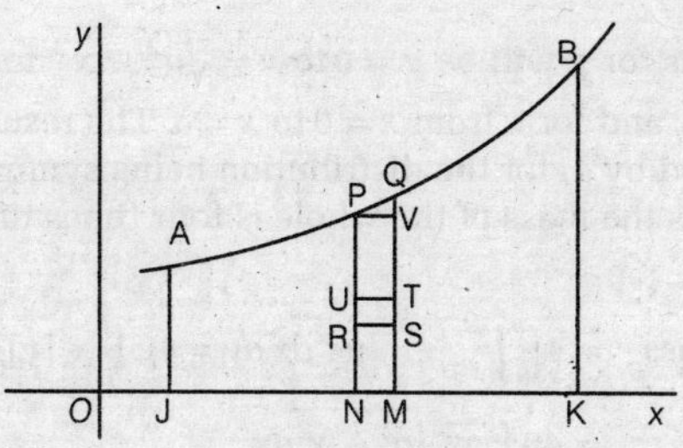

Fig. 46.

If then we search for the mass of the area *AJKB* all such strips as the above must be summed which lie between the ordinates *AJ*, *BK*, and the result may be written

$$Lt_{\delta x=0}\,\Sigma\left[\int \phi(x, y)\,dy\right]\delta x,$$

which may be written $\int\left[\int \phi(x, y)\,dy\right]dx$,

the limits of the integration with regard to x being from $x = a$ to $x = b$.

Thus mass of area

$$AJKB = \int_a^b\left[\int_0^{f(x)} \phi(x, y)\,dy\right]dx \quad \text{or} \quad \int_a^b\int_0^{f(x)} \phi(x, y)\,dy\,dx.$$

164. Notation.

This is often written $\int_a^b\int_0^{f(x)} \phi(x, y)\,dx\,dy$,

the elements dx, dy being written in the reverse order. There is no *uniformly* accepted convention as to the order to be observed, but as the latter appears to be the more frequently used notation, we shall in the present volume adopt it and write

$$\int\int \phi(x, y)\,dx\,dy$$

when we are to consider the first integration to be made with regard to y and the second with regard to x, and

$$\int\int \phi(x, y)\,dy\,dx$$

when the first integration is with regard to x. That is to say, the right-hand element indicates the first integration.

Ex. If the surface-density of a circular disc bounded by $x^2 + y^2 = a^2$ be given to vary as the square of the distance from the y-axis, find the mass of the disc.

Here we have μx^2 for the mass of the element $\delta x\,\delta y$, and its mass is therefore $\mu\, x^2\delta x\,\delta y$, and the whole mass will be

$$\int\int \mu x^2 dx\,dy.$$

The limits for y will be $y = 0$ to $y = \sqrt{a^2 - x^2}$ for the positive quadrant, and for x from $x = 0$ to $x = a$. The result must then be multiplied by 4, for the distribution being symmetrical in the four quadrants the mass of the whole is four times that of the first quadrant.

$$\text{Thus mass} \quad = 4\int_0^a \int_0^{\sqrt{a^2 - x^2}} \mu x^2 dx\, dy = 4\mu \int_0^a x^2 [y]_0^{\sqrt{a^2 - x^2}} dx$$

$$= 4\mu \int_0^a x^2 \sqrt{a^2 - x^2} dx.$$

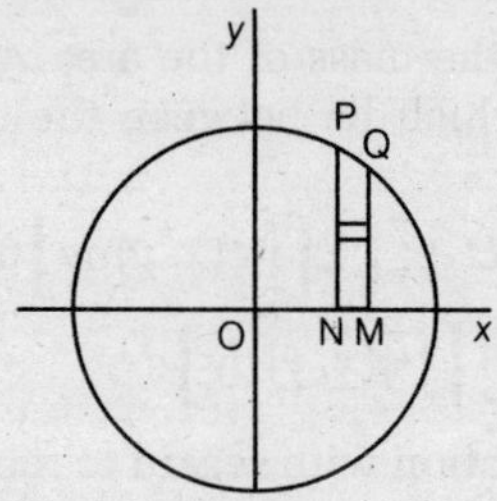

Fig. 47.

Putting $x = a \sin\theta$ and $dx = a \cos\theta\, d\theta$, we have

$$\text{mass} \quad = 4\,\mu a^4 \int_0^{\frac{\pi}{2}} \sin^2\theta \cos^2\theta\, d\theta$$

$$= 4\,\mu a^4 \frac{\Gamma\left(\frac{3}{2}\right)\Gamma\left(\frac{3}{2}\right)}{2\Gamma(3)} = 4\,\mu a^4 \frac{\frac{1}{2}\sqrt{\pi}.\frac{1}{2}\sqrt{\pi}}{2\cdot 2} = \frac{\pi\mu a^4}{4}.$$

165. Other Uses of Double Integrals.

The same theorem may be used for many other purposes, of which we give a few illustrative examples, which may serve to indicate to the student the field of investigation now open to him. But our scope in the present work does not admit exhaustive treatment of the subjects introduced.

Ex. Find the statical *moment* of a quadrant of the ellipse

$$\frac{x^2}{a^2} + \frac{y^2}{b^2} = 1$$

about the y-axis, the surface-density being supposed uniform.

Here each element of area $\delta x\, \delta y$ is to be multiplied by its surface density σ (which is by hypothesis constant in the case supposed) and by its distance x from the y-axis, and the sum of such elementary quantities is to be found over the whole quadrant.

The limits of the integration will be from $y = 0$ to $y = \frac{b}{a}\sqrt{a^2 - x^2}$ for y; and from $x = 0$ to $x = a$ for x. Thus we have

$$\text{moment} = \int_0^a \int_0^{\frac{b}{a}\sqrt{a^2 - x^2}} \sigma x \, dx \, dy = \frac{\sigma b}{a} \int_0^a x\sqrt{a^2 - x^2} dx$$

$$= \frac{\sigma b}{a} \left[-\frac{(a^2 - x^2)^{\frac{3}{2}}}{3} \right]_0^a = \frac{\sigma b a^2}{3}.$$

166. Centroids. Cartesians.

The formulae proved in statics for the coordinates of the centroid of a number of masses $m_1, m_2, m_3, \ldots$, at points $(x_1, y_1), (x_2, y_2)$ etc., are

$$\bar{x} = \frac{\sum mx}{\sum m}, \ \bar{y} = \frac{\sum my}{\sum m}.$$

We may apply these to find the coordinates of the centroid of a given area. (See also Arts. 158, 159.)

For if σ be the surface-density at a given point, then $\sigma \, \delta x \, \delta y$ is the mass of the element, and

$$\bar{x} = \frac{\Sigma(\sigma \, \delta x \, \delta y) \, x}{\Sigma(\sigma \, \delta x \, \delta y)},$$

or, as it may be written when the limit is taken

$$\bar{x} = \frac{\iint \sigma x \, dx \, dy}{\iint \sigma \, dx \, dy}.$$

Similarly $$\bar{y} = \frac{\iint \sigma y \, dx \, dy}{\iint \sigma \, dx \, dy},$$

the limits of integration being determined so that the summation will be effected for the whole area in question.

Find the centroid of the elliptic quadrant of the Example in Art. 165.

It was proved there that the limit of the sum of the elementary moments about the y-axis was $\frac{\sigma b a^2}{3}$.

Also $\iint \sigma \, dx \, dy =$ mass of the quadrant $= \frac{\sigma \pi \, ab}{4}$.

Hence $$\bar{x} = \frac{\sigma b a^2}{3} \Big/ \frac{\sigma \pi \, ab}{4} = \frac{4a}{3\pi}.$$

Similarly $$\bar{y} = \frac{4b}{3\pi}.$$

167. Moments of Inertia.

When every element of mass is multiplied by the square of its distance from a given line, the limit of the sum of such products is called the Moment of Inertia, with regard to the line.

Such quantities are of great importance in Dynamics.

Ex. Find the moment of inertia of the portion of the parabola $y^2 = 4ax$ bounded by the axis and the latus rectum, about the x-axis supposing the surface-density at each point to vary as the nth power of the abscissa.

Here the element of mass is $\mu x^n \delta x\, \delta y$,

μ being a constant, and the moment of inertia is

$$Lt\, \Sigma \mu y^2 x^n \delta x\, \delta y \text{ or } \mu \iint y^2 x^n dx\, dy,$$

where the limits for y are from 0 to $2\sqrt{ax}$, and for x from 0 to a.

We thus get

$$\text{Mom. In.} = \frac{\mu}{3}\int_0^a [y^3]_0^{2\sqrt{ax}}\, x^n dx$$

$$= \frac{\mu}{3}\int_0^a 8a^{\frac{3}{2}} x^{n+\frac{3}{2}} dx$$

$$= \frac{8\mu}{3} a^{\frac{3}{2}} \left[\frac{x^{n+\frac{5}{2}}}{n+\frac{5}{2}}\right]_0^a = \frac{16\mu}{3\,(2n+5)} a^{n+4}.$$

Again, the *mass* of this portion of the parabola is given by

$$M = \int_0^a\int_0^{2\sqrt{ax}} \mu x^n dx\, dy = \mu \int_0^a [y]_0^{2\sqrt{ax}}\, x^n dx$$

$$= 2\mu\, a^{\frac{1}{2}} \int_0^a x^{n+\frac{1}{2}} d\,x = \frac{4\mu}{2n+3} a^{n+2}.$$

Thus we have Mom. In. about $Ox = \frac{4}{3}\frac{2n+3}{2n+5} Ma^2$.

EXAMPLES

1. In the first quadrant of the circle $x^2 + y^2 = a^2$ the surface density varies at each point as xy. Find
   (i.) the mass of the quadrant,
   (ii.) its centre of gravity,
   (iii.) its moment of inertia about the x-axis.

2. Work out the corresponding results for the portion of the parabola $y^2 = 4ax$ bounded by the axis and the latus rectum, the surface-density varying as $x^p y^q$.

3. Find the centroid of a rod of which the line-density varies as the distance from one end.

   Find also the moments of inertia of this rod about each end and about the middle point.

4. Find the centroid of the triangle bounded by the lines $y = mx$, $x = a$, and the x-axis, when the surface-density at each point varies as the square of the distance from the origin.

   Also the moment of inertia about the y-axis.

168. Polar Curve. Second-order Element.

For polar curves it is desirable to use for our element of area a second-order infinitesimal of different form.

Let OP, OQ be two contiguous radii vectors of the curve $r = f(\theta)$; Ox the initial line. Let $\theta, \theta + \delta\theta$ be the angular coordinates of P and Q. Draw two circular arcs RU, ST, with centre O and radii r and $r + \delta r$ respectively, and let $\delta\theta$ and δr be small quantities of the first order. Then

$$\begin{aligned}\text{area } RSTU &= \text{sector } OST - \text{sector } ORU \\ &= \frac{1}{2}(r + \delta r)^2 \delta\theta - \frac{1}{2} r^2 \delta\theta \\ &= r\,\delta\theta\,\delta r \text{ to the second order,}\end{aligned}$$

and to this order $RSTU$ may therefore be considered a rectangle of sides δr (RS) and $r\delta\theta$ (arc RU).

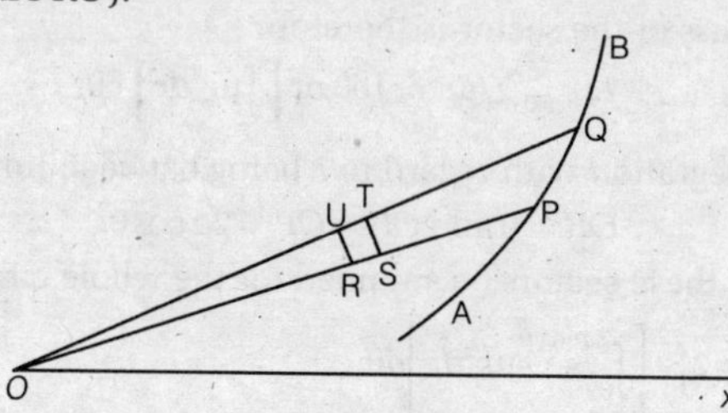

Fig. 48.

Thus if the surface-density at each point $R(r, \theta)$ is $\sigma = \phi(r, \theta)$, the mass of the element $RSTU$ is (to second-order quantities $\sigma r\,\delta\theta\,\delta r$, and the mass of the sector is therefore

$$Lt_{\delta r = 0} [\Sigma\, \sigma\, r\, \delta r]\, \delta\theta,$$

the summation being for all elements from $r = 0$ to $r = f(\theta)$, *i.e.*

$$\left[\int_0^{f(\theta)} \sigma\, r\, dr\right] \delta\theta,$$

in which integration θ is to be regarded as constant, and taking the limit of the sum of the sectors for infinitesimal values of $\delta\theta$ between any specified radii vectors OA $(\theta = \alpha)$ and OB $(\theta = \beta)$ we get the mass of the sectorial areaOAB

$$= \int_{\alpha}^{\beta}\left[\int_{0}^{f(\theta)} \sigma r\, dr\right] d\theta,$$

or as we have agreed to write it (Art. 164),

$$\int_{\alpha}^{\beta}\int_{0}^{f(\theta)} \sigma r\, d\theta\, dr.$$

Ex. Find the mass of a circle for which the surface-density at each point varies as the distance of that point from a point O on the circumference.

Taking O as the origin, and the diameter through O as the initial line, and a as the radius, the equation of the curve is

$$r = 2a\cos\theta.$$

Then we have density at R (r, θ) is μr, and mass of element $RSTU$ is $\mu r\,(r\,\delta\theta\,\delta r)$.

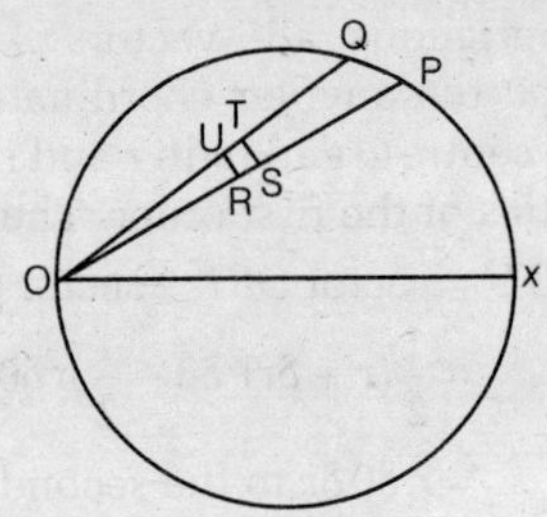

Fig. 49.

The mass of the sector is therefore

$$Lt_{\delta r=0}\, \Sigma(\mu r^2 \delta r)\,\delta\theta \text{ or } \left[\int \mu r^2 dr\right] \delta\theta,$$

the integration with regard to r being between limits

$$OR = 0 \text{ and } OR = OP = 2a\cos\theta.$$

And if these sectors be summed for the whole circle, we have

$$\text{mass} = 2\int_0^{\frac{\pi}{2}}\left[\int_0^{2a\cos\theta} \mu r^2 dr\right] d\theta$$

$$\text{or} \qquad (\text{Art. } 164) = 2\int_0^{\frac{\pi}{2}}\int_0^{2a\cos\theta} \mu r^2 d\theta\, dr$$

$$= 2\int_0^{\frac{\pi}{2}} \mu\left[\frac{r^3}{3}\right]_0^{2a\cos\theta} d\theta = \frac{2\mu}{3}\cdot 8a^3 \cdot \int_0^{\frac{\pi}{2}} \cos^3\theta\, d\theta = \frac{32\mu a^3}{9}.$$

169. Centroid. Polars.

The distance of the centroid of a sectorial area from any line may be found as before by finding the sum of the moments of the elementary masses about that line and dividing by the sum of the masses.

Thus $\sigma r\,\delta\theta\,\delta r$ being the element of mass and $r\cos\theta$ its abscissa, its moment about the y-axis is

$$r\cos\theta\cdot\sigma r\,\delta\theta\,\delta r.$$

Thus $$\bar{x}=\frac{\iint r\cos\theta\cdot\sigma r\,d\theta\,dr,}{\iint \sigma r\,d\theta\,dr},$$

and similarly $$\bar{y}=\frac{\iint r\sin\theta\cdot\sigma r\,d\theta\,dr}{\iint \sigma r\,d\theta\,dr}.$$

Ex. 1. Find the centroid of the upper half of the circle in the example of Art. 168.

We established the result for that semi-circle that

$$\iint \sigma r\,d\theta\,dr=\frac{16}{9}\mu a^3.$$

Also between the limits $r=0$ and $r=2a\cos\theta$ for r, and $\theta=0$ to $\theta=\frac{\pi}{2}$ for θ,

$$\iint r\cos\theta\ \sigma r\,d\theta\,dr=\int_0^{\frac{\pi}{2}}\mu\cos\theta\left[\frac{r^4}{4}\right]_0^{2a\cos\theta}d\theta$$

$$=4\mu a^4\int_0^{\frac{\pi}{2}}\cos^5\theta\,d\theta=4\mu a^4\,\frac{4}{5}\frac{2}{3}=\frac{32\mu a^4}{15},$$

and $$\iint r\sin\theta\ \sigma r\,d\theta\,dr=\int_0^{\frac{\pi}{2}}\mu\sin\theta\left[\frac{r^4}{4}\right]_0^{2a\cos\theta}d\theta$$

$$=4\mu a^4\int_0^{\frac{\pi}{2}}\sin\theta\cos^4\theta\,d\theta$$

$$=4\mu a^4\left[-\frac{\cos^5\theta}{5}\right]_0^{\frac{\pi}{2}}=\frac{4}{5}\mu a^4.$$

Hence $$\left.\begin{aligned}\bar{x}&=\frac{32\mu a^4}{15}\Big/\frac{16}{9}\mu a^3=\frac{6a}{5},\\ \bar{y}&=\frac{4}{5}\mu a^4\Big/\frac{16}{9}\mu a^3=\frac{9a}{20}.\end{aligned}\right\}$$

Ex. 2. Find the centroid of the area bounded by the cardioide $r = a(1 + \cos\theta)$, the surface-density being uniform.

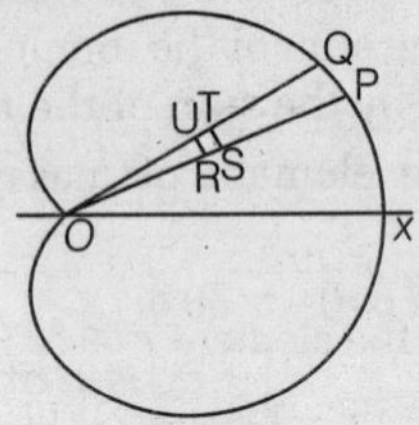

Fig. 50.

The centroid is evidently on the initial line. To find its abscissa we have

$$\bar{x} = \frac{\iint r\cos\theta \cdot r d\theta\, dr}{\iint r d\theta\, dr},$$

the limits for r being from $r = 0$ to $r = a(1 + \cos\theta)$, and for θ from 0 to π (and double, to take in the lower half).

$$\text{The numerator} = 2\int_0^{\pi}\left[\frac{r^3}{3}\right]_0^{a(1+\cos\theta)} \cos\theta\, d\theta$$

$$= \frac{2}{3}a^3\int_0^{\pi}(\cos\theta + 3\cos^2\theta + 3\cos^3\theta + \cos^4\theta)\, d\theta$$

$$= \frac{4}{3}a^3\int_0^{\frac{\pi}{2}}(3\cos^2\theta + \cos^4\theta)\, d\theta$$

$$= \frac{4}{3}a^3\left(3.\frac{1}{2}.\frac{\pi}{2} + \frac{3}{4}.\frac{1}{2}.\frac{\pi}{2}\right)$$

$$= \frac{4}{3}a^3\,\frac{3\pi}{4}.\frac{5}{4} = \frac{5}{4}\pi a^3.$$

$$\text{The denominator} = 2\int_0^{\pi}\left[\frac{r^2}{2}\right]_0^{a(1+\cos\theta)} d\theta$$

$$= a^2\int_0^{\pi}(1 + 2\cos\theta + \cos^2\theta)\, d\theta$$

$$= 2a^2\int_0^{\frac{\pi}{2}}(1 + \cos^2\theta)\, d\theta$$

$$= 2a^2\,\frac{\pi}{2}\left(1 + \frac{1}{2}\right) = \frac{3}{2}\pi a^2.$$

Hence $$\bar{x} = \frac{5}{4}\pi a^3 \Big/ \frac{3}{2}\pi a^2 = \frac{5}{6}a.$$

Ex. 3. In a circle the surface-density varies as the nth power of the distance from a point O on the circumference. Find the moment of inertia of the area about an axis through O perpendicular to the plane of the circle.

Here, taking O for origin and the diameter for initial line, the bounding curve is $r = 2a\cos\theta$, a being the radius. The density $= \mu r^n$.

Hence the mass of the element $r\,\delta\theta\,\delta r$ is $\mu r^{n+1}\delta\theta\,\delta r$, and its moment of inertia about the specified axis is $\mu r^{n+3}\delta\theta\,\delta r$.

Hence the moment of inertia of the disc is

$$\iint \mu r^{n+3} d\theta\, dr$$

where the limits for r and 0 to $2a\cos\theta$, and for θ, 0 to $\frac{\pi}{2}$ (and double).

$$\text{Thus Mom. Inertia } = 2\int_0^{\frac{\pi}{2}} \mu \frac{(2a\cos\theta)^{n+4}}{n+4} d\theta$$

$$= \frac{2\mu}{n+4}(2a)^{n+4}\int_0^{\frac{\pi}{2}} \cos^{n+4}\theta\, d\theta$$

$$= \frac{2\mu}{n+4}(2a)^{n+4}\frac{n+3}{n+4}\int_0^{\frac{\pi}{2}} \cos^{n+2}\theta\, d\theta.$$

Again, the mass of the disc is

$$M = 2\int_0^{\frac{\pi}{2}}\int_0^{2a\cos\theta} \mu r^{n+1} d\theta\, dr = \frac{2\mu}{n+2}(2a)^{n+2}\int_0^{\frac{\pi}{2}} \cos^{n+2}\theta\, d\theta.$$

$$\text{Hence Mom. Inertia } = 4\frac{(n+2)(n+3)}{(n+4)^2}Ma^2.$$

EXAMPLES

1. Find the centroid of the sector of a circle
   (α) when the surface-density is uniform,
   (β) when the surface-density varies as the distance from the centre.
2. Find the centroid of a circle whose surface-density varies as the nth power of the distance from a point O on the circumference.
   Also its moments of inertia
   (1) about the tangent at O, (2) about the diameter through O.
3. Show that the moment of inertia of the triangle of uniform surface-density bounded by the y-axis and the lines $y = m_1x + c_1$, $y = m_2x + c_2$, about the y-axis, is

$$\frac{M}{6}\left(\frac{c_1 - c_2}{m_1 - m_2}\right)^2,$$

where M is the mass of the triangle.

4. Find the moments of inertia of the triangle of uniform surface-density bounded by the lines

$$y = m_1 x + c_1,\ y = m_2 x + c_2,\ y = m_3 x + c_3,$$

about the coordinate axes; and show that if M be the mass of the triangle, they are the same as those of equal masses $\frac{M}{3}$ placed at the mid-points of the sides.

5. Show that the moments of inertia of a uniform ellipse bounded by $\frac{x^2}{a^2} + \frac{y^2}{b^2} = 1$ about the major and minor axes are respectively $\frac{Mb^2}{4}$ and $\frac{Ma^2}{4}$, and about a line through the centre and perpendicular to its plane, $M\frac{a^2+b^2}{4}$, M being the mass of the ellipse.

6. Find the area between the circles $r = a$, $r = 2a\cos\theta$; and assuming a surface-density varying inversely as the distance from the pole, find
   (1) the centroid,
   (2) the moment of inertia about a line through the pole perpendicular to the plane.

7. Find for the area included between the curves

$$\left.\begin{aligned} y^2 &= 4ax, \\ x^2 &= 4ay, \end{aligned}\right\}$$

   (1) the coordinates of its centroid (assuming a uniform surface-density),
   (2) the moment of inertia, about the x-axis,
   (3) the volume formed when this area revolves about the x-axis.

8. Find the moment of inertia of the lemniscate $r^2 = a^2 \cos 2\theta$ about a line through the pole perpendicular to its plane
   (1) for a uniform surface-density,
   (2) for a surface-density varying as the square of the distance from the pole.

9. Find
   (1) the coordinates of the centroid of the area of the cycloid

$$x = a(\theta + \sin\theta),\ y = a(1 - \cos\theta);$$

   (2) the volume formed by its revolution
   (*a*) about the base ($y = 2a$),
   (*b*) about the axis ($x = 0$),
   (*c*) about the tangent at the vertex.

DIFFERENTIAL EQUATIONS

CHAPTER XIII.

DIFFERENTIAL EQUATIONS OF THE FIRST ORDER.

VARIABLES SEPARABLE. LINEAR EQUATIONS.

170. It is proposed to add a brief account of the common methods of solution of the more ordinary forms of differential equations leading up to such as are required by the student in his reading of Analytical Statics, Dynamics of a Particle, and the elementary portions of Rigid Dynamics.

We shall not enter at all upon the solution of differential equations involving partial differential coefficients.

171. Genesis of a Differential Equation.

Let us examine for a moment how the " ordinary " differential equation is formed, and what kind of result we are to expect as its "solution."

Any equation, such as $f(x, y, a) = 0$, ...(1)

in which the form of the function is known, is representative of a certain family of curves, for each individual of which the constant a receives a particular and definite value, the same for the same curve but different for different curves of the family.

Problems frequently occur in which it is necessary to treat the whole family of curves together, as, for instance, in finding another family of curves, each member of which intersects each member of the former set at a given angle, say a right angle. And it will be manifest that for such operations, the particularizing letter a ought not to appear as a constant in the functions to be operated upon, or we should be treating one individual curve of the system instead of the whole family collectively.

Now a may be got rid of thus:–

Solve for a; we then put the equation into the form $\phi(x, y) = a$, ...(2)

and upon differentiation with regard to x, a goes out, and an equation involving x, y and y_1, replaces equation (1).

This is then the differential equation to the family of curves, of which equation (1) is the typical equation of a member.

In the formation of the differential equation it may be impracticable to solve for the constant. In this case we differentiate the equation

$$f(x, y, a) = 0 \qquad ...(1)$$

with respect to x and obtain

$$\frac{\partial f}{\partial x} + \frac{\partial f}{\partial y}\frac{dy}{dx} = 0, \qquad ...(3)$$

and then eliminate a between equations (1) and (3), thus obtaining a relation between x, y, and y_1, which is true for the whole family.

For example, consider the family of straight lines obtained by giving special values to the arbitrary constant in the equation

$$y = mx.$$

Solving for m, $\quad \dfrac{y}{x} = m,$

and differentiating, $\quad \dfrac{xy_1 - y}{x^2} = 0,$

or $\quad y = xy_1.$

Otherwise, without first solving for m, we have

$$y_1 = m,$$

and therefore $\quad y = xy_1.$

This then is the differential equation of all straight lines passing through the origin, and expresses the obvious geometrical fact that the direction of the straight line is the same as that of the vector from the origin at all points of the same line.

172. Again, suppose the representative equation of the family of curves to be

$$f(x, y, a, b) = 0, \qquad ...(1)$$

containing *two* arbitrary constants a, b whose values particularize the several members of the family. A single differentiation with regard to x will result in a relation connecting x, y, y_1, a, b; say

$$\phi(x, y, y_1, a, b) = 0, \qquad ...(2)$$

If we differentiate again with regard to x we shall obtain a relation connecting x, y, y_1, y_2, a, b ; say

$$\psi(x, y, y_1, y_2, a, b) = 0, \qquad ...(3)$$

and from these three equations a and b may theoretically be eliminated (if they have not already disappeared by the process of differentiation), and there will result a relation connecting x, y, y_1, y_2; say

$$F(x, y, y_1, y_2) = 0,$$

the differential equation of the family.

173. Order of an Equation.

We define the *order* of a differential equation to be the order of the highest differential coefficient occurring in it; and we have seen that if an equation between two unknowns contains *one* arbitrary constant the result of eliminating that constant is a differential equation of the *first* order; and if it contains *two* arbitrary constants the result is a differential equation of the *second* order. And our argument is general: so that to eliminate n arbitrary constants we shall have to proceed to n differentiations, and the result is a differential equation connecting $x, y, y_1, \ldots, y_n$, and is therefore of the nth order.

Ex. 1. Eliminate a and c from the equation $x^2 + y^2 = 2ax + c$.

Differentiating, $x + yy_1 = a$.

Differentiating again, $1 + y_1^2 + yy_2 = 0$,

and the constants having disappeared we have obtained as their eliminant a differential equation of the second order (y_2 being the highest differential coefficient involved,) which belongs to all circles whose centres lie on the x-axis.

Ex. 2. Form the differential equation of all central conics whose axes coincide with the axes of coordinates.

Here the typical equation of a member of this family of conics is

$$Ax^2 + By^2 = 1,$$

and we have $$Ax + Byy_1 = 0$$

and $$A + B(y_1^2 + yy_2) = 0,$$

Whence, $$x(y_1^2 + yy_2) - yy_1 = 0$$

is the differential equation sought.

174. Elimination an irreversible process.

Now this process of elimination is *not in general a reversible process*, and when we wish to discover the typical equation of a member of a family of curves when the differential equation is given, we are compelled to fall back, as in the case of integration, upon a set of standard cases, and many equations may arise which are not solvable at all.

We may infer, however, that in attempting to solve a differential equation of the nth order we are to search for an algebraical relation between x, y, and n arbitrary constants, such that when these constants are eliminated the given differential equation will result. Such a solution is regarded as the most general solution obtainable.

DIFFERENTIAL EQUATIONS OF THE FIRST ORDER.

175. There are five standard forms.

Case I. Variables Separable.

All equations in which it is possible to get dx and all the x's to one side, and dy and all the y's to the other, come under this head, and solve immediately by integration.

Ex. 1. Thus if
$$\sec y = \sec x \frac{dy}{dx},$$
we have
$$\cos x\,dx = \cos y\,dy,$$
and integrating,
$$\sin x = \sin y + A,$$
a relation containing one arbitrary constant A.

Ex. 2. If
$$\frac{x^2+1}{y+1} = xy\frac{dy}{dx},$$
we have
$$\left(x + \frac{1}{x}\right)dx = (y^2 + y)dy,$$
and therefore
$$\frac{x^2}{2} + \log x = \frac{y^3}{3} + \frac{y^2}{2} + A,$$
containing one arbitrary constant A.

EXAMPLES

Solve the following differential equations:—

1. $x\cos^2 y\,dx = y\cos^2 x\,dy.$

2. $\dfrac{dy}{dx} = \dfrac{x^2+x+1}{y^2+y+1}.$

3. $\dfrac{dy}{dx} + \dfrac{y^2+y+1}{x^2+x+1} = 0.$

4. Show that every member of the family of curves in Ex. 3 cuts every member of the set in Ex. 2 at right angles.

5. $xy\dfrac{dy}{dx} = \dfrac{1+y^2}{1+x^2}(1+x+x^2).$

6. $\dfrac{dy}{dx} = e^{x-y} + x^2e^{-y}.$

7. Show that all curves for which the square of the normal is equal to the square of the radius vector are either circles or rectangular hyperbolae.

8. Show that a curve for which the tangent at each point makes a constant angle (α) with the radius vector can belong to no other class than $r = Ae^{\theta \cot \alpha}$.

9. Find the equations of the curves for which
   (1) the Cartesian subtangent is constant,
   (2) the Cartesian subnormal is constant,
   (3) the Polar subtangent is constant,
   (4) the Polar subnormal is constant.

10. Find the Cartesian equation of the curve for which the tangent is of constant length.

176. Case II. Linear Equations.

[DEF. An equation of the form

$$y_n + Py_{n-1} + Qy_{n-2} + \dots + Ky = R$$

when $P, Q, \dots, K, R$ are functions of x or constants is said to be linear. Its peculiarity lies in the fact that no differential coefficient occurs raised to a power higher than the first.]

As, we are now discussing equations of the first *order*, we are limited for the present to the case

$$y_1 + Py = Q.$$

If this be multiplied throughout by $e^{\int P\,dx}$ it will be seen that we may write it

$$\frac{d}{dx}(ye^{\int P\,dx}) = Qe^{\int P\,dx}$$

Thus
$$ye^{\int P\,dx} = \int Qe^{\int P\,dx}dx + A,$$

a relation between x and y satisfying the given differential equation, and containing an arbitrary constant. It is therefore the solution required.

The factor $e^{\int P\,dx}$ which rendered the left-hand member of the equation a perfect differential coefficient is called an "integrating factor."

Ex. 1. Integrate $y_1 + xy = x$.

Here $e^{\int x\,dx}$ or $e^{\frac{x^2}{2}}$ is an integrating factor, and the equation may be written

$$\frac{d}{dx}(ye^{\frac{x^2}{2}}) = xe^{\frac{x^2}{2}},$$

or
$$ye^{\frac{x^2}{2}} = e^{\frac{x^2}{2}} + A,$$

i.e.
$$y = 1 + Ae^{-\frac{x^2}{2}}.$$

Ex. 2. Integrate $\frac{dy}{dx} + \frac{1}{x} y = x^2$.

Here the integrating factor is $e^{\int \frac{1}{x} dx} = e^{\log x} = x$, and the equation may be written

$$\frac{d}{dx}(xy) = x^3,$$

and
$$xy = \frac{x^4}{4} + A,$$

or
$$y = \frac{x^3}{4} + \frac{A}{x}.$$

177. Equations reducible to linear form.

Many equations, if not immediately of the linear form

$$\frac{dy}{dx} + Py = Q,$$

may be immediately reduced to it by change of the variables. One of the most important cases is that of the equation

$$\frac{dy}{dx} + Py = Q\, y^n,$$

or
$$y^{-n} \frac{dy}{dx} + Py^{-n+1} = Q.$$

Putting
$$y^{1-n} = z,$$

we have
$$y^{-n} dy = \frac{dz}{1-n},$$

or
$$\frac{dz}{dx} + (1-n)Pz = Q(1-n),$$

which is linear, and its solution is

$$ze^{(1-n)\int P\,dx} = (1-n) \int Qe^{(1-n)\int P\,dx} dx + A,$$

i.e.
$$y^{1-n} e^{(1-n)\int P\,dx} = (1-n) \int Qe^{(1-n)\int P\,dx} dx + A.$$

Ex. 1. Integrate $\frac{dy}{dx} + \frac{y}{x} = y^2$.

Here
$$y^{-2} \frac{dy}{dx} + \frac{y^{-1}}{x} = 1;$$

or putting
$$\frac{1}{y} = z, \quad \frac{dz}{dx} - \frac{z}{x} = -1,$$

and the integrating factor being

$$e^{-\int \frac{1}{x} dx} = e^{-\log x} = \frac{1}{x},$$

we have $$\frac{d}{dx}\left(\frac{z}{x}\right) = -\frac{1}{x},$$

i.e. $$\frac{z}{x} = \log\frac{1}{x} + A,$$

i.e. $$\frac{1}{y} = Ax - x\log x.$$

Ex. 2. Integrate the equation $\frac{dy}{dx} + x\sin 2y = x^3\cos^2 y.$

Dividing by $\cos^2 y$, we have

$$\sec^2 y\frac{dy}{dx} + 2x\tan y = x^3.$$

Putting $$\tan y = z,$$

we have $$\frac{dz}{dx} + 2xz = x^3,$$

and the integrating factor is $e^{\int 2x\,dx}$ or e^{x^2}, giving

$$ze^{x^2} = \int x^3 e^{x^2}dx + A$$

Let $$x^2 = \omega,$$

then $$2x\,dx = d\omega,$$

so that $$\int x^3 e^{x^2}dx = \frac{1}{2}\int \omega e^{\omega}d\omega = \frac{1}{2}e^{\omega}(\omega - 1).$$

$$\text{Thus } \tan y \cdot e^{x^2} = \frac{1}{2}e^{x^2}(x^2 - 1) + A$$

is the solution of the given equation.

It will be obvious that for examples of this kind considerable ingenuity may be called into play in order to effect the reduction to the linear (or other known) form.

EXAMPLES

Integrate the equations

1. $(1 + x^2)\frac{dy}{dx} + y = e\tan^{-1}x.$

2. $\frac{dy}{dx} + ay = \sin bx.$

3. $\frac{dr}{d\theta} + \frac{r}{\theta} = a\theta^n.$

4. $\frac{dx}{dy} + \frac{x}{y} = y^2.$

5. $(1 + y^2) + (x - e^{-\tan^{-1}y})\frac{dy}{dx} = 0.$

6. $\left(\frac{e^{-2\sqrt{x}}}{\sqrt{x}} - \frac{y}{\sqrt{x}}\right)\frac{dx}{dy} = 1.$

7. Show that no greater generality is obtained in the solution of Art. 176 by adding a constant to the index in obtaining the integrating factor $e^{\int P\,dx}$.

8. Find the curves for which the Cartesian subnormal varies as the square of the radius vector.

Integrate the equations

9. $\frac{dy}{dx} + \frac{y}{x} = \frac{y^2}{x^2}.$

10. $\frac{dy}{dx} + \frac{y}{x} = \frac{y^n}{x^n}.$

11. $\frac{dy}{dx} + xy = xy^n.$

12. $\frac{dy}{dx} + \frac{1}{x}\tan y = \frac{1}{x^2}\tan y \sin y.$ [Put $y = \sin^{-1} z$.]

13. $\frac{dz}{dx} + \frac{z}{x}\log z = \frac{z}{x^2}(\log z)^2.$ [Put $z = e^y$.]

14. $\frac{dz}{dx} + x = xe^{(n-1)z}.$ [Put $z = \log y$.]

15. Find the curves for which the sum of the reciprocals of the radius vector and the polar subtangent is constant.

16. Find the polar equation of the family of curves for which the sum of the radius vector and the polar subnormal varies as the nth power of the radius vector.

17. Show that the curves for which the radius of curvature varies as the square of the perpendicular upon the normal belong to the class whose pedal equation is $r^2 - p^2 = \frac{p}{k} + \frac{1}{2k^2} + Ae^{2kp}$, k being a given constant and A arbitrary.

18. Integrate the equations

(1) $\frac{dy}{dx} + \frac{1}{x} = \frac{e^y}{x^2}.$

(2) $\frac{dy}{dx} + a = e^{-y}\sin bx.$

(3) $\frac{dy}{dx} - \frac{\tan y}{1+x} = (1+x)e^x \sec y.$

(4) $\frac{dy}{dx} - \frac{f(y)}{f'(y)}\phi'(x) = \frac{\phi(x)\phi'(x)}{f'(y)}.$

CHAPTER XIV.

EQUATIONS OF THE FIRST ORDER-CONTINUED.

HOMOGENEOUS EQUATIONS. ONE LETTER ABSENT. CLAIRAUT'S FORM.

178. Case III. Homogeneous Equations.

Equations homogeneous in x and y may be written

$$x^n f\left(\frac{y}{x}, \frac{dy}{dx}\right) = 0.$$

(a) In this case we solve if possible for $\frac{dy}{dx}$, and obtain a result of the form

$$\frac{dy}{dx} = \phi\left(\frac{y}{x}\right).$$

Putting $$y = vx,$$

we obtain $$v + x\frac{dv}{dx} = \phi(v), \quad \text{or} \quad \frac{dv}{\phi(v) - v} = \frac{dx}{x},$$

and the variables are separated and the solution thus comes under Case I, giving as result

$$\log Ax = \int \frac{dv}{\phi(v) - v}.$$

(b) But if it be inconvenient or impracticable to solve for $\frac{dy}{dx}$, we solve for $\frac{y}{x}$, and write p for $\frac{dy}{dx}$, and we have

$$y = x\phi(p) \qquad \ldots(1)$$

Differentiating with respect to x,

$$p = \phi(p) + x\phi'(p)\frac{dp}{dx},$$

or $$\frac{dx}{x} = \frac{\phi'(p)\,dp}{p - \phi(p)}.$$

Integrating this equation we have x expressed as a function of p and an arbitrary constant

$$Ax = F(p)\,(\text{say}) \qquad \ldots(2)$$

Eliminating p between equations (1) and (2) we obtain the solution required.

Ex. 1. Solve $(x^2 + y^2)\dfrac{dy}{dx} = xy.$

Here $$\frac{dy}{dx} = \frac{xy}{x^2 + y^2};$$

and putting $$y = vx,$$

$$x\frac{dv}{dx} + v = \frac{v}{1 + v^2}.$$

or $$x\frac{dv}{dx} = -\frac{v^3}{1 + v^2};$$

$\therefore$ $$\frac{dx}{x} = -\left(\frac{1}{v^3} + \frac{1}{v}\right) dv,$$

or $$\log Ax = \frac{1}{2v^2} - \log v,$$

or $$Ay = e^{\frac{x^2}{2y^2}}.$$

Ex. 2. Suppose the equation to be

$$\frac{y}{x} = \frac{dy}{dx} + \left(\frac{dy}{dx}\right)^2,$$

i.e. $$y = x(p + p^2).$$

Then $$p = (p + p^2) + x(1 + 2p)\frac{dp}{dx},$$

or $$\frac{dx}{x} + \left(\frac{1}{p^2} + \frac{2}{p}\right)dp = 0,$$

giving $$\log Ax + 2\log p - \frac{1}{p} = 0,$$

i.e. $$Axp^2 = e^{\frac{1}{p}};$$

and the p-eliminant between

$$\left.\begin{aligned} p^2 + p &= \frac{y}{x} \\ Axp^2 &= e^{\frac{1}{p}} \end{aligned}\right\}$$

and

is the solution sought.

This eliminant is

$$\log\left\{\frac{Ax}{4}\left(-1\pm\sqrt{\frac{4y+x}{x}}\right)^2\right\}=\frac{x}{2y}\left\{+1\pm\sqrt{\frac{4y+x}{x}}\right\}.$$

But when it is algebraically impossible to perform the elimination of p, or when, if performed, the result will be manifestly unwieldy, it is customary to leave the two equations containing p unaltered, and to regard them as simultaneous equations whose p-eliminant if found would be the required solution.

EXAMPLES

Solve the differential equations

1. $\dfrac{dy}{dx}=\dfrac{x}{x+y}$.

2. $(3x+4y)=(5x+6y)\dfrac{dy}{dx}$.

3. $x^2\dfrac{dy}{dx}=y^2$.

4. $y=x\left\{\dfrac{dy}{dx}+\left(\dfrac{dy}{dx}\right)^3\right\}$.

5. $y=x\left\{A\left(\dfrac{dy}{dx}\right)^2+B\dfrac{dy}{dx}+C\right\}$.

179. A Special Case.

The equation $\dfrac{dy}{dx}=\dfrac{ax+by+c}{a'x+b'y+c'}$ is readily reduced to the homogeneous form thus:—

Put $\quad x=\xi+h.$

$\quad y=\eta+k.$

Then
$$\frac{d\eta}{d\xi}=\frac{a\xi+b\eta+(ah+bk+c)}{a'\xi+b'\eta+(a'h+b'k+c')}.$$

Now choose h, k so that

$$ah+bk+c=0,$$
$$a'h+b'k+c'=0$$

i.e. so that
$$\frac{h}{bc'-b'c}=\frac{k}{ca'-c'a}=\frac{1}{ab'-a'b}.$$

Then
$$\frac{d\eta}{d\xi}=\frac{a\xi+b\eta}{a'\xi+b'\eta}.$$

This equation being homogeneous we may now put $\eta=v\xi$, and the variables are separable as before shown.

180. There is one case, however, in which h, k cannot be chosen as above, *viz.*, when

$$\frac{a}{a'} = \frac{b}{b'} \neq \frac{c}{c'}.$$

Now let $$\frac{a}{a} = m \text{ and } ax + by = \eta.$$

Then $$\frac{dy}{dx} = \frac{1}{b}\left(\frac{d\eta}{dx} - a\right),$$

so that $$\frac{d\eta}{dx} - a = b\,\frac{\eta + c}{m\eta + c'},$$

or $$\frac{d\eta}{dx} = \frac{(am + b)\eta + ac' + bc}{m\eta + c'},$$

and $$dx = \frac{m\eta + c'}{(am + b)\eta + ac' + bc}\,d\eta$$

The variables being now separated, the integration may be at once performed.

181. One other case is worthy of notice, *viz*,

$$\frac{dy}{dx} = \frac{ax + by + c}{-bx + b'y + c'},$$

when the coefficient of y in the numerator is equal to that of x in the denominator with the opposite sign.

For then we may write the equation thus

$$(ax + c)\,dx + b(y\,dx + x\,dy) = (b'y + c')\,dy$$

an "exact" differential equation; the integral being

$$a x^2 + 2cx + 2bxy = b'y^2 + 2c'y + A,$$

A being the arbitrary constant.

Ex. 1. Integrate $\dfrac{dy}{dx} = \dfrac{2x + 3y - 8}{x + y - 3}$.

Put $x = \xi + h$, $y = \eta + k$, so that

$$\frac{d\eta}{d\xi} = \frac{2\xi + 3\eta + (2h + 3k - 8)}{\xi + \eta + (h + k - 3)}.$$

Choose h and k so that

$$\left.\begin{aligned} 2h + 3k - 8 &= 0, \\ h + k - 3 &= 0, \end{aligned}\right\} \text{i.e. } h = 1,\ k = 2,$$

then $$\frac{d\eta}{d\xi} = \frac{2\xi + 3\eta}{\xi + \eta}.$$

Now put $\eta = v\xi$, then

$$v + \xi\frac{dv}{d\xi} = \frac{2+3v}{1+v}, \; -\xi\frac{dv}{d\xi} = v - \frac{2+3v}{1+v} = \frac{v^2-2v-2}{v+1},$$

$$-\frac{d\xi}{\xi} = \frac{v+1}{\overline{v-1}^2 - 3}\,dv$$

$$= \left[\frac{v-1}{(v-1)^2-3} + \frac{1}{\sqrt{3}}\left(\frac{1}{v-1-\sqrt{3}} - \frac{1}{v-1+\sqrt{3}}\right)\right]dv,$$

$$\therefore \qquad -\log\xi = \frac{1}{2}\log\{(v-1)^2-3\} + \frac{1}{\sqrt{3}}\log\frac{v-1-\sqrt{3}}{v-1+\sqrt{3}} + A,$$

where $\qquad \xi = x - 1 \text{ and } v = \dfrac{y-2}{x-1}.$

Ex. 2. Integrate $\dfrac{dy}{dx} = \dfrac{x+y}{x+y-1}.$

Let $\quad x + y = \eta$, then

$$\frac{d\eta}{dx} = 1 + \frac{\eta}{\eta-1} = \frac{2\eta-1}{\eta-1},$$

and $$dx = \frac{\eta-1}{2\eta-1}\,d\eta = \frac{1}{2}\left[1 - \frac{1}{2\eta-1}\right]d\eta,$$

$$\therefore \qquad x = \frac{1}{2}\eta - \frac{1}{4}\log(2\eta-1) + A,$$

where $\qquad \eta = x + y.$

EXAMPLES

Integrate the equations:—

1. $\dfrac{dy}{dx} = \dfrac{2x+3y}{3x+2y}.$

2. $\dfrac{dy}{dx} = \dfrac{x+2y-3}{2x+y-3}.$

3. $\dfrac{dy}{dx} = \dfrac{2x+y-2}{3x+y-3}.$

4. $\dfrac{dy}{dx} = \dfrac{ax+by-a}{bx+ay-b}.$

5. $\dfrac{dy}{dx} = \dfrac{x+y+1}{x+y-1}.$

6. $\dfrac{dy}{dx} = \dfrac{x+y+1}{2x+2y+1}.$

7. $(2x+3y-5)\dfrac{dy}{dx} + 3x + 2y - 5 = 0.$

8. $(2x+3y-5)\dfrac{dy}{dx} + 2x + 3y - 1 = 0.$

9. Show that a particle x, y which moves so that

$$\frac{dy}{dt} = ax + hy + g, \quad \frac{dx}{dt} = -(hx + by + f),$$

will always lie upon a conic section.

10. Show that solutions of the general homogeneous equation $f\left(\frac{y}{x}, \frac{dy}{dx}\right)$ must always represent families of *similar curves*.

11. Show that solutions of $f\left(\frac{y}{x}, \frac{dy}{dx}\right)$ are homogeneous in x, y and some power of a single constant, and conversely that if the typical equation of a member of a family of curves be homogeneous in x, y and some power of one constant, the differential equation of the family is homogeneous and the family consists of similar curves.

12. State which of the following families of curves are similar sets:—

(1) $y^2 = 4ax$. (2) $y = a\cosh\frac{x}{a}$.

(3) $\frac{x^2}{a^2} + \frac{y^2}{b^2} = 1$. (4) $y = 2a^3 \log\frac{x}{a^3}$.

(5) $b\tan^{-1}\frac{y}{x} = a + y$. (6) $x^3 + y^3 = 3axy$.

for different values of a and b.

182. Case IV. One letter absent. x absent.

A. Suppose x absent from the differential equation, which then takes the form

$$f\left(y, \frac{dy}{dx}\right) = 0,$$

we now solve for $\frac{dy}{dx}$ or y, as may be most convenient.

(i.) If we solve for $\frac{dy}{dx}$ we throw the equation into the form $\frac{dy}{dx} = \phi(y)$.

Then
$$dx = \frac{dy}{\phi(y)},$$

and the integral is
$$x = \int \frac{dy}{\phi(y)} + A.$$

(ii.) If this be inconvenient or impossible we may solve for y and obtain $y = \phi(p)$, where p stands as before for $\frac{dy}{dx}$.

Differentiate *with regard to x, i.e. the absent letter.*

Then
$$p = \phi'(p)\frac{dp}{dx}, \quad \text{and} \quad dx = \frac{\phi'(p)}{p}dp.$$

Thus
$$x = \int \frac{\phi'(p)}{p}dp + A.$$

After the integration is performed we eliminate p between this equation and $y = \phi(p)$ and the solution of the given equation is obtained.

183. y absent.

B. Suppose y absent from the differential equation, which then takes the form

$$f\left(x, \frac{dy}{dx}\right) = 0.$$

Since $\frac{dy}{dx} = \frac{1}{\frac{dx}{dy}}$ this may be written $\psi\left(x, \frac{dx}{dy}\right) = 0,$

and therefore if y be regarded as the independent variable the foregoing remarks apply to this case also. Thus

(i.) if convenient we solve for $\frac{dx}{dy}$, and obtain a result of the form

$$\frac{dx}{dy} = \phi(x), \quad \text{then} \quad dy = \frac{dx}{\phi(x)},$$

and the integral is $\quad y = \int \frac{dx}{\phi(x)} + A.$

(ii.) But it this solution for $\frac{dx}{dy}$ be inconvenient or impossible we solve for x and obtain a result of the form $x = \phi(q)$ where q stands for $\frac{dx}{dy}$.

Then differentiating *with regard to y, the absent letter,*

$$q = \phi'(q)\frac{dq}{dy}. \quad \text{Thus} \quad dy = \frac{\phi'(q)}{q}dq,$$

and $\quad y = \int \frac{\phi'(q)}{q} dq + A.$

After the integration we eliminate q between this equation and $x = \phi(q)$, and the solution of the given equation is obtained.

The student should note that in either case, x absent or y absent, we solve for $\frac{dy}{dx}$ by preference, if possible. But when this is impossible or inconvenient we solve for the remaining letter and differentiate with regard to the *absent one*; thus considering the absent letter in either case as the independent variable.

Ex. 1. Integrate the equation $1 + x^2 - x\frac{dy}{dx} = 0.$

Here $\quad \frac{dx}{dy} = \frac{x}{1 + x^2}, dy = \left(x + \frac{1}{x}\right)dx,$

and $\quad y = \frac{x^2}{2} + \log x + A$

is the solution.

Ex. 2. Solve $x\dfrac{dy}{dx} = 1 + \left(\dfrac{dy}{dx}\right)^2$.

Then $$x = q + \frac{1}{q},$$

where $$q = \frac{dx}{dy}$$

Then differentiating with *regard to the absent letter y*,

$$q = \left(1 - \frac{1}{q^2}\right)\frac{dq}{dy},$$

or $$\frac{dy}{dq} = \frac{1}{q} - \frac{1}{q^3},$$

and $$y = \log q + \frac{1}{2q^2} + A,$$

and the q- eliminant between this equation and the original equation $x = q + \dfrac{1}{q}$ is the solution required.

EXAMPLES

Solve the equations:—

1. $\dfrac{dy}{dx} = y + \dfrac{1}{y}$.

2. $\dfrac{dy}{dx} = x + \dfrac{1}{x}$.

3. $\sqrt{a + x}\dfrac{dy}{dx} + x = 0$.

4. $(2ax + x^2)\dfrac{dy}{dx} = a^2 + 2ax$.

5. $(2ay + y^2)\dfrac{dy}{dx} = a^2 + 2ay$.

6. $y = \sin\left(\dfrac{dy}{dx}\right) - \dfrac{dy}{dx}\cos\left(\dfrac{dy}{dx}\right)$.

7. $y = A\left(\dfrac{dy}{dx}\right)^3 + B\left(\dfrac{dy}{dx}\right)^2$.

8. $x\left(\dfrac{dy}{dx}\right)^3 = A + B\dfrac{dy}{dx}$.

184. Case V. Clairaut's Form, $y = x\dfrac{dy}{dx} + f\left(\dfrac{dy}{dx}\right)$.

Writing p for $\dfrac{dy}{dx}$ we have

$$y = px + f(p) \qquad \ldots(1)$$

Differentiating with regard to x,

$$p = p + x\frac{dp}{dx} + f'(p)\frac{dp}{dx},$$

or $$\{x + f'(p)\}\frac{dp}{dx} = 0, \qquad \ldots(2)$$

whence either $\dfrac{dp}{dx} = 0$ or $x + f'(p) = 0.$

Now $\dfrac{dp}{dx} = 0$ gives $p = C$ a constant.

Thus $y = Cx + f(C)$ is a solution of the given differential equation containing an arbitrary constant C.

Again, if p be found as a function of x from the equation

$$x + f'(p) = 0, \qquad \ldots(3)$$

equation (2) will still be satisfied, and if this value of p be substituted in equation (1), or which is the same thing, if p be eliminated between equations (1) and (3) we shall obtain a relation between y and x which also satisfies the differential equation

Now to eliminate p between

$$\left.\begin{aligned} y &= px + f(p) \\ 0 &= x + f'(p) \end{aligned}\right\}$$

is the same as to eliminate C between

$$\left.\begin{aligned} y &= Cx + f(C) \\ 0 &= x + f'(C) \end{aligned}\right\}$$

i.e. the same as the process of finding the envelope of the line $y = Cx + f(C)$ for different values of C.

There are therefore two classes of solutions, viz.

(1) The linear solution, called the "complete primitive," containing an arbitrary constant.

(2) The envelope or "singular solution" containing no arbitrary constant and not derivable from the complete primitive by putting any particular numerical value for the constant in that solution.

The geometrical relation between these two solutions is that of a family of lines and their envelope. It is beyond the scope of this book to discuss fully the theory of singular solutions, and the student is referred to larger treatises for further information upon the subject.

Ex. Solve $y = px + \dfrac{a}{p}$.

By Clairaut's rule the complete primitive is $y = mx + \dfrac{a}{m}$,

and the envelope or singular solution is the result of eliminating m between the above equation and

$$0 = x - \frac{a}{m^2}. \qquad i.e. \qquad y^2 = 4ax.$$

The student will at once recognize in the singular solution $y^2 = 4ax$ the equation to a parabola, and in the complete primitive $y = mx + \dfrac{a}{m}$ the well known equation of a tangent to the parabola.

EXAMPLES

Write down the complete primitive, and find the envelope solution in each of the following cases:—

1. $y = px + p^2$. **2.** $y = px + p^3$.

3. $y = px + p^n$. **4.** $y = px + \sqrt{a^2p^2 + b^2}$.

5. $y = (x - a)\,p - p^2$. **6.** $(y - px)(p - 1) = p$.

185. The equation

$$y = x\phi(p) + \psi(p), \qquad \ldots(1)$$

may be solved by *differentiating with regard to x, and then considering p as the independent variable.*

For differentiating, we have

$$p = \phi(p) + x\,\phi'(p)\frac{dp}{dx} + \psi'(p)\frac{dp}{dx},$$

whence
$$\frac{dx}{dp} + x\frac{\phi'(p)}{\phi(p) - p} = -\frac{\psi'(p)}{\phi(p) - p},$$

which is linear, the solution being

$$xe^{\int \frac{\phi'(p)dp}{\phi(p)-p}} = -\int \frac{\psi'(p)}{\phi(p) - p} e^{\int \frac{\phi'(p)dp}{\phi(p)-p}} dp + A \qquad \ldots(2)$$

If now p be eliminated between equations (1) and (2), the complete primitive of the original equation will result.

Ex. Solve $y = 2px + p^2$. ...(1)

We have $p = 2p + 2x\dfrac{dp}{dx} + 2p\dfrac{dp}{dx}$,

or $p\dfrac{dx}{dp} + 2x = -2p$, *i.e.* $\dfrac{d}{dp}(p^2x) = -2p^2$,

giving $p^2x = -\dfrac{2}{3}p^3 - A$ ...(2)

The p-eliminant from these two equations may now be found be solving equation (1) for p, and substituting in equation (2).

But if it be an object to present the result in rational form, we may proceed thus:—

By equation (2) $2p^3 + 3p^2x + 3A = 0,$
from (1) $p^3 + 2p^2x - py = 0.$

Hence $p^2x - 2py - 3A = 0.$

And by cross-multiplication between this equation and

$$p^2 + 2px - y = 0, \quad \frac{p^2}{2y^2 + 6Ax} = \frac{p}{xy - 3A} = \frac{1}{2x^2 + 2y},$$

giving as the eliminant $4(y^2 + 3Ax)(x^2 + y) = (xy - 3A)^2$.

186. The algebraic process of eliminating p being in many cases difficult or impossible, the equations (1) and (2) are often regarded as simultaneous equations whose p - eliminant is the solution in question but the actual elimination not performed.

EXAMPLES

Solve the equations:—

1. $y = p^2x + p.$

2. $y = axp + p^2.$

3. $y = p^2x + p^3.$

4. $y = (p + p^2)x + \frac{1}{p}.$

5. $y = (p + p^n)x + \frac{1}{p^{n-1}}.$

6. $y = 2px + p^n.$

7. $y = apx + bp^3.$

8. The tangent at any point P of a curve meets the axis Oy in T, and OT^2 is proportional to the tangent of the inclination of PT to the axis Ox. Find the curve. [OXFORD, 1888.]

9. Find the differential equation of all curves which possess the property that the sum of the intercepts made by the tangent on the coordinate axes is constant. Obtain as the complete primitive the equation of the tangent, and as the singular solution the curves in question.

10. Obtain the curves for which the area of the triangle bounded by the axes and a tangent is constant.

11. Form the differential equation of curves for which the length of the portion of the tangent intercepted between the coordinate axes is constant. Obtain and interpret the complete primitive and the singular solution.

12. A curve satisfies the differential equation $y = p^2(x - p)$, and also that $p = 0$ when $x = \frac{1}{2}$; determine its equation. [OXFORD, 1889.]

13. Find the complete primitive and singular solution of the equation

$$e^{3x}\left(y - \frac{dy}{dx}\right) = c\left\{e^{2x} + \left(\frac{dy}{dx}\right)^2\right\}^{\frac{3}{2}}.$$ [OXFORD, 1890.]

14. Show that by putting $x^2 = s$ and $y^2 = t$, the equation $Axyy_1^2 + (x^2 - Ay^2 - B)y_1 - xy = 0$ is reduced to one of Clairaut's form. Hence write down its complete primitive and find its singular solution. Interpret the result.

CHAPTER XV.

DIFFERENTIAL EQUATIONS OF THE SECOND ORDER. EXACT DIFFERENTIAL EQUATIONS.

187. Second Order Equation.

We next come to the consideration of the differential equation of the second order, $\phi(x, y, y_1, y_2) = 0$.

There is no *general* method of solution, but particular forms arise which present but little difficulty.

188. Case I. Suppose the Equation linear.

The typical form will be $\dfrac{d^2y}{dx^2} + P\dfrac{dy}{dx} + Q\,y = R$,

where P, Q, R are functions of x.

The usual method is first to omit R and try to obtain or guess a solution of

$$\frac{d^2y}{dx^2} + P\frac{dy}{dx} + Q\,y = 0.$$

Suppose $y = f(x)$ to be such a solution. Put $y = zf(x)$.

Then $\quad y_1 = z_1 f(x) + zf'(x)\,;\ y_2 = z_2 f(x) + 2z_1 f'(x) + zf''(x)$.

Thus on substitution we get

$$z_2 f(x) + 2z_1 f'(x) + zf''(x) + Pz_1 f(x) + Pzf'(x) + Qzf(x) = R.$$

But $f''(x) + Pf'(x) + Q\,f(x) = 0$ by hypothesis.

Hence $$z_2 + \left\{\frac{2f'(x)}{f(x)} + P\right\} z_1 = \frac{R}{f(x)},$$

an equation which is linear for z_1.

The integrating factor is $e^{\int\left\{P + 2\frac{f'(x)}{f(x)}\right\}dx}$ or $\{f(x)\}^2\, e^{\int P\,dx}$,

and the first integral is $z_1\,\{f(x)\}^2\, e^{\int P\,dx} = \int R\,\{f(x)\}\, e^{\int P\,dx}\, dx + A$,

whence the second integral may be at once obtained and the solution effected.

Ex. Solve $\frac{d^2y}{dx^2} + x^3 \frac{dy}{dx} - x^2 y = x^3 e^{-\frac{x^4}{4}}$.

Here $y = x$ makes $\frac{d^2y}{dx^2} + x^3 \frac{dy}{dx} - x^2 y = 0$.

Put $y = xz$; then $y_1 = xz_1 + z$, $y_2 = xz_2 + 2z_1$.

Hence $xz_2 + 2z_1 + x^3(xz_1 + z) - x^2(xz) = x^3 e^{\frac{x^4}{4}}$

or $$z_2 + \left(\frac{2}{x} + x^3\right) z_1 = x^2 e^{\frac{x^4}{4}};$$

and the integrating factor is $e^{\int\left(\frac{2}{x} + x^3\right)dx}$ or $x^2 e^{\frac{x^4}{4}}$.

Thus $\frac{d}{dx}(z_1 x^2 e^{\frac{x^4}{4}}) = x^4$, and $z_1 x^2 e^{\frac{x^4}{4}} = \frac{x^5}{5} + A$,

i.e. $$z_1 = \frac{1}{5} x^3 e^{-\frac{x^4}{4}} + \frac{A}{x^2} e^{-\frac{x^4}{4}},$$

whence $$z = -\frac{1}{5} e^{-\frac{x^4}{4}} + A \int \frac{1}{x^2} e^{-\frac{x^4}{4}} dx + B,$$

and the solution required is $y = -\frac{x}{5} e^{-\frac{x^4}{4}} + Ax \int \frac{1}{x^2} e^{-\frac{x^4}{4}} dx + Bx$.

189. Case II. One letter absent.

A. **If x be absent**, let $y_1 = p$, then $y_2 = \frac{dp}{dx} = p\frac{dp}{dy}$,

and the equation $\phi(y, y_1, y_2) = 0$

takes the form $\phi\left(y, p, p\frac{dp}{dy}\right) = 0$,

and is of the first order.

B. **If y be the letter absent**, let $y_1 = p$, then $y_2 = \frac{dp}{dx}$,

and $\phi(x, y_1, y_2)$ becomes $\phi\left(x, p, \frac{dp}{dx}\right) = 0$,

and again is of the first order.

Ex. 1. Solve the equation $yy_2 + y_1^2 = 2y^2$.

Here x is absent. So putting $y_1 = p$ and $y_2 = p\frac{dp}{dy}$, we have

$$yp\frac{dp}{dy} + p^2 = 2y^2, \text{ or } \frac{dp^2}{dy} + \frac{2}{y}p^2 = 4y.$$

The integrating factor is $e^{\int \frac{2}{y} dy}$ or y^2,

$$\therefore \quad \frac{d}{dy}(p^2 y^2) = 4y^3,$$

or $\quad p^2 y^2 = y^4 + \text{constant} = y^4 + a^4$, say.

Hence $$\frac{y\,dy}{\sqrt{y^4 + a^4}} = dx, \quad \text{or} \quad \sinh^{-1}\frac{y^2}{a^2} = 2x + A.$$

i.e. $$y^2 = a^2 \sinh(2x + A).$$

Ex. 2. Solve $1 + y_1^2 = xy_2y_1$.

Here y is absent. So putting $y_1 = p$,

$$1 + p^2 = xp\frac{dp}{dx}, \quad \text{or} \quad \frac{dx}{x} = \frac{pdp}{1 + p^2},$$

i.e. $$\log x = \log\sqrt{1 + p^2} + \text{constant}$$

i.e. $$1 + p^2 = \frac{x^2}{a^2}, \text{ say,} \quad \text{or} \quad a\,dy = \sqrt{x^2 - a^2}\,dx,$$

giving $$ay = \frac{x\sqrt{x^2 - a^2}}{2} - \frac{a^2}{2}\cosh^{-1}\frac{x}{a} + b,$$

a and b being arbitrary constants.

EXAMPLES

Solve the following equations:—

1. $xy_2 = 1$.

2. $1 + y_1^2 = yy_2$.

3. $1 + y_1^2 = x^2y_2^2$.

4. $9y_2^2 = 4y_1$.

5. $ay_2 = (1 + y_1^2)^{\frac{3}{2}}$.

6. $y_2 + y_1^2 + y = 0$.

7. $y_1y_2 + y_1^2 + x = 0$.

8. $y_2 + xy_1 - y = \frac{1}{x}e^{-\frac{x^2}{2}}$.

9. $yy_2 = y_1^3 - y_1$. [OXFORD, 1889.]

10. Solve the equation $(1 - y^2)\frac{d^2y}{dx^2} - y\left(\frac{dy}{dx}\right)^2 = 2y^3$, having given that $\frac{dy}{dx} = 0$ when $y = 0$. [OXFORD, 1890.]

11. Given that x^2 is a value of y which satisfies the equation $x^2(\log x - 1)\frac{d^2y}{dx^2} - x(2\log x - 1)\frac{dy}{dx} + 2y\log x = 0$, find the complete solution. [I.C.S., 1894.]

190. General Linear Equation. Removal of a Term.

Let us next consider the more general equation

$$y_n + P_1 y_{n-1} + P_2 y_{n-2} + \dots + P_n y = Q,$$

where $P_1, P_2, \dots, Q$ are given functions of x.

Putting $y = vz$, we have $y_1 = vz_1 + v_1 z$,

$$y_2 = vz_2 + 2v_1 z_1 + v_2 z, \text{ etc.},$$

whence $$vz_n + nv_1 z_{n-1} + \frac{n(n-1)}{1 \cdot 2} v_2 z_{n-2} + \dots + v_n z$$

$$+ P_1 vz_{n-1} + (n-1) P_1 v_1 z_{n-2} + \dots + P_1 v_{n-1} z$$

$$+ P_2 vz_{n-2} + \dots + P_2 v_{n-2} z + \dots + P_n vz = Q.$$

The coefficient of z_{n-1} is $nv_1 + P_1 v$.

If then v be chosen so that $\dfrac{dv}{v} = -\dfrac{P_1 dx}{n}$ or $v = e^{-\int \frac{P_1 dx}{n}}$

the term involving z_{n-1} will have been removed.

Similarly, if v be so chosen as to satisfy the differential equation

$$\frac{n(n-1)}{1 \cdot 2} v_2 + (n-1) P_1 v_1 + P_2 v = 0,$$

the term containing Z_{n-2} will have been removed.

The coefficient of z is $v_n + P_1 v_{n-1} + P_2 v_{n-2} + \dots + P_n v$,

and if a value of v can be found or guessed which will make this expression vanish, we can, by writing $z_1 = \eta$, and therefore $z_2 = \eta_1$, etc., and $z_n = \eta_{n-1}$, reduce the degree of the equation by unity. The student should notice that this expression is the same in form as the left hand member of the given equation. Hence if any solution $y = v$ can be found or guessed of the given equation when the right hand member is omitted, we can, by writing $y = vz$, and then $z_1 = \eta$, reduce the degree of the equation.

191. Canonical Form.

In the case of the equation of the second degree $y_2 + P_1 y_1 + P_2 y = Q$, the substitution $y = e^{-\frac{1}{2}\int P_1 dx} z$

will by what has been above stated reduce the given equation to the sometimes simpler form $z_2 + P' z = Q'$.

But the *general* solution of this equation has not been at present effected.

"EXACT" DIFFERENTIAL EQUATION.

192. When p is $<q$, $x^p \dfrac{d^q y}{dx^q}$ is an exact differential, and can be integrated whatever y may be.

For denoting $\dfrac{d^q y}{dx^q}$ by y_q, $\int x^p y_q dx = x^p y_{q-1} - p\int x^{p-1} y_{q-1}\, dx$,

$$\int x^{p-1} y_{q-1} dx = x^{p-1} y_{q-2} - (p-1)\int x^{p-2} y_{q-2}\, dx, \text{ etc.,}$$

$$\int xy_{q-p+1} dx = xy_{q-p} - \int y_{q-p} dx = xy_{q-p} - y_{q-p-1}.$$

Thus
$$\int x^p y_q dx = x^p y_{q-1} - px^{p-1} y_{q-2} + p(p-1)x^{p-2} y_{q-3} - \ldots$$
$$+ (-1)^p p!\, y_{q-p-y}$$

It will be noticed that when $q = p$ or $< p$ the integration cannot be effected.

193. By aid of the above lemma we may often see quickly whether a given equation is "exact." For if all terms of the form $x^p y_q$ in which p is $< q$ be first removed, we can frequently tell at once by inspection whether the remainder is a perfect differential coefficient or not.

Ex. $x^2 y_5 + x^3 y_4 + xy_1 + y = \sin x$.

Here, by the lemma, $x^2 y_5$ and $x^3 y_4$ are perfect differential coefficients, and obviously $xy_1 + y$ is the differential coefficient of xy. Hence a first integral of this differential equation is obviously
$$x^2 y_4 - 2xy_3 + 2y_2 + x^3 y_3 - 3x^2 y_2 + 6xy_1 - 6y + xy = -\cos x + A.$$

194. A more General Test.

A more general test for an "exact" differential equation may be established in the general case $P_0 y_n + P_1 y_{n-1} + P_2 y_{n-2} + \ldots + P_n y = V$,

whatever forms the coefficients $P_0, P_1, \ldots, P_n, V$ may have, provided they be functions of x.

For denoting differentiations by dashes, we have upon integration by parts.

$$\int P_n y\, dx = \int P_n y\, dx, \int P_{n-1} y_1\, dx = P_{n-1} y - \int P'_{n-1} y\, dx,$$

$$\int P_{n-2} y_2\, dx = P_{n-2} y_1 - P'_{n-2}\, y + \int P''_{n-2} y\, dx,$$

$$\int P_{n-3} y_3\, dx = P_{n-3} y_2 - P'_{n-3}\, y_1 + P''_{n-3}\, y - \int P'''_{n-3}\, y\, dx, \text{ etc.}$$

Hence upon addition it is obvious that if

$$P_n - P'_{n-1} + P''_{n-2} - P'''_{n-3} + \ldots = 0,$$

the given equation is exact; and that its first integral is

$$(P_{n-1} - P'_{n-2} + P''_{n-3} - \dots)\, y + (P_{n-2} - P'_{n-3} + \dots)\, y_1 + (P_{n-3} - \dots)\, y_2 + \dots = \int V\, dx + A.$$

Ex. Is the equation $x^4 y_3 + 12x^3 y_2 + 36x^2 y_1 + 24xy = \sin x$ exact?

Applying the test, we have .

$$P_3 = 24x,\ P_2 = 36x^2,\ P_1 = 12x^3,\ P_0 = x^4,$$

and $P_3 - P'_2 + P''_1 - P'''_0 = 24x - 72x + 72x - 24x = 0.$

Thus the equation is exact; and its first integral is

$$(36x^2 - 36x^2 + 12x^2)\, y + (12x^3 - 4x^3)\, y_1 + x^4 y_2 = -\cos x + A,$$

or $$12x^2 y + 8x^3 y_1 + x^4 y_2 = -\cos x + A.$$

This again will be a perfect differential if

$$12x^2 - 24x^2 + 12x^2 = 0.$$

which is satisfied. Hence a second integral will be

$$(8x^3 - 4x^3)\, y + x^4 y_1 = -\sin x + Ax + B,$$

or $$4x^3 y + x^4 y_1 = -\sin x + Ax + B,$$

which may again be tested. But it is now obvious that the third and final integral is $x^4 y = \cos x + \dfrac{Ax^2}{2} + Bx + C.$

EXAMPLES

1. Show that the equation $x^5 y_3 + 15x^4 y_2 + 60x^3 y_1 + 60x^2 y = e^x$ is exact, and solve it completely.
2. Solve the equation
$$x^2 y_3 + 6xy_2 + 6y_1 + \sin x\,(y_3 - 3y_1) + \cos x\,(3y_2 - y) = \sin x.$$
3. Write down first integrals of the following equations:—
(a) $x^3 y_4 + xy_1 + y = e^x$.
(b) $x^3 y_4 + xy_1 - y = x^2 e^x$.
(c) $x^5 y_6 + x^4 y_5 + yy_1 + x = \log x$.
4. Show that if the equation $P_2 y + P_1 y_1 + P_0 y_2 = V$ admits of an integrating factor μ, then μ will satisfy the differential equation
$$P_2\, \mu - \frac{d}{dx}(P_1\, \mu) + \frac{d^2}{dx^2}(P_0\, \mu) = 0.$$

CHAPTER XVI.

GENERAL LINEAR DIFFERENTIAL EQUATION WITH CONSTANT COEFFICIENTS.

195. General Linear Differential Equation.

The form of the general linear differential equation of the nth order is

$$\frac{d^n y}{dx^n} + P_1 \frac{d^{n-1} y}{dx^{n-1}} + P_2 \frac{d^{n-2} y}{dx^{n-2}} + \dots + P_n y = V, \qquad \dots(1)$$

where $P_1, P_2, P_3, \dots, V$ are known functions of x.

Let us suppose that any particular solution $y = f(x)$

can be guessed, or obtained in any manner.

Then making the substitution $y = f(x) + z$

we obtain $$\frac{d^n z}{dx^n} + P_1 \frac{d^{n-1} z}{dx^{n-1}} + P_2 \frac{d^{n-2} z}{dx^{n-2}} + \dots + P_n z = 0, \qquad \dots(2)$$

Suppose $z = z_1, z = z_2, \dots, z = z_n$ to be solutions of this equation; then it is plain that $z = A_1 z_1 + A_2 z_2 + A_3 z_3 + \dots + A_n z_n$

is also a solution of equation (2) containing n arbitrary constants $A_1, A_2, \dots, A_n$.

Hence $y = A_1 z_1 + A_2 z_2 + A_3 z_3 + \dots + A_n z_n + f(x)$

is a solution of equation (1) containing n arbitrary constants, and is therefore the most general solution to be expected. No more general solution has been found.

The portion $f(x)$ is termed the Particular Integral (P.I.), and the remaining part containing the n arbitrary constants, which is the solution when the right-hand member of the equation is replaced by zero, is called the Complementary Function (C.F.). If these two parts can be found the whole solution can be at once written down as their sum.

196. Two Remarkable Cases.

There are two cases in which these solutions can be generally readily obtained.

(1) When the quantities $P_1, P_2, \dots, P_n$ are all constants.

(2) When the equation takes the form

$$x^n \frac{d^n y}{dx^n} + a_1 x^{n-1} \frac{d^{n-1} y}{dx^{n-1}} + a_2 x^{n-2} \frac{d^{n-2} y}{dx^{n-2}} + \dots + a_n y = V,$$

$a_1, a_2, \dots, a_n$ being constants and V any function of x.

The solution of the second case is readily reducible, as will be shown, to the solution of an equation coming under the first head.

EQUATION WITH CONSTANT COEFFICIENTS COMPLEMENTARY FUNCTION.

197. Let us therefore first determine the solution of such an equation as

$$y_n + a_1 y_{n-1} + a_2 y_{n-2} + \dots + a_n y = 0, \qquad \dots (1)$$

the coefficients being constants; *i.e.* for the present we confine our attention to the determination of the "Complementary Function" in the first case.

As a *trial* solution put $y = Ae^{mx}$, and we have

$$m^n + a_1 m^{n-1} + a_2 m^{n-2} + \dots + a_n = 0. \qquad \dots (2)$$

Let the roots of this equation be $m_1, m_2, m_3, \dots, m_n$, supposed (for the present) all different, then

$$A_1 e^{m_1 x}, A_2 e^{m_2 x}, A_3 e^{m_3 x}, \dots, A_n e^{m_n x},$$

are all solutions, and therefore also

$$y = A_1 e^{m_1 x} + A_2 e^{m_2 x} + A_3 e^{m_3 x} + \dots + A_n e^{m_n x}, \qquad \dots (3)$$

is a solution containing n arbitrary constants $A_1, A_2, A_3, \dots, A_n$, and is the most general to be expected.

198. Two Roots Equal.

If two roots of equation (2) become equal, say $m_1 = m_2$, the first two terms of the solution (3) become $(A_1 + A_2)e^{m_1 x}$, and since $A_1 + A_2$ may be regarded as a single constant, there is an apparent diminution by unity in the number of arbitrary constants, so that (3) is no longer the most general solution to be expected.

Let us examine this more closely.

Put $\qquad m_2 = m_1 + h.$

Then $\qquad A_1 e^{m_1 x} + A_2 e^{(m_1 + h)x}$

$$= A_1 e^{m_1 x} + A_2 e^{m_1 x} \left[1 + hx + \frac{h^2 x^2}{2!} + \dots \right]$$

$$= (A_1 + A_2) e^{m_1 x} + A_2 h \cdot x e^{m_1 x} + A_2 h e^{m_1 x} \left[\frac{hx^2}{2!} + \dots \right].$$

Now A_1 and A_2 are *two independent arbitrary quantities*, and we may therefore express them in terms of *two other independent arbitrary quantities* by two relations chosen at our pleasure.

First we will choose A_2 so large that ultimately A_2h when h is indefinitely small may be written B_2, an arbitrary finite constant.

Secondly, we will choose A_1 so large and of opposite sign to A_2 that $A_1 + A_2$ may be regarded as an arbitrary finite constant B_1. Then the terms

$$A_2he^{m_1x}\left[\frac{hx^2}{2!}+\ldots\right]$$

ultimately vanish with h since A_2h has been considered finite and the expression in square brackets is convergent and contains h as a factor.

Thus the terms $A_1e^{m_1x} + A_2e^{m_2x}$ may, when $m_2 = m_1$, be ultimately replaced by $B_1e^{m_1x} + B_2xe^{m_1x}$, and therefore the number of arbitrary constants in the whole solution remains n, and we therefore have obtained the *general* solution in this case.

199. Three Equal Roots.

Consider next the case when three of the roots of equation (2) become equal, viz., $m_1 = m_2 = m_3$. The terms, $A_1e^{m_1x} + A_2e^{m_2x} + A_3e^{m_3x}$, have already been replaced by $(B_1 + B_2x)e^{m_1x} + A_3e^{m_3x}$.

Let $\qquad m_3 = m_1 + k.$

Then $A_3e^{m_3x} = A_3e^{m_1x}e^{kx} = A_3e^{m_1x}\left(1 + kx + \dfrac{k^2x^2}{2!} + \ldots\right).$

Thus for $\qquad A_1e^{m_1x} + A_2e^{m_2x} + A_3e^{m_3x}$ we have

$$(B_1 + A_3)e^{m_1x} + (B_2 + A_3k)xe^{m_1x} + \frac{A_3k^2x^2e^{m_1x}}{2!}$$
$$+ A_3k^2x^2e^{m_1x}\left[\frac{kx}{3!} + \frac{k^2x^2}{4!} + \ldots\right],$$

and we may so choose A_3, B_2, and B_1, that

$$B_1 + A_3 = C_1,\ B_2 + A_3k = C_2,\ A_3k^2 = 2C_3,$$

C_1, C_2, C_3 being any arbitrary constants, whatever k may be, provided it be not absolute zero. But A_3k^2 being chosen a finite quantity, and the series within the square brackets being convergent, it is clear that ultimately, when k is indefinitely diminished, the limiting form of this expression is $(C_1 + C_2x + C_3x^2)e^{m_1x}$.

200. Several Roots Equal.

In a similar manner it will be obvious that if p roots of the equation (2) become equal, viz., $m_1 = m_2 = \ldots = m_p$,

there will be no loss of generality in our solution if we substitute the expression $(K_1 + K_2x + K_3x^2 + \ldots + K_p x^{p-1})e^{m_1x}$,

for the corresponding portion of the complementary function, viz.,

$$A_1e^{m_1x} + A_2e^{m_2x} + \ldots + A_pe^{m_px}.$$

201. Generalization.

More generally, if $A_1\phi(m_1) + A_2\phi(m_2) + A_3\phi(m_3) + \ldots + A_n\phi(m_n)$ be the complementary function of *any* linear differential equation with or without constant coefficients, what is to replace this expression so as to retain the generality when $m_1 = m_2$?

Let
$$m_2 = m_1 + h.$$

Then $\phi(m_2) = \phi(m_1 + h) = \phi(m_1) + h\dfrac{d\phi(m_1)}{dm_1} + \dfrac{h^2}{2!}\dfrac{d^2\phi(m_1)}{dm_1^2} + \ldots,$

and the terms $A_1\phi(m_1) + A_2\phi(m_2)$ become

$$(A_1 + A_2)\phi(m_1) + A_2h\frac{d\phi(m_1)}{dm_1} + A_2\frac{h^2}{2!}\frac{d^2\phi(m_1)}{dm_1^2} + \ldots$$

Now putting $A_1 + A_2 = B_1$, $A_2h = B_2$,

two arbitrary finite constants, the remaining terms ultimately disappear when we approach the limit in which h is indefinitely diminished.

Thus $A_1\phi(m_1) + A_2\phi(m_2)$ may be replaced by

$$B_1\phi(m_1) + B_2\frac{d\phi(m_1)}{dm_1},$$

thus retaining the same number (n) of arbitrary constants $B_1, B_2, A_3, A_4, \ldots, A_n$ in the complementary function as it originally possessed.

And as in Art. 200 we may proceed to show that if p roots become equal, viz. $m_1 = m_2 = \ldots = m_p$, the terms

$$A_1\phi(m_1) + A_2\phi(m_2) + \ldots + A_p\phi(m_p)$$

may be replaced by

$$B_1\phi(m_1) + B_2\frac{d\phi(m_1)}{dm_1} + B_3\frac{d^2\phi(m_1)}{dm_1^2} + \ldots + B_p\frac{d^{p-1}\phi(m_1)}{dm_1^{p-1}},$$

when the generality of the solution will be retained.

The results of Arts. 198, 199, 200 are of course particular cases of this, the form of $\phi(m_1)$ being e^{m_1x}.

202. Imaginary Roots

When a root of equation (2) of Art. 197 is imaginary, it is to be remembered that for equations with real coefficients imaginary roots occur in pairs.

Suppose, for instance, we have $m_1 = a + ib$, $m_2 = a - ib$,

where $\qquad i = \sqrt{-1}$.

Then the terms $A_1 e^{m_1 x} + A_2 e^{m_2 x}$

or $\qquad A_1 e^{(a+ib)x} + A_2 e^{(a-ib)x}$

may be thrown into a real form thus:—

$$\begin{aligned} & A_1 e^{ax} e^{ibx} + A_2 e^{ax} e^{-ibx} \\ &= A_1 e^{ax} (\cos bx + i \sin bx) + A_2 e^{ax} (\cos bx - i \sin bx) \\ &= (A_1 + A_2) e^{ax} \cos bx + (A_1 - A_2) i e^{ax} \sin bx \\ &= B_1 e^{ax} \cos bx + B_2 e^{ax} \sin bx, \end{aligned}$$

where the *two* arbitrary constants B_1 and B_2 replace $A_1 + A_2$ and $(A_1 - A_2) i$ respectively.

Let $B_1 = \rho \cos \alpha$, $B_2 = \rho \sin \alpha$,

then $\rho = \sqrt{B_1^2 + B_2^2}$

and $\alpha = \tan^{-1} \dfrac{B_2}{B_1}$.

Then $B_1 \cos bx + B_2 \sin bx = \rho \cos (bx - \alpha)$.

We may thus further replace

$$B_1 e^{ax} \cos bx + B_2 e^{ax} \sin bx \quad \text{by} \quad C_1 e^{ax} \cos (bx + C_2),$$

where C_1 and C_2 are arbitrary constants.

203. Repeated Imaginary Roots.

For repeated imaginary roots we may proceed as before, for it has been shown that when $m_2 = m_1$, $A_1 e^{m_1 x} + A_2 e^{m_2 x}$ may be replaced by $(B_1 + B_2 x) e^{m_1 x}$, and if $m_4 = m_3$, $A_3 e^{m_3 x} + A_4 e^{m_4 x}$ may be replaced by

$$(B_3 + B_4 x) e^{m_3 x}.$$

If then $m_1 = m_2 = a + ib$

and $\quad m_3 = m_4 = a - ib$, we may replace

$$A_1 e^{m_1 x} + A_2 e^{m_2 x} + A_3 e^{m_3 x} + A_4 e^{m_4 x}$$

by $\quad (B_1 + B_2 x) e^{ax} e^{ibx} + (B_3 + B_4 x) e^{ax} e^{-ibx}$,

that is by $e^{ax} [(B_1 + B_3) \cos bx + (B_1 - B_3) i \sin bx]$

$\qquad + x e^{ax} [(B_2 + B_4) \cos bx + (B_2 - B_4) i \sin bx]$, and therefore by

$$e^{ax}(C_1 \cos bx + C_2 \sin bx) + xe^{ax}(C_3 \cos bx + C_4 \sin bx),$$

that is by $e^{ax}(C_1 + xC_3)\cos bx + e^{ax}(C_2 + xC_4)\sin bx$,

or which is the same thing by

$$D_1e^{ax}\cos(bx + D_2) + D_3xe^{ax}\cos(bx + D_4).$$

Any of the last three forms contain four arbitrary constants which replace the original four arbitrary constants A_1, A_2, A_3, A_4, and thus retain intact the proper number (n) of arbitrary constants requisite to make the whole solution the most general to be expected. And this rule may obviously be extended to the case when any number of the imaginary roots are equal.

204. Ex. 1. Solve the equation $\dfrac{d^2y}{dx^2} - 3\dfrac{dy}{dx} + 2y = 0.$

Here our trial solution is $y = Ae^{mx}$, and we obtain

$$m^2 - 3m + 2 = 0,$$

whose roots are 1 and 2.

Accordingly $y = A_1e^x$ and $y = A_2e^{2x}$ are both particular solutions,

and $y = A_1e^x + A_2e^{2x}$

is the general solution containing two arbitrary constants.

Ex. 2. Solve $\dfrac{d^2y}{dx^2} - a^2y = 0.$

Here the auxiliary equation is $m^2 - a^2 = 0$ with roots $m = \pm a$, and the general solution is $y = A_1e^{ax} + A_2e^{-ax}$,

or as it may be written (if desired) $y = B_1 \cosh ax + B_2 \sinh ax$

by replacing A_1 by $\dfrac{B_1 + B_2}{2}$ and A_2 by $\dfrac{B_1 - B_2}{2}$.

Ex. 3. Solve $\dfrac{d^2y}{dx^2} + a^2y = 0.$

Here the auxiliary equation is $m^2 + a^2 = 0$ with roots $m = \pm ai$.

Hence the general solution is $y = A_1 \cos ax + A_2 \sin ax$,

or, which is its equivalent, $y = B_1 \cos(ax + B_2)$.

Ex. 4. Solve $\dfrac{d^3y}{dx^3} - 4\dfrac{d^2y}{dx^2} + 5\dfrac{dy}{dx} - 2y = 0$ or $(D-1)^2(D-2)y = 0$,

where D stands for $\dfrac{d}{dx}$.

Our auxiliary equation is $m^3 - 4m^2 + 5m - 2 = 0$

or $$(m-1)^2(m-2) = 0,$$

having roots 1, 1, 2. Accordingly the general solution is

$$y = (A_1 + A_2x)e^x + A_3e^{2x}.$$

Ex. 5. Solve $(D^2+1)(D-1)\,y=0$.

Our auxiliary equation is $(m^2+1)(m-1)=0$.

with roots $\pm\, i$, 1, and the general solution is therefore

$$y = A_1 \cos x + A_2 \sin x + A_3 e^x,$$

or
$$y = B_1 \cos (x + B_2) + A_3 e^x.$$

Ex. 6. Solve $(D^2+D+1)(D-2)\,y=0$.

Our auxiliary equation $(m^2+m+1)(m-2)=0$

has roots $-\dfrac{1}{2} \pm i\dfrac{\sqrt{3}}{2}$ and 2, and the general solution is

$$y = A_1 e^{-\frac{x}{2}} \cos \frac{x\sqrt{3}}{2} + A_2 e^{-\frac{x}{2}} \sin \frac{x\sqrt{3}}{2} + A_3 e^{2x},$$

or
$$y = B_1 e^{-\frac{x}{2}} \cos \left(\frac{x\sqrt{3}}{2} + B_3\right) + A_3 e^{2x}.$$

Ex. 7. Solve $(D^2+D+1)^2 (D-2)^3 (D-5)\,y=0$.

Here obviously the general solution is

$$y = (A_1 + A_2 x) e^{-\frac{x}{2}} \cos \frac{x\sqrt{3}}{2} + (A_3 + A_4 x) e^{-\frac{x}{2}} \sin \frac{x\sqrt{3}}{2}$$
$$+ (A_5 + A_6 x + A_7 x^2) e^{2x} + A_8 e^{5x},$$

containing eight arbitrary constants.

EXAMPLES

Write down the solutions of the following differential equations:—

1. $\dfrac{d^2y}{dx^2} - (a+b)\dfrac{dy}{dx} + aby = 0.$

2. $\dfrac{d^3y}{dx^3} - 6a\dfrac{d^2y}{dx^2} + 11\,a^2\dfrac{dy}{dx} - 6a^3\,y = 0.$

3. $\dfrac{d^3y}{dx^3} - 9\dfrac{d^2y}{dx^2} + 23\dfrac{dy}{dx} - 15y = 0.$

4. $\dfrac{d^3y}{dx^3} - 3\dfrac{dy}{dx} + 2y = 0.$

5. $\dfrac{d^3y}{dx^3} = y.$

6. $\dfrac{d^4y}{dx^4} = y.$

7. $(D-1)^2 (D-2)^2\, y = 0.$

8. $(D^2+1)(D^2+D+1)\, y = 0.$

9. $(D^2+1)^2 (D-1)^2\, y = 0.$

10. $(D^2+1)^3 (D^2+D+1)^2\, y = 0.$

11. $(D-1)^3 (D-2)(D^2+2D+2)^2\, y = 0.$

12. $(D^2+a^2)^2 (D^2+b^2)(D^4+c^2D^2+c^4)\, y = 0.$

THE PARTICULAR INTEGRAL.

205. Having considered the complementary function of such an equation as $F(D)y = V$ where $F(D)$ stands for

$$D^n + a_1 D^{n-1} + a_2 D^{n-2} + \dots + a^n,$$

$a_1, a_2, \dots, a_n$ being constants, and V any function of x, we next turn our attention to the mode of obtaining a particular integral, and propose to give the ordinary and most useful of the processes adopted.

We may write the above equation as $y = \frac{1}{F(D)} V$ (or $[f(D)]V$),

where $\frac{1}{F(D)}$ is such an operator that $F(D)\left[\frac{1}{F(D)} V\right] = V.$

206. "*D*" satisfies the fundamental laws of Algebra.

It is shown in the Differential Calculus that the operator D $\left(\text{denoting } \frac{d}{dx}\right)$ satisfies

(1) The Distributive Law of Algebra, viz.

$$D(u + v + w + \dots) = Du + Dv + Dw + \dots$$

(2) The Commutative Law as far as regards constants, *i.e.* $D(cu) = c(Du)$.

(3) The Index Law, *i.e.* $D^m D^n u = D^{m+n} u$,

m and n being positive integers.

Thus the symbol D satisfies all the elementary rules of combination of algebraical quantities with the exception that it is not commutative with regard to variables.

It therefore follows that any rational algebraical identity has a corresponding symbolical operative analogue. Thus since by the binomial theorem

$$(m + a)^n = m^n + nam^{n-1} + \frac{n(n-1)}{1 \cdot 2} a^2 m^{n-2} + \dots + a^n,$$

we have by an analogous theorem for operators which may be inferred without further proof

$$(D + a)^n y = \left\{D^n + naD^{n-1} + \frac{n(n-1)}{1 \cdot 2} a^2 D^{n-2} + \dots + a^n\right\} y$$

$$= D^n y + naD^{n-1} y + \frac{n(n-1)}{1 \cdot 2} a^2 D^{n-2} y + \dots + a^n y.$$

207. Operation $f(D)e^{ax}$.

It has been proved in the Differential Calculus that if r be a positive integer,

$$D^r e^{ax} = a^r e^{ax}.$$

Let us define the operation D^{-r} to be such that $D^r D^{-r} u = u$.

Then D^{-1} represents an integration, and we shall suppose that in the operation $D^{-1}u$ no arbitrary constants are added (for our object *now* is to obtain a *particular* integral and not the most general integral).

Now since $D^r a^{-r} e^{ax} = e^{ax} = D^r D^{-r} e^{ax}$, it follows that

$$D^{-r} e^{ax} = a^{-r} e^{ax}.$$

Hence it is clear that $D^n e^{ax} = a^n e^{ax}$ for all integral values of *n positive or negative.*

208. Let $f(z)$ be any function of z capable of expansion in integral powers of z, positive or negative $(= \Sigma A_r z^r$ say, A_r being a constant, independent of z).

Then
$$\begin{aligned} f(D)e^{ax} &= (\Sigma A_r D^r) e^{ax} \\ &= (\Sigma A_r D^r e^{ax}) \\ &= (\Sigma A_r a^r) e^{ax} = f(a) e^{ax}. \end{aligned}$$

The result of the operation $f(D)e^{ax}$ may therefore be obtained *by replacing D by a.*

Ex. 1. Obtain the value of $\dfrac{1}{D^3 + D^2 + D + 1} e^{2x}$.

Obviously by the rule this is

$$\frac{1}{2^3 + 2^2 + 2 + 1} e^{2x} \text{ or } \frac{e^{2x}}{15}.$$

Ex. 2. Obtain the value of $\dfrac{D+1}{(D+2)(D+3)(D+4)} e^{3x}$.

By the rule this is

$$\frac{4}{5 \cdot 6 \cdot 7} e^{3x} = \frac{2}{105} e^{3x}.$$

EXAMPLES

1. Perform the operations indicated by

(1) $\frac{1}{(D+1)^2} e^x$, (2) $\frac{1}{(D+1)(D+2)} e^{ax}$,

(3) $\frac{1}{(D+2)(D+3)(D+4)} \cosh x$.

2. Show that $\frac{D^2}{(D-a)(D-b)(D-c)} V = \Sigma \frac{a^2}{(a-b)(a-c)} \frac{1}{D-a} V$.

3. Apply Art. 208 to show that

$$f(D^2)\sin mx = f(-m^2)\sin mx,$$
$$f(D^2)\cos mx = f(-m^2)\cos mx,$$
$$f(D^2)\begin{Bmatrix}\sinh \\ \cosh\end{Bmatrix} mx = f(m^2)\begin{Bmatrix}\sinh \\ \cosh\end{Bmatrix} mx.$$

209. Operation $f(D)e^{ax}X$.

Next let $y = e^{ax} Y$, where Y is any function of x.

Then since $D^r e^{ax} = a^r e^{ax}$,

we have by Leibnitz's Theorem

$$y_n = e^{ax}(a^n Y + {}_nC_1 a^{n-1} DY + {}_nC_2 D^2 Y + \ldots + D^n Y),$$

which, by analogy with the Binomial Theorem (Art. 206) may be written

$$D^n e^{ax} Y = e^{ax}(D+a)^n Y,$$

n being a positive integer.

Now let $X = (D+a)^n Y$,

so that we may write $Y = (D+a)^{-n} X$.

Then from above $D^n e^{ax} Y = e^{ax}(D+a)^n Y$ or $D^n e^{ax}(D+a)^{-n} X = e^{ax} X$,

and therefore $D^{-n} e^{ax} X = e^{ax}(D+a)^{-n} X$.

Hence in all cases for integral values of *n positive or negative.*

$$D^n e^{ax} X = e^{ax}(D+a)^n X.$$

210. As in Art. 208 we shall have

$$f(D)e^{ax} X = \Sigma(A_r D^r)e^{ax} X = \Sigma(A_r D^r e^{ax} X)$$
$$= e^{ax}\, \Sigma A_r (D+a)^r X. = e^{ax} f(D+a) X.$$

That is, e^{ax} may be *transferred from the right side to the left* of the operator $f(D)$ *provided we replace* D by $D+a$.

Ex. 1. $\frac{1}{(D-1)^3} e^x x = e^x \frac{1}{D^3} x = e^x \cdot \frac{x^4}{2.3.4}$.

Ex. 2. $\frac{1}{D^2 - 4D + 4} e^{2x} \sin x = e^{2x} \frac{1}{D^2} \sin x = -e^{2x} \sin x$.

EXAMPLES

1. Perform the operations $\frac{1}{(D-1)^3}e^x x^2, \frac{1}{(D-1)^2}e^x \sin x, \frac{1}{D-1}e^x \log x.$

2. Show that $e^{ax}\frac{1}{(D+a-1)(D+a-2)}e^{bx} = e^{bx}\frac{1}{(D+b-1)(D+b-2)}e^{ax}.$

211. Operation $f(D^2)^{\sin}_{\cos}\, mx.$

We have $\quad D^2 \begin{smallmatrix}\sin\\ \cos\end{smallmatrix} mx = (-m^2) \begin{smallmatrix}\sin\\ \cos\end{smallmatrix} mx,$

and therefore $\quad D^{2r} \begin{smallmatrix}\sin\\ \cos\end{smallmatrix} mx = (-m^2)^r \begin{smallmatrix}\sin\\ \cos\end{smallmatrix} mx.$

Hence, as before, Arts. 208 and 210, it will follow that

$$f(D^2) \begin{smallmatrix}\sin\\ \cos\end{smallmatrix} mx = f(-m^2) \begin{smallmatrix}\sin\\ \cos\end{smallmatrix} mx.$$

Ex. $\int e^{ax} \sin bx\, dx = D^{-1}e^{ax} \sin bx = e^{ax}(D+a)^{-1} \sin bx$ (Art. 210)

$$= e^{ax}\frac{a-D}{a^2-D^2}\sin bx = \frac{e^{ax}}{a^2+b^2}(a-D)\sin bx \qquad \text{(Art. 211)}$$

$$= e^{ax}\frac{a\sin bx - b\cos bx}{a^2+b^2} = e^{ax}(a^2+b^2)^{-\frac{1}{2}}\sin\left(bx - \tan^{-1}\frac{b}{a}\right).$$

EXAMPLES

1. Find by this method the integrals of

$$e^{ax}\cos bx, e^x \sin^2 x, e^x \sin^3 x, \sinh x \sin x.$$

2. Perform the operations

$$\frac{1}{D^2+2}\sin 2x, \frac{1}{D^4+1}\cos x, \frac{D^2+1}{D^4+1}\sin 2x.$$

3. Obtain by means of the exponential values of the sine and cosine the results of the operations $f(D)\cos mx$, $f(D)\sin mx$.

212. Operation $\frac{1}{F(D)}\begin{smallmatrix}\sin\\ \cos\end{smallmatrix} mx.$

Let us next consider the operation $\frac{1}{F(D)}\sin mx$

where $F(z)$ is a function of z capable of expansion in positive integral powers of z.

Let $F(D)$ be arranged in powers of D, then if no odd powers occur the result may be written down by the foregoing rule of Art. 211.

Thus $\frac{1}{1+D^2+D^4+D^6}\sin 2x = \frac{1}{1-4+16-64}\sin 2x = -\frac{1}{51}\sin 2x.$

But if both even and odd powers occur we may proceed as follows:— Group the even powers together and the odd powers together, and then we may write the operation

$$\frac{1}{F(D)}\sin mx \equiv \frac{1}{\phi(D^2) + D\chi(D^2)}\sin mx$$

$$= \frac{\phi(D^2) - D\chi(D^2)}{[\phi(D^2)]^2 - D^2[\chi(D^2)]^2}\sin mx$$

$$= [\phi(D^2) - D\chi(D^2)]\frac{\sin mx}{[\phi(-m^2)]^2 + m^2[\chi(-m^2)]^2}$$

$$= \frac{\phi(-m^2)\sin mx - m\chi(-m^2)\cos mx}{[\phi(-m^2)]^2 + m^2[\chi(-m^2)]^2}.$$

Upon examination it will be seen that in practice we may write $-m^2$ for D^2 immediately after the step $\frac{1}{\phi(D^2) + D\chi(D^2)}\sin mx$,

writing immediately $\frac{1}{\phi(-m^2) + D\chi(-m^2)}\sin mx$,

or $\frac{\phi(-m^2) - D\chi(-m^2)}{[\phi(-m^2)]^2 - D^2[\chi(-m^2)]^2}\sin mx$, etc.

Ex. 1. Obtain the value of $\frac{1}{D^3 + D^2 + D + 1}\sin 2x$.

This is $\frac{1}{D^2 + 1 + D(D^2 + 1)}\sin 2x$,

or $\frac{1}{-3(1 + D)}\sin 2x$,

or $\frac{D - 1}{-3(D^2 - 1)}\sin 2x$,

or $(D - 1)\frac{\sin 2x}{15}$,

or $\frac{2}{15}\cos 2x - \frac{1}{15}\sin 2x$.

Ex. 2. Obtain the value of $\frac{1}{(D - 1)^3}e^{2x}\cos x$.

This expression $= e^{2x}\frac{1}{(D + 1)^3}\cos x$

$$= e^{2x}\frac{1}{D^3 + 3D^2 + 3D + 1}\cos x$$

$$= e^{2x} \frac{1}{-D-3+3D+1} \cos x \text{ [replacing each } D^2 \text{ by } -1]$$

$$= \frac{e^{2x}}{2} \frac{1}{D-1} \cos x = \frac{e^{2x}}{2} \frac{D+1}{D^2-1} \cos x$$

$$= \frac{e^{2x}}{2} (D+1) \frac{\cos x}{-2} = -\frac{e^{2x}}{4} (\cos x - \sin x).$$

EXAMPLES

1. Perform the operations indicated in the following expressions:

$$\frac{D}{D-1} e^x \sin x, \quad \frac{D^3}{(D-1)(D-2)} e^x \sin ax,$$

$$\frac{1}{D-1} e^x \sin x + \frac{1}{D+1} e^{-x} \sin x.$$

2. Show that $\frac{1}{(D+a)^n} V = e^{-ax} \int\int\int \ldots \int e^{ax} V \, dx \ldots dx$, there being n integral signs.

3. Show that by first expressing $\frac{1}{F(z)}$ in partial fractions, the operation $\frac{1}{F(D)} V$ may be expressed in terms of a set of common integrations.

213. Operator $\frac{1}{F(D)} V.V$ Algebraic.

If in the operation $\frac{1}{F(D)} V$, V be an algebraic function of x, rational and integral, we may expand $\frac{1}{F(D)}$ by any method in ascending powers of D as far as the highest power of x contained in V.

Ex. 1. For example, find $\frac{1}{1+D+D^2}(x^2+x+1)$.

This is $\frac{1-D}{1-D^3}(x^2+x+1)$,

or $(1 - D + D^3 - D^4 + \text{etc.})(x^2+x+1)$

$= (x^2+x+1) - (2x+1)$

$= x^2 - x.$

Ex. 2. Again, find $\frac{1}{D^3+3D^2+7D-1}e^x x^3$.

This expression is

$$= e^x \frac{1}{(D+1)^3+3(D+1)^2+7(D+1)-1}x^3$$

$$= e^x \frac{1}{10+16D+6D^2+D^3}x^3 = \frac{e^x}{10}\frac{1}{1+\frac{8}{5}D+\frac{3}{5}D^2+\frac{1}{10}D^3}x^3$$

$$= \frac{e^x}{10}\left(1-\frac{8}{5}D+\frac{4}{2}\cdot\frac{9}{5}D^2-\frac{5}{2}\frac{6}{5}\frac{9}{0}D^3 \ldots\right)x^3$$

$$= \frac{e^x}{10}\left(x^3-\frac{8}{5}.3x^2+\frac{4}{2}\frac{9}{5}.6x-\frac{5}{2}\frac{6}{5}\frac{9}{0}.6\right).$$

EXAMPLES

Perform the operations

1. $\frac{1}{(D+1)(D+2)}x^2, \frac{1}{D(D-1)}x, \frac{1}{D^2(D-1)^2}x.$
2. $\frac{1}{(D+1)(D+2)}e^x x^2, \frac{1}{D(D-1)}x\cos h\, x.$
3. $\frac{1}{(D-1)}x\cos h\, x\cos x.$

214. Cases of Failure.

In applying the above methods of obtaining a Particular Integral, cases of failure are frequently met with. We propose to illustrate the course of procedure to be adopted in such cases.

215. Ex. 1. Solve the equation $\frac{dy}{dx}-y=e^x$.

The Complementary Function is Ae^x.

To obtain the Particular Integral we have $\frac{1}{D-1}e^x$.

If we apply Art. 208, the result becomes $\frac{e^x}{1-1}$ or ∞.

We may *evade this difficulty* and obtain the result of the operation by applying Art. 210 when we have $\frac{1}{D-1}e^x = e^x.\frac{1}{D}1 = xe^x$,

which is the particular integral required.

Instead, however, of *substituting another method*, let us examine the operation $\frac{1}{D-1}e^x$ more carefully.

Writing $x(1+h)$ instead of x, we have

$$\frac{1}{D-1}e^x = Lt_{h=0}\frac{1}{D-1}e^{x(1+h)} = Lt_{h=0}\frac{1}{h}e^x e^{hx}$$

$$= Lt_{h=0}\frac{1}{h}e^x\left(1+hx+\frac{h^2x^2}{2!}+\frac{h^3x^3}{3!}+\ldots\right)$$

$$= Lt_{h=0}\left[\frac{e^x}{h}+xe^x+he^x\left\{\frac{x^2}{2!}+\frac{hx^3}{3!}+\ldots\right\}\right].$$

Of this expression the portion $Lt\ e^x/h$ becomes infinite, but may be *taken with the complementary function* Ae^x; and A being arbitrary we may regard $A+\frac{1}{h}$ has a new arbitrary constant B, for we may suppose A to contain a negatively infinite portion to cancel the term $1/h$.

The term xe^x is the *Particular Integral* desired.

The remaining terms *contain h and vanish* when h is decreased indefinitely.

The whole solution is therefore $y = Ae^x + xe^x$.

Ex. 2. Solve the equation $\frac{d^2y}{dx^2}+4y=e^x+\sin 2x$.

The complementary function is clearly

$$y = A\sin 2x + B\cos 2x.$$

The particular integral consists of two parts $\frac{1}{D^2+4}e^x$ or $\frac{1}{5}e^x$ and $\frac{1}{D^2+4}\sin 2x$. In this second part, if we apply the rule of Art. 211, we get $\frac{\sin 2x}{0}$, *i.e.* ∞, and so fail.

We now consider the limit, when $h=0$, of $\frac{1}{D^2+4}\sin 2x(1+h)$.

This expression

$$= \frac{1}{4}\frac{1}{1-(1+h)^2}\sin(2x+2hx)$$

$$= \frac{1}{4}\frac{1}{-2h-h^2}(\sin 2x\cos 2hx + \cos 2x\sin 2hx)$$

$$= -\frac{1}{8}\frac{1}{h+\frac{h^2}{2}}\left[\sin 2x\left(1-\frac{4h^2x^2}{2!}+\ldots\right)+\cos 2x\,(2hx-\ldots)\right]$$

$$= -\frac{1}{8}\frac{\sin 2x}{h} - \frac{1}{4}x\cos 2x + \text{powers of } h$$

= (a term which may be included in the complementary function)

$$-\frac{x\cos 2x}{4} + \text{(terms which vanish with } h).$$

Thus the whole solution of the differential equation will be

$$y = A\sin 2x + B\cos 2x + \frac{1}{5}e^x - \frac{x\cos 2x}{4}.$$

Ex. 3. Solve the equation

$$(D^2 + 3D)(D-1)^2\, y = e^x + e^{2x} + \sin x + x^2.$$

Here the complementary function is plainly

$$A_1 + A_2e^{-3x} + (A_3 + A_4x)e^x.$$

The particular integral consists of four parts, viz.,

$$\frac{1}{(D^2+3D)(D-1)^2}e^x = \frac{1}{(D-1)^2}\cdot\frac{e^x}{4} = \frac{e^x}{4}\cdot\frac{1}{D^2}\cdot 1 = \frac{x^2e^x}{8}$$

[or consider $\dfrac{1}{(D-1)^2}\cdot\dfrac{e^{x(1+h)}}{4} = \dfrac{1}{4h^2}e^x\left(1 + hx + \dfrac{h^2x^2}{2!} + \ldots\right)$

= (a part going into the complementary function)

$+\dfrac{x^2}{8}e^x$ + (terms which vanish with h)] .

$$\frac{1}{(D^2+3D)(D-1)^2}e^{2x} = \frac{1}{10}e^{2x}.$$

$$\frac{1}{(D^2+3D)(D-1)^2}\sin x = \frac{1}{(-1+3D)(-2D)}\sin x = \frac{1}{-6D^2+2D}\sin x$$

$$= \frac{1}{6+2D}\sin x = \frac{3-D}{2(9-D^2)}\sin x$$

$$= (3\sin x - \cos x)/20.$$

$$\text{Finally } \frac{1}{(D^2+3D)(D-1)^2}x^2 = \frac{1}{3D}\left(1+\frac{D}{3}\right)^{-1}(1 + 2D + 3D^2 + \ldots)x^2$$

$$= \frac{1}{3D}\left(1+\frac{D}{3}\right)^{-1}(x^2 + 4x + 6)$$

$$= \frac{1}{3D}\left(1 - \frac{D}{3} + \frac{D^2}{9} - \ldots\right)(x^2 + 4x + 6)$$

$$= \frac{1}{3D}\left(x^2 + 4x + 6 - \frac{2}{3}x - \frac{4}{3} + \frac{2}{9}\right)$$

$$= \frac{1}{3D}\left(x^2 + \frac{10}{3}x + \frac{44}{9}\right) = \frac{1}{3}\left(\frac{x^3}{3} + \frac{5}{3}x^2 + \frac{44}{9}x\right).$$

Hence the whole solution is $y = A_1 + A_2 e^{-2x} + (A_3 + A_4 x)e^x$

$$+ \frac{x^2 e^x}{8} + \frac{e^{2x}}{10} + \frac{3 \sin x - \cos x}{20} + \frac{x^3}{9} + \frac{5x^2}{9} + \frac{44}{27} x.$$

Ex. 4. Solve the equation $\frac{d^4 y}{dx^4} - y = x \sin x$.

The C.F. is $A_1 \sinh x + A_2 \cosh x + A_3 \sin x + A_4 \cos x$.

To find the P.I. we have $\frac{1}{D^4 - 1} x \sin x$,

which is the coefficient of i in $\frac{1}{D^4 - 1} x e^{2x}$,

i.e. in $\quad e^{ix} \frac{1}{(D + i)^4 - 1} x$,

i.e. in $\quad e^x \frac{1}{-4i D - 6D^2 \ldots} x$,

i.e. in $\quad e^{ix} \frac{1}{-4iD} \frac{1}{1 - \frac{3}{2} iD \ldots} x$,

i.e. in $\quad e^{ix} \frac{i}{4} \frac{1}{D} \left(x + \frac{3}{2} i \right)$,

i.e. in $\quad e^{ix} \left(\frac{ix^2}{8} - \frac{3}{8} x \right)$

Thus the P.I. is $\frac{x^2 \cos x}{8} - \frac{3}{8} x \sin x$,

and the whole solution is

$$y = A_1 \sinh x + A_2 \cosh x + A_3 \sin x + A_4 \cos x + \frac{x^2 \cos x}{8} - \frac{3}{8} x \sin x.$$

EXAMPLES

1. Obtain the Particular Integrals indicated by

(1) $\frac{1}{D^2 + 1} \sin x$. (2) $\frac{1}{D^2 + 4} \cos 2x$.

(3) $\frac{1}{D^2 - 1} \sinh x$. (4) $\frac{1}{D^3 - 1} e^x x$.

(5) $\frac{1}{(D - 1)(D - 2)(D - 3)} e^x$. (6) $\frac{1}{D^4 - 1} (\sinh x + \sin x)$.

(7) $\frac{1}{(D^2 - a^2)(D^2 - b^2)} (e^{ax} + \cosh bx)$.

(8) $\frac{1}{(D^2 + 1)(D^2 + 4)} \cos \frac{x}{2} \cos \frac{3x}{2}$.

2. Solve the differential equations

(1) $\dfrac{d^2y}{dx^2} - y = e^{2x}$.

(2) $\dfrac{d^2y}{dx^2} - y = \cosh x$.

(3) $\dfrac{d^2y}{dx^2} + y = e^{-x} + \cos x + x^3 + e^x \sin x$.

(4) $(D^2 - 1)(D^3 - 1)\, y = xe^x$.

(5) $(D - 1)(D + 1)\, D^3 y = x$.

(6) $(D^3 - 3D^2 - 3D + 1)\, y = e^{-x} + x$.

(7) $(D^3 - 1)\, y = x \sin x$.

(8) $(D^2 - 1)\, y = xe^x \sin x$.

(9) $(D^2 - 1)\, y = \cosh x \cos x + a^x$.

(10) $(D - 1)^2 (D^2 + 1)^2\, y = \sin^2 \dfrac{x}{2} + e^x + x$.

216. The Operator $x\dfrac{d}{dx}$.

A transformation which renders peculiar service in reducing an equation of the class

$$x^n \frac{d^ny}{dx^n} + A_1 x^{n-1} \frac{d^{n-1}y}{dx^{n-1}} + A_2 x^{n-2} \frac{d^{n-2}y}{dx^{n-2}} + \dots + A_n y = V,$$

where $A_1, A_2, \dots,$ are constants, to a form in which all the coefficients are constants, arises from putting $x = e^t$.

In this case $\dfrac{dx}{dt} = e^t$, and therefore $x\dfrac{dy}{dx} = \dfrac{dy}{dt}$.

It is obvious therefore that the operators $x\dfrac{d}{dx}$

and $\dfrac{d}{dt}$ are equivalent. Let D stand for $\dfrac{d}{dt}$. Then we have

$$x\frac{d}{dx}\left(x^{n-1}\frac{d^{n-1}y}{dx^{n-1}}\right) = x^n \frac{d^ny}{dx^n} + (n-1)x^{n-1}\frac{d^{n-1}y}{dx^{n-1}},$$

or

$$x^n \frac{d^ny}{dx^n} = \left(x\frac{d}{dx} - n + 1\right) x^{n-1} \frac{d^{n-1}y}{dx^{n-1}}$$

$$= (D - n + 1)\, x^{n-1} \frac{d^{n-1}y}{dx^{n-1}},$$

Now putting n in succession 2, 3, 4, ... , we have

$$x^2 \frac{d^2y}{dx^2} = (D-1)\, x\frac{dy}{dx} = (D-1)\, Dy$$

$$x^3 \frac{d^3y}{dx^3} = (D-2)\, x^2 \frac{d^2y}{dx^2}$$

$$= (D-2)(D-1)\, Dy, \text{ etc.}$$

Hence generally $\quad x^n \dfrac{d^ny}{dx^n} \equiv (D-n+1)(D-n+2)\ldots(D-1)\, Dy$

or reversing the order of the operations

$$= D(D-1)(D-2)\ldots(D-n+1)\, y.$$

Ex. Solve the differential equation

$$x^3 \frac{d^3y}{dx^3} + 2x^2 \frac{d^2y}{dx^2} + 3x\frac{dy}{dx} - 3y = x^2 + x$$

Putting $x = e^t$, the equation becomes

$$D(D-1)(D-2)\, y + 2D(D-1)\, y + 3Dy - 3y = e^{2x} + e^t,$$

or $\quad (D^3 - D^2 + 3D - 3)\, y = e^{2t} + e^t,$

i.e. $\quad (D-1)(D^2+3)\, y = e^{2t} + e^t.$

giving $y = Ae^t + B\cos t\sqrt{3} + C\sin t\sqrt{3} + \dfrac{e^{2t}}{7} + \dfrac{te^t}{4},$

or $y = Ax + B\cos(\sqrt{3}\log x) + C\sin(\sqrt{3}\log x) + \dfrac{x^2}{7} + \dfrac{x\log x}{4}.$

EXAMPLES

Solve the differential equations

1. $x^2 \dfrac{d^2y}{dx^2} + x\dfrac{dy}{dx} + q^2y = 0.$

2. $x^2 \dfrac{d^2y}{dx^2} + x\dfrac{dy}{dx} + q^2y = [\log x]^2 + x\sin\log x + \sin q\log x.$

3. $x^3 \dfrac{d^3y}{dx^3} + 3x^2 \dfrac{d^2y}{dx^2} + x\dfrac{dy}{dx} + y = x + \log x.$

4. $x^3 \dfrac{d^3y}{dx^3} + 2x^2 \dfrac{d^2y}{dx^2} - x\dfrac{dy}{dx} + y = x + x^3.$

5. $(a+bx)^2 \dfrac{d^2y}{dx^2} + b(a+bx)\dfrac{dy}{dx} + q^2y = 0.$

CHAPTER XVII.

ORTHOGONAL TRAJECTORIES. MISCELLANEOUS EQUATIONS.

ORTHOGONAL TRAJECTORY.

217. Cartesians.

The equation $f(x, y, a) = 0$ is representative of a family of curves. The problem we now propose to investigate is that of finding the equation of another family of curves each member of which cuts each member of the former family at right angles.

And in such a problem as this it has been already pointed out that it is necessary to treat all members of the first family collectively, so that the particularizing constant a ought not to appear in the equation of the family. It has been shown in Art. 171, that the quantity a may be eliminated between the equations

$$f(x, y, a) = 0,$$
$$\frac{\partial f}{\partial x} + \frac{\partial f}{\partial y}\frac{dy}{dx} = 0.$$

Let this eliminant be

$$\phi\left(x, y, \frac{dy}{dx}\right) = 0.$$

This is the differential equation of the first family.

Now at any point of intersection of a member of the first system with a member of the second system, the tangents to the two curves are at right angles.

Thus if ξ, η be the current coordinates of a point on a curve of the second family at its intersection with one of the first family, and x, y the current coordinates of the same point regarded as lying upon the intersected curve of the first family, we have

$$\xi = x, \eta = y, \frac{d\eta}{d\xi} = -\frac{dx}{dy}.$$

The differential equation of the second family is therefore

$$\phi\left(\xi, \eta, -\frac{d\xi}{d\eta}\right) = 0,$$

and when this is integrated we have the family of "Orthogonal Trajectories" of the first system.

The rule is therefore:

Differentiate the given equation, *eliminate the constant*, write $-\frac{dx}{dy}$ in place of $\frac{dy}{dx}$, and integrate the new differential equation.

218. Polars.

If the curve be given in polars the angle the tangent makes with the radius vector is $r\frac{d\theta}{dr}$, so our rule is now:

Differentiate the equation, *eliminate the constant*, write $-\frac{1}{r}\frac{dr}{d\theta}$ in place of $r\frac{d\theta}{dr}$, and integrate the new differential equation.

219.

Ex. 1. Find the orthogonal trajectory of the family of circles

$$x^2 + y^2 = 2ax, \qquad \ldots (1)$$

each of which touches the y-axis at the origin.

Here $\quad x + y\frac{dy}{dx} = a,$

and, eliminating a, $x^2 + y^2 = 2x\left(x + y\frac{dy}{dx}\right),$

i.e. $\quad x^2 + 2xy\frac{dy}{dx} - y^2 = 0 \qquad \ldots (2)$

Hence the new differential equation must be

$$x^2 - 2xy\frac{dx}{dy} - y^2 = 0,$$

or $\quad y^2 + 2xy\frac{dx}{dy} - x^2 = 0, \qquad \ldots(3)$

which is a homogeneous equation, and the variables become separable by the assumption $y = vx$.

However, this being the same as equation (2) with the exception that x and y are interchanged, its integral must be

$$y^2 + x^2 = 2by,$$

another set of circles, each of which touches the x-axis at the origin.

Ex. 2. Find the orthogonal trajectory of the curves

$$\frac{x^2}{a^2+\lambda}+\frac{y^2}{b^2+\lambda}=1, \quad \ldots (1)$$

λ being the parameter of the family

Here $$\frac{x}{a^2+\lambda}+\frac{yy_1}{b^2+\lambda}=0, \quad \ldots (2)$$

and λ must be eliminated between these two equations.

(2) gives $x(b^2+\lambda)+yy_1(a^2+\lambda)=0$,

or $$\lambda=-\frac{b^2x+a^2yy_1}{x+yy_1}, \quad \text{so that } a^2+\lambda=\frac{(a^2-b^2)x}{x+yy_1},$$

and $$b^2+\lambda=-\frac{(a^2-b^2)yy_1}{-x+yy_1}.$$

Thus the differential equation of the family is

$$\frac{x^2(x+yy_1)}{(a^2-b^2)x}-\frac{y^2(x+yy_1)}{(a^2-b^2)yy_1}=1,$$

or $$x^2-y^2+xy\left(y_1-\frac{1}{y_1}\right)=a^2-b^2. \quad \ldots (3)$$

Hence changing y_1 into $-\frac{1}{y_1}$, the differential equation of the family of trajectories is

$$x^2-y^2+xy\left(-\frac{1}{y_1}+y_1\right)=a^2-b^2 \quad \ldots (4)$$

But this being the same as equation (3) must have the same primitive, viz. :

$$\frac{x^2}{a^2+\mu}+\frac{y^2}{b^2+\mu}=1.$$

i.e. a set of conic sections confocal with the former set.

Ex. 3. Find the orthogonal trajectories of the family of cardioides $r=a(1-\cos\theta)$ for different values of a.

Here $$\frac{dr}{d\theta}=a\sin\theta,$$

and, eliminating a, $$r\frac{d\theta}{dr}=\frac{1-\cos\theta}{\sin\theta}=\tan\frac{\theta}{2}.$$

Hence for the family of orthogonal trajectories we must have

$$-\frac{1}{r}\frac{dr}{d\theta}=\tan\frac{\theta}{2},$$

or $$\log r=2\log\cos\frac{\theta}{2}+\text{constant},$$

or $$r=b(1+\cos\theta),$$

another family of coaxial cardioides whose cusps point in the opposite direction.

EXAMPLES

1. Find the orthogonal trajectories of the family of parabolas $y^2 = 4ax$ for different values of a.
2. Show that the orthogonal trajectories of the family of similar ellipses $\frac{x^2}{a^2} + \frac{y^2}{b^2} = m^2$ for different values of m is $x^{a^2} = Ay^{b^2}$.
3. Find the orthogonal trajectories of the equiangular spirals $r = ae^{\theta \cot \alpha}$ for different values of a.
4. Find the orthogonal trajectories of the confocal and coaxial parabolas $\frac{2a}{r} = 1 + \cos\theta$ for different values of a.
5. Show that the families of curves $\left.\begin{array}{r} x^3 - 3xy^2 = a \\ 3x^2y - y^3 = b \end{array}\right\}$ are orthogonal.
6. Show that the curves $r\sin^2\alpha = a(\cos\theta - \cos\alpha)$ and $r\sinh^2\beta = a(\cosh\beta - \cos\theta)$ are orthogonal.
7. Show that if $f(x + iy) = u + iv$ the curves

$$\left.\begin{array}{l} u = a \\ v = b \end{array}\right\}$$

form orthogonal systems.
8. Prove that for any constant value of μ the family of curves
$\cosh x \operatorname{cosec} y - \mu \cot y = \text{constant}$
cut the family $\mu \coth x - \operatorname{cosech} x \cos y = \text{constant}$
at right angles. [LONDON, 1890.]

SOME IMPORTANT DYNAMICAL EQUATIONS.

220. The equation $\frac{d^2u}{d\theta^2} + u = f'(u)$

is the general form of the equation of motion of a particle under the action of a central force.

Multiplying by $2\frac{du}{d\theta}$ and integrating we have

$$\left(\frac{du}{d\theta}\right)^2 + u^2 = 2f(u) + A,$$

which we may write as

$$\int \frac{du}{\sqrt{A + 2f(u) - u^2}} = \theta + B$$

and the solution is therefore effected.

221. Equations of the form

$$\frac{d^2u}{d\theta^2} + n^2u = f(\theta)$$

have already been discussed as being linear with constant coefficients. The solution may however be conducted thus :—
Multiply by $\sin n\theta$, which will be found to be an integrating factor.
Integrating,

$$\sin n\theta \frac{du}{d\theta} - nu \cos n\theta = \int_0^\theta f(\theta') \sin n\theta' d\theta' + A.$$

Similarly, $\cos n\theta$ is an integrating factor and the corresponding first integral is

$$\cos n\theta \frac{du}{d\theta} + nu \sin n\theta = \int_0^\theta f(\theta') \cos n\theta' d\theta' + B.$$

Eliminating $\frac{du}{d\theta}$,

$$nu = \int_0^\theta f(\theta') \sin n(\theta - \theta')\, d\theta' + B \sin n\theta - A \cos n\theta.$$

222. The equation of motion of a body of changing mass often takes some such form as

$$\frac{d}{dt}\left\{\phi(x)\frac{dx}{dt}\right\} = \psi(x),$$

and for this equation $\phi(x)\frac{dx}{dt}$ will be found to be an integrating factor.

For $$\phi(x)\frac{dx}{dt}\frac{d}{dt}\left\{\phi(x)\frac{dx}{dt}\right\} = \psi(x)\phi(x)\frac{dx}{dt}$$

leads at once to $$\frac{1}{2}\left\{\phi(x)\frac{dx}{dt}\right\}^2 = \int \psi(x)\phi(x)\, dx + A,$$

or $$\frac{1}{\sqrt{2}} \frac{\phi(x)\, dx}{\sqrt{\int \psi(x)\phi(x)\, dx + A}} = dt,$$

and the variables are separated.

FURTHER ILLUSTRATIVE EXAMPLES.

223. Many equations may be solved by reducing to one or other of the known forms already discussed by special artifices.

Ex. 1. $\frac{dy}{dx} = f(ax + by)$.

Let $$ax + by = z.$$

Then $$a + b\frac{dy}{dx} = \frac{dz}{dx}.$$

Thus $$a + bf(z) = \frac{dz}{dx},\ dx = \frac{dz}{a + bf(z)},$$

or $$x + A = \int \frac{dz}{a + bf(z)}.$$

Ex. 2. $x^2 \frac{dy}{dx}\left(y + x\frac{dy}{dx}\right) + 1 = 0.$

Put $$xy = z.$$

Then $$y + x\frac{dy}{dx} = \frac{dz}{dx},$$

$\therefore$ $$x\left(\frac{dz}{dx} - y\right)\frac{dz}{dx} + 1 = 0,$$

or $$z = x\frac{dz}{dx} + \frac{1}{\frac{dz}{dx}}$$

which is of Clairaut's form, and the complete primitive is

$$xy = xC + \frac{1}{C}.$$

Ex. 3. Solve $e^{2(x+y)}\left(1 - \frac{dy}{dx}\right)^2 = e^{2x} + e^{2y}\left(\frac{dy}{dx}\right)^2$.

Let $$e^y = \eta, e^x = \xi.$$

Then, since this equation may be arranged as

$$\left(e^y - \frac{e^y dy}{dx}\right)^2 = 1 + \left(\frac{e^y dy}{e^x dx}\right)^2,$$

we may write it as $$\eta - \xi\frac{d\eta}{d\xi} = \sqrt{1 + \left(\frac{d\eta}{d\xi}\right)^2},$$

which being of Clairaut's form the complete primitive may be written

$$\eta = C\xi + \sqrt{1 + C^2},$$

or $$e^y = Ce^x + \sqrt{1 + C^2}.$$

Ex. 4. $Axy\left(\frac{dy}{dx}\right)^2 + (x^2 - Ay^2 - B)\frac{dy}{dx} - xy = 0$

(an equation occurring in Solid Geometry)

Put $x = \sqrt{s}$ and $y = \sqrt{t}$.

Then the equation becomes

$$A\sqrt{st}\left(\frac{\sqrt{s}\,dt}{\sqrt{t}\,ds}\right)^2 + (s - At - B)\left(\frac{\sqrt{s}\,dt}{\sqrt{t}\,ds}\right) - \sqrt{st} = 0,$$

or $$As\left(\frac{dt}{ds}\right)^2 + (s - At - B)\frac{dt}{ds} - t = 0,$$

i.e. $$t\left(1 + A\frac{dt}{ds}\right) = s\frac{dt}{ds}\left(1 + A\frac{dt}{ds}\right) - B\frac{dt}{ds},$$

giving $$t = s\frac{dt}{ds} - \frac{B\frac{dt}{ds}}{1 + A\frac{dt}{ds}},$$

which is of Clairaut's form and has the complete primitive

$$t = sC - \frac{BC}{1 + AC},$$

or $$Cx^2 - y^2 = \frac{BC}{1 + AC},$$

and singular solution the four straight lines

$$x \pm \sqrt{-A}\,y = \pm\sqrt{B}.$$

Ex. 5. Solve the equation

$$(1 + ax^2)\frac{d^2y}{dx^2} + ax\frac{dy}{dx} + q^2y = 0.$$

Let the transformation be such that $\frac{dx}{\sqrt{1 + ax^2}} = dt,$

then x is known by direct integration as a function of t.

Now $$\frac{dy}{dx} = \frac{\frac{dy}{dt}}{\sqrt{1 + ax^2}},$$

and $$\frac{d^2y}{dx^2} = \frac{\frac{d^2y}{dt^2}}{1 + ax^2} - \frac{dy}{dt}\frac{ax}{(1 + ax^2)^{\frac{3}{2}}}.$$

Thus $$(1 + ax^2)\frac{d^2y}{dx^2} = \frac{d^2y}{dt^2} - ax\frac{dy}{dt}\cdot\frac{dt}{dx},$$

and the given equation thus reduces to

$$\frac{d^2y}{dt^2} + q^2y = 0,$$

whose solution is $y = A\sin qt + B\cos qt$,

and when the value of t in terms of x is substituted, the solution is complete.

[If a be positive we have

$$\frac{1}{\sqrt{a}} \frac{dx}{\sqrt{\frac{1}{a} + x^2}} = dt,$$

$$\frac{1}{\sqrt{a}} \sinh^{-1}(x\sqrt{a}) = t.$$

If a be negative we have

$$\frac{1}{\sqrt{-a}} \frac{dx}{\sqrt{\frac{1}{-a} - x^2}} = dt,$$

$$\frac{1}{\sqrt{-a}} . \sin^{-1}(x\sqrt{-a}) = t.]$$

Ex. 6. Solve the simultaneous differential equations (which are *linear with constant coefficients*)

$$\left.\begin{aligned} 4\frac{dx}{dt} + 9\frac{dy}{dt} + 44x + 49y &= t, \\ 3\frac{dx}{dt} + 7\frac{dy}{dt} + 34x + 38y &= e^t. \end{aligned}\right\}$$

We may write these equations as

$$\left.\begin{aligned} 4(D + 11)x + (9D + 49)y &= t, \\ (3D + 34)x + (7D + 38)y &= e^t, \end{aligned}\right\}$$

where D stands for $\frac{d}{dt}$.

Operating upon these equations respectively by $7D + 38$ and by $9D + 49$ and subtracting, we eliminate y and obtain

$$[(4D + 44)(7D + 38) - (3D + 34)(9D + 49)]x = 7 + 38t - 58e^t,$$

or $\quad (D^2 + 7D + 6)x = 7 + 38t - 58e^t,$

giving $\quad x = Ae^{-t} + Be^{-6t} + \frac{1}{D^2 + 7D + 6}(7 + 38t - 58e^t),$

or $\quad x = Ae^{-t} + Be^{-6t} + \frac{7}{6} + \frac{19}{3}\left(t - \frac{7}{6}\right) - \frac{29}{7}e^t.$

To obtain y let us eliminate $\frac{dy}{dt}$ from the original equations.

Multiply the first by 7 and the second by 9 and subtract.

This gives $\quad \frac{dx}{dt} + 2x + y = 7t - 9e^t.$

Thus $$y = 7t - 9e^t - 2x - \frac{dx}{dt}$$

$$= 7t - 9e^t - 2\left(Ae^{-t} + Be^{-6t} + \frac{19}{3}t - \frac{56}{9} - \frac{29}{7}e^t\right)$$
$$- \left(-Ae^{-t} - 6Be^{-6t} + \frac{19}{3} - \frac{29}{7}e^t\right)$$

$$= -Ae^{-t} + 4Be^{-6t} + \frac{55}{9} - \frac{17}{3}t + \frac{24}{7}e^t.$$

Thus
$$\left.\begin{aligned} x &= Ae^{-t} + Be^{-6t} + \frac{19}{3}t - \frac{56}{9} - \frac{29}{7}e^t, \\ y &= -Ae^{-t} + 4Be^{-6t} - \frac{17}{3}t + \frac{55}{9} + \frac{24}{7}e^t. \end{aligned}\right\}$$

[The student should notice the elimination of $\frac{dy}{dt}$. This avoids the introduction of supernumerary constants.]

Ex. 7. Solve the simultaneous equations

$$\left.\begin{aligned} \frac{d^2x}{dt^2} + 3\frac{dy}{dt} + 16x = 0, \\ \frac{d^2y}{dt^2} - 5\frac{dx}{dt} + 9y = 0. \end{aligned}\right\}$$

These equations may be written

$$\left.\begin{aligned} (D^2 + 16)x + 3Dy = 0, \\ -5\,Dx + (D^2 + 9)\,y = 0, \end{aligned}\right\}$$

whence operating upon these in turn by $D^2 + 9$ and by $3D$ and subtracting, we eliminate y and obtain

$$[(D^2 + 16)(D^2 + 9) + 15D^2]x = 0,$$

or $$(D^4 + 40D^2 + 144)x = 0,$$

i.e. $$(D^2 + 4)(D^2 + 36)x = 0,$$

whence $$x = A\sin 2t + B\cos 2t + C\sin 6t + D\cos 6t.$$

Differentiating the first equation and subtracting three times the second to eliminate differential coefficients of y, we have

$$\frac{d^3x}{dt^3} + 31\frac{dx}{dt} = 27y,$$

whence we obtain the value of y *without any new constants, viz.*:—

$$y = -2B\sin 2t + 2A\cos 2t + \frac{10}{9}D\sin 6t - \frac{10}{9}C\cos 6t.$$

EXAMPLES

Solve the equations

1. $2xy\dfrac{dy}{dx} - (1-x)y^2 = x^4.$

2. $\sec^2 y\dfrac{d^2y}{dx^2} + 2\dfrac{\sin y}{\cos^3 y}\left(\dfrac{dy}{dx}\right)^2 + \tan y = x.$

3. $(a+bx)^2\dfrac{d^2y}{dx^2} + A(a+bx)\dfrac{dy}{dx} + By = x.$

4. $(1+x^2)^2\dfrac{d^2y}{dx^2} + 2x(1+x^2)\dfrac{dy}{dx} + y = 0.$

5. $(1-x^2)\dfrac{d^2y}{dx^2} - x\dfrac{dy}{dx} + n^2y = 0.$

6. $\dfrac{dy}{dx} = e^{x-y}(e^x - e^y).$

7. $\dfrac{dy}{dx} = 2\sin\dfrac{(x-y)}{2}\cos\dfrac{(x+y)}{2}\dfrac{\cos x}{\cos y}.$

8. Obtain the integrals of the following differential equations:—

(*a*) $\dfrac{d^3y}{dx^3} - 3\dfrac{d^2y}{dx^2} + 9\dfrac{dy}{dx} + 13y = 0.$

(*b*) $\dfrac{d^2y}{dx^2} + 6\dfrac{dy}{dx} + 9y = 25\cos x.$

(*c*) $x^2\dfrac{d^2y}{dx^2} - 5x\dfrac{dy}{dx} + 10y = 0.$ [I. C. S., 1894.]

9. Integrate the simultaneous system

$$\frac{d^2y}{dx^2} + 15y + 3z + 30 = 0,$$

$$\frac{d^2z}{dx^2} + 2y + 10z + 4 = 0.$$ [I. C. S., 1894.]

10. Find the form of the curve in which the tangent of the inclination of the current tangent to the *x*-axis is proportional to the product of the coordinates of the point.

11. Find the form of the curve for which the curvature varies as the cube of the cosine of the inclination of the tangent to the *x*-axis.

12. Show that in the curve for which the projection of the radius of curvature on the *y*-axis is of constant length

(1) $s \propto \log\tan\left(\dfrac{\pi}{4} + \dfrac{\psi}{2}\right),$

(2) $y \propto \log\sec\dfrac{x}{a}.$

ANSWERS

CHAPTER I.

PAGE 10.

1. Area. $= e^b - e^a$.

2. Vol. $= \frac{\pi}{2}(e^{2b} - e^{2a})$.

3. Area $= \frac{1}{2}a^2 \tan\theta$, Vol. $= \frac{\pi}{3}a^3 \tan^2\theta$.

4. Vol. $= \frac{4\pi a^3}{5}$.

5. Vol. $= \frac{4}{3}\pi a^3$.

6. (α) Area $= \frac{3}{4}a^{\frac{2}{3}}h^{\frac{4}{3}}$, Vol. $= \frac{3}{5}\pi\, a^{\frac{4}{3}}h^{\frac{5}{8}}$.

(β) Area $= \frac{n}{n+1}a^{\frac{n-1}{n}}h^{\frac{n+1}{n}}$, Vol. $= \frac{n}{n+2}\pi a^{2\frac{n-1}{n}}h^{\frac{n+2}{n}}$.

(γ) Area $= \frac{1}{n+1}\frac{h^{n+1}}{a^{n-1}}$, Vol. $= \frac{1}{2n+1}\pi\frac{h^{2n+1}}{a^{2n-2}}$.

(δ) Area $= \frac{1}{12}\frac{h^3}{a^2}(3h+4a)$, Vol. $= \frac{\pi}{105}\frac{h^5}{a^4}(15h^2 + 35ah + 21a^2)$.

7. $\frac{2}{3}\pi\mu a^3$.

8. Mass of half the spheroid $= \frac{1}{4}\pi\mu a^2 b^2$.

CHAPTER II.

PAGE 13.

1. $\frac{1}{11}(b^{11} - a^{11})$.

2. $\frac{1}{11}$.

3. $\frac{2^{n+1}-1}{n+1}$.

4. $\log_e\frac{3}{2}$.

5. 1.

6. 1.

7. $\sqrt{2} - 1$.

8. $\frac{\pi}{4}$.

9. $\frac{\pi}{2}$.

10. $\frac{b^2 - a^2}{2} + (\sin b - \sin a)$.

PAGE 17.

1. $\frac{x^2}{2}, x, C, \frac{x^{100}}{100}, \frac{x^{1000}}{1000}, \frac{x^{1001}}{1001}$. 2. $-\frac{x^{-10}}{10}, -\frac{x^{-100}}{100}, -\frac{x^{-98}}{98}$.

3. $\frac{2}{3}x^{\frac{3}{2}}, \frac{5}{8}x^{\frac{8}{5}}, \frac{3}{8}x^{\frac{8}{3}}$. 4. $2x^{\frac{1}{2}}, 6x^{\frac{1}{6}}, 3x^{\frac{1}{3}}$.

5. $\frac{ax^2}{2} - \frac{b}{x}, ax + b\frac{x^2}{2} - \frac{1}{9}\frac{c}{x^9}$.

6. $a\log x - \frac{b}{x} - \frac{c}{2x^2}, a\frac{x^2}{2} + b\frac{x^3}{3} + c\frac{x^4}{4}$.

PAGE 18.

1. $\frac{ax^2}{2}, \frac{x^{a+1}}{a+1}, ax + \frac{x^2}{2}, ax - \frac{x^2}{2}, ax - \frac{x^{a+1}}{a+1}$.

2. $a\log x, \frac{x^2}{2a}, a\log x, x, \log(a+x)$.

3. $x - a\log(a+x), -\frac{1}{b}\log(a-bx), \frac{1}{a-x}, \frac{1}{n-1}\frac{1}{(a-x)^{n-1}}$.

4. $\log\frac{a+x}{a-x}, \log(x^2-a^2), \frac{2x}{a^2-x^2}$.

PAGE 19.

1. $\frac{(e^x+a)^{n+1}}{n+1}, \log(e^x+a), \frac{(ax^2+bx+c)^{n+1}}{n+1}$.

2. $\log(e^x - e^{-x}), \log\tan x, -\frac{1}{ax^2+bx+c}$.

3. $\log\tan^{-1}x, \log\sin^{-1}x, \log(\log x)$.

PAGE 21.

1. $\log(x+1), \log_e\frac{e^x}{x+1}, \frac{1}{2}\log(x^2+1), \frac{1}{3}\log(x^3+1), \frac{1}{n}\log(x^n+a^n)$.

2. $\frac{2^x}{\log 2}, \frac{x^4}{4} + \frac{3^x}{\log 3}, ax + \frac{b^x}{\log b} + \frac{c^{2x}}{\log c^2}$.

3. $\frac{x+\sin x}{2}, -\frac{\cos^4 x}{4}, \frac{\tan^{n+1} x}{n+1}$.

4. $\log\tan x, \log\sin x - \operatorname{cosec} x$.

5. $\sin^{-1}x, \frac{1}{3}\tan^{-1}\frac{x}{3}, \frac{1}{2}\sec^{-1}\frac{x}{2}$.

6. $\text{vers}^{-1} 2x, \frac{1}{2\sqrt{2}} \sec^{-1} \frac{x}{2}, \frac{1}{\sqrt{2}} \sin^{-1} \frac{x}{2}, x - 2\tan^{-1} \frac{x}{2}$.

7. $\frac{1}{2}(\tan^{-1} x)^2, \frac{1}{2}(\sin^{-1} x)^2, \frac{1}{2}(\sec^{-1} x)^2$.

8. $\frac{1}{e} \log (x^e + e^x), \log (\log \sin x), \log (\sec^{-1} x)$.

CHAPTER III.

PAGE 24.

1. $\sin e^x, \sin x^n, \sin (\log x)$.

2. $\tan^{-1} x^2, \tan^{-1} x^3$.

3. $a \sin x + \frac{b}{4} \tan^{-1} x^4, - a \cos e^x + b \log \cos h\, x$.

4. $\frac{1}{\sqrt{2}} \tan^{-1} \frac{1}{2\sqrt{2}}$.

5. $\sin^{-1} \frac{2}{\sqrt{6}} - \sin^{-1} \frac{1}{\sqrt{6}}$.

6. $\frac{\pi}{3}$.

7. $\tan^{-1} \sqrt{x}$.

8. $\sin^{-1} \sqrt{x}$.

9. $\sec^{-1} \sqrt{x}$.

PAGE 31.

1. $\sin^{-1} x, \cos h^{-1} x, \sin h^{-1} x, \frac{x\sqrt{1 - x^2}}{2} + \frac{1}{2} \sin^{-1} x,$

$\frac{x\sqrt{x^2 - 1}}{2} - \frac{1}{2} \cos h^{-1} x, \frac{x\sqrt{1 + x^2}}{2} + \frac{1}{2} \sin h^{-1} x.$

2. $\cos h^{-1}(x + 1), \sin^{-1} \frac{x - 1}{\sqrt{3}}, \sin h^{-1}(x - 1),$

$\frac{(x + 1)\sqrt{x^2 + 2x}}{2} - \frac{1}{2} \cos h^{-1}(x + 1), \sin^{-1} \frac{x + 2}{\sqrt{5}}$.

3. $-\sqrt{1 - x^2}, \sqrt{x^2 - 1}, \frac{1}{2} \sin^{-1} x - \frac{x\sqrt{1 - x^2}}{2}, \frac{x\sqrt{x^2 + 1}}{2} - \frac{1}{2} \sinh^{-1} x$.

4. $\frac{1}{3}(x^2 + 1)^{\frac{3}{2}}, \frac{1}{3}(x^2 + 1)^{\frac{3}{2}} + \frac{1}{2} x(x^2 + 1)^{\frac{1}{2}} + \frac{1}{2} \sin h^{-1} x, \sqrt{x^2 + 1} + \sin h^{-1} x$.

5. $\frac{1}{n + 2}(x^2 + a^2)^{\frac{n + 2}{2}}, \frac{1}{n + 2}(x^2 + 2x + 3)^{\frac{n + 2}{2}}$.

6. $\frac{7}{2} \sin^{-1} x - 2\sqrt{1 - x^2} - \frac{1}{2} x\sqrt{1 - x^2}, \frac{5}{2} \sin h^{-1} x + 2\sqrt{1 + x^2}$

$+ \frac{1}{2} x\sqrt{1 + x^2}, \; \frac{15}{8} \sin h^{-1} \frac{2x + 1}{\sqrt{3}} + \frac{1}{4}(2x + 5)\sqrt{x^2 + x + 1}$.

7. $\sqrt{x^2-1}+\cosh^{-1}x, \sin^{-1}x-\sqrt{1-x^2},$

$\frac{1}{2}\sin^{-1}x-\frac{1}{2}(2+x)\sqrt{1-x^2}, 4\cosh^{-1}\frac{x}{2}+\frac{x+6}{2}\sqrt{x^2-4}.$

8. $\frac{1}{2}\log\tan x, \frac{1}{a}\log\tan\frac{ax+b}{2}, \frac{1}{2}\log\tan\left(\frac{\pi}{4}+x\right),$

$\frac{1}{2}\log\tan\left(\frac{\pi}{4}+x\right), \frac{1}{3}\log\tan\frac{3x}{2}.$

9. $\frac{1}{\sqrt{2}}\log\tan\left(\frac{x}{2}+\frac{\pi}{8}\right), \frac{1}{\sqrt{a^2+b^2}}\log\tan\left(\frac{x}{2}+\frac{1}{2}\tan^{-1}\frac{b}{a}\right).$

13. $\log(\log x), \log\{\log(\log x)\}, \log[\log\{\log(\log x)\}], l^{r+1}(x).$

CHAPTER IV.

PAGE 35.

1. $(x-1)e^x, (x^2-2x+2)e^x, (x^3-3x^2+6x-6)e^x,$

$x\sinh x-\cosh x, (2+x^2)\sinh x-2x\cosh x.$

2. $x\sin x+\cos x, (x^2-2)\sin x+2x\cos x, \frac{x\sin 2x}{2}+\frac{\cos 2x}{4},$

$\frac{x^3}{4}+\frac{x\sin 2x}{4}+\frac{\cos 2x}{8}, \frac{1}{36}[3x(\sin 3x+9\sin x)+\cos 3x+27\cos x].$

3. $\frac{1}{8}(\sin 2x-2x\cos 2x),$

$\frac{1}{4}\left[\frac{\sin 2x}{4}+\frac{\sin 4x}{16}-\frac{\sin 6x}{36}-x\left(\frac{\cos 2x}{2}+\frac{\cos 4x}{4}-\frac{\cos 6x}{6}\right)\right].$

4. $\frac{x^3}{9}\log\left(\frac{x^3}{e}\right), \frac{x^{n+1}}{(n+1)^2}\log\left(\frac{x^{n+1}}{e}\right), \frac{x^{n+1}}{n+1}(\log x)^2-\frac{2x^{n+1}}{(n+1)^3}\log\left(\frac{x^{n+1}}{e}\right).$

5. $\frac{1}{2\sqrt{5}}e^x\sin(2x-\tan^{-1}2), \frac{1}{4\sqrt{17}}e^x\sin(4x-\tan^{-1}4).$

6. $\frac{1}{4}e^{ax}\Sigma(a^2+n^2)^{-\frac{1}{2}}\sin\left(nx-\tan^{-1}\frac{n}{a}\right)$, for the values of n,

$p+q-r, q+r-p, r+p-q, -p-q-r.$

7. $\pi, \frac{\pi^2}{4}, \pi^2-4.$

9. $x\sin^{-1}x+\sqrt{1-x^2}, \frac{1}{4}(2x^2-1)\sin^{-1}x+\frac{1}{4}x\sqrt{1-x^2},$

$\frac{x^3}{3}\sin^{-1}x+\frac{1}{3}\sqrt{1-x^2}-\frac{1}{9}(1-x^2)^{\frac{3}{2}}.$

PAGE 37.

1. $e^x(x^4-4x^3+12x^2-24x+24), (x^3+6x)\sinh x-3(x^2+2)\cosh x,$
$(x^5+20x^3+120x)\cosh x-5(x^4+12x^2+24)\sinh hx.$

2. $(2-x^2)\cos x+2x\sin x, (6x-x^3)\cos x+(3x^2-6)\sin x,$

$$\frac{x^4}{8}-\frac{1}{4}\left\{\left(x^3-\frac{3}{2}x\right)\sin 2x+\left(\frac{3x^2}{2}-\frac{3}{4}\right)\cos 2x\right\}.$$

$$\frac{1}{8}\{2(2x^3-3x)\sin 2x-(2x^4-6x^2+3)\cos 2x\}.$$

3. $\pi^5-20\pi^3+120\pi, -5\pi^4+60\pi^2-240, 265e-720.$

PAGE 38-40.

1. (*a*) $(m^2+1)^{-\frac{1}{2}}e^{m\theta}\cos(\theta-\cot^{-1}m)$, where $x=\sin\theta$.

(*b*) $\frac{1}{4}\left(\theta\sin\theta+\cos\theta-\frac{\theta\sin 3\theta}{3}-\frac{\cos 3\theta}{3^2}\right)$, where $x=\sin\theta$.

(*c*) $x\tan x+\log\cos x$.

(*d*) $x\tan^{-1}x-\frac{1}{2}\log(1+x^2)$.

(*e*) $\frac{x^4-1}{4}\tan^{-1}x-\frac{x^3-3x}{12}$.

(*f*) $x\sec^{-1}x-\cosh^{-1}x$.

2. (*a*) $x-\sqrt{1-x^2}\sin^{-1}x$.

(*b*) $\theta(\sec\theta+\cos\theta)-\sin\theta-\log\tan\left(\frac{\theta}{2}+\frac{\pi}{4}\right)$, where $x=\sin\theta$.

(*c*) $(a+x)\tan^{-1}\sqrt{\frac{x}{a}}-\sqrt{ax}$.

(*d*) $\frac{a^2}{4}(\sin\phi-\phi\cos\phi)$, where $x=2a\cos\frac{\phi}{2}$.

3. (*a*) $\frac{1}{m}e^{m\tan^{-1}x}$.

(*d*) $\frac{(m+x)}{1+m^2}\frac{e^{m\tan^{-1}x}}{\sqrt{1+x^2}}$.

(*b*) $\frac{1}{2}e^{m\theta}\left[\frac{1}{m}+\frac{1}{\sqrt{m^2+4}}\cos\left(2\theta-\tan^{-1}\frac{2}{m}\right)\right]$, where $\tan\theta=x$.

(*c*) $\frac{1}{4}e^{m\theta}\left\{\frac{3}{\sqrt{m^2+1}}\cos\left(\theta-\tan^{-1}\frac{1}{m}\right)+\frac{1}{\sqrt{m^2+9}}\cos\left(3\theta-\tan^{-1}\frac{3}{m}\right)\right\}$,

where $\tan\theta=x$.

4. (*a*) $e^x \sin x$.

(*b*) $\frac{1}{2}e^x(x-1) - \frac{e^x}{10}\{\sqrt{5}\,x\cos(2x - \tan^{-1}2) - \cos(2x - 2\tan^{-1}2)\}$.

(*c*) $\frac{(a\sin bx\sinh ax - b\cos bx\cosh ax)}{a^2+b^2}$.

(*d*) $$\frac{1}{2}\left\{\frac{x}{r}e^{ax}\sin(bx-\phi) - \frac{e^{ax}}{r^2}\sin(bx-2\phi) - \frac{x}{r}e^{-ax}\sin(bx+\phi) - \frac{e^{-ax}}{r^2}\sin(bx+2\phi)\right\},$$

where r and ϕ are as in Art. 53.

(*e*) $2^x(P\sin 2x - Q\cos 2x)$, where

$$P = \frac{x^2}{r}\cos\phi - \frac{2x}{r^2}\cos 2\phi + \frac{2}{r^3}\cos 3\phi,$$

$$Q = \frac{x^2}{r}\sin\phi - \frac{2x}{r^2}\sin 2\phi + \frac{2}{r^3}\sin 3\phi,$$

and $$r^2 = 4 + (\log 2)^2 \text{ and } \tan\phi = \frac{2}{\log 2}.$$

(*f*) $\frac{x}{\sqrt{b^2+1}}\cos\left(b\log\frac{x}{a} - \tan^{-1}b\right)$.

5. $x\sin^{-1}x\log\frac{ae}{x} + \sqrt{1-x^2}\log\frac{ae^2}{x^2} + \log\frac{x}{1+\sqrt{1-x^2}}$.

6. $\frac{e^x}{1+x}$.

7. $-\cot\theta\log(\cos\theta + \sqrt{\cos 2\theta}) - \theta - \cot\theta + \frac{\sqrt{\cos 2\theta}}{\sin\theta}$.

8. $\sin\theta\cos\theta\log(1+\tan\theta) - \frac{\theta}{2} + \frac{1}{2}\log\sin\left(\theta + \frac{\pi}{4}\right)$.

9. (*a*) $e^x\tan\frac{x}{2}$.

(*b*) $-e^x\cot\frac{x}{2}$.

11. $\frac{a+c}{2}e^x + \frac{b}{\sqrt{5}}e^x\sin(2x - \tan^{-1}2) + \frac{c-a}{2\sqrt{5}}e^x\cos(2x - \tan^{-1}2)$.

CHAPTER V.

PAGE 43.

1. $\frac{1}{2}\log(x^2+2x+3)-\frac{1}{\sqrt{2}}\tan^{-1}\frac{x+1}{\sqrt{2}}$.

2. $\log(x+1)+\frac{1}{x+1}$.

3. $\frac{1}{2}\log(x^2+4x+5)-\tan^{-1}(x+2)$.

4. $-\log(3-x)$.

5. $x-2\log(x^2+2x+2)+3\tan^{-1}(x+1)$.

6. $2x-\frac{9}{2}\log(x^2+6x+10)+11\tan^{-1}(x+3)$.

PAGE 47, 48.

1. (i.) $\frac{1}{a-b}\log\frac{(x-a)^a}{(x-b)^b}$. (ii.) $\log\frac{(x^2-1)^{\frac{1}{2}}}{x}$.

(iii.) $x-\frac{a^2}{a-b}\log(x+a)+\frac{b^2}{a-b}\log(x+b)$.

(iv.) $\log\frac{x^2-1}{x}$. (v.) $\frac{1}{6}\log\frac{(x+1)^6(x-1)^2}{(2x+1)^5}$.

(vi.) $\frac{1}{3}\log x(x^2-3)^4$. (vii.) $\Sigma\frac{a^2}{(a-b)(a-c)}\log(x-a)$.

(viii.) $x+\frac{(c-a)(c-b)}{(c-d)}\log(x-c)+\frac{(d-a)(d-b)}{(d-c)}\log(x-d)$.

(ix.) $x+\frac{(a_1-a)(a_1-b)(a_1-c)}{(a_1-b_1)(a_1-c_1)}\log(x-a_1)+$ etc.

(x.) $\frac{1}{30}\log\frac{(x-2)^8(x+3)^{27}}{(x+1)^5}$.

2. (i.) $-\frac{1}{2}\frac{1}{x-1}+\frac{1}{4}\log\frac{x+1}{x-1}$.

(ii.) $-\frac{1}{6}\frac{1}{(x-1)^3}+\frac{1}{8}\frac{1}{(x-1)^2}-\frac{1}{8(x-1)}+\frac{1}{16}\log\frac{x+1}{x-1}$.

(iii.) $\frac{1}{27}\log\frac{x+2}{x-1}+\frac{1}{9}\frac{1}{x+2}-\frac{2}{9}\frac{1}{x-1}$.

(iv.) $-\frac{1}{ax}+\frac{b}{a^2}\log\frac{a+bx}{x}$.

(v.) $\frac{1}{4}\log\frac{x+1}{x-1}-\frac{1}{2}\frac{x}{x^2-1}$.

(vi.) $\frac{1}{(b-a)^2(b-c)}\log(x-b)+\frac{1}{(c-a)^2(c-b)}\log(x-c)$

$-\frac{2a-b-c}{(a-b)^2(a-c)^2}\log(x-a)-\frac{1}{(a-b)(a-c)}\frac{1}{x-a}$.

3. (i.) $\frac{1}{a(b^2-a^2)}\tan^{-1}\frac{x}{a}+\frac{1}{b(a^2-b^2)}\tan^{-1}\frac{x}{b}$.

(ii.) $x+\frac{(a^2-c^2)(b^2-c^2)}{c(d^2-c^2)}\tan^{-1}\frac{x}{c}+\frac{(a^2-d^2)(b^2-d^2)}{d(c^2-d^2)}\tan^{-1}\frac{x}{d}$.

(iii.) $\tan^{-1}x-\frac{1}{\sqrt{2}}\tan^{-1}x\sqrt{2}$.

(iv.) $\frac{1}{3\sqrt{2}}\tan^{-1}\left(\frac{3}{\sqrt{2}}\frac{x}{1-x^2}\right)$.

4. (i.) $-\frac{1}{\sqrt{3}}\tan^{-1}\frac{\sqrt{3}}{2x^2+1}$. (ii.) $\frac{1}{\sqrt{3}}\tan^{-1}\frac{x\sqrt{3}}{1-x^2}-\frac{2}{\sqrt{3}}\tan^{-1}\frac{\sqrt{3}}{2x^2+1}$.

(iii.) $\frac{1}{\sqrt{2}}\tan^{-1}\frac{x\sqrt{2}}{1-x^2}$. (iv.) $\tan^{-1}\frac{x}{1-x^2}$.

(v.) $\frac{1}{a\sqrt{3}}\tan^{-1}\frac{ax\sqrt{3}}{a^2-x^2}$. (vi.) $\frac{1}{2a}\log\frac{x^2-ax+a^2}{x^2+ax+a^2}$.

(vii.) $\frac{1}{\sqrt{3}}\tan^{-1}\frac{x\sqrt{3}}{1-x^2}-\sqrt{3}\tan^{-1}\frac{\sqrt{3}}{2x^2+1}$.

(viii.) $\frac{1}{4\sqrt{2}}\log\frac{x^2+x\sqrt{2}+1}{x^2-x\sqrt{2}+1}+\frac{1}{2\sqrt{2}}\tan^{-1}\frac{x\sqrt{2}}{1-x^2}$.

5. (i.) $\frac{1}{3}\log\frac{x-1}{\sqrt{x^2+x+1}}+\frac{1}{\sqrt{3}}\tan^{-1}\frac{2x+1}{\sqrt{3}}$.

(ii.) $\log\frac{x^2-1}{x\sqrt{x^2+1}}$.

(iii.) $\frac{1}{16}\log\frac{(x-2)^2}{x^2+4}-\frac{1}{8}\tan^{-1}\frac{x}{2}$.

(iv.) $x-2\log x+\frac{3}{4}\log(x-1)+\frac{1}{4}\log(x+1)+\frac{1}{2}\log(x^2+1)$

$-\frac{1}{2}\tan^{-1}x$.

(v.) $-\log(x+1)+\frac{1}{2}\log(x^2+1)$.

(vi.) $\frac{1}{20}\log\frac{x-1}{x+1}-\frac{1}{30}\tan^{-1}\frac{x}{3}$.

(vii.) $\frac{1}{6}\log\frac{x-1}{(x+1)^3}+\frac{1}{6}\log(x^2+x+1)-\frac{1}{\sqrt{3}}\tan^{-1}\frac{2x+1}{\sqrt{3}}.$

(viii.) $\frac{1}{2}\log\frac{x^2+1}{x^2-x+1}+\frac{1}{\sqrt{3}}\tan^{-1}\frac{2x-1}{\sqrt{3}}.$

(ix.) $\frac{1}{2}\log(x+1)-\frac{1}{4}\log(x^2+1)+\frac{1}{2}\tan^{-1}x.$

(x.) $\frac{x^3}{3}+2x^2+15x+\frac{1024}{17}\log(x-4)-\frac{2}{17}\log(x^2+1)+\frac{1}{17}\tan^{-1}x.$

6. (i.) $\frac{1}{2}\log(x-2)-\frac{1}{x-2}-\frac{1}{4}\log(x^2-2x+4)-\frac{1}{2\sqrt{3}}\tan^{-1}\frac{x-1}{\sqrt{3}}.$

(ii.) $\frac{2}{3}\log(1+x)-\frac{1}{3}\log(1+2x+4x^2)-\frac{1}{3}\frac{1}{1+x}+\frac{2}{3\sqrt{3}}\tan^{-1}\frac{4x+1}{\sqrt{3}}.$

(iii.) $x+\frac{18}{25}\log(x-1)+\frac{16}{25}\log(x^2+4)-\frac{1}{5}\frac{1}{x-1}-\frac{24}{25}\tan^{-1}\frac{x}{2}.$

(iv.) $\frac{1}{4}\log\frac{(x+1)^2}{x^2+1}-\frac{1}{2}\frac{1}{x+1}.$

(v.) $\frac{1}{4}\log\frac{x^2+1}{(x-1)^2}-\frac{1}{2}\frac{1}{x-1}.$

(vi.) $\log\frac{x}{x-1}-\frac{1}{2}\frac{1}{x-1}+\frac{1}{2}\tan^{-1}x.$

(vii.) $\frac{1}{3}\log\frac{x^3(1+x^3)}{(1+2x^3)^2}.$

(viii.) $\frac{1}{a^3}\log\frac{(x-a)\sqrt{x^2+a^2}}{x^2}+\frac{1}{a^2x}.$

(ix.) $\frac{1}{4}\log\frac{x^2+1}{(x+1)^2}+\frac{1}{2}\frac{x-1}{x^2+1}.$

(x.) $\frac{1}{2}\log\frac{x^2}{1+x^2}+\frac{1}{2}\frac{1}{1+x^2}+\frac{1}{4}\frac{1}{(1+x^2)^2}.$

7. $\frac{1}{\sqrt{2}}\left[\frac{\pi}{2}-\log(\sqrt{2}+1)\right],\frac{1}{\sqrt{2}}\left[\frac{\pi}{2}-\log(\sqrt{2}-1)\right].$

8. $\frac{\pi}{2}.$

9. $\log\frac{4}{3}.$

CHAPTER VI.

PAGE 51.

1. $\sinh^{-1}\dfrac{x+1}{\sqrt{2}}, \dfrac{1}{\sqrt{2}}\sinh^{-1}\dfrac{2x+1}{\sqrt{5}}.$

2. $\dfrac{1}{\sqrt{2}}\sin^{-1}\dfrac{4x-3}{5}, \dfrac{1}{\sqrt{2}}\sin^{-1}\dfrac{4x+3}{5}.$

3. $(b^2 < ac)\dfrac{1}{2c^{\frac{3}{2}}}\left[(cx+b)\sqrt{c\,(cx^2+2bx+a)}+(ac-b^2)\sinh^{-1}\dfrac{cx+b}{\sqrt{ac-b^2}}\right],$

$(b^2 > ac)\dfrac{1}{2c^{\frac{3}{2}}}\left[(cx+b)\sqrt{c\,(cx^2+2bx+a)}-(b^2-ac)\cosh^{-1}\dfrac{cx+b}{\sqrt{b^2-ac}}\right].$

4. $\dfrac{1}{2c^{\frac{3}{2}}}\left[(cx-b)\sqrt{c\,(a+2bx-cx^2)}+(b^2+ac)\sin^{-1}\dfrac{cx-b}{\sqrt{b^2+ac}}\right].$

PAGE 52.

1. $\sqrt{x^2+2x+3}.$

2. $\sqrt{x^2+a^2}.$

3. $\sqrt{x^2+a^2}+b\sinh^{-1}\dfrac{x}{a}.$

4. $2\sqrt{x^2-1}+3\cosh^{-1}x.$

5. $2\sqrt{x^2+x+1}+2\sinh^{-1}\dfrac{2x+1}{\sqrt{3}}.$

6. $\dfrac{x\sqrt{x^2+4}}{2}-\sinh^{-1}\dfrac{x}{2}.$

7. $\dfrac{1}{2}(x-1)\sqrt{x^2+2x+3}.$

8. $\dfrac{1}{3}(x^2+2x+3)^{\frac{3}{2}}-(x+1)\sqrt{x^2+2x+3}+2\sinh^{-1}\dfrac{x+1}{\sqrt{2}}.$

PAGE 57.

1. $\dfrac{x}{2}-\dfrac{\sin 2x}{4}, -\dfrac{3}{4}\cos x+\dfrac{1}{12}\cos 3x$ or $-\cos x+\dfrac{\cos^3 x}{3},$

$\dfrac{1}{8}\left(\dfrac{\sin 4x}{4}-2\sin 2x+3x\right), \dfrac{1}{2^4}\left(-\dfrac{\cos 5x}{5}+\dfrac{5\cos 3x}{3}-10\cos x\right)$

or $$-\cos x + \frac{2\cos^3 x}{3} - \frac{\cos^5 x}{5}$$

$$-\frac{1}{2^5}\left(\frac{\sin 6x}{6} - \frac{3\sin 4x}{2} + \frac{15\sin 2x}{2} - 10x\right),$$

$$\frac{1}{2^6}\left\{\frac{\cos 7x}{7} - \frac{7\cos 5x}{5} + 7\cos 3x - 35\cos x\right\}$$

or $$-\cos x + \cos^3 x - \frac{3}{5}\cos^5 x + \frac{1}{7}\cos^7 x.$$

$$\frac{(-1)^n}{2^{2n-1}}\left\{\frac{\sin 2nx}{2n} - {}^{2n}C_1\frac{\sin(2n-2)x}{2n-2} + {}^{2n}C_2\frac{\sin(2n-4)x}{2n-4} - \ldots\right\},$$

$$\frac{(-1)^n}{2^{2n}}\left\{-\frac{\cos(2n+1)x}{2n+1} + {}^{2n+1}C_1\frac{\cos(2n-1)x}{2n-1} - {}^{2n+1}C_2\frac{\cos(2n-3)x}{2n-3} + \ldots\right\}$$

or $$-\cos x + {}^nC_1\frac{\cos^3 x}{3} - {}^nC_2\frac{\cos^5 x}{5} + {}^nC_3\frac{\cos^7 x}{7} - \ldots$$

2. $\frac{1}{3}\sin^3 x - \frac{1}{5}\sin^5 x, \frac{1}{4}\sin^4 x - \frac{1}{6}\sin^6 x, -\frac{1}{3}\cos^3 x + \frac{1}{5}\cos^5 x,$

$$\frac{1}{128}\left\{3x - \sin 4x + \frac{1}{8}\sin 8x\right\},$$

$$\frac{1}{512}\left\{6x + \sin 2x - 2\sin 4x - \frac{1}{2}\sin 6x + \frac{1}{4}\sin 8x + \frac{1}{10}\sin 10x\right\}.$$

3. $\frac{1}{3}\tan^3 x, -\frac{1}{3}\cot^3 x, \tan x - \cot x, \frac{1}{3}(\tan^3 x - \cot^3 x) + 3(\tan x - \cot x).$

4. $\frac{\pi - 2}{8}, \frac{43}{60\sqrt{2}}, \frac{15\pi + 44}{192}.$

5. $-\frac{1}{2}\cos^4 x, \frac{3}{2}\sin^2 x - \frac{7}{4}\sin^4 x + \frac{2}{3}\sin^6 x,$

$$-\frac{1}{2n}\cos nx - \frac{1}{4(n+2)}\cos(n+2)x - \frac{1}{4(n-2)}\cos(n-2)x.$$

PAGE 63-65.

1. $2\sqrt{\tan x}.$

2. (i.) $\frac{1}{\sqrt{a^2+b^2}}\log\tan\frac{1}{2}\left(x + \tan^{-1}\frac{a}{b}\right).$

(ii.) $-\frac{1}{a^2+b^2}\cot\left(x + \tan^{-1}\frac{b}{a}\right).$

3. (i.) $[a\theta + b\log(a\cos\theta + b\sin\theta)]/(a^2+b^2).$

(ii.) $[(ac+be)\theta + (bc-ae)\log(c\sin\theta + e\cos\theta)]/(c^2+e^2).$

4. $\frac{\pi}{8}(\alpha-\beta)^2.$

5. (i.) $\frac{1}{a\sqrt{a^2-b^2}}\tan^{-1}\left(\frac{a}{\sqrt{a^2-b^2}}\tan x\right).$

(ii.) $\frac{2}{3}\tan^{-1}\left(\frac{1}{3}\tan\frac{x}{2}\right).$

(iii.) $\frac{1}{\sin a}\cosh^{-1}\frac{1+\cos a\cos x}{\cos a+\cos x}.$

(iv.) $\cosh^{-1}\frac{3\cos(x-\tan^{-1}3)-\sqrt{10}}{3-\sqrt{10}\cos(x-\tan^{-1}3)}.$

(v.) $\frac{2}{\sqrt{3}}\tan^{-1}\frac{1}{\sqrt{3}}\tan\left(\frac{x}{2}-\frac{\pi}{8}\right).$

(vi.) $\frac{1}{ab}\tan^{-1}\left(\frac{a}{b}\tan\theta\right).$

(vii.) $x\cos a+\sin a\cosh^{-1}\frac{1+\cos a\cos x}{\cos a+\cos x}.$

6. (i.) $\frac{2}{3(b-a)}\left\{(x-a)^{\frac{3}{2}}-(x-b)^{\frac{3}{2}}\right\}.$

(ii.) $\frac{2}{a-b}\left\{\sqrt{a(x-b)}-\sqrt{b(x-a)}-\sqrt{ab}\left(\tan^{-1}\sqrt{\frac{x-b}{b}}-\tan^{-1}\sqrt{\frac{x-a}{a}}\right)\right\}.$

(iii.) $\frac{2}{a-a'}\left\{\sqrt{ax+b}-\sqrt{a'x+b'}-\frac{\sqrt{a'b-ab'}}{\sqrt{a-a'}}\right.$

$\left.\times\left(\tan^{-1}\frac{\sqrt{a-a'}}{\sqrt{a'b-ab'}}\sqrt{ax+b}-\tan^{-1}\frac{\sqrt{a-a'}}{\sqrt{a'b-ab'}}\sqrt{a'x+b'}\right)\right\}.$

if $a>a'$ and $a'b>ab'$, with analogous forms for other cases

7. $\frac{3}{68}\tan^{-1}\left(\frac{1}{2}\tan\frac{\theta}{2}\right)-\frac{5}{68}\tanh^{-1}\left(2\tan\frac{\theta}{2}\right).$

8. $\frac{1}{3}\log\frac{\sin x(1+\cos x)}{(1+2\cos x)^2}.$

9. $\frac{\sin 2\theta}{2}\log\frac{\cos\theta+\sin\theta}{\cos\theta-\sin\theta}-\frac{1}{2}\log\sec 2\theta.$

10. $\cosh x\tan\frac{x}{2}.$

11. $-2\sqrt{1-\sin x}.$

12. $-2\sqrt{1-\sin x}-\sqrt{2}\log\tan\left(\frac{x}{4}+\frac{\pi}{8}\right).$

13. $\frac{1}{4}\log\frac{1+\sin x}{1-\sin x}+\frac{1}{2}\frac{1}{1+\sin x}$.

14. $\frac{1}{\sqrt{b-a}}\cos^{-1}\left[\sqrt{\frac{b-a}{b}}\cos x\right]$.

15. π.

16. $\log\log\tan x$.

17. $-\cosh^{-1}(\cos\theta+\sin\theta)$.

18. $\theta+\frac{1}{\sqrt{3}}\log\frac{\tan\theta-\sqrt{3}}{\tan\theta+\sqrt{3}}$.

19. $-\frac{2}{na^{\frac{n}{2}}}\sinh^{-1}\left(\frac{a}{x}\right)^{\frac{n}{2}}$.

20. $\frac{\sin x-x\cos x}{\cos x+x\sin x}$.

21. $-\frac{2}{b^2}\left\{\log(a+b\cos x)+\frac{a}{a+b\cos x}\right\}$.

22. $\operatorname{cosec}^{-1}\left(2\cos^2\frac{\theta}{2}\right)$.

23. $\cos^{-1}\frac{\sin x}{2}+2\sqrt{3}\tanh^{-1}\left[\sqrt{3}\tan\frac{1}{2}\left\{\cos^{-1}\left(\frac{\sin x}{2}\right)\right\}\right]$.

24. $\operatorname{cosec}^{-1}(1+\sin 2\theta)$.

25. $\sec^{-1}(\cos\theta+\sec\theta)$.

26. $2x\tan^{-1}x-\log(1+x^2)$.

27. $\frac{1}{2}\log\frac{1-\sin\theta}{1+\sin\theta}-\frac{1}{\sqrt{2}}\log\frac{\frac{1}{\sqrt{2}}-\sin\theta}{\frac{1}{\sqrt{2}}+\sin\theta}$, where $\theta=\tan^{-1}x$.

28. $\frac{1}{2}\log\tan\left(\frac{x}{2}+\frac{\pi}{4}\right), \frac{1}{2\sqrt{3}}\log\frac{\sqrt{3}+\tan x}{\sqrt{3}-\tan x}$,

$$\frac{1}{8}\log\frac{1-\sin x}{1+\sin x}-\frac{1}{4\sqrt{2}}\log\frac{\frac{1}{\sqrt{2}}-\sin x}{\frac{1}{\sqrt{2}}+\sin x}.$$

CHAPTER VII.

PAGE 71.

6. $\dfrac{x^{m+1}}{m+1}\left(\log x - \dfrac{1}{m+1}\right), \dfrac{x^{m+1}}{m+1}\left\{(\log x)^2 - \dfrac{2}{m+1}\log x + \dfrac{2}{(m+1)^2}\right\},$

$$\frac{x^{m+1}}{m+1}\left\{(\log x)^3 - \frac{3}{m+1}(\log x)^2 + \frac{6}{(m+1)^2}\log x - \frac{6}{(m+1)^3}\right\}.$$

7. If $\qquad I_m = \int x^m\sqrt{2ax - x^2}\,dx,$

$$I_0 = \frac{(x-a)\sqrt{2ax-x^2}}{2} + \frac{a^2}{2}\text{vers}^{-1}\frac{x}{a},$$

and $\qquad I_1 = -\dfrac{(2ax-x^2)^{\frac{3}{2}}}{3} + aI_0,$

$$I_2 = -\frac{x(2ax-x^2)^{\frac{3}{2}}}{4} + \frac{5}{4}aI_1,$$

$$I_3 = -\frac{x^2(2ax-x^2)^{\frac{3}{2}}}{5} + \frac{7}{5}aI_2.$$

Between limits 0 and $2a$,

$$I_1 = \frac{\pi a^3}{2}, I_2 = \frac{5}{8}\pi a^4, I_3 = \frac{7}{8}\pi a^5$$

PAGE 72.

1. $\int \sin^p\theta\cos^q\theta\,d\theta = \dfrac{\sin^{p+1}\theta\cos^{q+1}\theta}{p+1} + \dfrac{p+q+2}{p+1}\int\sin^{p+2}\theta\cos^q\theta\,d\theta,$

and similarly for 2, 3, 4, 5.

6. $\int\sin^4 x\,dx = -\dfrac{\cos x\sin^3 x}{4} + \dfrac{3}{4}\left(\dfrac{x}{2} - \dfrac{\sin 2x}{4}\right),$ and similarly for $\int\sin^6 x\,dx$, etc.

7. $\int\cos^n x\,dx = \dfrac{\sin x\cos^{n-1}x}{n} + \dfrac{n-1}{n}\int\cos^{n-2}x\,dx.$

8. (i.) $-\dfrac{\sin^3 x\cos^3 x}{6} + \dfrac{1}{2}\left\{-\dfrac{\sin x\cos^3 x}{4} + \dfrac{1}{4}\left(\dfrac{x}{2} + \dfrac{\sin 2x}{4}\right)\right\} = \text{etc.}$

(ii.) $\dfrac{\sin^3 x}{\cos x} - \dfrac{3}{2}(x - \sin x\cos x).$

(iii.) $\tan x - 2\cot x - \dfrac{1}{3}\cot^3 x.$

PAGE 77, 78.

1. $\frac{\pi}{4}, \frac{3\pi}{16}, \frac{35\pi}{256}, \frac{128}{315}.$

2. $\frac{3\pi}{2^9}, \frac{8}{693}, \frac{8}{693}, \frac{1}{60}.$

4. $\frac{1}{8}\sin^8\theta, \frac{1}{8}\sin^8\theta - \frac{1}{10}\sin^{10}\theta, \frac{1}{8}\sin^8\theta - \frac{1}{5}\sin^{10}\theta + \frac{1}{12}\sin^{12}\theta,$

$$-\frac{1}{3}\cos^3\theta + \frac{3}{5}\cos^5\theta - \frac{3}{7}\cos^7\theta + \frac{1}{9}\cos^9\theta,$$

$$-\frac{1}{10}\sin^5\theta\cos^5\theta + \frac{1}{128}\left(\frac{3}{2}\theta - \frac{1}{2}\sin 4\theta + \frac{1}{16}\sin 8\theta\right).$$

5. $\frac{128 - 71\sqrt{2}}{1680}, \frac{3\pi - 8}{32}, \frac{3\pi + 4}{192}, \frac{289}{4480}.$

6. $\frac{\pi}{8}, \frac{2}{9}, \frac{5\pi}{192}.$

PAGE 78-82.

2. If $I_{m,n}$ denote the given integral,

$$I_{m,n} = \frac{x^{m-1}(1+x^2)^{\frac{n}{2}+1}}{m+n+1} - \frac{m-1}{m+n+1} I_{m-2,n},$$

$$I_{5,7} = (1+x^2)^{\frac{9}{2}}\left\{\frac{x^4}{13} - \frac{4x^2}{13\cdot 11} + \frac{4.2}{13\cdot 11\cdot 9}\right\}.$$

6. With a similar notation,

$$(\alpha)\ I_{n,p} = \frac{x^n(a+bx)^{p+\frac{3}{2}}}{\left(p+n+\frac{3}{2}\right)} - \frac{an}{\left(p+n+\frac{3}{2}\right)b} I_{n-1,p}.$$

$$(\beta)\ I_{n,p} = \frac{x^{2n-1}(x^2+a^2)^{p+\frac{3}{2}}}{2n+2p+2} - \frac{(2n-1)a^2}{2n+2p+2} I_{n-1,p}.$$

$$(\gamma)\ (m-n+1)\, I_{m,n} = \frac{x^{m-2}}{(a^3+x^3)^{\frac{n}{3}-1}} - (m-2)a^3 I_{m-3,n}.$$

$$(\delta)\ mI_m = x^{m-2}(x^3-1)^{\frac{2}{3}} + (m-2)\, I_{m-3},$$

$$(x^3-1)^{\frac{2}{3}}\left(\frac{x^6}{8} + \frac{6x^3}{8\cdot 5} + \frac{6.3}{8\cdot 5\cdot 2}\right).$$

7. $I_n = e^{ax}\cos^{n-1} x \dfrac{a\cos x + n\sin x}{a^2+n^2} + \dfrac{n(n-1)}{a^2+n^2} I_{n-2}.$

$$I_4 = \frac{e^{ax}}{a^2+4^2}\left[\cos^3 x\,(a\cos x + 4\sin x) + \frac{4\cdot 3}{a^2+2^2}\left\{\cos x\,(a\cos x + 2\sin x) + 2\cdot 1\cdot \frac{1}{a}\right\}\right].$$

8. $I_n = -x^n \cos x + nx^{n-1}\sin x - n(n-1)I_{n-2}.$

$I_n = e^{ax}\sin^{n-1} x \dfrac{a\sin x - n\cos x}{n^2+a^2} + \dfrac{n(n-1)}{n^2+a^2} I_{n-2},$

$I_n = -\sin^{n-1} x \dfrac{a\sin x \sin ax + n\cos x \cos ax}{n^2-a^2} + \dfrac{n(n-1)}{n^2-a^2} I_{n-2}.$

12. $I_n = \dfrac{2}{2n+1} x^n \sqrt{x-1} + \dfrac{2n}{2n+1} I_{n-1}.$

17. $\dfrac{1}{3m} + \dfrac{m}{3m(3m-2)} + \dfrac{m(m-1)}{3m(3m-2)(3m-4)} + \ldots$

$+ \dfrac{m(m-1)\ldots 2}{3m(3m-2)\ldots(m+2)} + \dfrac{m(m-1)\ldots 1}{3m(3m-2)\ldots(m+2)}\dfrac{1}{m}\left(1-\cos\dfrac{m\pi}{2}\right).$

20. $(m \text{ even}) \dfrac{m(m-1)(m-2)(m-3)\ldots 2\cdot 1}{(n^2+m^2)\{n^2+(m-2)^2\}\ldots(n^2+2^2)} \cdot \dfrac{2\sinh \dfrac{n\pi}{2}}{n}.$

$(m \text{ odd}) \dfrac{m(m-1)(m-2)(m-3)\ldots 3\cdot 2}{(n^2+m^2)\{n^2+(m-2)^2\}\ldots(n^2+3^2)} \cdot \dfrac{2\cosh \dfrac{n\pi}{2}}{n^2+1^2}.$

23. $I_n = 2\dfrac{\sin(n-1)x}{n-1} + I_{n-2}.$

28. $(n-1)u_{m\cdot n} = -\dfrac{x^{m+1}}{(\log x)^{n-1}} + (m+1)u_{m,\,n-1}$

29. $amI_m + (2m-1)b\,I_{m-1} + (m-1)c\,I_{m-2} = x^{m-1}\sqrt{ax^2+2bx+c}.$

31. (α) $I_n = I_{n-2} - \dfrac{\tanh^{n-1} x}{n-1}.$

(β) Deduce from 25.

(γ) $I_n = -\dfrac{(n-2)x\cos x + \sin x}{(n-1)(n-2)\sin^{n-1} x} + \dfrac{n-2}{n-1} I_{n-2}.$

CHAPTER VIII.

PAGE 87.

1. $\log \dfrac{\sqrt{x+1}-1}{\sqrt{x+1}+1}, \dfrac{1}{\sqrt{3}} \log \dfrac{\sqrt{x+2}-\sqrt{3}}{\sqrt{x+2}+\sqrt{3}},$

$2\sqrt{x+2} + \dfrac{2}{\sqrt{3}} \log \dfrac{\sqrt{x+2}-\sqrt{3}}{\sqrt{x+2}+\sqrt{3}}, \dfrac{2}{3}(x-1)^{\frac{3}{2}} + 2\sqrt{3} \tan^{-1} \dfrac{\sqrt{x-1}}{\sqrt{3}}.$

2. $-\text{cosech}^{-1} x, -\dfrac{1}{\sqrt{2}} \sinh^{-1} \dfrac{1-x}{1+x}, \sinh^{-1} x + \dfrac{1}{\sqrt{2}} \sinh^{-1} \dfrac{1-x}{1+x},$

$\sqrt{x^2+2x+3} - \sinh^{-1} \dfrac{x+1}{\sqrt{2}} - \dfrac{1}{\sqrt{2}} \text{cosech}^{-1} \dfrac{x+1}{\sqrt{2}}.$

3. $\dfrac{1}{2\sqrt{2}} \log \dfrac{x+\sqrt{2x}+1}{x-\sqrt{2x}+1} + \dfrac{1}{\sqrt{2}} \tan^{-1} \dfrac{\sqrt{2x}}{1-x},$

$\dfrac{1}{2\sqrt{2}} \log \dfrac{x+\sqrt{2(x+1)}+2}{x-\sqrt{2(x+1)}+2} - \dfrac{1}{\sqrt{2}} \tan^{-1} \dfrac{\sqrt{2(x+1)}}{x},$

$\dfrac{1}{\sqrt{2}} \log \dfrac{x+2-\sqrt{2(x+1)}}{x+2+\sqrt{2(x+1)}},$

$2\sqrt{x+1} + \dfrac{3}{2\sqrt{2}} \log \dfrac{x+2+\sqrt{2(x+1)}}{x+2-\sqrt{2(x+1)}} + \dfrac{1}{\sqrt{2}} \tan^{-1} \dfrac{\sqrt{2(x+1)}}{x}.$

PAGE 90.

1. $a^2 > b^2, \dfrac{1}{\sqrt{a^2-b^2}} \tan^{-1} \sqrt{\dfrac{x^2+b^2}{a^2-b^2}},$

$a^2 < b^2, \dfrac{1}{2\sqrt{b^2-a^2}} \log \dfrac{\sqrt{x^2+b^2}-\sqrt{b^2-a^2}}{\sqrt{x^2+b^2}+\sqrt{b^2-a^2}}.$

2. $-\dfrac{1}{\sqrt{2}} \sinh^{-1} \sqrt{\dfrac{x^2+1}{x^2-1}}.$

3. $\dfrac{1}{\sqrt{2}} \sinh^{-1} \sqrt{\dfrac{x^2-1}{x^2+1}}.$

4. $\dfrac{\sqrt{x^2-1}}{x}.$

5. If a, b, c are in ascending order of magnitude

$$\frac{1}{(b^2-a^2)^{\frac{1}{2}}(c^2-b^2)^{\frac{1}{2}}}\cos^{-1}\sqrt{\frac{b^2-a^2}{c^2-a^2}}\sqrt{\frac{x^2+2ax+c^2}{x^2+2ax+b^2}},$$

with modifications for other cases.

6. $-\sqrt{\dfrac{x+1}{x-1}}.$

7. $\dfrac{10}{19}\cosh^{-1}\dfrac{4}{\sqrt{3}}\sqrt{\dfrac{4x^2-2x+1}{5x^2+8x}}-\dfrac{9}{19}\sinh^{-1}\sqrt{\dfrac{4x^2-2x+1}{5x^2+8x}}.$

PAGE 92.

1. $\dfrac{1}{\sqrt{3}}\log\dfrac{\cos x-\cos\frac{\pi}{6}}{\cos x+\cos\frac{\pi}{6}}.$ **2.** $2(\sin x + x\cos a).$

3. $\sin 2x + 4\sin x\cos a + x(4\cos^2 a - 1).$.

4. Prove (n being a positive integer)

$$\frac{\cos nx-\cos na}{\cos x-\cos a}=2\operatorname{cosec} a\sum_{r=1}^{r=n-1}\sin ra\cos(n-r)x+\frac{\sin na}{\sin a}.$$

Then $\displaystyle\int\frac{\cos nx-\cos na}{\cos x-\cos a}dx=\frac{2}{\sin a}\sum_{r=1}^{r=n-1}\frac{\sin ra}{n-r}\sin(n-r)x+x\frac{\sin na}{\sin a}$.

5. $2\sin x + 2\sin a\log(\sin x-\sin a)+2\sin a\log\dfrac{\tan\frac{x}{2}-\cot\frac{a}{2}}{\tan\frac{x}{2}-\tan\frac{a}{2}}.$

6. $\dfrac{1}{\sin^2 a}\log\cot\dfrac{x}{2}+\dfrac{\cos a}{2\sin^2 a}\log\left(\tan\dfrac{x+a}{2}\tan\dfrac{x-a}{2}\right).$

PAGE 98-102.

1. (i.) $2\tan^{-1}\sqrt{x}.$ (ii.) $2\tan^{-1}\sqrt{1+2x}.$

(iii.) $-\dfrac{1}{\sqrt{2}}\cosh^{-1}\dfrac{4-3x}{x}.$ (iv.) $-\sinh^{-1}\dfrac{1}{\sqrt{3}}\dfrac{1-x}{1+x}.$

(v.) $\sqrt{x^2+x+1}-\dfrac{1}{2}\sinh^{-1}\dfrac{2x+1}{\sqrt{3}}-\sinh^{-1}\dfrac{1}{\sqrt{3}}\dfrac{1-x}{1+x}.$

(vi.) $\dfrac{x\sqrt{x-1}}{\sqrt{x+1}}.$ (viii.) $2\operatorname{cosec}^{-1}\left(\sqrt{x}+\dfrac{1}{x}\right).$

(vii.) $-\dfrac{2}{na^{\frac{n}{2}}}\sinh^{-1}\left(\dfrac{a}{x}\right)^{\frac{n}{2}}.$

2. (i.) $\dfrac{1}{2ab}\sin^{-1}\dfrac{(a^2+b^2)x^2-a^4-b^4}{(b^2-a^2)\,x^2+a^4-b^4}.$

(ii.) If $a>c$

$$I=\frac{1}{\sqrt{a^2-c^2}}\tan^{-1}\sqrt{\frac{x^2+c^2}{a^2-c^2}}+\frac{b}{a\sqrt{a^2-c^2}}\cosh^{-1}\frac{a}{c}\sqrt{\frac{x^2+c^2}{x^2+a^2}},$$

with a corresponding real form if $a<c$.

(iii.) $-\dfrac{1}{\sqrt{a+c}}\cosh^{-1}\dfrac{1}{\sqrt{b+c}}\dfrac{\sqrt{a\cos^2\theta+b\sin^2\theta+c}}{\sin\theta}.$

3. (i.) $\dfrac{1}{\sqrt{(\cos\alpha-\cos\beta)(\cos\alpha-\cos\gamma)}}.$

$$\times\cosh^{-1}\frac{\dfrac{2}{\cos x+\cos\alpha}-\dfrac{1}{\cos\alpha-\cos\beta}-\dfrac{1}{\cos\alpha-\cos\gamma}}{\dfrac{1}{\cos\alpha-\cos\beta}-\dfrac{1}{\cos\alpha-\cos\gamma}}.$$

for the case $\cos\alpha>\cos\beta$ or $\cos\gamma$ with modifications for other cases.

(ii.) $-\dfrac{1}{\sqrt{\sin(\alpha-\beta)\sin(\alpha-\gamma)}}.$

$$\times\cosh^{-1}\frac{\dfrac{2}{\tan x-\cot\alpha}+\dfrac{1}{\cot\alpha-\cot\beta}+\dfrac{1}{\cot\alpha-\cot\gamma}}{\dfrac{1}{\cot\beta-\cot\alpha}-\dfrac{1}{\cot\gamma-\cot\alpha}}.$$

6. (i.) $\dfrac{1}{4}\log_e(2e)$. (ii.) $\dfrac{1}{2a}$. (iii.) $\dfrac{2\sqrt{2}-\sqrt{3}-1}{2}\pi$.

9. (i.) $\dfrac{\pi}{3\sqrt{3}}$. (ii.) $\dfrac{1}{3}\log 2$. (iii.) $\dfrac{\pi}{1-a^2}$.

13. $(n>1)\ I_n=\dfrac{n(n-1)}{n^2+1}I_{n-2}.$

14. (i.) $\log_e 2-1$. (ii.) $-\dfrac{\pi^2}{24}$. (iii.) 0.

15. (i.) $\dfrac{\pi}{2ab}$. (ii.) $\dfrac{\pi}{4}$.

27. (i.) $\log_e 2$. (ii.) $\dfrac{\pi}{4}$.

(iii.) $\dfrac{\pi}{2}$. (iv.) $\dfrac{\lfloor 2k}{\{2^k\lfloor k\}^2}$.

29. $2e^{\frac{\pi-4}{2}}$. **30.** e^{-1}.

CHAPTER IX.

PAGE 107-109.

1. $a(\beta - \alpha)$.

7. (i.) $a(\theta_2 - \theta_1)$. (iii.) $\frac{a}{2}[\theta\sqrt{1+\theta^2} + \sin h^{-1}\theta]_{\theta_1}^{\theta_2}$.

(ii.) $(r_2 - r_1)\frac{\sqrt{1+m^2}}{m}$. (iv.) $2a\left(\cos\frac{\theta_1}{2} - \cos\frac{\theta_2}{2}\right)$.

11. $2\frac{c^2 - a^2}{a}$. **12.** $\frac{4a}{\sqrt{3}}$.

PAGE 115, 116.

1. $\frac{a}{2}\left[\sqrt{3}\cos h^{-1}\frac{6x - 7a}{a} + 2\sqrt{\frac{4a - 3x}{a - x}}\right]_{x_1}^{x_2}$.

2. $8a$.

3. The Cycloid.

8. $a\left[\frac{\sqrt{1 + 3\cos^2\theta}}{\cos\theta} - \frac{\sqrt{3}}{2}\log\frac{\sqrt{1+3\cos^2\theta} + \sqrt{3}\cos\theta}{\sqrt{1+3\cos^2\theta} - \sqrt{3}\cos\theta}\right]_{\theta_1}^{\theta_2}$.

9. $\frac{1}{2}\left[(x_2^{\frac{2}{3}} + y_2^{\frac{2}{3}})^{\frac{3}{2}} - (x_1^{\frac{2}{3}} + y_1^{\frac{2}{3}})^{\frac{3}{2}}\right]$.

15. $5a$.

CHAPTER X.

PAGE 120, 121.

1. $\frac{4a^2}{3}$.

2. (a) $c^2 \sin h\frac{h}{c}$. (b) $e^h - 1$.

(c) $\frac{\pi ab}{4} - \frac{b^2}{2a}\sqrt{a^2 - b^2} - \frac{ab}{2}\sin^{-1}\frac{\sqrt{a^2 - b^2}}{a}$.

(d) $\frac{1}{2}(e^{h^2} - 1)$. (e) $\log\frac{b^b}{a^a} - b + a$.

(f) $k^2 \log\frac{b}{a}$.

3. $\dfrac{16a^2}{3}$.　　**4.** $\dfrac{\pi ab}{2} \mp \left(\dfrac{ac}{b}\sqrt{b^2 - c^2} + ab \sin^{-1}\dfrac{c}{b}\right)$.

5. $4a^2$.　　**6.** $3\pi a^2$.

7. $\dfrac{a^2}{2}(4 - \pi)$.

PAGE 123.

1. $\dfrac{\pi}{2}(a^2 + b^2)$.　　**2.** $\dfrac{\pi a^2}{8}$.　　**3.** $\dfrac{\pi a^2}{16}$.

4. $\dfrac{\pi a^2}{4n}$. Total area $= \dfrac{\pi a^2}{2}$ (n even), or $\dfrac{\pi a^2}{4}$ (n odd).

5. $\dfrac{a^2 \tan a}{4} e^{2\beta \cot \alpha}(e^{2\gamma \cot \alpha} - 1)$.　　**6.** $\dfrac{a^2}{6}\dfrac{\beta^3 - \alpha^3}{\alpha^3\beta^3}$.

7. $\dfrac{a^2}{2}\log\dfrac{\beta}{\alpha}$.　　**8.** $\dfrac{a^2}{2}\dfrac{\beta - \alpha}{\alpha\beta}$.　　**9.** $\dfrac{3\pi a^2}{2}$.

PAGE 128.

1. $3\pi a^2$.　　**3.** $\dfrac{c^2}{2}\left(\tan\psi + \dfrac{1}{3}\tan^3\psi\right)$.

4. $\dfrac{A^2B}{4}[B(\psi_2 - \psi_1) + \sin B(\psi_2 - \psi_1)\cos B(\psi_2 + \psi_1)]$.

5. $\dfrac{A^2B}{4}(e^{2B\psi_2} - e^{2B\psi_1})$.

PAGE 136-139.

1. $\dfrac{8}{15}a^2$.　　**2.** $\dfrac{4a^2}{3}$.

5. $(\pi - 2)a^2$.　　**7.** $\dfrac{3\pi a^2}{4}$.

9. (i.) $\dfrac{3}{8}\pi ab$.　　(ii.) $\dfrac{15\pi ab}{128}$.

(iii.) $2mab\dfrac{\Gamma\left(\dfrac{m}{2}+1\right)\Gamma\left(\dfrac{m}{2}\right)}{\Gamma(m+1)}$, m being supposed odd.

10. $a^2\left(\dfrac{19\pi}{12} + 1 + \dfrac{\sqrt{3}}{2}\right)$ and $a^2\left(\dfrac{\pi}{12} - 1 + \dfrac{\sqrt{3}}{2}\right)$.

11. $a^2\left[2\log(\sqrt{2} + 1) - \dfrac{11}{24}\sqrt{2}\right]$.

12. $4c^2\sqrt{2}\sin^{-1}\frac{1}{\sqrt{3}}$.

13. $c^2\left(\frac{\sqrt{3}}{2}+\frac{\pi}{3}\mp\frac{\pi}{2}\right)$.

14. $\frac{a^2}{6}(32+24\sqrt{3}-3\pi)$.

17. $\frac{352}{15}a^2\sqrt{2}$.

21. $\frac{3a^2}{2}$; 2 : 1.

22. $$\left[\frac{a^2}{8b^3}e^{2b\theta}\{2b^2(e^{4\pi b}-1)\theta^2+2b\,(4b\pi e^{4\pi b}-e^{4\pi b}+1)\theta + 8\pi^2b^2e^{4b\pi}-4\pi be^{4b\pi}+e^{4b\pi}-1\}\right]_{\theta_1}^{\theta_2}.$$

23. $\frac{\pi a^2}{16}\left(\frac{\pi^2}{6}-1\right)$.

24. n even, $\frac{\pi a^2}{2}$; n odd, $\frac{\pi a^2}{4}$.

25. $\pi\frac{a^2+b^2}{12}$.

28. $\pi\left(b^2+\frac{a^2}{2}\right)$.

29. $\frac{a^2}{3}(10\pi+9\sqrt{3})$.

30. $\frac{5\pi a^2}{4}$.

32. $a^2\left(1-\frac{\pi}{4}\right)$.

34. $a^2(\pi+2)$.

39. $\frac{\pi a^2}{4}$.

40. $\pi a\,(a-b)$.

41. a^2.

42. $\pi a^2\sqrt{2}$.

43. $\frac{a^2n^2-b^2m^2}{2m^3n^3}\tan^{-1}\frac{an}{bm}+\frac{ab}{2m^2n^2}$.

44. (i.) $\frac{7\pi a^2}{2^9}$, (ii.) $\frac{7\pi a^2\sqrt{2}}{2^{14}}$.

CHAPTER XI.

PAGE 144.

1. $4\pi a^2$.

3. $\pi a^2\{3\sqrt{2}-\log(\sqrt{2}+1)\}$, $\frac{4\pi a^3}{5}$.

PAGE 146.

1. $2\pi^2a^2b$.

2. $4\pi a^2\sqrt{2}$, $\pi a^3\sqrt{2}$.

3. If the sides be a, b, c ; s the semiperimeter ; and h_1, h_2, h_3 the distances of the midpoints from the given line,

surface $= 2\pi\,(ah_1+bh_2+ch_3)$,

volume $= \frac{2\pi}{3}(h_1+h_2+h_3)\sqrt{s\,(s-a)(s-b)(s-c)}$.

PAGE 148, 149

1. If a = rad. of base,

h = altitude,

l = slant height,

surface = πal,

volume = $\frac{1}{3}\pi a^2 h$.

2. $\frac{4}{3}\pi ab^2$.

5. $2\pi a^3\left(\log_e 2 - \frac{2}{3}\right)$.

6. Surface = $\frac{32}{3}\pi a^2$,

volume = $\pi^2 a^3$.

8. $\frac{1}{2}\pi^2 a^3$.

10. $\frac{1}{12}\pi^2 a^3$.

12. $\frac{8\sqrt{2}\pi a^3}{15}$.

CHAPTER XII.

PAGE 154, 155

1. (i.) Mass = $\frac{\mu a^4}{8}$, (ii.) $\bar{x} = \bar{y} = \frac{8a}{15}$, (iii.) $M\frac{a^2}{3}$. (M = mass.)

2. (i.) $M = \frac{\mu 2^{q+2} a^{p+q+2}}{(q+1)(2p+q+3)}$,

(ii.) $\bar{x} = \frac{2p+q+3}{2p+q+5}a$, $\bar{y} = 2\frac{q+1}{q+2}\cdot\frac{2p+q+3}{2p+q+4}a$,

(iii.) $4Ma^2\frac{q+1}{q+3}\cdot\frac{2p+q+3}{2p+q+5}$.

3. $\frac{2}{3}$ of length of rod from end of zero density.

If a = length, $\frac{Ma^2}{2}, \frac{Ma^2}{6}, \frac{Ma^2}{12}$.

4. $\bar{x} = \frac{4a}{5}$, $\bar{y} = \frac{3a}{5}m\frac{m^2+2}{m^2+3}$; $\frac{2}{3}Ma^2$.

PAGE 159, 160.

1. Let 2θ be the angle, a the radius, the median the initial line,

$(\alpha)\ \bar{x} = \frac{2}{3}\frac{a \sin\theta}{\theta}$, $(\beta)\ \frac{3}{4}a\frac{\sin\theta}{\theta}$.

2. $\bar{x} = 2a\frac{n+2}{n+4}$, about tang., $4Ma^2\frac{(n+2)(n+3)(n+5)}{(n+4)^2(n+6)}$,

about diam., $-4Ma^2\frac{(n+2)(n+3)}{(n+4)^2(n+6)}$.

4. If $p_1 = -\frac{c_2 - c_3}{m_2 - m_3}$ and $q_1 = \frac{m_2c_3 - m_3c_2}{m_2 - m_3}$,

Mom. In about x-axis $= M\{(q_2+q_3)^2 + (q_3+q_1)^2 + (q_1+q_2)^2\}/12$.

about y-axis $= M\{(p_2+p_3)^2 + (p_3+p_1)^2 + (p_1+p_2)^2\}/12$.

6. Area. $= (2\pi + 3\sqrt{3})a^2/6$,

$$\bar{x} = \frac{3a\sqrt{3}}{2(3\sqrt{3}-\pi)},$$

Mom. In. $= \frac{Ma^2}{3}\cdot\frac{9\sqrt{3}-\pi}{3\sqrt{3}-\pi}$.

7. (1) $\left(\frac{9a}{5}, \frac{9a}{5}\right)$, (2) $\frac{144}{35}Ma^2$, (3) $\frac{96\pi a^2}{5}$.

8. (1) $M\frac{\pi a^2}{8}$, (2) $M\frac{16a^2}{9\pi}$.

9. (1) $\bar{x} = 0, \bar{y} = \frac{7a}{6}$.

(2) (a) $5\pi^2a^3$, (b)$\pi a^2\left(\frac{3\pi^2}{2} - \frac{8}{3}\right)$, (c) $7\pi^2a^3$

CHAPTER XIII.

PAGE 166, 167.

1. $x\tan x - \log\sec x = y\tan y - \log\sec y + C$.

2. $\frac{x^3 - y^3}{3} + \frac{x^2 - y^2}{2} + x - y = C$.

3. $2xy + x + y + C(x + y + 1) = 1$.

5. $\log\sqrt{1 + y^2} = \log x + \tan^{-1}x + C$.

6. $3(e^y - e^x) = x^3 + C$.

9. (1) $y = Ce^{\frac{x}{a}}$. (2) $y^2 = 2ax + C$.

(3) $r(C - \theta) = a$. (4) $r = a\theta + C$.

10. $x = \sqrt{a^2 - y^2} + \dfrac{a}{2}\log\dfrac{a - \sqrt{a^2 - y^2}}{a + \sqrt{a^2 - y^2}}$ if $y = a$ when $x = 0$.

PAGE 169, 170.

1. $2ye\tan^{-1}x = e^{2\tan^{-1}x} + C$.

2. $(a^2 + b^2)y = a\sin bx - b\cos bx + Ce^{-ax}$.

3. $r\theta = a\dfrac{\theta^{n+2}}{n+2} + C$.

4. $4xy = y^4 + C$. **5.** $xe^{\tan^{-1}y} = \tan^{-1}y + C$.

6. $ye^{2\sqrt{x}} = 2\sqrt{x} + C$. **8.** $x^2 + y^2 + ax + \dfrac{a^2}{2} = Ce^{\frac{2x}{a}}$.

9. $\dfrac{1}{xy} = \dfrac{1}{2x^2} + C$. **10.** $\left(\dfrac{1}{xy}\right)^{n-1} = \dfrac{1}{2x^{2n-2}} + C$.

11. $\dfrac{1}{y^{n-1}} = 1 + Ce^{(n-1)\frac{x^2}{2}}$. **12.** $\dfrac{1}{x\sin y} = \dfrac{1}{2x^2} + C$.

13. $\dfrac{1}{x\log z} = \dfrac{1}{2x^2} + C$. **14.** $e^{-(n-1)z} = 1 + Ce^{(n-1)\frac{z^2}{2}}$.

15. $\dfrac{1}{r} = \dfrac{1}{a} + Ce^{\theta}$. **16.** $\dfrac{1}{r^{n-1}} = \dfrac{1}{a^{n-1}} + Ce^{(n-1)\theta}$.

18. (1) $\dfrac{e^{-y}}{x} = \dfrac{1}{2x^2} + C$.

(2) $(a^2 + b^2)e^y = a\sin bx - b\cos bx + Ce^{-ax}$.

(3) $\dfrac{\sin y}{1 + x} = e^x + C$.

(4) $f(y) + \phi(x) + 1 = Ce^{\phi(x)}$.

CHAPTER XIV.

PAGE 173.

1. $\dfrac{1}{2}\log(v^2 + v - 1) + \dfrac{1}{2\sqrt{5}}\log\dfrac{2v + 1 - \sqrt{5}}{2v + 1 + \sqrt{5}} + \log x = C$, where $v = \dfrac{y}{x}$.

2. $\frac{1}{2}\log(6v^2+v-3)+\frac{9}{2\sqrt{73}}\log\frac{12v+1-\sqrt{73}}{12v+1+\sqrt{73}}+\log x=C,$

where $v=\frac{y}{x}$.

3. $\frac{1}{x}-\frac{1}{y}=C.$

4. The p - eliminant of $y=x(p+p^3),$ and $x=\frac{c}{p^3}e^{\frac{1}{2p^2}}.$

5. The p-eliminant of $y=x(Ap^2+Bp+C)$, and

$$\log x\{Ap^2+(B-1)p+C\}+\frac{2}{\sqrt{4AC-(B-1)^2}}\tan^{-1}\frac{2Ap+B-1}{\sqrt{4AC-(B-1)^2}}=\text{const.}$$

PAGE 175, 176.

1. $(y-x)^5=C(y+x).$
2. $(y-x)^3=C(y+x-2).$
3. $\frac{2+\sqrt{3}}{2\sqrt{3}}\log\left(\frac{y}{x-1}+1-\sqrt{3}\right)-\frac{2-\sqrt{3}}{2\sqrt{3}}\log\left(\frac{y}{x-1}+1+\sqrt{3}\right)+\log(x-1)=C.$
4. $(a+b)\log(y-x+1)+(a-b)\log(y+x-1)=C.$
5. $x-y+\log(x+y)=C.$
6. $6y-3x=\log(3x+3y+2)+C.$
7. $3x^2+4xy+3y^2-10x-10y+C=0.$
8. $x+y-4\log(2x+3y+7)=C.$

PAGE 178.

1. $y^2+1=Ce^{2x}.$

2. $y=\frac{x^2}{2}+\log x+C.$

3. $y+\frac{2}{3}(a+x)^{\frac{3}{2}}-2a(a+x)^{\frac{1}{2}}=C.$

4. $x(x+2a)^3=Ce^{\frac{2y}{a}}.$

5. $4ax=y^2+3ay-\frac{3a^2}{2}\log(2y+a)+C.$

6. $\cos\left\{\frac{\sqrt{1-(A-x)^2}-y}{A-x}\right\}=A-x.$

7. $\left.\begin{aligned}x&=\frac{3}{2}Ap^2+2Bp+C,\\ y&=Ap^3+Bp^2.\end{aligned}\right\}$

8. $\left.\begin{aligned}y&=\frac{3}{2}Aq^2+2Bq+C,\\ x&=Aq^3+Bq^2.\end{aligned}\right\}$

PAGE 180.

1. $y = Cx + C^2, x^2 + 4y = 0.$

2. $y = Cx + C^3, 27y^2 + 4x^3 = 0.$

3. $y = Cx + C^n, n^n y^{n-1} + (n-1)^{n-1} x^n = 0.$

4. $y = Cx + \sqrt{a^2C^2 + b^2}, \dfrac{x^2}{a^2} + \dfrac{y^2}{b^2} = 1.$

5. $y = (x-a)C - C^2, (x-a)^2 = 4y.$

6. $(y - Cx)(C-1) = C, \sqrt{x} + \sqrt{y} = 1.$

PAGE 181.

1. $$\left.\begin{aligned} y &= p^2x + p, \\ x &= \frac{\log p - p + C}{(p-1)^2}. \end{aligned}\right\}$$

2. $$\left.\begin{aligned} y &= apx + p^2, \\ x &= \frac{2p}{1-2a} + Cp^{\frac{a}{1-a}}. \end{aligned}\right\}$$

3. $$\left.\begin{aligned} y &= p^2x + p^3, \\ x(p-1)^2 &= -p^3 + \frac{3}{2}p^2 + C. \end{aligned}\right\}$$

4. $$\left.\begin{aligned} y &= (p + p^2)x + \frac{1}{p}, \\ p^2x &= 1 + Ae^{\frac{1}{p}}. \end{aligned}\right\}$$

5. $$\left.\begin{aligned} y &= (p + p^n)x + \frac{1}{p^{n-1}}, \\ p^nx &= (n-1) + Ae^{\frac{1}{(n-1)p^{n-1}}}. \end{aligned}\right\}$$

6. $$\left.\begin{aligned} y &= 2px + p^n, \\ p^2x &= -\frac{n}{n+1}p^{n+1} + A. \end{aligned}\right\}$$

7. $$\left.\begin{aligned} y &= apx + bp^3, \\ xp^{\frac{a}{a-1}} &= -\frac{3b}{3a-2}p^{\frac{3a-2}{a-1}} + A. \end{aligned}\right\}$$

8. A rectangular hyperbola.

9. Parabolae touching the axes.

10. Hyperbolae.

11. A four-cusped hypocycloid $x^{\frac{2}{3}} + y^{\frac{2}{3}} = a^{\frac{3}{2}}$.

12. $8y = (2x - 1)^2$.

13. $y = Ae^x + c(1 + A^2)^{\frac{3}{2}}$.

$$\left.\begin{aligned} y &= c\,\frac{3\sin^2\theta - 1}{\cos^3\theta} \\ x &= \log\frac{3\,c\sin\theta}{\cos^2\theta} \end{aligned}\right\}.$$

14. $y^2 = Cx^2 - \dfrac{BC}{AC + 1}$, a series of conics touching the four straight lines $x \pm \sqrt{-A}\,y = \pm\sqrt{B}$, the singular solution.

CHAPTER XV.

PAGE 184.

1. $y = x\log x + Ax + B$.

2. $y = a\cos\text{h}\left(\dfrac{x}{a} + b\right)$.

3. $2y = \dfrac{x^2}{2a} - a\log x + b$.

4. $y = \dfrac{(x + 3a)^3}{27} + b$.

5. $(x - A)^2 + (y - B)^2 = a^2$.

6. $x + b = \displaystyle\int \frac{dy}{\sqrt{ae^{-2y} + \frac{1}{2} - y}}$.

7. $y + b = \displaystyle\int \sqrt{ae^{-2x} + \frac{1}{2} - x}\;dx$.

8. $\dfrac{y}{x} = \displaystyle\int\left(\frac{1}{x} + \frac{a}{x^2}\right)e^{-\frac{x^2}{2}}\,dx + b$.

9. $y = b\tan\dfrac{x + y + a}{2b}$.

10. $x + A + \dfrac{\sqrt{1 - y^2}}{y} + \sin^{-1} y = 0$.

11. $y = B\,x^2 - A\,x\log x$.

PAGE 187.

1. $x^5y = e^x + Ax^2 + Bx + C$.

2. $(x^2 + \sin x)y = \cos x + Ax^2 + Bx + C$.

3. (*a*) $x^3y_3 - 3x^2y_2 + 6xy_1 + (x - 6)y = e^x + A$.

(*b*) $xy_3 - y_2 + \dfrac{y}{x} = e^x + A$.

(*c*) $x^5y_5 - 4x^4y_4 + 16x^3y_3 - 48x^2y_2 + 96xy_1$

$$- 96y + \frac{1}{2}(x^2 + y^2) = x(\log x - 1) + A.$$

CHAPTER XVI.

PAGE 194.

In the results of the following set all capitals denote arbitrary constants:—

1. $y = Ae^{ax} + Be^{bx}$.
2. $y = Ae^{ax} + Be^{2ax} + Ce^{3ax}$.
3. $y = Ae^{x} + Be^{3x} + Ce^{5x}$.
4. $y = (A + Bx)e^{x} + Ce^{-2x}$.
5. $y = Ae^{x} + Be^{-\frac{x}{2}} \sin \frac{x\sqrt{3}}{2} + Ce^{-\frac{x}{2}} \cos \frac{x\sqrt{3}}{2}$.
6. $y = Ae^{x} + Be^{-x} + C\sin x + D\cos x$.
7. $y = (A + Bx)e^{x} + (C + Dx + Ex^2)e^{2x}$.
8. $y = A\sin x + B\cos x + Ce^{-\frac{x}{2}} \sin \frac{x\sqrt{3}}{2} + De^{-\frac{x}{2}} \cos \frac{x\sqrt{3}}{2}$.
9. $y = (A + Bx)\sin x + (C + Dx)\cos x + (E + Fx)e^{x}$.
10. $y = (A + Bx + Cx^2)\sin x + (D + Ex + Fx^2)\cos x$
$$+ (G + Hx)e^{-\frac{x}{2}} \sin \frac{x\sqrt{3}}{2} + (I + Jx)e^{-\frac{x}{2}} \cos \frac{x\sqrt{3}}{2}.$$
11. $y = (A + Bx + Cx^2)e^{x} + De^{2x} + (E + Fx)e^{-x} \sin x + (G + Hx)e^{-x} \cos x$.
12. $y = (A + Bx)\sin ax + (C + Dx)\cos ax + E\sin bx + F\cos bx$
$$+ Ge^{-\frac{cx}{2}} \sin \frac{cx\sqrt{3}}{2} + He^{-\frac{cx}{2}} \cos \frac{cx\sqrt{3}}{2} + Ie^{\frac{cx}{2}} \sin \frac{cx\sqrt{3}}{2} + Je^{\frac{cx}{2}} \cos \frac{cx\sqrt{3}}{2}.$$

PAGE 197.

1. (1) $\frac{e^x}{4}$; (2) $\frac{e^{ax}}{(a+1)(a+2)}$,

(3) $\frac{e^x}{120} + \frac{e^{-x}}{12}$.

PAGE 198.

1. $\frac{e^x x^5}{60}, -e^x \sin x, xe^x \log_e\left(\frac{x}{e}\right)$.

PAGE 198.

1. $e^{ax}(a^2+b^2)^{-\frac{1}{2}}\cos\left(bx-\tan^{-1}\frac{b}{a}\right), \frac{e^x}{2}-\frac{e^x}{2\sqrt{5}}\cos(2x-\tan^{-1}2),$

$\frac{e^x}{4}\left\{\frac{3}{\sqrt{2}}\sin\left(x-\frac{\pi}{4}\right)-\frac{1}{\sqrt{10}}\sin(3x-\tan^{-1}3)\right\},$

$\frac{1}{2}(\sin x\cos h\,x-\cos x\sin h\,x).$

2. $-\frac{1}{2}\sin 2x, \frac{1}{2}\cos x, -\frac{3}{17}\sin 2x.$

PAGE 200.

$e^x(\sin x-\cos x), e^x\,\frac{4a(a^2-1)\sin ax+(a^4-6a^2+1)\cos ax}{a(a^2+1)-2\cos x\cos hx.},$

$-2\cos x\cos h\,x.$

PAGE 201.

1. $\frac{x^2}{2}-\frac{3}{2}x+\frac{7}{4}, -\frac{x^2}{2}-x, \frac{x^3}{6}+x^2.$

2. $e^x\left(\frac{x^2}{6}-\frac{5}{18}x+\frac{19}{108}\right), e^x\left(\frac{x^2}{4}-\frac{x}{2}\right)+e^{-x}\left(\frac{x}{4}+\frac{3}{8}\right).$

3. $\frac{1}{2}e^x(x\sin x+\cos x)-\frac{e^{-x}}{10}\left\{\left(2x+\frac{3}{5}\right)\cos x-\left(x+\frac{4}{5}\right)\sin x\right\}.$

PAGE 204.

1. (1) $-\frac{x\cos x}{2}.$ (2) $\frac{x\sin 2x}{4}.$

(3) $\frac{x}{2}\cos h\,x.$ (4) $e^x\left(\frac{x^2}{6}-\frac{x}{3}\right).$

(5) $\frac{xe^x}{2}.$ (6) $\frac{x}{4}(\cos h\,x+\cos x).$

(7) $\frac{x}{2(a^2-b^2)}\left(\frac{e^{ax}}{a}-\frac{e^{bx}}{2b}+\frac{e^{-bx}}{2b}\right).$

(8) $\frac{x}{6}\sin x\sin^2\frac{x}{2}.$

2. (1) $y = A_1 e^x + A_2 e^{-x} + \frac{1}{3} e^{2x}$.

(2) $y = A_1 e^x + A_2 e^{-x} + \frac{1}{2} x \sin hx$.

(3) $y = A_1 \sin x + A_2 \cos x + \frac{1}{2} e^{-x} + \frac{x \sin x}{2} + x^3 - 6x + \frac{e^x}{5} (\sin x - 2\cos x)$.

(4) $y = (A_1 + A_2 x) e^x + A_3 e^{-x} + A_4 e^{-\frac{x}{2}} \sin \frac{x\sqrt{3}}{2} + A_5 e^{-\frac{x}{2}} \cos \frac{x\sqrt{3}}{2} + \frac{e^x}{72} (2x^3 - 9x^2)$.

(5) $y = A_1 + A_2 x + A_3 x^2 + A_4 e^x + A_5 e^{-x} - \frac{x^4}{24}$.

(6) $y = A_1 e^{-x} + A_2 e^{(2+\sqrt{3})x} + A_3 e^{(2-\sqrt{3})x} + \frac{x}{6} e^{-x} + x + 3$.

(7) $y = A_1 e^x + A_2 e^{-\frac{x}{2}} \sin \frac{x\sqrt{3}}{2} + A_3 e^{-\frac{x}{2}} \cos \frac{x\sqrt{3}}{2} + \frac{1}{2} \{(x-3)\cos x - x \sin x\}$.

(8) $y = A_1 e^x + A_2 e^{-x} - \frac{e^x}{25} \{(10x+2)\cos x + (5x-14)\sin x\}$.

(9) $y = A_1 e^x + A_2 e^{-x} - \frac{1}{5} \cos x \cos h\, x + \frac{2}{5} \sin x \sin h\, x + \frac{a^x}{\log (ae) \log \left(\frac{a}{e}\right)}$.

(10) $y = (A_1 + A_2 x) e^x + (A_3 + A_4 x) \sin x + (A_5 + A_6 x) \cos x + \frac{1}{2} - \frac{1}{32} x^2 \sin x + \frac{x^2 e^x}{8} + x + 2$.

PAGE 206.

1. $y = A_1 \sin (q \log x) + A_2 \cos (q \log x)$.

2. $y = A_1 \sin (q \log x) + A_2 \cos (q \log x) + \frac{(\log x)^2}{q^2} - \frac{2}{q^4} + x \frac{q^2 \sin (\log x) - 2\cos (\log x)}{q^4 + 4} - \frac{\log x \cos (q \log x)}{2q}$.

3. $y = \frac{A_1}{x} + A_2 \sqrt{x} \sin \left(\frac{\sqrt{3}}{2} \log x\right) + A_3 \sqrt{x} \cos \left(\frac{\sqrt{3}}{2} \log x\right) + \frac{x}{2} + \log x$.

4. $y = \frac{A_1}{x} + A_2 x + A_3 x \log x + \frac{x (\log x)^2}{4} + \frac{x^3}{16}$.

5. $y = A_1 \sin \left\{\frac{q}{b} \log (a + bx)\right\} + A_2 \cos \left\{\frac{q}{b} \log (a + bx)\right\}$.

CHAPTER XVII.

PAGE 210.

1. $2x^2 + y^2 = b.$ **3.** $r = be^{-\theta \tan a}.$

4. $\dfrac{2b}{r} = 1 - \cos.$

PAGE 216.

1. Put $y^2 = xz$; $y^2 = x^3 - 2x^2 + 2x + Cxe^{-x}.$

2. Put $\tan y = z$; $\tan y = A\cos x + B\sin x + x.$

3. Put $a + bx = e^x$; $y = C(a+bx)^{m_1} + D(a+bx)^{m_2} - \dfrac{a}{Bb} + \dfrac{a+bx}{b(B+AB)}$

where m_1, m_2 are the roots of the equation

$$b^2m^2 + (Ab - b^2)m + B = 0.$$

4. Put $z = \tan^{-1} x$; $y = (Ax + B)/\sqrt{1 + x^2}.$

5. Put $z = \sin^{-1} x$; $y = A\sin(n\sin^{-1} x) + B\cos(n\sin^{-1} x).$

6. Put $e^x = \xi, e^y = \eta$; $(e^y - e^x + 1)e^{e^x} = A.$

7. Put $\sin x = \xi, \sin y = \eta$; $(\sin y - \sin x + 1)e^{\sin x} = A.$

8. (a) $y = Ae^{-x} + Be^{2x}\sin 3x + Ce^{2x}\cos 3x.$

(b) $y = (A + Bx)e^{-3x} + 2\cos x + \dfrac{3}{2}\sin x.$

(c) $y = Ax^3 \sin(\log x) + Bx^3 \cos(\log x).$

9. $\left.\begin{aligned} y + 2 &= A\sin 3x + B\cos 3x + C\sin 4x + D\cos 4x, \\ 3z &= -6(A\sin 3x + B\cos 3x) + (C\sin 4x + D\cos 4x). \end{aligned}\right\}$

10. $y = Ae^{kx^2}.$

11. $y = kx^2 + Ax + B.$